Foreword

CW01500462

This edition is part of a series of publications, sponsored by the Universities of Wales Association for the Study of Welsh Writing in English, bringing together collected editions of Welsh authors writing in English. The field has received relatively little attention in the past and it is hoped that, with the re-publication of major literary works from earlier this century and before, critical interest will be stimulated in writers who will handsomely repay such attention. The editions are conceived of on scholarly lines and are intended to give a rounded impression of the author's work, with introductions, bibliographical information and notes.

JOHN PIKOULIS
General Editor

The Complete Poems of
T. H. Jones

General Editor

John Pikoulis

Volume Editors

Don Dale-Jones
P. Bernard Jones

The Complete Poems of T. H. Jones

Edited by

Don Dale-Jones

and

P. Bernard Jones

UNIVERSITY OF WALES PRESS
CARDIFF
2008

British Library Cataloguing-in-Publication Data
A catalogue record for this book is available from the British Library.

ISBN 978-0-7083-1967-3

THE ASSOCIATION FOR
WELSH WRITING IN ENGLISH
CYMDEITHAS LÊN SAESNEG CYMRU

Typeset by Columns Design Ltd, Reading RG4 7DH
Printed and bound in Great Britain by CPI Antony Rowe, Wiltshire

For Madeleine

Contents

Foreword   ix

Introduction   xi

The Complete Poems of T. H. Jones   1

Notes on the poems   372

Index of titles   447

Index of first lines   464

Introduction

Early on the summer's evening of 29 January 1965 T. H. Jones, charismatic poet, critic, lecturer and acting Head of the Department of English at University College, Newcastle, New South Wales, was found drowned in the sea-bathing pool known as The Bogey Hole. To all appearances a successful and happy family-man, he had published three important volumes of poetry with Rupert Hart-Davis and was looking forward to a sabbatical year in the United States. He had apparently overcome his addiction to alcohol and was writing the finest poetry of his life. America, he believed, would enable him to transcend his most recent and constraining persona, that of 'the poor colonial's Dylan Thomas', achieve international recognition and return in triumph to Wales.

The forty years since his death have not been kind to Jones's personal or literary reputation. He is by a long way the last significant twentieth century Anglo-Welsh poet to be accorded a major critical biography, and the sculpture set up to honour him in his native town, Builth Wells, was apologised for by local dignitaries, vandalised and finally, amid controversy and farce, exiled to the obscurity of a country-house hotel. It has taken a new century for a revival of interest sufficient to justify major critical reappraisal of this paradigm of the dichotomy at the heart of personal and national identity in twentieth century Wales. This complete poems comes forty years late. Of the three most significant Welsh poets of the period writing in English, R. S. Thomas, Dylan Thomas and T. H. Jones, only Jones offers us convincing insight into that century's most anguished preoccupation and neurosis – sexual passion.

Thomas Henry Jones, 'Harri' to his family and friends, but as a writer always and only 'T. H. Jones', was born on 21 December 1921 at Cwm Crogau, a remote hillside shepherd's cottage in the huge rural parish of Llanafan Fawr in what was then Breconshire. His father, Llewelyn, a disillusioned veteran of the First World War employed by the County Council as a roadman, had married Ruth Teideman, a servant girl from Porth in the Rhondda valley. Harri was their firstborn:

> 'My grandfather came down from the hills to have a look at me ...' he would write in his short story, 'My Grandfather Would Have me Be a Poet', '... he said, "He's going to be a poet."'

Son of a Welsh-speaking labourer, grandson of a shepherd and nephew of Daniel Jones, the bardd gwlad of the 'bro' (Welsh language poet of the locality), T. H. Jones might well have followed the example of that other great Welshman of the parish, Thomas Price, Carnhuanawc (1787–1848), friend of Iolo Morganwg and fellow progenitor of the nineteenth century's reinvention of Welsh cultural identity. The circumstances of his life dictated, however, that his way would be that of Price's great contemporary from neighbouring Builth Wells, the proto-Anglo-Welshman, Thomas Jeffrey Llywelyn Prichard (1790–1862), antiquarian, travelling player and first Anglo-Welsh novelist. Although Welsh-speaking, Prichard was a tireless polemicist for what he considered the inevitable and natural union of Wales and England by means of the 'superior' English language.

In the autobiographical short stories written for the most part in his early twenties, T. H. Jones would adopt the first of his many personae, the romantic boy from the hills pre-destined to be, not a 'bardd gwlad' like his Uncle Dan, but a famous poet in the English language. These stories trace the development of a sensitive child born in a remote, claustrophobic valley and destined to be a poet. They portray a handsome, feckless father, a Welsh 'mam' of great fortitude: 'a woman of power and knowledge, a wise woman old as the hills', and a grandfather to be confused with the God 'who was a great voice and might appear at any time as a flaming bush to announce the end of the world', as well as a large cast of minor local characters who would not be out of place in the short stories of Caradoc Evans. The tales foreground an early alienation from Welsh roots – at his mother's behest he spoke no Welsh – and dramatise the emerging temptations of the flesh. They reveal an early recognition of 'the triple intoxication' stimulated by 'knowledge, power and freedom of choice' which leads to rejection of Welsh nonconformity with its reductive god imprisoned within the walls of Llanafan's Pisgah Chapel and further circumscribed by the language of that chapel's devotions.

At the age of five Jones entered Llanafan Church School. Its headmaster, 'Proud Salop', was a 'red-faced bully ... a man who would always be looking up at the heavens and taught with a huge stick, thick as a wrist, which he applied impartially to head, back or arms.' These early school years, recollected among the pubs of Fitzrovia, read like a psychoanalyst's primer. The shy schoolboy bullied by the head teacher and the rough boys from the farms is saved by a sympathetic young female teacher who cultivates his reading:

> 'despite a home that possessed only four books: the Bible, Sankey and Moody, Pilgrim's Progress, and Mrs Beeton which was exotic and unfailing of delights but which I was only allowed to look at on special occasions such as birthdays and when I had the measles.'

In this persona Jones reads all the books the small school can provide and becomes the only child in his year to qualify for entry to the County

School. Dislocation follows inevitably and he acquires 'an adequate carapace of indifference to the ordinary world', and confirms in his own mind once and for all 'that God was shut up in the little dirty white chapel which smelled of soap, lamp oil and deacons.' The teenager undergoes rites of passage which confirm that the certainties of Pisgah Chapel, so important to his mother, have for him no significance beyond winning recitations at eisteddfodau, outdoing his contemporaries and devouring iced buns at the anniversary tea. What was for his Mam the agoraphobia of the annual outing to the seaside at Aberystwyth (for her and the rest of the family its highlight being interminable shopping at Woolworths) was for him, when eventually permitted to tread the grey, sandy beach, a liberating vision: 'the great mystery of blue waters covering the face of the earth and holding the wonders of the Lord.'

Builth Secondary School in 1933 was a relaxed and, by the standards of the time, a surprisingly enlightened, classless institution where talent could flourish. The working-class Jones became best friends with Robson Davies, the headmaster's son, and Donald John Jones, son of a local solicitor. Both had libraries at home to supplement the limited provision of the W. H. Smith library, and Donald Jones collected Penguin publications from their inception in 1935. Another seminal influence was F. J. Anthony, an inspirational teacher of English and French who encouraged independent reading beyond a narrow curriculum typified by Shakespeare and Palgrave's 'Golden Treasury', 'that bit of victoriana that haunted my youth and almost killed my poetic ambition'. Jones's early preference for robust Salvationist poetry such as Briggs' 'The Modern Village Blacksmith' and the popular verse of A. G. Prys-Jones was succeeded by an interest in the work of D. H. Lawrence, in particular *Sons and Lovers*.

By the time he entered the Sixth Form the academically precocious Jones was taking himself seriously as a writer. His juvenilia, which still appear fresh, are tinged with humour and irony. He edited some particularly good editions of the school magazine and played rugby and soccer wildly and well. His life was already a double one: at weekends he worked for his keep on farms or in the forestry and acquired his next persona, that of the hard-drinking teenage rebel. Jones drank from an early age, but it was for smoking in school that he was briefly suspended. The waiting-room at Builth Wells G.W.R. station became the comfortable club-room of a sixth form coterie, led by him, that met to read poetry, discuss politics and fear for the future of a Europe descending rapidly into war.

In 1939 Jones won the county scholarship to the University College of Wales, Aberystwyth, and went up shortly after the German invasion of Poland. His father 'spat his disappointment into the fire': he had wished his son to become a clerk with the Breconshire County Council. For his mother, her hopes of a priestly vocation not yet entirely dashed, his success was a reward for twenty years' unhappiness and toil. She prepared food-parcels and warned against the two notorious pitfalls of what she thought of as the cosmopolitan university town, actresses and boxing. Jones, ideologically Marxist and in politics a pacifist, was emotionally combative. A good amateur boxer, he became, with lodgings to pay for, an excellent poker player; the actresses would keep until after the War. He distributed Marxist literature on the promenade and campaigned for peace and for Communism, but in 1941 the progress of the war overcame his pacifism and he volunteered for the Navy, leaving behind his first love, Clara (Claire) Jones, and a prize-winning eisteddfod essay which proposed a post-war world that would substitute 'power and planning' for the false 'prophets and kings' of the 1930s.

The emotional bond with 'the sea which he loved so passionately' established on the Pisgah Chapel outings was cemented and qualified by three years' convoy duty in the Mediterranean. Long periods of boring but tense routine, which gave him time to develop his poetic craft, were punctuated by terrifying, savage action such as the dramatic capture of the Italian submarine, Bronzo: 'She ran the white flag up, and still our gunners/Pressed their automatic fingers/To make her run with blood.' Despite his best efforts, Jones failed to place until after the war even one of the many poems which he wrote while on active service – virtually all of them are published for the first time in this volume – and it was not long before Clara Jones informed him that she had found someone else.

No anthology of Second World War poetry is complete without the memorable 'Lucky Jonah', a retrospective distillation of naval war experience that fuses, with the catalyst of childhood memories, a sailor's perception of love and death, 'the patient erotic sea' and 'the lullaby and catalogue of the drowned'. As is usual with writing derived from first-hand experience of conflict, it was not until 1959 that the experience became capable of being given artistic form. Jones's immediate feelings were expressed in an untitled poem written in Algiers in 1944:

> O you who sit so easily over tea
> Or, in the cosy pub, the well-earned beer
> Regretting this and that and the other
> and the price of things – 'ridiculous, my dear' –
> to whom a drowned ship is a paragraph
> to be glossed over in the breakfast paper,
> and a bridgehead a tiresome term
> from which we are so slow to make advances –
> what can we wish you, to express our hate?
> ('Algiers, January 1944')

In 1946, awaiting demobilisation, Jones met and married the potter, Madeleine Scott.

'It was a wonderful coincidence that your father and I ever met', she would tell her daughters. 'He was a man from the mountains of Breconshire and I was brought up in Dulwich.' The contrast was, however, even more extreme: her father, William McDonald Scott, son of a medical missionary, was a highly qualified pathologist who had worked at Edinburgh, Munich and Paris; her mother, Alice Mollard, the daughter of a French senator, had been educated at the Sorbonne.

Leaving her to complete her studies at the Camberwell College of Art, he returned to Aberystwyth to complete his studies and publish, under the influence notably of Dylan Thomas, his first serious adult poems:

> In no proud walking,
> But the waved form awoke
> Broke the gulled promenade
> To rippled laughter. The tall hills
> Bent down to mark my coming
> Home
>   ('Aberystwyth, March 1946')

Immediate post-war life at Aberystwyth was a wild affair. It is easy, sixty years on, to underestimate the impact upon this small seaside university town of a large number of war-hardened, mature students. Jones's close friends included the future historian, Gwyn Alf Williams (1925–95), who remembered him as 'gaunt, craggy, and permanently stooping, with a lock of dark dank hair falling over his forehead like something out of the Celtic twilight'. Another friend was the actress, Rachel Roberts (1927–80), who, in addition to enriching Jones's personal life, starred in his experimental verse-play, 'The Weasel at the Heart' (1947). Jones resumed his political activities with the Socialist Society and edited the undergraduate magazine, 'The Dragon'. His academic talents and his poetry impressed his formidable mentor, Professor Gwyn Jones (1907–99), who was, however, rather nervous of his social behaviour during that immediate post-war lacuna recalled by T .H. Jones's friend, Tom Sallis, as 'a lost weekend that lasted a year'. Jones famously drank his way to first class honours.

He then read for an M.A. on the imagery of the Metaphysical Poets and moved up the coast to Borth for a period of regeneration. There he cultivated the friendship of Ted Richards, occasional short story writer, antique dealer, part-time fisherman and proprietor of the Welsh Kitchen café where Jones worked alongside Rachel Roberts. On one of his frequent visits to Madeleine at Camberwell he met the sculptor, John Glanville, whose wife, Delia, presented Jones with the 'Black Book', the leather-bound octavo volume into which, between 11 May 1949 and 28 September 1964, he copied every poem which he completed, together with the date of its entry.

His M.A. completed, and with poems and reviews accepted by 'Life and Letters', 'Wales', 'Dock Leaves' and the 'Dublin Magazine', but now under pressure to provide for his wife and firstborn daughter, Sian, he settled in London and attempted to secure an academic appointment. Like Dylan Thomas before him, he haunted Fitzrovia in the persona of a neo-romantic poet, supporting his family by teaching English as a foreign language and reviewing. Poverty would not permit him to drift for long and he coveted the respectability and freedom of university teaching, preferably in Wales. All applications were unsuccessful, however, and the disappointment fuelled hiraeth and stimulated creativity:

> Remembering among the unlovely London voices
> A man who said, out of enthusiasm and love,
> 'You live upon your grandparents' memories',
> I am vexed and despondent; where my unruly heart rejoices
> I am tongue-tied, having not gratitude enough
> To speak in my own language or to hold my peace.
>   ('The Anglo-Welsh', October 1949)

The poem is addressed to Aneirin Talfan Davies (1909–80), critic, poet and broadcaster.

In 1951 Jones was obliged to settle for a post teaching English to apprentices at the Royal Dockyard School, Portsmouth, and a comfortable semi-detached home in the suburbs. He was a popular teacher at the college and an inspirational one for the W.E.A., his family expanded with the birth of two more daughters: Rhiannon (1953) and Ruth (1954), and his reputation as an Anglo-Welsh writer of some promise grew. His predominantly neo-romantic and confessional poems were frequently published in magazines and anthologies in Britain, Europe and the United States and attracted further interest through his dramatic readings on the BBC's *Third Programme* where their consciously self-referential elements were foregrounded by the bardic nature of their performance. There were also a few Welsh Home Service broadcasts, but, despite poems such as 'Out of Wales' (18 May 1950)

> Remembering today the land from which
> You come, the huddled nonconformist hills,
> The short grass sweetening the mountain sheep,
> The stubborn ponies proof against the weather,
> A shepherd's hazel stick and favourite bitch,
> (My best-loved image of remembered Wales)

he remained very much on the fringe of the Welsh literary establishment.

By 1957, now every inch the provincial Angry Young Man, he had found a sympathetic and prestigious publisher in Rupert Hart-Davis, whose eclectic list included R. S. Thomas, Charles Causley, Edmund Blunden, Andrew Young and Ronald Duncan. 'The Enemy in the Heart' (1957), Jones's first collection, was a great success. The 'Times Literary Supplement' reviewer in particular found the poems 'turbulent, raging, ecstatic ... and accomplished' and that his 'quest for the ideal ends in restlessness, disillusion, despair, rage.' There was strong support from Morwyth Rees in 'Dock Leaves', and Padraic Fallon, in 'The Dublin Magazine', compared him favourably to Thom Gunn, whose own juxtaposition of a quintessential metaphysical Englishness with the more exotic subject matter of 'leather boy' Hell's Angels, Elvis Presley and mescaline in his Californian collection, *The Sense of Movement* (1957), gave rise to a poetic tension between form and content, traditional poetic structures and intellectual abstraction, that were also so transparent in T. H. Jones.

Whilst working for the W.E.A. Jones had developed an interest in American Literature. In 1958 he attended the Salzburg Seminar, where he became friends with the American poet, Louise Bogan, poetry reviewer for the 'New Yorker', who would champion his poetry in the U.S.A. Another important friendship of this time was with the Italian poet, Roberto Sanesi, a friend of Vernon Watkins and translator of Dylan Thomas. Soon after his return to England Jones was recruited by Norman Jeffares to the staff of the rapidly expanding Newcastle college of the University of New South Wales. A letter to his apprehensive mother explained that it was 'a much better job ... more interest, more money, better prospects and university teaching is what I have always wanted to do'. As a valedictory for the old world and recommendation to the new he hurriedly assembled a number of unpublished poems and persuaded a rather reluctant Hart-Davis to bring out his second collection, 'Songs of a Mad Prince' (1960). This comprised thirty-five poems rejected for his first collection, six translations of Sanesi's work and only twenty-three new poems. The 'Times Literary Supplement' reviewer was unenthusiastic as was Roland Mathias in the 'Anglo Welsh Review', but Douglas Phillips, for the 'Western Mail', was perceptive and generous:

> 'His poems are for the most part short, highly disciplined, the work of a man of rare and acute intelligence shot through with the sardonic humour that is black and bleak enough to scare the pants off anyone whose mind is wrapped in the grey flannel clichés of our admass world ... I regard this as one of the most impressive books of new verse by a Welshman since [*Dylan Thomas's*] "Deaths and Entrances" (1946).'

Newcastle, New South Wales, was paradoxically both Eden and industrial wasteland, a dark, satanic steel town and a surfers' paradise. The as yet embryonic university college was peopled with English expatriates and there was a large Welsh community. Drink was cheap and campus life a round of parties. Jones perfected his charismatic lecturing style and enhanced his academic credentials by reviewing, publishing and developing his acquaintance with American literature. He attempted, with mixed success, to balance family commitments against playing the Dionysiac and increasingly frank and lucid confessional poet.

Some students thought that T. H. Jones's poetry was becoming influenced by the new focus of his critical attention, American poetry. To Julian Croft it seemed not dissimilar to what Lowell was writing at this time: 'It was metaphysical in origin and influenced by New Criticism techniques.' The Canadian, Northrop Frye, was a seminal influence at the cognitive level, in particular his *Fearful Symmetry* in which he contended that the product of the imaginative life 'is most clearly seen in the work of art which is a unified mental vision of experience'. Perception is superior to abstraction, says Frye, and vision is 'the goal of all freedom, courage and wisdom'. Frye's standpoint is Christian and holistic, concerned with unity rather than dislocation: 'there is', he maintains, 'a single visionary conception which the mind of man is trying to express, a vision of a created and fallen world which has been redeemed by divine sacrifice'. This formulation was particularly attractive to Jones, the alienated exile.

The problem was how to achieve personal regeneration. Many poems of this period are consistent with such terms, current during the 1960s, as 'poems of experience', 'confessional', 'open', 'poetry of involvement'. Lowell's *Life Studies* (1959) and *For the Union Dead* (1964) were the significant texts, but Jones had also lectured on and performed poetry by Roethke, Berryman and W. D. Snodgrass. His own mature poetry had now achieved simplicity, directness, a language close to common speech; its preoccupation is often with psychological truths and obsessions and he reveals with wry regret intimate, sometimes sordid or humiliating details of a physical decline that included alcohol-induced impotence:

> Drunk on duty, not for the first time,
> Private Ianto stands limply to attention,
> Thankful that though being unable's a crime
> At least it can't be punished by detention.
> (*Drunk on Duty*, 27 June 1961)

compulsive promiscuity:

> Waking with the taste still of your nipples
> In my mouth, I groan and stretch my empty arms,
> Remembering too well I have a member
> And rise reluctantly to write a poem.
> (*Who'd be an Erotic Poet Anyway*, 6 June 1961)

and more promiscuity:

> As malefactors once were branded, so
> I hoped your bites would stay upon my body
> That the whole envious world might know
> This was my guerdon when I served you nightly.
> (*She Bit Me, but not in Anger*, 17 April 1961)

The habit of self-scrutiny is central to American literature. At its purest it dominated the discourse of New England Puritanism; twentieth-century America wholly embraced its extension, psychoanalysis. The significance of language in the process of self-scrutiny has been discussed by Perry Miller (*The New England Mind: The Seventeenth Century*, Harvard University Press, 1939): 'the doctrine of regeneration caused the founders of New

England to become experts in psychological dissection', he writes. Herbert Leibowitz says of Lowell's early poetry that 'his ambivalent attitude to the Puritans is central to an understanding of his poetry' (*Robert Lowell: ancestral voices*, in: *Robert Lowell: a Portrait of the Artist in His Own Time* (ed.) Michael London and Robert Boyers, New York, David Lewis, 1970). Anthony Giddens suggests that Puritanism was one of the main stimuli for 'a take-off' into the more inclusive internally referenced ordering of society and nature (*Modernity and Self-Identity*, Stanford U.P. 1991, 155). Just as Lowell was preoccupied with the strange figure of Jonathan Edwards (*For the Union Dead*), so T. H. Jones used characters like Cotton Mather and Frances Higginson to give perspective to puritanical Welsh characters, such as the referential Uncle Daniel Jones who influenced his childhood.

A student of his, Marion Halligan, fictionalised Jones as 'Tom Lloyd' in her novel, *Self-Possession*: 'Literature was the only topic of conversation apart from sex ... and even that was a form of literature with him.'

> 'His classes sat fascinated, absorbing, silent. Often they forgot to write anything down, which was irritating afterwards, but they never forgot the experience ... He took a book from the shelf behind him. "Life is short, art is long, the crooked worm will have us in the end, and that's the way it should be," he said ... He read slowly, and the words came so lovingly out of his mouth that it seemed he were inventing them. "Secret by the unmourning water ... After the first death, there is no other".'

His role became that of the proverbial 'spoiled preacher' and the more he drank and womanised the better his poetry became. He 'dried out' at least once:

> But after two days' drying out
> I am no more inclined to shout,
> I do not even whisper poetry
> Except inside the quiet of my head,
> Not loud enough to disturb the other dead.
> ('You Can Have More Than One Breakdown
> If You Try Hard Enough', October 1964)

and his wife, Madeleine, supported him to the bitter, unexpected end and beyond.

The Jones family album contains an anachronistic photograph of a rather overweight father in sandals and Hawaiian shirt with his three daughters and their horse. Tightly grouped, they stand in a wide, dusty street; the shadows are short and crisp; there are no hills on the horizon. As Jones explained in a letter to Aneirin Talfan Davies, 'I came here in the first place because I could get an academic job – this, like the convicts of the old days, tends to be one-way traffic. And of course my children, despite their Welsh names, are thoroughly Australian.' The comment contains an unconscious irony, for it was those very 'one-way' exiles who had carved out The Bogey Hole in which this one was eventually to drown.

Jones's Australian poems achieve the simplicity and directness appropriate to the time and place of their creation. Their language is close to the vernacular and they deal transparently with psychological truths and obsessions: alcoholism; promiscuity; impotence. In major poems of the period he adopts various personae, most notably that of the American Puritan minister, writer and witch-finder, Cotton Mather:

> Is God's good wilderness now purified?
> Or must we fear and go in constant sorrow
> That we are still afflicted, that tomorrow
> May bring back to Salem that delirium?
> ('Cotton Mather Remembers the Trial of
> Elizabeth How', September 1964)

Australia's two major contemporary poets, A. D. Hope and James McAuley, encouraged Jones and published him both as poet and reviewer. The creative burst that followed his arrival in Australia enabled him to suggest to Hart-Davis a third collection, 'The Beast at the Door', sales of which he felt would benefit from his forthcoming monograph on Dylan Thomas (Oliver and Boyd, 1963). Published in the same year, the volume received a negative response from the 'Times Literary Supplement', and even Glyn Jones, in the 'Western Mail', reviewing it alongside R. S. Thomas's 'The Bread of Truth', found no more than twenty or so poems 'that speak without mimicry and ventriloquism'. He missed the point, however, that these poems, particularly the satirical ones, consciously undermine any certainty of knowledge and by so doing exhibit an extraordinary reflexive dynamism in their radical appropriation and transformation of that 'knowledge'. In particular, Jones revisits 'hiraeth' (nostalgia/longing) through the half-empty dark glass of his 'exile' so that, for the first time in Anglo-Welsh poetry, this characteristic becomes fertile ground for deconstruction, a repudiation of the certainties of the ever-present 'I' and reified past.

Since his death, and in particular because of the manner of it, Jones's very being appears to have been subsumed into a mythology of his own making. A posthumous volume, 'The Colour of Cockcrowing', in which his widow and her friend, Gillian Stowell, collected some of the less obviously 'confessional' and occasional poems of his last years, appeared in 1965. Elizabeth Jennings noted that these 'last verses were sombre and pulsating with life'. Bernard Bergonzi concluded that 'Jones was an excellent poet who was clearly moving into a new phase of maturity.' Herbert Williams found him a striking and original talent and Terence Hawkes summarised his achievement as steering a course between the contrasting visions of Wales represented by Dylan and R. S. Thomas: 'the polarities of body and soul, order and disorder, boozer and Bethel, Saturday night and Sunday morning'.

Harri Webb, who had heard a lot about him 'as a larger than life character who'd had a blazing affair with Rachel Roberts ... (and) lived a conspicuously poetic life' eulogised him in 'In Memory of Harri Jones':

From Irfon, guilty water
And up the Chwefri where
A dead prince and a dead poet
Called me ...
You did well to get out of
This hole in the middle of Wales,
Only there is nowhere else
Anywhere ...
Were you perhaps lucky
Not to come back to this land
Of dead villages and ruined harvests?

In the decade following his death Jones's reputation declined in Australia, paradoxically because he was seen as an essentially Welsh writer and emigré. Meic Stephens, always an admirer, commissioned a monograph in the 'Writers of Wales' series (Julian Croft, 1976) and Gomer Press published the collected poems (Julian Croft and Don Dale-Jones, 1977) comprising the four volumes plus 29 poems selected by Julian Croft from the 'Black Book'. The occasional critical essay reminded readers of the existence of Jones's poetry, but it was not until 2001 that a major re-assessment of him ('T. H. Jones, Poet of Exile', by Bernard Jones and Don Dale-Jones) was published by the University of Wales Press.

We suggested then, and reassert now, that Jones shares many of the preoccupations and characteristics of writers seen today as postmodern. In an unpublished essay (c.1955), 'A Refusal to Write Autobiography', Jones adopts a view identical to that of the quintessential postmodern writer damned with faint praise as ('merely' understood) 'experimental', B. S. Johnson. Jones presents his own 'job' of 'writer' as 'just a little sweet lying' and, purporting to analyse his practice, adds, 'Let me be deceitful'. Johnson, in 1973, preferred to define the process with, 'Life is chaotic fluid random ... Telling stories really is telling lies.'

As Jones's life disintegrated, he came to believe that it was impossible, in a fragmenting world, to say with certainty anything of permanence. Paradoxically, as that of a rootless transported 'taffy', his writing celebrates discontinuity and chaos, discards control and creates a bricolage of poetry from loss of faith in the metanarratives of his childhood – redemptive Christianity, Welshness, Marxism, sometimes even language itself.

I am troubled by my own old poems:
Own poems: would, Judas, do better not to
What he or I made in what garden do,
Could be kissed away, turned by, into rhymes.
I weed the garden for my metaphors,
Desert into, from, the legion of the curse.
    ('On Taking Part in a Recital of Baroque Music and
    Poetry at Newcastle Cathedral, Sunday, 4 October 1964')

In his last poem he takes as signifier of his condition the isolated, windswept hawthorn of the hills of his childhood:

> The thorn through all its punishment
> In March and in October
> Would not have any wind relent,
> No mercy ever.
>   ('Thorn', December 1964)

This is the defiance of Shakespeare's *Macbeth* at bay: 'They have tied me to a stake; I cannot fly,/But bear-like I must fight the course ...'. Macbeth, however, was justly punished for defying an harmonious order established and enforced by a just and loving God; in Jones's world, as in ours, no such order existed or exists.

Thomas Henry Jones invented the designation, T. H. Jones, under which all of his published work appeared. He did so to dare comparison with W. B. Yeats, T. S. Eliot and W. H. Auden and to resist submersion in Dylan Thomas. Only to family and friends was he known as 'Harri'. We may broadly summarize his achievement in terms of the signpost works which mark its progress. 'The Welsh Hills' (*c.*1939), the schoolboy essay which first claims the Llanafan landscape as his own; 'Visions' (1940), the undergraduate eisteddfod essay which shows the awakening intellect, the already wide reading and the Marxist/Blakean idealism. 'The Enemy in the Heart' (1946), technical *tour de force* and first clear statement of the dangers of passionate love. 'Poem for Wales' (1946) and other associated nationalistic declarations mark his return from the war and reassert Welsh nationality as the basis of his writing. 'Lucky Jonah' (1959), requiem for the war years, elegy for lost companions but, unfortunately, no exorcism of the nightmares, is literally transitional, written as it was on passage to Australia. 'The Colour of Cockcrowing' (1959), one of the few wholehearted celebrations of the beauty, life, sexuality of the postlapsarian world which is the only one we know. The short story, 'The First Christmas' (*c.*1962) is an unflinching assertion of individual identity even in the face of God, and acceptance of the consequences of sin; in contrast, 'Girl Reading John Donne' (1964) and 'Welsh Bastard' (1964) may stand together to exemplify the 'concealed art' of the many mature poems in which deceptively easy colloquial language and an apparently casual deployment of allusions convey a wealth of postmodernist significance. 'Cotton Mather' (1964) moves to a bleak exploration of the man caught between a rigorous religion, a sense of human frailty and an awareness of change.

> . . . the land where every wind
> > Is a breath of guilt
> Is home . . .
>
> My paradise will be despair
> > And the cold winds that blow
> About the rocks, about your hair
> > And the grief I know.
> > (*My Country, My Grief*, 1 January 1964)

> Crow, cock, until this woman and this man
> Return to dust, crow until their children
> And their children's children too are dust,
> Crow until God revokes his first decree
> That Earth and all the inhabitants thereof
> Should wear forever the colour of cockcrowing.
> In the world we know it was always the colour of the cockcrow.
> > (*The Colour of Cockcrowing*, 2 December 1959).

Viewed from the early years of a new century T. H. Jones is neither transitional nor marginal even though he was, or made himself, most unjustly marginalized. In his distinctive Anglo-Welshness, he ranks with Dylan and R. S. Thomas, sharing the romanticism of the one, the intellect and sense of Wales of the other. All three are, in quite different ways, religious poets; all three are, also in quite different ways, international in their appeal and relevance. They remind us that writing out of the myth of a small nation is no bar to universality. Yeats is their paradigm, each his own justification. As a love-poet T. H. Jones is unique among Welsh writers who have written in English. That his private imagination was dismantled by war, that he was never quite able to rebuild for himself a sense of the unfractured home he desired, is as certain as that final feeling of futility which caused him to cry out:

> Put not your trust in words or anything.
> Put not your trust in really saying enough.
> Birds in the hand can't be compelled to sing.
> Despair suffices. Love's something else, ah! something.
> > (*Useless Advice to a Young Man Hopelessly in Love*,
> > 14 June 1962)

Sonnet on a Lost Mistress

There was a time, not over-long ago,
When I could claim her love, and she would bend
Her fair head over me, and 'To the end,
My love,' would say: this gallant, fruitless show
Is over now; yet would I gladly go
To Hell for her if I could be her friend,
Only her friend, again;– the years' slow trend
Will come and I be here alone. But no! –
I have her sacred mem'ry yet; her love
Remains in memory although 'tis gone
In actual fact;– her golden hair and eyes
Of candid blue still from the mists above
Bend over me when I'm asleep at dawn,
Her shadow rises with me when I rise.

The Pacifist

When I see old heads bowed in shame
at things the world has long forgot,
and young men seeking empty fame
or going, blindly, to be shot,–
I think of that hare's collar-bone
through which Yeats laughed across the water,
and carve a mindless face on stone
for which a king would sell his daughter;
and go and join the skeletons
and laugh with them their lipless grin
that men should be such simpletons
as not to look beneath the skin;
and meditate on suicide,
toying with death's pale trophies,– then
I think of all who vainly died
to make the world more fit for men,
and with a broken-hearted laugh
I mutter underneath my breath:
Let all the grain be free from chaff
in God's good granary after death.

Acrobat

Your heart is an acrobat that will not stand still
But swings in mad evolutions from the earthfast trapeze
you have made of my heart. When will you learn
that stillness is desirable? that the whirl of movement
is maddening? that I am not to be spurned?
For, one day, if your acrobatics cease not, the trapeze
will vanish, you will crash to earth, all movement gone,
all motion ceased for ever.

(Calling within us the spring)

Calling within us the spring
Answering itself in the blood
Foretelling function of summer
Pregnant with increase of autumn
Nescient of winter's decay;

Calling within us the spring,
Poetry leaping to answer
The call of the flux of us the blood
Love, a bacchanal dancer . . .
Calling within us, and answering
Only the wind in the rigging,
Waves susurrus and laughing

Calling within us the spring
And the urge in the blood upsurging.

(In the duality of man)

In the duality of man
Lies confusion's cause.
That he should have this Janus' face
Obscures the issue.
This reveller, this rutting stag
Sets up a pedestal
And worships chastity.
In the abstract only?
But how in this little pause
Of time sum up the account
Balance the ledger, say

This or that he did,
Was chaste or not.
Here's debit and here's credit,
Much duality of motive,
More of action, loss and gain.
It is no easy sum.

(Cool pity covers us)

Cool pity covers us
to hear the sorrow of the amorous
nightingale.
What for the story
of their sudden glory
who flashed kingfisherwise
across the unrecording skies?
They have gone beyond lament
who had for element
the bare bright air
and wrote their honour there.

(Why should I be afraid?)

Why should I be afraid?
I who have walked with Merlin
Through the caves of thought
And sat among the dead
And listened to their sly laughter
At our follies.

(No more for you and I, my love)

No more for you and I, my love, the warm retreat
In pub or cinema; the privacy of the sheet,
The intimate coffee, or the long, slow walks
Around the old town, or the quiet talks
Watching the moonlight silver all the beach,
The midnight passion when each leant to each
We kissed and said goodnight and kissed again,
No more the joy we had in wind and sun and rain
Together – (now, for me, a world of discipline and sudden fears,
The swan's way whaleback, long, long years

Of danger hardship and the lack
Of you –
and for you my love, the lonely, black
Existence, fearing, hoping, loving).

Landward

Landward you linger, and the western air,
The wanton, caresses you capriciously,
And I am dumb to send my yearning there
Where you wait upon the white edge of the sea.

Landward you linger in the quiet light
When evening smiles upon you, and you smile
As dreams of me come to you. A mile
Of beach I recollect, of silvered sand
Where once we walked, and hand-in-hand,
And all the merry little waves sang free.

And we were young and love is dark to be unlocked
To find our passions tender and unmocked.
Landward you linger, linger there for me.

(Reaching towards the light)

Reaching towards the light;
Only the heat of the afternoon, and the sea,
The still sea, and the unmoving sky;
And all the restlessness of mind diluted
To this thin fluid delicately dropping
In contemplation even.

Epitaphs

All we are is epitaphs
'They shall not be forgotten'
While round us the wave breaks, laughs
On the beaches where the corpses are rotting.

For us no forest fires
Crumble the ivory towers
Of apathy; the minutes fall away

From us endlessly, irretrievably,
With the poems unwritten, the words unspoken,
The plays not staged, the murders left undone,
Not even hearts are broken.
The windows of our sensibility
Are leaded over with monotony.

Once there was a young girl, was a tree
One word that leaped from all the other words,
One bird that dazzled as it flashed
Beneath the bridge and up the silver stream.
These are behind us; all around
The unreflecting sky.

Holds the sun to a rippled sea
Behind the glory; dream
Is dissipated, epitaphs
Contain us; shall we be forgotten
When no more the bird laughs, laughs
The wave; shall we be forgotten?

No songs or sonnets

No songs or sonnets now take time away,
No passion plucks us for the tearing minutes
That builded islands in our life before.
Oh! the King's shilling hires oblivion for us
And we, abstracted from the flux of life we knew,
Feeling the sun of life come faintly only
Through the burning glass of love, know
In our veins blood thickens, sap coagulates,
Know the entries of the mind grow hard;
The crannies of our wall – so picturesque – are filled
With the cement of this monotony.
No songs or sonnets; and our passion dies.

Love, lust, pride, passion moved us once
To take up arms, but in long use of arms
Passion and pride, lust, love, fade, die;
And all that's left us is this robot body,
Briefly loaned to cheat oblivion with.

Let us but have our songs and sonnets back,
Restore our pride and passion, to upraise
Us islands in this grey flat sea,

Let us be wild again with morning joy,
And in the evening know the ecstasy
Of one white face montaged in moonlight.
Give us back our songs and passions.
Better to die like Marlowe in a tavern,
Hot with the moment's fancy. Than to rot
In the corruption of monotony.

Time flies by us irrevocably,
A flat plain; we desire the peaks, the pause
Of songs and sonnets, pride and passion – love
The word to mean the city in the plain.
People the dust with children. Fill the page
With linked sweetness, the bare boards
With the riot and the colour and the thought.
Let us disturb with islands this flat sea!

Contemplation

In the afternoon, the Indian summer,
When the seed of the land is shrivelled, and the sea
Is rocked in stillness, contemplation only
Is left to us; only to look
And listen not for the quiver of sap
The last, faint protest of the dying leaf,
The babe's stir in the belly.
Not these for us, but only contemplation,
Only calmness, looking-on.

When I threw out my first branches,
Reaching towards the sky,
Nothing was ever dry,
There was no stillness,
And contemplation was an old man's idleness.
Now with all twigs unbudded,
And the branches bare, decaying,
I sleep.
Serenity enwraps me,
And the sea is rocked in stillness,
No words disturb the silence,
No thoughts, no spring
Of sap to bud in fierceness,
Reaching towards the light;
Only the heat of the afternoon, and the sea,

The still sea, and the uninviting sky;
And all the restlessness of mind diluted
To this thin fluid delicately dropping
In contemplation even.

(Fear not the pettiness of time)

Fear not the pettiness of time,
The compromise of age.

With the danger of anger now gone, the horizon
From grieving to loving is scanned by our yearning
Eyes that for years were empty and hollow
The city we see now is bravely illumined.
No faces are loose now as memory holds them
That bitter winter of our disillusion.
A tower in the air we will build now
Straight and white wherein to ring out bells
In a fine frenzy, frantic with anticipation
Of our dream that came to be true in the morning.

(Waiting the onslaught of the light)

Waiting the onslaught of the light
Be silent now;
And from the stillness of the night
Take, grieving heart,
No sense of hurt.

Sad heart, be silent now, an hour
Waiting the light,
The sudden spear shaft's flashing power,
The leaping voice
The naked joys.

Dream yet, sad heart, dream on your grief,
Until day comes,
Dream till the falling of the leaf
And take no hurt,
Sad, and lovely heart.

(Before the bright bird write his epitaph)

Before the bright bird write his epitaph of wing
With flash of beak and sunlit glitter
In the rippled air with his thrill of song,
His brief ambition, laugh
His sorrow out of countenance,
Before this epilogue of song and dance
What legend of his bitter wayfaring
Is born to make his sons or daughters strong
In wisdom to uphold his faith
Win from his death
His half-believed-in vision?

This is our decision.
Rear up his pillowed hours
Against the principalities and powers
And through the mists of fate
Reach for his higher dreams.
And let his heirs inherit
The flowering of his fine spirit.

(Oh! you who have been there)

Oh! you who have been there, at the end
Of the transitory inglorious power
Of this fleeting hour,
You who have been all the way,
and are still my friend,
Will you not now return and say
Was it worthwhile, your journey, after all?

Similes in Exile

Similes of sunlight at thought of you occur,
Patterning their brightness on the parched air
Of this exile like birds' song descending
From its high tower, or waves befriending
A lonely beach.
        Within this envelope
Of flesh, this crumbling keep
Of bones and blood, are images
Of you; symbols are in the sky; and these

Are timeless though your beauty's mortal.
Time is a prison; and its granite portal
Opens upon eternity; the key is love,
And though we love now at remove
Of space and time, I still hold in my hand
Your heart fluttering like a caught bird.
We are out of focus; but adjust your mind,
Tune in the wavelength of the whispered word,
And you shall hear me: the mutual response
Of our two hearts will outlive our mere romance.

(I remember the house)

I remember the house
In an attitude of imprecision
There was neither the chill dawn wind advancing
Nor the cool night wind retreating
But the stagnation of the after-dinner chance
But the prolongation of our no-decision.
Poised there an endless moment we swung
Between the choices; then we chose but did not choose.
And all was over, and we went the middle way
Not starting from the destined end
Nor going from the preordained beginning.
Old griefs are useless now
For these new scars.
Can time and the power of weeping
Take away wars?

(The singing wonder of the stars)

The singing wonder of the stars
Shall heal these scars,
The shadowed beauty of the night
Yet give delight
To mind and body, ease
Be found beneath tall trees,
And all lost joys
Recaptured in her face and voice.
The singing wonder of the stars
Shall heal these scars.

Winter Beeches

These wan woods now are winter's care
Imprisoned in the iron air
Keeping the promise of spring
an unbound and lissom thing
like a young dancer's classic grace
and wanton limbs and lyric face.

Love Song

Be human only now, and warm,
and calmly lie with me
in no romantic ecstasy,
but face to face and form to form
Forget the facile response
the automatic reply to the old traditions.

Be human only now, the tale of
rose and nightingale and moon
(which rhymes too easily with June)
forget, know only this, the fact of love.
This is our present situation
and we must not be deceived by preconceptions.

Be human only now, relax in love
forget the future, the pictured past
and do not ask, 'Can moments last?'

Salvationist's Dream

The lion sleeps upon the stair
The lamb rampages through the sky
And shiny in the shimmery air
Behold the scarlet dragons lie
And stumbling on the ribbon road
is God beneath his heavy load
Of all our unredeemed desires
fuel for everlasting fires
while crowned about the jewelled sky
Man no longer doomed to die,
Sees at last his destined end
With God become his mighty friend

Raging lamb, tender lion
redeemed Gomorrah, glorious Sion
man deserving of his pardon
and God relieved of his great burden.

(Jack Christ was kind to me)

Jack Christ was kind to me, a poor thief,
For my grave-soaked gallows-pocked grief
gave me to suck of his nipples of pity
and builded for me for my hedgerow home
a glass palace in a crystal city.

Would I not then feel the pain of his nails,
be crucified in all their lousy jabs
just to ease the strain of his great burden
relieve his pain (his pain of pity for me)
be deserving of his pardon?

(In this white courtyard where the not-to-be-imprisoned sun)

In this white courtyard where the not-to-be-imprisoned sun
floodlights my fantasy of being free
I write to you, who, in that milder climate of the heavy lunch
and tea at five o'clock, and closing time,
butter your mind to my uncomfortable fact.
O you who sit so easily over tea
Or, in the cosy pub, the well-earned beer
Regretting this and that and the other
and the price of things – 'ridiculous, my dear' –
to whom a drowned ship is a paragraph
to be glossed over in the breakfast paper,
and a bridgehead a tiresome term
from which we are so slow to make advances –
what can we wish you to express our hate?
We do not really hate you, but we fear
that your indifference will cost us dear.
Fear is hate's well-spring, and so we
to whom fear and hope are the pole of living
hate, as we love, fiercely.

(Moondappled memories)

Moondappled memories of beloved midnights
Make a tree top patterning of awaited rain
In the parched forests of my exiled madness;
And being, concentrated to a point of pain,
Makes an escape-hatch of these memories
To reach the larger air of its desires.

When we were young we felt the tortured cities

When we were young we felt the tortured cities
Writhe in our bowels. Austria and Spain
Were more than symbols to us. Our own pain
And China more than a theme for heroic ditties.
More than the object of our too-ironic pities
The people dying on the huddled plain,
The dreamer's loss the manufacturer's gain.
But in our blood the feuds and aunties.
Where are we now who sang that tortured time?
What is the mask now of our tragic mime?
Compassion still the fluid in the vein
And in our bowels still the cities weep
And through our thoughts the tortured peoples creep
And the world is still our personal pain.

Journey from a War

The war being only, when you look at it, a state of mind,
and not belonging to me like head or heart or hand,
I took a journey outward, tangent-wise, to where
memory holds open still an uninhibited door.
This was my sole freedom which I took in liberal fashion
Cutting myself off deliberately from communication
With the warfare, I succeeded in isolating
Myself, becoming lonely as a runic writing.
And when I got to my before planned destination
alighting at the other end, alone with my own ration
I looked down the long, deserted platform
searching the desert eagerly – for whom?
Why, I was looking for the one who did not come
the nameless one who has no need of name
since she was always with me in the time before
on all adventurous journeys a Pole star.

This Hero Now

This hero now, a gauche cynic,
holds Europe helpless in the hollow of hand and skull.
Will the moon of his perfection ever come to the full
in a flurry of seas
incarnadined with his own sacrificial blood;
or, sliding between the knees
of these antique gods now crumbling for ever away,
will he see on the edge of this horror of guts and blood
new dawn his pastoral day?
He is heavy-booted and browed.
There seems to smoulder
a heavy faggot of care on his broad shoulder,
and his belly is big with his mind's increase of wonder.
Shall he thirst then, shall he for ever hunger
after those bright pavilions of his domestic ease,
his hearth of comfort, his enduring peace?
When he lies jewelled in elegiac verse
shall they, the inheritors of his desperate renown,
play out the part he would so patiently rehearse;
riot of spring and tumult of honeyed breath
take away this salt-tang-bitter smell of death;
or their clay kingdoms too come tumbling down?
He needs no gilded hearse,
no pillared pomp nor monument
of storied verse
to legend his fulfilled intent
to reach across the black, tumultuous seas
his new America.
        (When will he sprawl at ease
again among his neighbours, telling tales
of an old bitterness, with apple-blossom light
softening his scarred face; and the quiet oncoming of night
make him think only of slumber?)
Whom eloquence could not win,
nor power's rhetoric seduce wholly,
who wants no vision of glory,
but only cessation of this battle-folly;
he is the hero, the cynic,
the clumsy guard behind a sullen wall
of universal hopes and dreams.
Before the bright bird write his epitaph
with flash of beak and sunlit glitter of wing
in the rippled air, mock with his trill of song

his brief ambition, laugh
his sorrow out of countenance;
before this epilogue of song and dance,
what legend of his bitter wayfaring
is born to make his sons and daughters strong
in wisdom to uphold his faith,
win from his death
his half-believed-in vision?

This now is our decision:
Rear up his pillared hours
against the principalities and powers;
and through the mists of fate
reach for his higher dream;
and let his heirs inherit
the flowering of his fine spirit.

(It was a lovely lady)

It was a lovely lady came riding by
down the old road of dreams and dreaming towers
and straightway I forsake all other paramours
to make a music of the glory of that day.

Her body's whiteness was so marvellously fair
so sweet her perfumes exhaled on the wind
that she has echoed since in the corridors of my mind
like some entrancingly sweet old country air.

All the land was endowed with graciousness as she went
by, and I there gazing on her in speechless wonder
tore the bonds of aestheticism asunder
and dedicated my muse to astonishment.

Exercise in Blank Verse: the Dancing Girl

And so fawn-like she came
Before us dancing; nor was there any stir,
Nor any sound, save our muted breathing.
Among us some were very wise, some witty,
And some had travelled far, and seen all things,
And some had sung the praise of women
In more cities than Cino's three, but all

Were still to marvel at this girl's dancing
And all were hushed before her fathers grace.
Plum blossom waving in the air she seemed,
Her body motion, and her motion breath.
Then when at last she stopped, and stood before us,
White bird alighted on a branch, a snowflake fallen,
We raised our eyes to look into her eyes,
And read there. Death.

(But that was yesterday)

We were the last romantics – chose for theme
Traditional sanctity and loveliness . . .

W. B. Yeats ('Coole Park and Ballylee', 1931)

But that was yesterday.
Now all those lovely landscapes are a dream,
A plaintive echo dying down the glades,
And we phantom pursuers of faint shades,
Travellers on a dank nostalgic stream,
Sigh for the lost romantic loneliness,
The high tradition, which, like the Holy Grail,
Ever eludes us.
This is a twice-told tale
Of long endeavour, with some bitterness,
Much folly, and all that's left to say
Is – That was yesterday.

Mountain Scene

Here stone and sky are married,
and breed fantastic peace,
a bleak golgothic nightmare.
The winds cross and re-cross
a home of friendly,
of pilgrim fancies,
haunt of high-hovering buzzard
where the loved heart dances
in sculptured fancies.

Nostalgia

Waves whelm me westwards from this antique sea
to read my own land's verdant scripture.
Time is here a mirror
for its own failures.
I would see a river
and a mountain lonely in the sky,
and the dark friendliness of trees.
Antiquity's monotone
is reflected in this changing, unchanging sea.
I want to feel again a modern fever
and see a pithead, a town's crucifix,
and the long street struggling down the mountainside,
the huddled cottages,
and the twin comfort of the pub and chapel.

Sailor's Return

Dazedly watching from a railway window
The landscape sliding by to final peace
The sailor rubs his unbelieving eyes
Feels no emotion but a sense of wonder
That all the pain and boredom and the separations
Have receded, and that his next station
Is home, the longed for, inconceivable
Joy and bliss where love and loved ones dwell.

Desertion

On the horizon a funereal gleam
was all that remained of the unquiet lands
from which we fled in our romantic dream.
We did not see the clasped despair of hands,
The anguished sweat upon the pallid brows
of those whose piteous moans we did not hear,
We watched the burning from beneath Arcadian boughs
And did not feel the chilling wind of fear.

Invocation

Unlatch those lids.
Their beauty hides
a deeper magic under them,
a coral dream to which I plunge,
seeking a rich sea-change,
unsealing with a kiss
the loveliness that glides
beneath the magic of those tides,
sea-green Atlantis.
Let your waves break over
me, your bright waves cover
me with tang and glitter
of sun and wind and water;
in your sun – and water shine
let me, o let me drown;
deep in your multitudinous waves
reap the rich harvest of our loves.

Dear Lady

Dear Lady,
	In another age
I would by now have reached the stage
Of writing sonnets, jewelled things
Richer than all the gifts of kings,
Fairer than flowers, far
More lovely than the evening star –
To you, dear goddess of my dream;
But now perforce a lowlier theme
Must occupy my eager pen
For in these lesser times, both men
And circumstance can only fail
– In brief, I am no nightingale
And in this unenlightened time
Can only in unworldly rhyme
Commemmorate (*sic*) your many charms –
Great Virgil say of man and arms
Milton of God, his way, and men,
And Eliot with a bitter pen
Showed us the waste and desolate land,
And Spenser leads us by the hand
Through many an enchanted place.

With Shakespeare we have gazed upon the face
Of all the world, been almost blind
To see such workings of man's mind.
But leave these dazzling heights awhile,
Upon me bend your brilliant smile,
Come down O Maid, as Tennyson said,
From yonder mountain heights, he said,
For love is of the valleys, come
Thou down to find him; some
There be who deem him worthy, I
For him would live and die.

(I have been one that loved)

I have been one that loved
Beneath night skies to brood,
Shaping the world anew
In starlit solitude.
So might I once have sung
In the flamboyant days when I was young
But now the mood
Has gone, the ancient spell is broken.

Beloved hands I once felt in my hair
beloved voices that might once have spoken
are now but fragments shored against my ruins,
but dreams. And mockings of the wanton air.

Be wise, oh grief, the poet sang,
and hold yourself more calm.
But once the praises all about me rang,
and mine once were the laurel and the palm.

(Sweet sleeper, do not wake)

Sweet sleeper, do not wake
Lest you find
The brightness gone from the air
Your images all broken,
Youth dead, and
Dust, the quick dust of oblivion, everywhere.

Sweet dreamer, do not shatter
Your own dreams,
For there are no others now,
It will be time to wake later.
Waking dims
Your splendour, and puts out your glow.

Sweet sleeper, o sweet sleeper
Do not waken.
Dream on your happy sleep.
For Time, the relentless sapper,
Soon will weaken
Your defences – sleep now, dream, hope.

(It was a voice serene and placid as)

It was a voice serene and placid as
A river between meadows in summer
With each halt for breath as pregnant as the pause
That comes before the headlong fall of water.
It tumbled on, quietly, melodiously,
Telling the tales with just a hint of malice
Such as might make its quiet surface glitter
As sun does water, but no storm disturbed
Ever its ear-soothing monotone.

Inaccessibility

Safe islanded in ravening seas,
remote and inaccessible, she dwells,
hoarding a store of timeless days,
remorseless calm and indolent ease,
against the fate that never falls.

Though I have charted her, there's no approach.
The tides of passion bear me to her,
but in her cliff can make no breach,
and I stay helpless, out of reach,
and she is calm among the ocean's stir.

Severe among the waves she stays,
and smiles serenely, looking on,
nor all my force of passionate days

can ever touch her splendid ease,
nor all my wit discover a lagoon

To enter in and take her by surprise,
explore her island and possess her charm.
Of my high towering waves her eyes
are not afraid. Untouched, she lies
amid my passion ocean's storm.

Love Gone

There was a chemistry I knew,
a swift and intimate analysis
that in the crucible of a kiss
revealed the mystery of you.

There was a map I once could trace,
swelling hills and fertile plains
and forests welcoming love's rains,
– love's map, your body and your face.

O there were dreams once, there was love,
and youth and high romance,
and morning in the lovelight of your glance
and music – and all this was love.

Where now the chemistry I knew?
my skill the magic map to trace
of love in you? a haunting face?
where is my love now? where are you?

Lament

He will not come again
In the corrosive intimacy
Of critic or lover,
Nor bloody with loud stain
The room of anger,
Nor fat the threatening sea.

The knife of days
Has found his armoured hurt,
His wounded centre.

Under the waves of praise
The psalm of his murder
Escapes the sorrows of art.

Am I Christshape
To him now in that dazzling dark?
Virtue and song
Wreath round his bones like hope
Where his sleep is long.
And memory is my work.

He is kept by the tides.
Not as critic or lover
Will he ever again
Over the bright seeds
Be sun or rain.
Praise is too late, and there is no time for anger.

Requiescat

Rest from intolerable living
Cease from pain of taking and giving
In the coolness of earth alone
Give to the worms your whiteness of bone,
Give to the worms your flesh that was fair,
Go from the ache of the brightness of air
And in the grave seek rest from loving
Rest from intolerable living.

(Darlings)

Darlings,
          Once again I sit,
And rack my brains, and stretch my wit
To write a little note to you
Which shall say more than, 'How d'you do?'
I haven't time to tell the tale
Of how I upped and set my sail
For foreign lands across the seas,
Although I know that that would please
You, for you like to hear
Such stories; but I fear
I simply haven't got the time

To tell you now in babbling rhyme,
And that must wait another day.
The question is, what shall I say
Tonight. It's really no fit season
For any sort of rhyme or reason.
Outside, it's lovely. Overhead
The stars are shining; from her bed
The silver moon has stolen slow
To watch those brave star-captains go.
Outside it's lovely. – Here's the but –
Within this barren, oblong hut,
The fact must really now be told,
It's bitter, wicked, freezing cold,
And I lie writing in my bed,
With a jersey pulled up round my head.
It's warmer so, without a doubt,
But I would like to wander out,
And walking briskly, with a star
For guide, go northwards far
From here to where the lovely Wye
Comes sliding, slipping, roaring by,
And walking at blood warming pace,
Almost as fast as in a race,
At last with joyful heart I'd come
To you, my dears, for welcome home.
Then would we sit beside the fire,
And talk all night, – we'd never tire.
We'd have a hearty supper, then
We'd sit down by the fire again.
Sometimes we'd look out at the night;
Then, shivering, we'd pull up tight
Against the fire, and we'd chat,
Old Harri, Val, and little Pat,
Each like a large and comfy cat,
Sitting at ease upon the mat.
I'd tell you lots of wondrous stories
Of all the marvels and the glories
I've seen while roaming o'er the seas,
(And that, I know, would greatly please.)
I'd tell of Africa, Jerusalem,
And all the golden lands that hem
The middle sea; the marvellous blue
Of that sea I'd describe to you,
What Alexandria looks like, what Algiers,
And how the sight of Cyprus cheers

The voyager, and the lovely view
Of Naples in its bay so blue.
Then, my dears, for variety's sake,
I'd get up and down would take
Some old book from the shelves above,
Full of those poems that you love,
And you would read with eyes a-glisten,
While I would sit and smoke and listen.

So, while the stars shine overhead,
I lie a-writing in my bed,
And think and dream always of you,
Although my nose is frozen blue.
And I look forward to the day
When with a merry voice I'll say
'I'm home again, and what's for tea?'
And you will climb upon my knee,
And kiss me, laugh, and stare
At my strange clothes, and pull my hair.

But now, before I say Goodnight,
I really hope that you will write
And tell me all the latest news.
Then someday, my new wishing-shoes
Will bring me to you once again;
And be it sunshine, be it rain,
Or hail or frost or driving snow,
This one thing I surely know,
I shall be very glad to be
With you once more to have my tea.

This for the moment must suffice.
I hope you find it rather nice
And the last line my pen will write
Will be, dear Val, dear Pat, Goodnight.

Poem for Wales

This is a poem I must make for you,
The tale of all your passionate sons,
The violent men who sometimes knew
A blade-bright clearness sifting their dark questions
Reveal the gentleness they sought,
I am their son, and by my fathers taught,

Those obstinate old men with cymbal lungs
Whose honoured heir I am, in whom
– O rich inheritance in little room! –
Lives on the challenge of their thundering tongues.

Dark hills for whom I feel this chemic love,
Who stir in me the furious syllables
That make an agony of my tower of words,
Hearing my fathers with one voice reprove
My weakness, my lost faith, – o sheltering hills
Help me to sing like all your vowelled birds.
Dark hills, there is a poem I must make,
The triumph of your singing sons,
The angry men who now awake
Their dream-bound heir to their own foundering passions,
And from their ancient keep of song
Proclaim the pride of blood, and the heart's wrong.
Their flesh is perished, but in me I trace
– Recurrent miracle of abiding bone,
Perpetual phoenix from the grave's corruption –
The still-proud outline of my fathers' face.
And shall I wear their mask, and not like them
Be proud and violent and passionate,
And sing the joy of love's returning seasons,
Wear on my forehead like a diadem
My forbears' loving and my enemies' hate,
And make a triumph of our lamentations?

That were indeed betraying the glad morning,
A life-in-death, a neural treason,
And the blood leaps to give its warning,
Spirit remembers it is bred of bone;
The sea of darkling syllables,
Rising in richly sounding surges tells
My old inheritance, my welcomed doom
(The passionate heir of passionate men)
To undam the streams of eager blood again,
And with that redness the old hills illume,
Time is no knotted string, no flowing river;
I am my fathers' son, and they in me
Walk the dark valleys with their ancient pride;
Their strong, sweet tongues are sounding ever
Like the unending music of the sea;
Dark hills, in me my fathers have not died.

Beneath that goat-skinned tent of sky
Whose hairy hovering my old hills
Love reciprocally, I lie
And suck the wonder of those syllables;
Those thundering syllables, those words
That wheel and circle in my heart like birds
In a storm-haunted cove, those antique sounds
That trumpet me to darkening towers
To war with hope against the fatal powers,
Cry Resurrection from the burial mounds
Of all my fathers buried in dark places,
And with a bardic fury proud proclaim,
In me my fathers are not dead; they live,
Not only in the fading lines of faces,
Not only in the splendour of our name,
Not only in this tribute which I give.

But when I lie in proud and perfect peace
With a dark-haired woman of my race
Whose raven eyes will never cease
To lighten my hell-murky earthly place,
In me my fathers have not died;
And in the loftiest eyrie of my pride
My soul – my father's soul, and hers –
Sings in a towering exultation,
Making a vast reverberation
Through the dim centuries its singing stirs;
And cries, not only in the fading face,
Not only in the perishing trace of bone,
Not only in the little gifts you give,
Lives on the splendour of your ancient name;
Not in these brief mortalities alone,
But in your sons shall your great fathers live.

Dark hills, I sing not like your vowelled birds,
Your choral waters, preaching stones;
My craft of moulding sullen words
To echo the sweet trumpeting of your tones
Is feeble, but I sing, I sing
Always the glory of your triumphing.
O sombre hills who gently brood and wait,
O valleys in your bridal green,
O places all my sires have seen
And loved and blessed, I too have loved, though late,
Dark hills, green valleys, this is marriage-song,

Epithalamium I sing today,
Wedding your beauty to my towering pride.
Dark hills, dark hills, be spousal to me long,
So when I die I may with honour say,
Dark fathers, O in me you have not died.

Song of Hope

Coiled within us waiting for release
the mainspring of the blood is taut and hard,
the face may be a mask, the sinews
slack, eyes sullen, song unheard,
the god clay-footed, the machine
rusted and tangled, the bird's neck broken,
the morning sun in premature decline,
the young man dead, the maids, the arts, forsaken, –
all this may be, as from a railway train
the landscape slides from symbols of content
to images of sorrow, signs of pain,
that rob the traveller of all fresh intent.
But coiled within us waiting for release
the mainspring of the heart lies taut and hard.
And as a ploughshare, rusty, old, forsaken,
may yet cleave furrows in an eager earth,
so when the catch is slipped, bonds broken,
our dogs of war unleashed, towards the south
beyond all frontiers, to the new, bright land,
the fertile beauty and the heart's increase
of wisdom with the lips' decay
run forth the rainbows of our reckoning.
This is to live, to feel within the surge
of seas uncharted, the rush of blood,
the flood of sex, the quick uncoiling
of the spring, the calyx' flutter,
blossoming of buds, release in action
of the old, dry thoughts, the barren plains
become emotion, the bare twigs of thought
put on green dress, oil take away rust stains.
So, pistons running smoothly,
currents flowing, earth joyfully travailing,
the spring that lies within us coiled and waiting
released, we wake up in the warm new world,
beyond all frontiers, where the first
tree welcomes life we enter loving,

machines make bacchic dance, we laugh,
robots dance minuets, mermaidens
grace our shores, satyrs our suburbs,
the spring released we leap
like dogs unleashed not to new havoc
but a culmination
                the last frontier passed,
last barrier broken, creed and cult and hate
forgotten, plough and furrows
make new railway lines for passengers
to the Grand Central of the longer life
and build Parnassus not a film location.

For a Proud Beauty

Being older now I said
I'll no more endure
The folly and the smart,
These in me are dead
And I'll no more
Grieve my too-loving heart.
Such was my wisdom, such
The little that I knew
(And thought it much).
All ignorant of you,
I thought my craft of song
Would now content
Me. I was wrong.
Love, I repent,
That, ignorant, blamed thee.

Sea Voices

The speaking voices of the sea
across the intervening land
assail me, voices of the blind,
amorphous, bitter-lovely sea.

Caressingly on sunlit shores
the languorous waves insidiously invite
me to the memory of delight,
warm whisper of the waves on sunny shores.

And I remember an old sailor
who had a certain sea-green speech
in which you heard the sullen bells
far down toll muffled sombre chimes
in glaucous memory of those dim souls
who listened to the languid syllables
of waters lisping on those sunsoaked shores
and found their graves in those betraying seas.
You heard and saw the molten joy
of tropic isles, the suck and splash of surf,
the peacock-plumaged afternoons, the palms
waving, the golden maids, the heat
and then, chill as that last embrace of the grave,
felt death, the last all-swallowing wave.

So charmed the murmur of his seagreen voice
the distant languors of his tropic eyes,
so charmed and so betrayed.

So now I listen to the sea's urgent voice,
its distant languors, tropical delights,
its promise
                    and I am again betrayed.

Homage

Under his downy arm's
delicious terror
legendary eves
behind our bird-bare walls
waiting his windy coming
his mountain walking
we suckled song
when he towered and struck
his muscles' rippled magic
fluttered us caught
in his great grasp but seeing
the harvest-promise in his eyes
we loved and legended
his fingers' mastery
under his downy arm's
delicious fervour
suckled song
and laughed to find his strength was gentleness.

You

Could with love's rhetoric
seduce my art
to making idols of your heart
a hawthorn metaphysic.

Could with mirroring eyes
or that profound despair
of poets your black depth of hair
turn sonnets sacrifice.

Could with insolent charm
make me forget
my craft the reason of it
do me this subtle harm.

This is within your power
this is the scope of love
end of all else I have
in this my foundering hour.

The Enemy in the Heart

In the heart alone is the last enemy
The fatal friend who in the dim cathedrals
Of the towered and toppling waves
Makes you an image of all lost remembered loves
And kills the corn with terror of the sea
Rapes the rich earth with his sea-green betrayals.
Cast out romantically that spent savour
That lurking enemy whose glaucous veins
Spoiled the rich promise of your spousal saviour
And drowned your green blades in his greener veins.
But when you come to that last house of bone
His are the last embraces you discover
Though you go to your narrow bed alone
In no fond convoy with a friend or lover
That is the last speck on the unfolding chart
The murderer the foul the vulture heart.

Found Love

In the dissolving churches of her smiles
    In humility and heart's ease
      I loving pray
      Under the sky
    Of her undying charm of days
My flower heart unfolds adoring petals.

This is the windless corner of heaven
    Where comforting hearts may beat
      That tropic sea
      In whose waves I may
    Now find my loving last retreat
From terror, and my welcome harbour haven.

Her eyes' and lips' memorial smiles I keep
    Secure within a secret pocket
      On this leaved bough
      Heart you are happy now
    Love is immortal agate
In her cathedral is undying hope.

And safe within her windless waveless cove
    I rock at anchor Peace
      In all her smiles
      Her murmured syllables
    The wonder of her cloudless eyes
My chapel of contentment my found love.

Metamorphosis

    Being older now, I said,
    I'll no more endure
    That folly and that smart;
    My green, romantic heart
    Is withered, dead,
    And I am wiser, sure,
    Now I shall find my peace
    In a sullen pride of craft,
    And in certain learned men,
    Wits, or who lewdly laughed
    At the world's fools, and these
    My ancient, mothering hills,

I am eased of the arctic ills
Of foolish love, I said,
I am older, love is dead.

This was my thought, – and then, –
O blessed miracle of fire,
Unsealing blinded eyes again –
You came and talked my dialect
With my own accent, you
Epitomised with grace
All that I loved and knew
– You had a lovely face –
O bride of heart and intellect
And all desire
I was proud to realise
Myself again in your two eyes.

Aberystwyth, March 1946

In no proud walking,
But the waved form awoke
Broke the gulled promenade
To rippled laughter. The tall hills
Bent down to mark my coming
Home, the roaming sea
Stilled, and the awakened town
Of waves recalled lost loves
Of all the hills I never climbed
Clambered the seaweed to embrace
My memoried face
Curled the little towers of foam
To make me an unfading home
O home and wave and hill
My last dear hospital
And let me hide
Where I am no more afraid
In the curled sheltering
Of your quick welcoming.

(Pay no more adulation)

Pay no more adulation
to those slack dishevelled stars
who in their wandering wreak
havoc on sheltering peace
with disregard of their or your configuration.

(What original or rare)

What original or rare
Precious or costly gift
Can I offer to her?
These only are left:
The arrogance of intellect,
The surly pride of craft,
And the certain delight
In what of rhythm or wit
I might discover
In manners or books or men
The humility of a lover
And the pride of desire.

(He had a certain seagreen speech)

He had a certain seagreen speech
in which you heard a sullen bell
far off toll muffled sombre chimes
a glaucous memory of those dim souls
who listened to the languid syllables
of waves lisping on a summer shore
and found a graveyard in the cheating sea.
You heard and saw the molten joys
of tropic isles, the suck and splash of surf,
the peacock plumaged afternoons, the palms
waving, the golden maids, the heat,
– And then the thrill as that last embrace of the grave
felt death the last all-swallowing wave.
So charmed the murmur of his seagreen voice
the distant languor of his tropic eyes,
so charmed, and so betrayed.

(My heart is now an unlocked lucky room)

My heart is now an unlocked lucky room
wherein you move with more than sensuous bliss
lighting its former shut and dusky gloom
with this sun miracle of your witness kiss.
Now is it seen to be repository
of all the ages gifts of rich and rare
which waited only for two kissing glory
to be revealed in your enchanting air.
My heart, my heart is now your tribal tent
your home, your garden and your tower from care.
O love be still now be at peace content
this little room is now an everywhere.
This is my history and this your art
to live on kisses in my lucky heart.

Builth

After his grief he woke
after the indolences and the barrenness
the ennui of remorse, lost love,
the crawling towns across his eyelids broke
the shuttering seals

And after silence spoke
after the quiet in the stony places
after the desolation in the sunlit lands
the quickening rainfall on his eyelids woke
the sleeping spirit

And the full heart broke
sharded to syllables the angry heart
the annunciate singing heart
after his griefs, the silence, broke
when he awoke.

In My Returning

In my returning, the proud, flowered walking
Again in the loved, remembered land,
The valleys and hills of fact and legend,
Dear hospital and home of hopes and the sweet light,

I hear my heart a hedge of singing-birds,
And fill my eyes with the welcome of the hills;
Walking with pride of race and singing craft
I magnify mountains, and suck in the air
Wales wears with memoried grace;
In the green cwms I am again at home.

This is the blossomed quaystone where I end
My tattered seasons where begun;
The flowered and feathered landscape
No longer a fading map of unloving strategy,
But a weight and a wonder of words
Not to be silently borne on my tender tongue;
A pride and humility in my home-returning
To the dear and dark hills of legend
And fact that must be unleashed
In triumphant chorus to the bird-thronged air.

So to the dear land back I sing my own
Welcome, and in my tumbling pride
Hear it re-echoed by the rain-washed winds.
Wales wears an air, a grace, as a loved face
Motions to kisses on the letters of exile;
And the intricate maps of farms
Welcome me back to a singing service,
A wonder of work, and the toil of love
In the green cathedrals of the sea-lapped,
Lovely, enduring landscape of fact and legend.

(Now after many journeys)

Now after many journeys
on barren seas, through empty lands,
I am come to the last, imagined,
lovely, impossible landscape
to find you too had been a traveller
near always though never seen
through the same forests, over the same
heartchilling mountains, across
the same uncharted seas
to make landfall at last
on this dear island where I waited
impatiently for you, my fated
guest and only lover.

Poem

I am the poet walking in the wind,
The ploughman following furrows in the sky;
I have no house but your enhancing mind,
And the most I can hope for is to make my cry
Articulate, and carve my death
In warm words issuing on your passionate breath.

My furrows fade even as I follow them,
My poems die into the freezing air;
Your beauties vanish as I image them,
And the wind plucks away your hair,
Already I am gone from you, and dead,
And come back only for the words you said.

Now I am gone into my narrow grave,
Tracked my last furrow to its barren end,
No words can be powerful to save
The houseless poet, ploughman without friend,
Who never had a home but in the wind,
And in the bare rooms of your loving mind.

(No pity nor prophylactic)

No pity nor prophylactic
We ask, nor the peace
Of your wilful charity
Nor your aloof didactic
Preachings of common sense
Your moral clarity.
We in the cloudy glory
Of our personal heaven
Ask only to be together
To tell our sensuous story
Nor ponder whether
Our heaven and your heaven
Coincide or not.
We have deliberately forgot
Your prophecies and find all charms
In the warm circle of each other's arms.

Idyll

The long legs of my love were walking like swans
In the green legend where I was happy once
With a book in my pocket and my country eyes
Flowers in my hair and my head on her breast
Living on poems and a bite of bread and cheese.
The birds in my lively ears were singing certainties.
O the long legs of my love and her bare white breast.

The laughter of my love was the summer song of birds
In the happy hedges of my landscape of green words
Where my head was on her lap and a sonnet in my eyes
And the clouds were not softer than the whiteness of her breast
When the birds carolled clear and all the rest was lies
When I lay like a poet in my country paradise.
O the long legs of my love and her bare white breast.

But now there is no laughter nor no long legs like swans
And ashen is the landscape where I was happy once
With her kisses on my lips and poems in my eyes
And praises for the loving of the lilies of her breast.
Faded are the flowers and the birds are out of tune
Winter overtook me when I went to bed at noon.
O the long legs of my love and her bare white breast.

(From my singing sullenness)

From my singing sullenness
I do not bring
insipid elegies
the heart to ease
nor sing
to lighten love's distress.

(We are in love. The miracle is this)

We are in love. The miracle is this
That, though when we love we mortal two
Do only that which other lovers do,
Our act remains unique, and, when we kiss,
As others do in love or passion, this
For us is more than other lovers do,

More than sweet union of our loving two,
Ah more, much more, the miracle of our kiss,
For when we kiss and love our bodies meet
And mingle as do other lovers when
They kiss and love, and though the meeting's sweet
It is not this marks us from other men.
No, when we love, all else is in eclipse
And our two souls mingle as do our lips.

(Once I wanted to make)

Once I wanted to make
A poem for a Poem's sake,
Elaborate and well-designed,
Purely evolved out of my mind,
A perfect poem that should be
Essence alone of poetry.
But when my love at last I knew
Poems could only be for you.

First Kiss

At that miraculous unlooked-for moment
the world was suddenly happy with birds
and on seas too vast for my cockleshell words
I fled from the land of my lonely torment
to islands of flowers, and in my happy blood
heard the unrivalled notes of the trumpeting
the golden thunder of our marrying
the touch of solitude with solitude.
I walked in streets that were lovely as summer
hedgerows, and my blood was jealous
that the great sea could run more freely.
In courts and palaces I was the crowned newcomer
the lusty, tender, the mighty, amorous,
the king, the lover – yours immutably.

(And I would send you argosies of words)

And I would send you argosies of words
commemorating each miraculous moment
of our love with ardent ode or lapidary sonnet,
and in your ears make always the music of birds.

I would clothe you in the beauty of a legend
so that all men might have your memory
like Venus rising from that violet sea
to make men mad and lovers violent,
I would invent for you an antique story
of how you were made from the spring's flowers
and the warm riches of those summer hours
when life achieves a gold abundant glory.
But what wild wonder could ever equal this
sweet promise, sweet fulfilment of our kiss.

(Were I that cold commemorative ghost)

Were I that cold commemorative ghost
who still keeps sleepless chill parade
along those futile streets where he once lost

his passion, but still wants the heartless jade;
were I that cold unsleeping ghost
still mouthing to the wind a lorn tirade

of constancy to love for ever lost;
were I that ghost drowned in cascade
of his own weeping, and self-pitying most

the wanton way in which he was betrayed
and made this working, waiting ghost
for ever on a futile chill parade

along the empty streets of a faded past;
would you not laugh at the poor waiting ghost?

(Legends ago)

Legends ago
She who is now my miracle of morning
Rose like a flower from violet, dolphined seas
And lovers knew
The bright exultance of her beauty burning
And the sun shone on their hearts' certainties.

Legends ago
She who is now my more than beauty's legend

Was born in a poet's making marrying mind.
And lovers knew
How hands could twine an ever-living garland
And love be everywhere a healing wind.

Legends ago
She who is legendary now of love
Gave lovers their immortal catalyst
And lovers knew
Why the blood leaps and the quick pulses move
O we created love and legends when we kissed.

(Grief's unscarred wounds)

Grief's unscarred wounds are treasured up,
The salt tears fill a brimming cup,
Sad images of happier days,
Distorted by our passionate praise,
Dazzle the retina. There's no release
From sorrow's bitter, binding peace.

Prayer

Purge me those images of idol days.
Bright winds receding from my fevered hair,
Come now and re-create the wisdom there
Beyond all folly and all need of praise.

Purge me the uncreated commerce of delight,
O bright skies fading from my longing eyes,
Make the enfolding light which never dies
Into the dark despairing of the night.

Purge me all prayers of mere profanity,
Dear flowers withering as I gather you,
Suck earth's ripe sustenance and healing dew
To fit the vessels of my vanity.

Bright winds and skies and flowers, enduring earth
Purge me my intellectual poverty,
And from abundant riches give to me
The vital seed I need for my rebirth.

Epithalamion

But never until the meeting making hour
Waking the dream-bound princess with a kiss
The listening chorus of his haunting words
Heard no such music of his sweet descending
To end the terror and fatuity of loneliness
And bless this marriage when he harbours there.

The air is sweet with auras of his doves
Moving upon them as they lie at peace
Eased of all subterranean terrors now
And ploughing fearlessly green fields again.

O rain, sweet love, benignant influence
Upon the senses of these lovers here.
They fear no longer, know no discontent,
Bent are the boughs now and they pluck the fruit,
Mute is the chorus now and dumb the birds
But eyes, lips, hands tell more than all his words.

(Bodies are poems)

Bodies are poems lovers learn
Patterned with intricate device
For their most sweet, most strange delight.
Love is the wisdom poets earn
Whom all God's fools cannot entice
To dim their eyes' wild-burning light.
Now wise one learn this poetry
With hands and lips and making mind,
Poem you never will forget
When all your longings are set free
And all the arts are left behind
And all the suns, save hers, are set.

That other I, the unhappy lover
and proud talker

That other I, the unhappy lover and proud talker
You will not know now for his time-belled tongue
Is stilled, is hushed in all your seas of silence,
And the voice you hear is his, yet is another's.
So, my love, when you go lithely walking

On the bright mountains in your brighter morning
Stop not to listen to the grass-ruffling wind
Or the forlorn bleat of sheep; the distant buzzards
Wheeling in lovely, fatal circles do not mark,
Nor how the mountains are like ribs of man,
But go walking in the morning, darling,
Only in golden fertilising of the sun
Hearing no mocking voices from the unburied past
But only this half-inarticulate
Soliloquy of this most happy talker, your proud lover.

Two Poems

I

In the shop-front of your magnificence
Is no evasion, but the unshuttered stare
Of beauty beautiful beyond prim care,
Preening the feathers of its indolence;
Or you veer off with sudden insolence
Of the lone sexless place agleam in air;
You have no warm humility to share,
Aloof in your displayed indifference.
What if I shatter now your plate-glass splendour?
Force you to a sharp, complete surrender
Of the cold beauty you so heartlessly parade?
Shatter that facade of your bright disdain?
Mar its white coldness with a spreading stain
Of tenderness my human hands have made?

II

Believing in no grief save that alone
Which takes my love and leaves the bare white bone,
How should my verses for your loss atone?
So you are captured in time's fine-spun mesh;
Yet I should only make you mockery afresh
To weep for what I have not lost, the flesh.
Weep then, dear wanton, without thought of me;
Mourn the sweet loss of your virginity,
While I, love's lord, turn now to poetry.
But, my dear mourner, when necessary night
Replaces this despairing, clarifying light,
Build we again our tiny world and bright.
And never till the flesh fade from your bone,
Again, dear wanton, shall you lie alone.

The Enemies

The enemies are walking, walking
In the grey fields of our devoured youth
With gun and bayonet, bent on shattering
The vowelled towers of our green desire.
Our bell of love gives warning, warning
Of their cold approach, their quick, most deadly coming,
But heart and mouth can only pray for succour,
We have no weapons but our feeble limbs
Fit only for warm love's most harmless warfare.
The enemies are winning, winning
The uncontested fight upon our pastures,
The towers of our love are falling, falling,
The flowers of our pride are fading, fading,
And all the green sounds of our songs are dying.
The enemies in pride are walking
Over the fields of our love, our youthful pastures,
Shading their faces, – yours and mine, my friend.

(I would send you words)

I would send you words
as warm and tender as children
and as clear, as rejoicing
as the summer music of birds.

I would show you like Venus
warm-stepping from the foam
and golden, and lovely
as she, oh! and amorous.

I would give you my pride,
the greatest gift of all,
but if you had that you would know
that my love had died.

(It was always easy)

It was always easy to imagine idylls
With the extravagance of intellect,
The summer seasons in the lover's lap,
And all love's usual adoring symbols.

The blood's hot knocking would not let me rest
But on the beauty of some visioned breast.

It was too easy also to imagine
The wintry end of all those golden idylls,
The breast become repulsive, and the light no longer
Provoking desire feeding on itself,
The intellect subduing the hot blood.
Proclaiming chastity the mental good.

Such the succession of those imagined idylls,
Cold season quick succeeding to the list,
And summer with like ease displacing winter,
Till the poor brain and body were bemused
And thought themselves a wanton sacrifice
To love's idolatrous inanition.

But all those idylls were imagined only.
What shall I say of this enduring summer,
This warm reality of you and I
Who want no images to mirror splendour
Of our love; what can a fool relate
Of his miraculous translated state?

So then I picture in my arrogant mind
No more confusion of those earlier idylls,
Expect no winter to succeed this season
Of our most warm, most human passion.
O love lie still by me. We will create
An idyll that shall armour us from fate.

Renunciation

I have forsaken them all,
The public pleasures and the private pain,
The rituals of loving and of separation,
Even forgiveness and the need of pardon;
I have laid down the burden of my youth,
Memory's insistence, and the fool's delight
In recollection of lithe limbs: the treasons
Of the over-eager mind, and the rebellions
Of the body; I have put away from me
The passionate acceptance of uncertain symbols,
And all idolatry of men and women,

And the warm regard I had once
In skilful making, in a subtle craft.
I have forsaken them all.
Cold, loveless, forlorn, I am become
This nothingness, who have laid down
Soul's burden, and is alone, but cannot die,
Still conscious of the folly of forsaking.

Benghazi, Christmas 1942

Unreal this ruined city in the unredeeming
revelation of the sunlight, as unreal
as Tintagel's distant ruins in their storied
twilight, or those forgotten cities under water.
Here is no reward or remedy
nor any end to our bitter, unsought journey.
White wreck of a city in the noon glare
with no more meaning than a heap of casual bones
in the desert, stumbling one's foot,
and more unreal than the fallen towers of Troy,
too lifeless even to symbolise the mockery
of our peace on earth, goodwill to men,
unstoried ruins, o sunlit wreck
of a white city, why are we here?
Who could bother to build you, or destroy.

(From what high heaven)

From what high heaven of thought
over the landscapes of words
the flattened contours of feeling
will he suddenly swoop the unseen
the fatal the moral hawk
from whom we cower in love
but cannot hide or escape?

(Djinn-master Solomon)

Djinn-master Solomon
Had never such delight
From all his wives
As I from one
Dark princess of my mind.

(Images of adventure and desire)

Images of adventure and desire
Symbols and similes of the dear and daring,
And the great metaphors of praise and passion,
I seek, not altogether blindly, that I may fashion
A poem as hard and lovely as the faring
That brought me to you, as fierce as the fire
Eyes and lips kindled, and as tender
As my first kiss, or your surrender.

For I would be for you the paragon
Of art, as you for me of nature,
And would make in the tourbillion of my pride
Such a poem for you as would have satisfied
Ulysses' self when for every feature
Of Penelope he yearned being absent alone.
But words are weaklings and I should invent
New language to tell you all I meant.

A Wish

I would walk always in gardens,
Dreaming unhurriedly of summer,
And noting how the pale light flakes
And falls round flowers in the evening,
And bearing the sensuous, elusive moment
Of dark women walking where I do not see them.

I would live forever in gardens,
In the low evening light, with flowers,
And the voices of dark women,
And an uninterrupted dream of summer.

Portrait

Inhibited, he walks his narrow stage
In a soft, diffused and shadow-forming light,
Making faint mock and meagre irony
Of the robust passions that in others rage,
Fearing the brightness of the day, the dark of night,
And too much virtue, too much villainy.

Don't break his musings with impetuous tread,
For the poor creature is already dead.

Ulysses

Ulysses, self-satisfied though travel-weary,
Sunburned but happy in his enduring prowess,
And confident in his subtle craftiness
Of his ability to outwit or placate
The gods and men, the exile longed for home
And Penelope, but meanwhile was never long
Without some woman to share his mighty bed.

Late Love

I who was never handsome nor very tall,
Never Prince Hamlet nor the Squire of Dames,
And always timid at the sound of drums,
The normal hero of a normal tale,
Who crossed no frontiers and hauled down no flags,
And shunned both Venus and the trampling boar,
For no good ale let back and sides go bare,
Sipped cautiously the wine and left the dregs,
I, the poor, shivering and abject man,
The slave, the coward, prudent and alone,
What have I done for this great misery,
This stiffening of my sinews, this great pride,
The weight and wonder of this love's great load,
This sweet denial of nonentity.

(O broken by bright eyes my crusoe mind)

O broken by bright eyes my crusoe mind
now has a yearning irrevocably
for bodies that are nohow so unkind

As the encompassing, estranging sea,
and the tensed body powerfully longs
for your wise mind, unbroken, clean and free.

So mind to body, flesh to mind belongs
in dreams and longings all the dancing day,
and since you are absent I must make mad songs
As porpoises about the urgent vessels play
who find dark water no impediment
to love or laughter, but are always gay.

But o from me the sea withholds consent
of your white arms, your bright and breaking eyes,
and all the mercy of your loving advent.

O broken by bright eyes my body cries
to be released in your clear element.
My mind reciprocates my body's cries:
O broken and remade by lovelit eyes.

(I see the sad cities)

I see the sad cities but I cannot reach them
With the gloved hands of charity on the naked fingers
Of pity. But only with remote and troubled eyes
Which see in my morning mirror the despair
Of being an impotent liberator who might as well curse
The stricken cities and their weeping multitudes
As so weep with them, but so far removed.

(Across the unresponsive oceans)

Across the unresponsive oceans and the listless lands,
Over monotonous mountains, through forests of fear,
The pampas of pride and the meadows of indolence
        The sunburned travellers come
        To their imagined home.

(Traced on the dark skies of my mind)

Traced on the dark skies of my mind
The fitful gleaming of your flesh
Awakens all desire afresh
To be no longer blind
To the wild white wonder of flesh,
And the stranger beauty of your loving mind.

(The young men who admired themselves in mountain pools)

The young men who admired themselves in mountain pools,
The mirror-haunting, lonely, glimmering girls,
Have come together now and look with wondering gaze
On lonelier pools and mirrors of unloving eyes.

But the wild roaring riders on the windy heights,
The madcap girl who ran unclothed at nights
To dance in forests, these have come together now –
Each girl a fallow field, each man a mighty plough.
So you my dear and distant one o be no more
Lonely with mountain pool in your admiring mirror
But ride wild horses with me on the windy heights
And learn love's wisdom with me in unsleeping nights.

(I would not have you otherwise)

I would not have you otherwise
Than as you so magnificently step
Challenging mirrors and the eyes
Of others to match your love-engendered
Beauty.

(Now is the time to remember the other landscapes)

Now is the time to remember the other landscapes
The deserts and the green fields of our earlier visions
Our profit and loss from all the impossible mountains
We crossed in the hectic winters of our youth
And the swamps we floundered in for gasping summers.
It is well to hold these landscapes in our memory
The desolate and drear and challenging
And the lush and luxurious and inviting
Landscapes of warning which we should record
Against corruption of our truer vision.

(Surrender that which is already given)

Surrender that which is already given,
Love's prouder symbol, self-enriching token,
No words for what is powerless to be spoken.
No portrait of this unimagined heaven.

(Agony is not to be encountered in islands)

Agony is not to be encountered in islands.
The suffering of the Jews across the water
Could at the most teach us only to suffer

And to wear nobly our rhetoric garlands
But nothing of the moment of consummation
The beautiful and irrevocable crossing
Of the last frontier where in their passing
They left behind them the guards and the concentration
Camp and the beatings, and could laugh again
Because they were dead and could not be hurt.
How shall we ever imagine that agony
Who have this lust for living and terror of pain
O put us up against walls and shoot
Us that we too may learn how to die.

(Who dealt in dogmas of delight)

Who dealt in dogmas of delight
And now like Leda feel the downy weight
Of the greater mystery upon them
The inexpressible in man and woman
What would they do with the folly of words
Though they sang like the impassioned birds.

(Because of that great company)

Because of that great company
I walked with in my waking dreams
You were even afraid of me
When I was awake it seems.
My fearful one, could you not have guessed
When I was torn by dreams and thought
That only on the sureness of your breast
Was the peace I sought?

(Refusing now to sing)

Refusing now to sing I am cast out
and left alone like lovers in the dark,
and my secret pride is thus my only wages.
But it is terrible too to be so lonely
seeing in the heart's clear and pitiless mirror
the sullen meanings and impotent longings
to be without art and again have a place in the sun.

(Do not look for me in that foreign place)

Do not look for me in that foreign place
Where even kisses are forgotten,
But smile and turn your lovely face.
I shall be rotten,
And corpses never can embrace.

(Of course that was no country for young men)

Of course that was no country for young men
With their loves in their arms and their poetic eyes
Their deep heartsearching, and their dim romantic cries
That land we found but could not find again
Over the since obliterated borders of pain
Where all that young men live for quickly dies
And death itself loses its element of surprise
Soaking the whole of consciousness like monsoon rain;
O no, it was no country for the poetic young
That land where no romances were ever sung
Where kisses could not be imagined and the breath
Was a burden, and one sought for ease
In the oblivion of insatiable seas
In uncorrupted cold, a sea-green death.

(Winter's shadowed hour)

Winter's shadowed hour
Breaks at last in flower
And summer grows
As swiftly as a kiss
To the last magnificent rose
And dies again to this
Winter's shadowed hour
Which will break again in flower.

(Seeking the last deformity)

'and all in flight and all
Deformed because there is no deformity
But saves us from a dream.'
                    – W. B. Yeats

Seeking the last deformity,
The Hunchback, Saint, or Fool,
To save us from the dream
We fled from school to school,
Physics, philosophy,
The summers of love that seem
To warm the soul for ever,
Or the dark, Lethean river,
But, fast as we fled,
The pervading dream pursued,
The dream of the quick and the dead,
Alone, or the multitude
Around us, we could not escape
The dream for our perfect shape,
And because of our broken mind
Could never find
The saving deformity
Of Hunchback, Saint, or Fool.

(Winter can be deceitful)

Winter can be deceitful.
After the waiting,
the heart's expectancy,
the flowers breaking
can bring only a sour spring.
And such deceits of seasons
harden the heart.
We long for winter always,
the cold, the animal sleep,
with no spring following,
no pomp of summer,
fertility of autumn,
but only winter,
no promises, no deceit,
no hope.

After the Funeral

After the funeral with none to praise
The widowed voices that forget to mourn
Turn from the grave to ordinary days

After the funeral the bodies turn
The voices fade, the pitiless grief betrays
And mourning accents soon forget to mourn

Grief has no meaning in the following days
Loved body from the grave cannot return
To thank us for our memory or praise

After the funeral forget to mourn,
Grief is an anodyne that soon betrays
The dung-sick soul. Bodies do not return.

After the funeral forget the grave.
She has the peace we all would wish to have.

(Hot summer in the blood)

Hot summer in the blood
And love is dumb
To tell the lovers of the coming winter
When the smothering ice
Will fasten flesh
And freeze the mind
And love will have no meaning in the grave.

(It is not death I fear)

It is not death I fear
Nor elemental pain,
But the still, small space within
The shuddering brain.

(Where no light breaks)

Where no light breaks
Dumb lovers and the little worms embrace
And cannot tell us
Or the singing seeds
We too shall fade to bone from this hot fever
Fade to that same cold kiss
Though now hands' commerce
And the limbs' warm labour
Make love's delight
We too shall end
Where no light breaks
Dumb in the chill embraces of the worm
And dumb to tell
The singing seeds
How lovers end
Grumbling, cold, in the dark loneliness
Dumb darkness and the worm's cold kiss.

(Oh! who would follow singing seas to his death?)

Oh! who would follow singing seas to his death?
Or listen to the fatal lure of distant stars?
Beautiful are the waves indeed for those who have faith,
Beautiful the siren song, the sweet salt breath
of morning golden on the seas, the seas of death.
All beautiful in memory,
          What waves shall wash away these scars?
What peace efface the bitter memory of wars?

Forget now then the ancient dream,
The antique call the waves sing through the blood,
Recall
Only the bitterness of it all,
The lonely aching ever in the blood,
The seas for ever breaking, the ache
Of the lonely, breaking seas, the salt death
At the heart of beauty, making all
The beauty sterile as a broken heart
O follow singing seas no more, my sailors,
No more depart
From peaceful fertile fields and happy home
The wandering ways of gulls and waves to roam,
Be deaf now to the music of the stars.

(The limbs of summer in their glory)

The limbs of summer in their glory
Dazzle my winter bleary sight.
Before the uncut wealth of wheat
My eyes close, my heart is sorry,
Remember the winter ruins,
The greyness, the unending rain,
The isolation that is gone,
Leaving me still in ruins, sorry.

(If I should lyrically lament)

If I should lyrically lament
The summer gone for you and me,
The passing of the sensuous days
Quicker than we could stop to praise,
Should I herald the spring for you and me
After this season of discontent.

(The separated limbs)

The separated limbs are lovelier
Than in an empty room a flaunting mirror;
Always, they wait
To recreate their lithe delight
Outpacing time with swift and urgent prayer
For meeting, and the end to heart's despair
When the desiring hands
Shall have their dominion
And the eyes see more sweetly
Their brighter kingdom
The summer season in its imaged glory
The lovers at their ease
And the proud limbs no longer lonely.

(Love's weather changed to thunder in my ears)

Love's weather changed to thunder in my veins.
The golden torments came
And filled my lap with oceans of desire.
Nor, till he suck

My sea-bed dry
Shall water lack again in all my land.

Fear not, then, portents in the ponderous heavens.
Love's thunder will condemn
All parched and dying creatures to dear oblivion
In his wide waters
His creating rain
That fills my lap unto the ends of earth.
And love makes wisdom's weather through the land
The sun shines on the sea
And I am warmed by that creating spirit
Nor shall be sucked
My sea-bed dry
Nor love's wide waters drained from out my lap.

(So I was ruined in that hectic summer)

So I was ruined in that hectic summer
And when the sun shone on my sea-bed face
Love's tides flung up the wrecks of richer wonders,
The drowned armadas of my stormy days,
And gold and bones and hollow shapes of ships
Cargoed with skulls came to the brighter surface.
The sun of summer syllabled my ruin
The revelation of my hoarded truth
And treasure and my thoughts like corpses
Under the weight of waters the green pressure.
Love's sun shone on them on the tidal trove
Revealed in that hot summer of my ruin
And laughter ran across the sky like lightning
Because my ruin was a battering prelude
To still more golden days and new armadas.

(So I beget you in a lyric mood)

So I beget you in a lyric mood
O dearer than my dreams of summer days
And image you about my solitude
Because I could not otherwise so praise
Our nearer marriage in my making mind
Where first I saw you as an untouched dream
That I should ask for ever, but not find,

In my heart's desert a deceiving stream.
But when my dream puts on the fairer flesh
What images could I then magnify
That wit and wonder should both satisfy,
Or hammer out sufficient praise afresh
From older poets to bless your loving heart
Or murmur kisses when we are apart.

(From brooding on the possible event)

From brooding on the possible event
Hot catalyst of love deliver us
Before the future grow so ominous
We fear to meet its over-imaged advent.

(I would have you remain)

I would have you remain
In just such venust eloquence
As when your nakedness
Irradiates the foamy seas
You rise from, and the day.

(Prince Hamlet:- but not with
very much to say)

Prince Hamlet:- but not with very much to say
Looks on his lost and latent Elsinore,
And still the tension tears the thickening day.
The ghost has gone – but what can he do more?
No sentry now, his jaded spirit peers
Over the edge into the deepening dark.
Has rottenness but increased with the years?
Is Osric now the only vital spark?
Prince Hamlet with a sigh leaves Elsinore
And this time does not wish to leave his name
Or to return to prod his pitying heirs.
Hamlet has died, still bigger is the sore;
And Claudius says his prayers and plays his game
The queen still warms him with her golden hairs.

(The lone mister in the park)

The lone mister in the park
Derided by boys
Feels the stab of winter
Murdering his praise
Of girls and the lift
Of their breasts and their arms,
And their welcoming eyes
Like the promise of summer.

The sad mister in the park
Has only a violent friend
As he sits, derided by boys,
In the deepening dark,
Feeling the stab of winter
Murder his dreamed-of days.

(A summer of birds made the wild morning wonder)

A summer of birds made the wild morning wonder
When I awoke to the bright day of a poem
The singing sun ascended in the limbs
And the tears of sleep were dried

And I walked nearer to heaven with the birds on my shoulders
With sunlit imagery of eyes
A sky blue song above the deep green hedges
A carol in the morning
Praising the birds and the sun

The blue song of the green hedgehidden birds
Filling the sky and my unparadised eyes
Made this carol of summer
When I awoke on a morning of wonder
To hear the sun announce
The bright day of a poem
A poem to praise the coming of summer.

Alone

I would not ache tonight
For all the sounds of the world
But only my private loss
That, lonelier than a star,
I rage alone with my heart.

No longer proud tonight
Do I spurn or solicit the world
But weep alone for my loss
But weep alone for my star
And rage alone with my heart.
Not proud or brave tonight
Nor conscious of the world
Beyond my private loss
I am lonelier than a star
As I rage alone with my heart.

For a Dead Sailor

He found the countless pities of the sea.
Among green navies now he sleeps content,
Is stayed and comforted by the great weight
Of waters, is lulled in a green night.

Refuse to mourn now for this long sleeper
Whose clean bones lie so lost.
Deep with the dead of all the tempests
Deeper than plummet and beyond torpedoes
Deeper than that great diver, the old whale,
He sleeps, secure against another death.

Under green pressure, among ancient crews
He has found the countless pities of the sea.

Ferdinand to Miranda

In the conspiracy of love
we dream the pattern of our dance
moving like waves into the pastoral
long-coveted country, the happy island.

Let the kind tyrant frown,
we know his power,
we can play chess quietly, and watch
each other with unloosed delight,
and wait the inevitable coming
of love's warm night.

Or let him smile upon us,
we know his power,

and the conspiracy of love
eludes him, if he smile or frown.
And we are cunning, and obedient,
following the patterns of our dance.
And the island is ours.

The rock of wisdom in our waves
is lost, the tyrant's voice is drowned,
the mystery is brighter and more deep.

The waves dance, and the golden minutes fall
in patterns at our dancing feet.
The quick conspiracy of love
has conquered all. The rites are done,
the music of the richer storm begun,
the golden tempest in each other's arms.

War Widow

Whose hands were blessing on my breasts
When by his dreaming side I lay
Is now a broken thing.

Who came in glory like the morning
To wound me with his spears of light
Is now a broken thing.

Whose murmur in my willing ears
Was singing, whose words were joy
Now lies silent.

And shall his singing not be justified?
Shall not the blessing that he laid
Upon my breast before he died
Flower within me?
Or am I, too, broken,
Our love a barren thing?

To exist is enough
We cry in the tousled bed
But the heart grows frightened
In a lonely place.

(When in the tousled bed we lie)

When in the tousled bed we lie
Secure against alarms
And softly into sleep we die
In one another's arms
Our bodies with the confidence of love
Cry 'To exist is enough'.

(It was a winter night and cold to the heart)

It was a winter night and cold to the heart,
The pale air drew me to dreams,
And the moving moon became
The symbol of my desire, restless and dimmed.
The air was suddenly filled with whispers, ghosts,
Half-articulate presences, vague hints of you,
And the cold was everywhere,
And the silver hostile stars.

(Let me make you a poem that is everywhere)

Let me make you a poem that is everywhere,
Even in the desire your absence makes,
The passionate poem with which the morning wakes,
The expressive moving of the evening air.

Let me make you the poem of the daring day,
The sun's fierce ode, the miracle of the light;
And the cool elegy of the coming night,
When I make poems for you as others pray.

Let me make you the poem of the singing birds,
The vivid lyric of grass, of splendid trees,
The magnificence and terror of lonely seas,
And all the wonder not to be caught with words.

Let me make you the poem of my without-end love,
The magnificent song I endeavour to raise
In vain for your beauty sufficient praise,
Let me make you a poem 'til we again can love.

(The greenness of the heart)

The greenness of the heart
Unseasoned by art
Can be cut, can bleed
In bitter need.
But the older heart,
Like the older wood,
Will warp and split
When you pressure it.

(The mind alone has not its own defence)

The mind alone has not its own defence.
It giddies, fails, when looking on the steep
Cliffs that fall sheer to the unfathomed deep
Where reason mocks at its own vain pretence
And logic shows no hold to its weak sense.
Mind reels when maddened eyes forget to weep,
When sleep is dark, when waking more than sleep
Is awful, dreams foretell still worse events.

Oh then the only refuge is the heart,
The unshaken heart in which alone abide
The memory and the hope of quiet days,
The instinct and the surety of art,
The animal rhythm, the blood's consoling tide,
And love, the knowledge of her gracious ways.

(Though we lie now in this dead land)

Though we lie now in this dead land
Of separation, remember the flowers,
The spring, and the riches of harvest.
To be alone is to be more fully aware
Of the need of love.

(At the close of a winter day)

At the close of a winter day
The grey world darkens, and the heart is cold
Because the sunlight and you are away
And even lovers grow old.

I am afraid in this cold air
And long to sleep on your breast
The peace and the warmth that is there.

Descending dark, and the loneliness
Of separated lovers, the dark unrest,
The cold air chills my heart
Because we are apart.

At the dying of a winter day
I long to lie on your breast.

Song

Were I as wise as Solomon
And had as many queens
I would not love the pack of them
As I so love my one
Dark woman of my dreams
– Sang the poet dancing with the skeleton.

Were I as bold as Nelson
And had such charms on land
There's not a lady I would love
As I so love my one
Dark woman of my dreams
– Sang the poet dancing with the skeleton.

Were you the Queen of Sheba
And I the wise old king
I would not love you half so much
As now you are the one
Dark woman of my dreams
– Sang the poet dancing with the skeleton.

Poems in Separation

I

My world is weeping, and the driven blood
Floods me like ocean,
The stark seas violently invade
The emptied land, drown the heart's waste.
My world is water, and a bitterness,
A barren flood, heaven in an imaged kiss.

My world is blood, the driven weeping
Floods me like rain.
Stark showers violently invade
Denuded heart, drowning the empty land,
My world is bitter, is salt to touch and taste,
The barren floods leave me unquenched, unkissed.

My world is the weeping of blood, the driven
Floods of ocean, of rain,
Stark waters violently invade
And drown the longing world of heart,
My world is bitter water while you stand
Afar with your kiss from my love-drowned land.

II

The windy oceans that around me sorrow
Fall in a flood from brain to bone
The dark tides driven, the tired light dies
The woes of the body, the waves, complain.

The wastes of water and the moaning winds
Unrib me of my dream of love
In seas of blood are poems drowned
The winds are mighty spellers of my love.

Night on the waters, a sea of sorrow,
The dumb flesh crying in the wind,
The tides of blood are surging with my love,
I come to you to dawn to land.

The windy waters, but I am your lover,
Tomorrow the ocean will have been crossed over.

Poem

The hand that dreams of poems at my side
My violent friend who dreams me in the dark
Blood-spilling down the pathways of the stars
Seed scattering in many a summer field
Could conquer kingdoms, burn all cities down
Or lay a benediction on the breasts
Of her who lies so white and dreamless in my sleep.
What is the monstrous imagining
That could so move this curved and passionate friend
To such tall deeds? what is the hidden metre
That moves these crooked bones? what song
Sings in the nerves and moans along the blood
Impelling them to vast and prodigal deeds?

Only the slim curved whiteness of the hands
The bones' strength and the sensitive finger-tips
Whorled round their mystery, revealing nothing
Can spell the answer in a frantic scribble
Or in curved gentleness around her breasts.

My passionate ally dreaming at my side
Conceiving poems in my chapelled dark
Apocalyptic fingers grasping stars
And scattering their seed across the summer
White hand, curved hand, o dreaming hand
Be always passionate for me, and dream
Me poems down the pathways of the stars.

Apologia pro Carmina Sua

If I make a dark song,
A wounded crying,
If I am not that lyrical boy
Celebrating the long
Bourgeois summers, and their heroic dying
Into the legend of Troy,
Can love construe my bitterness
Into the bright emblems of imagined peace?

Because of an old violence
Men are afraid
Of poems born of a great passion.
Because of violence
I have not whispered, but have made
Some songs of an old passion,
Can love construe my cryptic face,
Transmute the iron of my bitterness?

Hear my dark singing,
My wounded cries;
And do not weep for the lyric boy,
Or the slow dying
Of the bright heroic seasons. Everything dies
Into legend like Troy.
Concern yourself only with the peace
That love construes out of my bitterness.

(This circling dancer is the whirling world)

This circling dancer is the whirling world
All passionate thinking dreamed into a moment
Clear and symbolic as the flight of geese
Clamorous across blue, frigid dawns,
All violence become artistic as a brush
Held lightly, with firm purpose, in the delicate hand
Of some painter in that timeless China.
All knowledge caught and held a moment
An endless moment in a wave of the sea.

The Weasel at the Heart (A Verse Play in Two Scenes)

Characters: Poet
             Woman/Queen
             Old Man
             Chorus
             Two Soldiers

Scene 1

(The stage is at first in darkness, and only the poet's voice is heard)

POET: Summer for the lovers, a gift of sun,
    Cries love's evangelist;
        And let not winter, that cold anatomist
        Come when they have with tender fierceness kissed
    To shroud them, when bright day is done.

    Summer for the lovers, a gift of light,
    Cries love's evangelist;
        And let no cold and wintry elegist
        Bewail the tenderness with which they kissed,
    Or their passing into the night.

    Summer for the lovers, a gift of love,
    Cries love's evangelist;
        Ward off the winter, that sharp satirist,
        From coming when they have so sweetly kissed;
    End not their summer love.

(As the poet speaks, the stage is gradually lighted, revealing a rough, simple hearth. Suspended above the fire a large, black pot. R. an old ragged man, seated. L. a handsome woman, also seated. At her side the young poet. The wind can be heard without.)

WOMAN: The old wives say that we are born to weep.
    Never a woman had more cause than I,
    Queening this rude sty, on this barren hill.
    Imprisoned by those black and tearing winds.
    And nobody to keep me warm at nights –
    An old mumbling, sapless stick of a man,
    And an unshaven boy whose mind
    Runs more on rhymes than the white limbs of women.

POET (*kneeling*): Have I not made songs in the honour
    Of your white limbs so that all men
    Cannot forget my songs or your great beauty?

WOMAN: Songs! What good are songs
    To a woman when she stretches in her bed
    And cries for a likely lad to cover her?
    O I am sick with loneliness and hatred,
    And great desire,
    And wishing for a rich exultant life.
    The old fool babbles, and the young one dreams,
    And all my blood goes lonely.

(She leans forward and stirs viciously the pot. The poet gazes at her pouting face. The old man's mumbling suddenly becomes distinct.)

OLD MAN: Enormous visions haunted me all day,
    Black horses thundering across the sky,
    Ridden by women with long, rippled hair
    Into a bloody and tremendous sun.
    And I who watched, an old and weary man,
    With bitten lips, cried in impotent fury
    To hold those horses and their naked riders,
    To keep them from that red triumphant death,
    To read a secret in their love-crazed eyes.
    I have seen nothing like that wild loveliness,
    Those horses galloping with their white riders
    Into the sun, the beauty of those riders.
    What was the urgency of their desire?
    What the magnificence of their red doom.

POET (*musingly*): The old men shall see visions.
    It is written.

WOMAN: And the young men dream dreams.
    And neither dreams nor visions feed
    The starving body, quiet the blood,
    Or kill the weasel biting at the heart.

POET (*rising slowly to his feet*)
    The old men see visions,
    But the wise have bitter power
    To interpret them. And what this means
    Is a cold shuddering in all my veins.
    Old men see visions. So the writing says.
    But who ordained the telling of such visions?
    Old men who see such sights should tell them
    Only to their unresponsive beards.

(he turns passionately to the woman)

Will you not be content with life,
With the protecting air of love
And all the honour my songs make of your beauty,
And so avoid the doom that has been seen?

WOMAN: And even were it true, that this old fool
        Has seen a vision of some awful doom,
        I would not change.
        I want a lover,
        The warm night's desecration in his arms,
        And to be queen in the cold light of day.

POET: I have power. I have an ancient art.
       The vision has been seen. The doom must come.
       You will be queen. You will have many lovers.
       And in the end, you will despoil your beauty,
       And weep for the old simpleness and my great homage.

WOMAN: Never.

POET: For the last time I make a song for you.

WOMAN: I am content to listen.
        Tomorrow when I am taken in strong arms
        I will command a hundred singers
        To make a golden marriage-song.
        Tonight I'll hold your hands, and you may sing.

POET: Complexity of passion
       Makes a song
       From the tumult of dung,
       Raises a flower
       From blood and mire.
       But cannot keep the flesh upon the bone.

       Intellect and passion
       Violently mixed
       Have always vexed
       Unexultant hearts,
       Given great hurts.
       But cannot keep the flesh upon the bone.

       A singing passion
       Is a monstrous thing,
       A brazen clang

In the wild throat
Of our defeat.
But cannot keep the flesh upon the bone.

Only this passion
Makes me sing.
Only this troubled dung
Raises this flower.
Passions endure
But cannot keep the flesh upon the bone.

(*As the Woman kisses the Poet the curtain falls*)

Scene II

(*A Throne-room, pillared. On the throne sits the woman, now robed and crowned, as a Queen. The Old Man, now in official dress, stands at a respectful distance. The light is the cold, grey light of dawn.*)

QUEEN: The light comes to look upon my royalty.
    Well, I have had a night –
    In such strong arms so to be clipped and caught,
    Who would have thought that dawn would ever come,
    Or daylight birds eclipse my warm heart's music?
    My dreams, my wishes all fulfilled – not all.
    I said that after the sweet night of love
    I would be Queen in the cold light of day,
    And hear the homage of a hundred singers.
    O vision-haunted man, old crazy fool,
    Bring me the singers to enhance my glory.

OLD MAN: When visions terrify the eye,
    Affright the mind,
    My poor madness yearns to be dead or blind –

QUEEN: Bring me the singers.

OLD MAN: When in the bed of lust
    The beauty that I scorned
    Begets its own corruption, though I warned -

QUEEN: The singers.

OLD MAN: The birds sing in the dawn.

QUEEN: I, the Queen, command
　　　　Bird-throated singers with dark, human faces
　　　　And pulsing blood to be brought to pay me homage.

OLD MAN: The birds sing.
　　　　But you will have these others.
　　　　I obey.

(*He beats a gong, and the Chorus enter.*)

CHORUS: Everything is created by desire.
　　　　This the mother and the poet know.

　　　　Out of the half-apprehended world
　　　　All black and crying weathers
　　　　Suddenly vanish in a bright storm,
　　　　And what remains is fabulous,
　　　　The coloured artifice for which we crave.

　　　　Everything is created by desire.

　　　　The desire of the water for passion,
　　　　The sensual, devouring flame;
　　　　The desire of our whimpering tension
　　　　For the final peace;
　　　　Of worship for abandon,
　　　　Of lust for release.
　　　　This the mother and the poet know.

　　　　All our desire is crying for creation,
　　　　Our blood for the forming of small bones,
　　　　Our voices for the making of rich words,
　　　　Our present to create a history.

　　　　Everything is created by desire.
　　　　This the mother and the poet know.

QUEEN: Bird-throated singers to the Queen of love
　　　　Pay homage. All the day is mine,
　　　　The warm, dark hours, and the cold, bright hours,
　　　　All, all exist to honour the great Queen.
　　　　The old man, crazed with visions,
　　　　And the golden singers
　　　　All, all exist to mirror the Queen's glory.
　　　　The blood is satisfied, and the fierce weasel

Bites no longer at the desiring heart.
All exist because the Queen is loved.
All – all but one. My poet.
Where is the bitter scorner,
He who would sing no more,
He who foretold an agony to follow
My night of love, my day of royalty?

OLD MAN: My visions are a fever in my blood.
      Wild riders to a bloody death –

(*The Poet enters and stands before the Queen.*)

QUEEN: My poet. So my triumph is complete.
      The night of love is hot within my veins.
      The light of day salutes my queenliness.
      The bright song has been sung to honour me.
      Sing for me now, my poet,
      And all rewards are yours.

POET: The old men see visions. It is written.
      I foretold the night of love, the royal day.
      And said that I would sing for you no more.

QUEEN: Your choice is – sing, or die.

POET: To die is less than sing without the heart.

QUEEN: To die is horror when a queen commands.

POET: When you were lonely on the barren hill,
      And your desires as wild as the great winds,
      Then I would sing for you. But now
      You have ridden the black horse into the sun.

QUEEN: Forget your fantasies, and sing – or die.

POET: To die is but to be a breaking wave,
      To find the angel aching in the blood,
      The god among the bitter elder-branches.

      To die is but to consummate great love,
      To lose life's sores in time's great fountain-head,
      To lose the bitterness of elder-branches.

To die is but to end all dreams in dream,
All vision in annihilating light,
And hear the endless and unspoken word.

To die is better than to live a dream,
Yearning to make again a poet's night.
I go to find love in a wordless god.

QUEEN: Sing but one song to praise my royal beauty.

POET: I cannot sing.

QUEEN: The guard. His head, that I may dance before it.

(*The Old Man beats his gong again. Two soldiers enter and lead away the Poet.*)

OLD MAN: When visions riot in the veins
          When dreams are dances
          When the cold blood runs
          Away from the heart's defences.
          When in the labyrinth of lust
          The bewildered heart is lost
          When madness has had its desire
          When the poet sings no more –

QUEEN: O stop your miseries, old croaking raven,
          Or I will dance before your head as well.

(*The two soldiers re-enter, and set the head before the Queen. She looks at it with mounting horror, while the Chorus sings.*)

CHORUS: Legends ago
          She who is now my miracle of morning
          Rose like a flower from violet, dolphined seas.
          And lovers knew
          The bright exultance of her beauty burning,
          And the sun shone on their heart's certainties.

          Legends ago
          She who is now my more than beauty's legend
          Was born in a poet's making marrying mind,
          And lovers knew
          How hands could twine an ever-living garland,
          And love be everywhere a healing wind.

Legends ago
She who is legendary now of love
Gave lovers this immortal catalyst.
And lovers knew
Why the blood leaps and the quick pulses move.
O we created love and legends when we kissed.

QUEEN: What have I done?
　　　My praiser, my bright praiser, sings no more.
　　　And I am doomed.
　　　My lusty night, my royal day,
　　　Are gone with the windy hillside I rejected.
　　　My strong-armed lovers and bird-throated singers
　　　Are gone with the proud poet I have killed.
　　　The vision. The doom foretold.
　　　I was a queen and I had many lovers;
　　　I could contract eternity into a night
　　　Of love, a day of honour and of song.
　　　All's gone. My blood is dry and cold.
　　　My limbs, my royal love-flushed limbs,
　　　But now quick from the commerce of delight,
　　　The joy of poets and of mighty lovers,
　　　Are feeble. And I have to dance,
　　　To dance before his head,
　　　Into that bloody and tremendous sun.

(*She dances away, slowly, despoiling herself, into the red sunlight which has flooded the scene during her speech.*)

OLD MAN: Dreams are short, and life is long.
　　　A woman must have love, a poet song.
　　　Passion and pride and pain.

　　　Birth is death, and sleep is waking.
　　　All our lives our hearts are aching.
　　　Passion and pride and pain.

　　　Wild riders on wild horses.
　　　Brute instruments and forces.
　　　Passion and pride and pain.
　　　When all the fire of life is gone
　　　A bloodless man is left alone.
　　　Passion and pride and pain.

Curtain

Poet

To die is but to be a breaking wave,
To find the angel aching in the blood,
The god among the bitter elder-branches.

To die is but to consummate great love,
To lose life's sorrows in time's great fountainhead,
To lost the bitterness of elder branches.

To die is but to end all dreams in dream
All vision in annihilating light
And the endless and unspoken word.

To die is better than to live a dream
Yearning to make again a poet's might.
I go to find love in a wordless god.

(Death is within us like a child)

Death is within us like a child
Waiting the leaping moment of his triumph
The priested minute of burial and beckon
The seeded second we have carried from the womb.

We are childed with death and know
The quiet terror of his certain coming
The seed springs from the shroud
The curtaining darkness of our graved corruption
Blossoms the purple of his victory.
Death is the only heir of our corruption.

A Woman and Some Men

A dark woman, passionate in a public place
Can put all about her to scorn.
For her intricate service
A ceremony is born,
And we are nothing but fools in public places.

All the delusions of our intellect are lost
In the dark tides of her hate
And love, the demands of a passionate woman,
Her assumption of fate,
And we are nothing but fools in public places.

We are whipped children before the bitter scorn
Of a dark woman's eyes
Publicly declaring us to be fools and knaves,
Our faiths and visions lies.
And we are nothing but fools in public places.

The Sailor Speaks

After my many bitter journeys,
Over cold seas, over warm seas,
Here in this fertile land
I had hoped to understand,
To see, however dimly,
The elusive light you sometimes see
Above the waters, but always lose.
I had hoped that this time I would not lose
That light, that somewhere here
Among the stubborn and half-hidden cheer
Of these hills and little farms
Where life is order, where the only harms
Are the expected ones of rain
And no rain, of the crooked seasons
Which were always over the horizon
At sea.
But here there is none.

'Love is Like the Lion's Tooth'

– W. B. Yeats

Caught in the singing foliage of youth
Bright limbs trembling in a silver dance
Beneath the dreaming mockery of the moon
When all the drunken treetops seem aswoon
And the pale sky is heavy as with trance
Nostalgic hearts have found the lion's tooth.,

Burdened with the filthy weight of years
Brine-sodden from implacable, dancing waves
Respectable men have eased their unbent backs
And found the certainty each moment lacks
Have found, before the assurance of their graves
A thunderous solace for their wistful tears.

Old men, abandoned to dim innocence
Have had a coloured woodland dream

Beneath the pale insistence of the moon,
And sung again the insolent bodily tune
Which only lovers know but all men dream.
And lust has always danced with innocence.

Caught in the singing foliage of youth
Nostalgic hearts have found the lion's tooth.

Prologue to 'Love For Love'

A comedy we offer you tonight
Which will, we hope, afford you more delight,
More profit too, than all the Sunday news
Of rapes, and nations, Communists, and Jews;
More too, than will your average modern play,
Written, produced, forgotten in a day.
Congreve, who wrote for a robuster stage
Is not confined to one particular age:
We represent for you his men and women
Because they're witty, spirited and human,
If you resent their follies and their crimes
Be sure they are those of modern times
As well as Congreve's; if you feel his whip,
Take solace from your neighbour as we strip
His hypocritic mask away as well. –
The play itself tells this: I'm here to tell
You only that we strive for your delight
In playing 'Love for Love' for you tonight.

Poem

In the mean parishes of my desire
The nagging knives of time
Have chastened with laborious artifice
The innocent luxuriance of my care,
Whittled the singing folly of my days
To a thin stick of crime.

Is there a wisdom to be found in ease?
A green tide like a sleep
To wash over the defeated land
To drown the worn and unrepentant days?
An end to foolishness, a quiet end
To the need to weep?

Nothing is left within my emptied acres.
The razored tongues of time
Have cut away the fragrance of my youth.
A lonely ploughman in the barren pastures
Turns me the haggard face of truth
And calls me Crime.

For My Unborn Child

Out of my stubborn passion comes this prayer
For you whom mixed bloods bring to genesis.
May you burn through life as through some rare
And intricate dancing ceremony
Turbulently consummated with a kiss.
Too proud to care for either praise or blame
Know nothing but deliberate happiness
And may you have no enemy but time.

Song

By violent, ambiguous ways
I came to the proud bed of love,
Travelling for many stubborn days
Bitterly through the stricken grove.

Now in the dark peace of the night
I mouth brave words, and fear no more
The unguessed dogmas of delight,
The vast, anonymous desire.

The sober morning shall not tell
My old pedantic sullenness,
Nor any hectic day reveal
The spindrift of my voyages.

Nor shall my liberated art
Spill out its broken images
To mourn the unregenerate heart
Burning upon fantastic seas.

No artifices shall remove
The mask from my obscure days
Now I have reached the bed of love
By violent, ambiguous ways.

The Heart of the Winter

In a cold season
In a bitter weather
I made in the green arms of the sea
A lonely music, a troubled pastoral
Of nostalgia for the familiar landscape
And the security of the established hills.
Abandoned by legends and remote from love
Among the unkind pastures of the dolphin
I made an idyll of defeat
Despairing through the dark night of the waves,
The green annihilation, the cold death.

In a cold season
In a bitter weather
When all my visions were a green hunger
The great seas sucked the marrow from my bones
The salt weed scrawled a chilly epitaph
Across my drowning face a love receded.

In a cold season,
In a bitter weather
But the sea gave up its dead. The storm
Broke into a golden weather, and the waves,
The dank and turbulent tides, bore me like triumph
To the green island beyond the black horizon
Where love and legends flourish, and the day
Is fabulous.

In a cold season
In a bitter weather
The sad heart of the winter shattered
And desire unfolded, and the day is fabulous
Of love and legends in the green island
I came to in the springtime of my blood
After the cold horror of my drowning.

In a cold season,
In a bitter weather
I made a bitter music in the green acres,
Nostalgic hymns for the imagined island.
Now that sad heart is broken, may the birds
Be the only choristers of our desire
The sun the only witness of our legend.

(Tonight I see an image)

Tonight I see an image
Of an old house,
Bare, ruinous,
Half-hidden by dark foliage
In a sullen wood.

Is it the moon that crazes me
To wander there
In the dark night air
Though fearful of the mystery
In a sullen wood.

An old and ruined house
Affrights my mind.
The baffled wind
Moans low and venomous
In a sullen wood.

Poem

The innocent frenzy of the wind
Making the cold seas murderous
Creates an image in the mind
Of how the body's pitilessness
Begets upon the foolish heart
The exotic violence of art.

O innocent, o murderous seas
When the wind drops you cease to rage:
Will the complex fury of images
Stop in the mind when doldrum age
Asserts its bitter calm, or will
This lust torment and drive me still?

The Conquest of the West

A female voice out of the East
Aroused that sleeping and bull-chested hero
To cross the seas in a vague, murderous frenzy.

The hieroglyphic sun scarred his hot brain;
The spoiling tides made mock inside his body;

The East receded as the hero travelled
Viciously on towards the voice.
And still the inexorable voice lured on
To pain and some obscure mystery.

He found no comfort in his creed of murder.
The voice remained elusive, and still called.
The patient nations were subdued in vain;
Their splendour held no secrets. And he travelled on,
For ever seeking an exacter passion.

The tale ends vaguely. Some report
Cathay was his last landfall,
And he came alone to where the voice
Splintered his spirit and gave him peace at last.
This much is known for certain. He did not come back.

Biography

Virgins and heroes in his eclectic youth
Made the sensed valleys ardent, and his mountains seemed
But the romantic nudity from which he dreamed
His fatal bright descent to find the truth.

The windswept years went by. He grew more loth
To screw his mind against the lowering sky
For manna. The valleys called. One day,
Crammed with his visions, he asserted both
His hunger and his pride, and left the hills.
What if the virgins proved all harlots, and the fair
Chivalric champions smaller than himself?

Experience had not rotted him upon a shelf,
Nor had the cold winds stripped his spirit bare
Before he found the poison cures and kills.

Peace

What then if there were no power to crave,
No fear of the hereafter, no desire
Whimpering through the blood for a kinder grave,
No pity, no deceit, no descending terror?
What if there were no possibility of error,

No blind wandering through the groves of love,
No fitful urge to mask, betray, or squander,
No crying for the moon we may not have?

Such a great peace is unimaginable,
Fantastic as our sour ancestors' hell;
And yet there is a moment in between

Two sufferings when such peace may come
Like a great water spoiling and making clean.
And leaving us to a new martyrdom.

History

The blind old empires crumble to decay
Appeasing the barbarians on their borders;
Each subtle civilisation has its day
And disappears in imbecile disorders.

We sit at school and learn the obvious lesson,
But once outside deny it any force.
Believing history becomes the capital treason,
We have our lives, and let things take their course.

And when our own imperium weakens,
Despairs, and finally collapses, our alarms
Are greater for the unlit, untended beacons
That should have summoned us before to arms

And we condemn, no, not ourselves, but others,
And in the ruins call our conquerors brothers.

Legends

In the last chapter he grew sick and died,
And so the myth came to an ordinary end.
Perhaps it had been better not to read
So far, to disobey the vague command

That seemed to reach us from a distant country
Saying, Believe. This genuine oracle
Will never disappoint you. Liberty
Is in obedience. The last page reveals the miracle.

But we read on, to the last bitter page
To be again cheated and disappointed.
Bewilderment and ignorance afflict our age.
The myth's a failure, and the times disjointed.

Tomorrow is another book, another hero.
We must have legends, though they end in sorrow.

Poem

The sensual landscape in his mind
Flowered in sudden fury, made him blind
To everything but that cathartic pain
Loosening the bonds of order in his brain.
He found the animals behind his eyes
Could take that verdant kingdom by surprise.
And when the brutal ravishing was done
He rested easily, took solace from the sun.

Morning over the Valleys

My intricate and massy image
Sprawled on the sleeping mountains
Calls me to fever
And the quick spilled syllables
The fountained orators of no defeat.

That coupling in the dawn should be a symbol
The urgent index
And the fiery sermon
Love-crossed, the valleys whimper
As the light grows flagrant.

Dive then, my plummet, in your disregard.
The peaks, kissed crimson, can no longer hold you.
My dissipated image
In the valleys' darkness
Tongues its escape from the cold silent dawn.

Stanzas in Dejection

Autumnal Hamlet sees the spies of grief
Crawl through the sap to wither the wild branch.

The hunted moon, a tell-tale and a thief,
Blanches the blood the brain the bone
And the defeated heart is sullen.

The kingly courts are lost, the poets dumb,
All lovers with Ophelia drowned.
Reason and passion are like winter numb
And no bird sings behind the mocking eyes.
The self-spawned world decays.

Depraved the tigers have forgotten spring.
The hunters in the ravaged land sleep easily.
Armoured with adultery and prayers the king
Ranges the big battalions on his side.
The players eyes are sad.

Hamlet, alone in autumn, weeps
Seeing king's havoc and a frosty sky.
And the cool water where the maiden sleeps.
The branch is withered, and no flamboyant leaf
Disturbs the spies of grief.

Song

Ten weathers at my finger-tips
May make me wise
When the lost kingdoms of my eyes
Are branch and blossom on my lips.

A cloud and thunder on my brow
May make me sad
When the rough blood turns dark and bad
To stop the singing on the bough.

A rising sun within my heart
May wither me,
Drying the sap, burning the tree,
And killing all my country art.

O weathers, thunder, golden sun,
Make me sad and numb,
And all my singing branches dumb,
To see my stolen countries gone.

Poem

In that rich dark, that midnight wood,
The ambiguity of your surrender
Taught me a suffering eloquence,
In ravelled prayers to sift and sunder
The cruel politics of the blood,
The vague platonic dissidence.

The treasured spilling of the wine
Showed me a panic imagery,
Your wisdom in that subtle wood
To coil and catch the mystery
In urgent symbols and profane,
The bitter idols of the blood.

But your dear thievery of time,
That dark encounter in the wood,
Has only this obscure result,
The purging of my sullen blood
From contemplation of its crime,
From solemn rapture in its guilt.

In that deep, that secret wood
Flowered these sermons of my art,
Baroque, indecorous, to spurn
And spill the tears of the fanatic heart,
The cold and unbelieving blood,
The passions in the callous urn.

Your forest wisdom harvests now
My singing seasons; from the wine
We spilled within the ancient wood
The reckless odours rise again;
The birds exult on every bough
The midnight victory of the blood.

Poem

Mortal, miraculous,
You lie within my sleep,
Where, old and venomous,
The ornate dragons keep
Their dark dominion.

Their ancient, evil charm
Suffers not loneliness,
The waking fever, or harm
To fret your loveliness
In their dominion.
You dream within my dream
While the vexed dragons keep
Their watches as we seem
Immortally to sleep
In their dominion.

But mortal, faithless, we wake
In cold questioning light,
And only a fable make
Of our enchanted night
In dragons' dominion.

Ennui, Mediterranean

The bridge to that romantic country
Is broken, and the avid enemy
Smiles in the poisoned shadow of his swords
To see my dumb hand and expectant eye.

Let anarchy be rampant in the night,
A tide of blood to drown the shrinking light
In passionate and innocent festival
For all my voices and the pangs of sight.

Distant, the suave lions of Africa
Sleep in the avid indolence of day.
My immemorial rendezvous is with
These violent waters and the heart's decay.

Brutal unreason of this classic sun
Reveals the certain working of the poison;
No lion roused within my tawny sides
Startles my enemy or breaks the tension.

O innocent passion, loose the bloody tide
Of anarchy, let the rich waters ride
In savage triumph round the frenzied world,
And let my hands sing what my heart has cried.

Elegy

The various poems answer for my hero
Who, fabled, lies remote and harboured
From the articulate urgency of my desire.

The strange light does not wake him where he sleeps.

Beautiful the image of his disregard
In that eternal lullaby of waters
Denies the ultimate symbolism of sorrow,
Grief's unkind climate, the heart's withering.

He said, 'Look for me in romantic countries'.

The poems are his only passions now
To speak to us with any certain voice,
The spelled configuration of impatience,
His trembling fever for the distant conquest,
The sombre conflagration in his blood
Those passionate answers predicate our journeys
Harassed in subtleties of light and darkness
To those romantic countries that he spoke of,
To find tomorrow's angel in the clouds of fear,
Wearing a hairy mask, annunciation
Bladed and trumpeted to break
The centuried sleep, the long endurance.

The poems call us from his fabled darkness.

Venus Anadyomene

Trample on that sea-born innocence
The antic watchers cry; our inland loves,
Furtive and musty in the horrid groves,
Are stricken by that naked insolence
Of flesh foam-gendered; our sordid reverence
Is troubled by that brightness which the waves
Flung up in passion; an envious shudder moves
Through our decrepit sanctuaries of sense.

And did they vex the glory of the hour
With their hot slanders, spoil that nudity
The amorous parting of the waters bore,
What second birth could the foam's agony
Cast up had those impotent ones the power
To trample that bright life upon the shore.

Stages to a Modern Prelude: 'The Uncreated Conscience'

I

A dream which I translated to a painted stage,
A personal document of bitterness and rage
And speculative passion, to torment the knowledge of the proud,
Startle the meek, offend the earnest crowd;
How guess those ceremonious symbols of delight
Could bring the desecration of the poet's right?
Or that the gaudy cunning of those innocent toys
Should call to exile with such imperious voice?
The passionate heraldic emblems which were worn
For gaiety became a burden not to be borne,
And the brute darkness and the impious silence came
To reap my anger with narrow scythes of blame.
The bestial images that slavered at the doors
Broke in, and danced and copulated on the floors
Where the players, gracious idols of my mind
Had moved with serious charm unconscious of the wind
Howling for sacrifice in the crowd's empty heart,
The bloated enemies of my paraded art.
I, who in moving visions had only sought to please
The body's mental pride and the sensual heresies,
Was made a mockery by the arrogant intellect,
The sober demon which the reckless hearts reject;
And the careful idols I had made for men to stare
Upon exposed and spat on in the frigid air.
The dull ass triumphed, and the lean spirit went
To hungry lands, the discipline of discontent.

II

I have kept the rust from the tragic mirror of my blade
So that all grim and fanciful things therein portrayed
Are seen with cold clearness and unflinching eye
Like the flight of birds against a pallid sky.
I have kept the disillusioned weapons of my anger
Clean with my passions and sharpened with my hunger.
I have kept the animal alive with bitter bread,
And scorned the timid pity of the half-dead,
The braggart dunces who bargain in my place
With snuffling nostrils, blood-dimmed eyes and anxious face,
For life controlled and ordered in easy grooves,
For belly's comfort, empty minds, expensive graves.

III

Let the tyrannical generations be, and find
A delicate mask for the unforgiving mind.
Let the fools drink the impure water in the ditch;
Disdain whatever coin or chamber tempt to fetch
Me back to that blind and unheroical school
To be lessoned by impotents, or censured by a fool,
Grow old in loneliness; the heart's terrible pride
Cares not if old lover or old enemy have died,
So that the body feels no cold or abstract joy
In the conflicts which burned the will of girl or boy;
So that the ash of the mind can still create
A dancing image, the proud deceit of the tongue relate
Old heroic stories and legends of amorous women,
Beautiful houses, eager ships, magicians, courteous foemen.
Grow old behind the shield's terrible brilliance,
The lusty heart's vexed and vexing arrogance,
The passions which endure, the mind which is always sad
Because only in troubled sadness is to be had
The contentment of the monotonous artifice which lights
A comforting candle in our impassioned nights.

IV

So I have made my peace at last with my turbulent self
And lie at ease upon my cold and solitary shelf
Above the water's swirl; and like any burning boy
Can kill an enemy or take a quick remorseless joy
In coupling; or make some bright romantic image which
Shall lead men as they please into or out of the ditch.
Salt in my blood, and a tameless violence in my eye,
In the wisdom of the artifice I am prepared to die.

(The beauty lies with the fool)

The beauty lies with the fool
And the strong man lies alone
And in the churchyard moulders
The solitary bone.
O heart, is this the end of pride?

The withering intellect
And the beauty that turned many heads
Had only a brief daytime
Before finding narrow beds.
O heart, is this the end of pride?

The king lies with the beggar-maid,
The harlot with the priest,
The wise man with the brutal one,
The worst with the best.
O heart, is this the end of pride?

Nightmare

The dragons crawl about the mountains
With sexy and discordant cries;
The cripples and the drunken soldiery
Put on a lecherous disguise,
Perform the ceremony of evil,
And couple in the bestial trance.
The innocence of day is gone;
Night is a foul traditional dance.
Obscenity of raddled puppets
Sprawls in mockery of delight;
The beggars do their ulcered ministry;
The squalid monsters lech and fight.
The ceremony of evil done,
And all the foul traditional dance,
The innocence of day is gone,
Remains the intolerable trance.

Sonnet

No rich complexity of flower or woman
    Could tease him from the clichés of remorse
Or his cold pondering on the inhuman
    Zodiac where he'd run his course.

He had no dreams to sabotage his tower,
    (There was a dream at first, and then no other).
In the selfconscious circle of his power
    Despair was faithful to him like a brother.

And yet decrepitude subtle as a thief
    Mocked him obscenely, and made him rage.
The grave refusal of passion became grief
    When the obstinate years made him aware of age.

Weeping he left the tower for the park
    To watch the lovers waiting for the dark.

From a Play?

Loneliness came quietly like a pain
Upon the old man's trivial innocence.
His nomadic discipline seemed suddenly vain
Before the tattered magnificence
Of the riders sweating and laughing on the shore.

But when he went among the easy crowd
His broken poise was cause for mockery.
Their laughter was vulgar and unduly loud
And they threatened to throw him in the sea
Or trample him under the feet of horses.

Brothel in Algiers: Wartime

Where the dark sisters paid
Their coins and charities
In landscapes of disgust
Waters and memories
Elusive, sad
Heretically recalled
Lust's younger season
And the ritual denied
The dance.

Here the humbling anonymity
Lost among the ascending spirals
The meagre ceremonies
Furtive observance
Wears and welcomes
Meek brutes and arrogant
And the world's wandering sons.

Ithyphallic demented choirs
Perform their unexultant rites
The sad priest blesses.

Dance, o my daughters
For their short delight
Dance.

These weary gyres are broken by small rooms
Where dirty beds invite

Where the sisters of charity display
Where the sons of violence are not afraid
Where is the deed
Walk nonchalantly up the crowded stairs
Through the smell of sweat
The smoke patterns and the stale, sour wine-breath
On the top floor they keep the rarities
Lean from the landing
And look down the gyres.
Who planted the great tree in the court?
Who plucks the tarnished fruit
From the insidious branches?

Sisters of mercy
I bring my prayer and the plucked fruit
To join you in the dance.

The priest dreams in the wilderness
The tall tree flowers
And the circles descend
And narrow
And the dance goes on.

The sons of fear are violent
The sisters of display are charitable.

Noise
And many smells
And coin changing hands.

The deed
The dance
The darkness.

The Need for Pardon

The bitter thoughts that flowered in the garden
Made him afraid and lonely; he was tired
Of the patterned richness he had once admired,
And conscious now of the great need for pardon.

Spurning the florid landscapes of his pride,
He eased his stiffness over the dark fence,
Thinking to climb back into innocence
Or a country where wisdom had grown old and died.

His long exotic sojourn had made him daft
Perhaps; or possibly he had nurtured his mind
Too long on the formalism of solitude.

Pardon was not to be had where the lovers laughed,
Nor where the music was comfort to the blind.
He wept quietly, alone in the wood.

Judgement Day

And many were afraid and his their faces
When the secret suburbs flowered into light,
And others cried the day had come too late,
And some were desperate and wore disguises.
And all were unaware of how the myth
Had failed them, how the terrible peace
Had come at last and had not brought them ease,
Because they found no mercy in that death.

Art Poetique

The golden hammers of my tongue beat out
Gold handiwork, the singing tree ascends
Within your ear, the sober dancing there;
And how can I deride with battered shout,
– Bedraggled bird of that magnificence, –
The brightness or the darkness of the air?

Let drowsy soldiers, drunken emperors lie
Dreaming in bed or on the sensual floor
– We know the waking ardours of our sweat.
Let the sad women in the doorways cry
– We have no alms for beggar, saint or whore,
Only the artifice our pains beget.

The gold invention sings within your ear,
The tall trees laden with the golden birds,
The hammered miracle of innocence,
And all that dancing, all that singing there,
A drunken miracle, a toil of words,
A tower from the brute and lonely sense.

O that gold handiwork, that blossomed dawn,
That miracle of golden singing birds,
The prostitute, the beggar and the saint
Wailing their wounds outside our towered dance
How shall they tell the speakers from the words?
How shall we comfort beggar, whore and saint?

Soldiers and emperors in their bestial beds,
Beggars and saints about the innocent streets,
And women crying from their shadowed doors,
All who have aching or have empty heads,
The singing tree is not compact of sweets,
There is no comfort for beggars, saints or whores.

Garden of Eden

On the edge of the horrible wood
I heard the painted parrots scream,
I heard the bright and angry apes,
I saw the rampant tigers make
Their hostile patterns of delight,
I saw the cold ecstatic snake
And the innocent sensual woman.
I saw the flare and fall of light
Upon their sinewed, coloured shapes,
I heard the laughter, cold, inhuman,
I felt their anger and their fear,
The consummation in the wood.

That peacock-plumaged afternoon
The parrots' bright metallic sneers,
The laughter of the angry apes,
The cold ecstatic snake
Made fearful patterns of delight
Such as heraldic tigers make
In the erotic and inhuman
Albums of some classic night,
Twisting their sinewed, coloured shapes
Against an innocent sensual woman
In agonies and cruel fears
Tearing the ragged afternoon.

On the edge of the horrible wood
That peacock-plumaged afternoon
I heard the painted parrots scream
And fled in hot heraldic fear.

The Country Drunkard

The country drunkard desiring
Ordered kingdoms, coherent myths,
The hero of some landscapes and some loves,
Is epitaphed by a chill worm of pathos
Across the sprawled horizon of the cities.

Fabulous darkness hides him,
Vocative to pity and nostalgia,
The conscience of his song,
And the hurt, aimless townlands,
Where no thorn of grief can penetrate,
And no ironic tear wash out his sins.

An urban winter holds
His passionate seeds, a jagged landscape
Mars the green coherence of his dreams.
Only a vague and unauthentic legend
Troubles the frosty ignorance of the city,
Murmurs uncertainly in the pale air
Where once he was a hero and desired.

Orpheus

He drew the hyperbolic draperies
about him where the stone woman sat
and she arose, taking his hand again.
Out to the distant light they faltered
while the stone animals looked on in wonder.
But on the very edge of darkness
he stopped his music and looked back
to see the miracle dissolve,
the curtains reassume rigidity,
and all the animals looked on in pity.

Ancestral

Where we were born, a windy place,
A broken landscape of regrets,
High curlews calling, the careful men
Nursed their rocky memories in silence,
Avoiding the fat plains and their brute inhabitants.

Sullen or silver, the quick waters strained
Away from the bare ridges,
Seeking the fertile lands, the distant sea.
But the quiet men, the burdened women,
Aloof as foxes, clung to the ferned hillsides,
The stubborn memory, the confidence of God.

Eclogue

At wedding-feast or country fair
No seasonal metaphors disturb
    The nonconformist ghost.
Remote as myth, he hovers where
Ancestors, foaming on the curb,
    Are ridden by the lost.

And easy in his craft he prays
Purgation of such vanities.
    The guests endure and smile.
Though he denies their holidays,
The sailors on the broken seas
    Laugh at his sullen tale.

The unregenerate at feast
Or fair or straddled on the seas
    Are dabbled in the blood;
But he, his victim and his priest,
Is swaddled in such fantasies
    Of evil and of good

As turn about his sorry heart
In formal, convoluted prayers
    For those who, smiling, lost,
Ignore his preordaining art
To damn them at their feasts and fairs
    And make them pay the cost

For sins too readily forgiven
By easier churches, milder gods.
    That unrelenting ghost
Is tenant of a narrow heaven,
And checks with terror of his rods
    The future in the past.

(I am the spindrift ghost)

I am the spindrift ghost of many sailors, whose white bones now lie without lust or hampering of flesh beneath the green and ancient pressure of the seas.

I am the ghost, the disembodied longing, of all those poor bodies who for long and empty watches have starved upon ship's biscuits and unavailing dreams of women, and cursed, or confronted themselves with, the incredible romance of deep waters.

I am the ghost of those restless crews for ever swinging with the swinging tides, signed on for an everlasting and a watery commission, to endure the pluck of the waters until the end of time.

The Prisoner

Nursing a brittle passion,
Romantic discipline,
I sang in my prison
Mad like an angel.

That voice of birds
Broke the bright air
About the coloured freedom
Of my mocked enemies,
They fled in terror.

My passion splintered
And my voices faded
As the air darkened
Discipline failed.

But still that angel madness
Held me prisoner.

Lost Love

The old extravagance of love eludes us.
The furtive seasons mock our torn regrets,
Desire, harsh as sunlight upon rock,
Lays sinewy hands upon us where we wait
For some forgotten symbol to announce
That water has been found, the wilderness
Hides somewhere the well, the sheltering trees,
The promised country we would not take by force.

(At midnight, in deserted towns)

At midnight, in deserted towns
An alien pastoral displays
The white integrity of innocence;
The drunken hero's bonds of sense
Are slackened, his lack-lustre gaze
Encounters those deep, breaking seas
Where all experience fails and drowns.
He sees, and knows not that he sees.

For a Play (Chorus for the Undefeated)

Ambiguous omens
Assault our generations,
The lessons of history
Escape our troubled search,
And the leaders are absent,
The tall men with certainty
Frowning their bright brows
Or making their smiles dazzling.
We consult the omens,
And weep for our bewildered fate,
Having no certain knowledge
And no tall leaders.

And all this helps to fatten the false prophets.

The convincing fables,
The enchanting chorus
Are hushed, and lost
Beneath the bloodied seas.
Our sullen bones
Picked clean of myth and miracle
Swing with the dangerous tides,
Nuzzled by monsters,
Or simply lie
Under the green nightmare's pressure.

And this makes it easier for the lying poets.

Anarchy has no landscape
For the eye or heart
To caress or remember.
And the shadowy symbols,

The amorous summer airs,
The ragged winters,
Dismay the patience
Of the broken generations.

It is easy to be deceived by the eye or the heart.

(In love's outrageous slums)

In love's outrageous slums
My father, tiger in my heart, has built
A tower where he spills his words
Making a tremble in the rippled air
Before the angry breasts of the sea's murder.

Star-crossed, where none may stalk him,
He treads, oiled knives and images hung loose,
Seeking a goosegirl in a lonely meadow
To share his bread and wine.

And always those bright breasts beat down his anger.
From the ruined forest women
See his drowning, and their wounds
Weep music where they once gave suck.

Poem

From these five witnesses
Five deaths I read
When the assassin love conducts
Me where the black seas wait,
The funeral of grief
And terror, the endless insult of the night.

For there is no escape
From symbols or from loving.
The iron walkers come
At last to that cold shore,
The final shiver, the five separate deaths,
The callous concupiscence of the night.

Winter

The secret scripture of the grass
Is knocking at my tell-tale heart,
The squandered blood is dumb to tell the time.

Winter is written by the winds
About the oppression of the hills.
The frozen blood is frightened by those scrawls.

And where time lies, my gossip heart
Reads, but in vain, the secrets of the grass,
Hears, but in vain, the scripture of the winds.

The squandered blood is dumb,
My tell-tale heart uneasily hears
The frozen howl of winds, the words of grass.

The Shapes of Pity

The shapes of pity reluctantly displayed
In dreams of daylight or the vivid darkness
Convince like fables; the anarchy of hope
Is mute memorial to the griefs we made
Immortal animals to pad across the night,
To nuzzle us with centuries of fear.
The coloured dreams dissolve; the faded past
Is crystal in the memory of a tear.

Pity is neither kindness nor cruelty,
But only witness to a world of sins.
The immemorial wilderness is weeping
Always, a desolation that in pain begins
And never ends but in some idiot laughter.
Across the desert wing the hideous birds
Whose cry is the remembered childhood nightmare,
The sweating Adam stammering for words.

Mirrored, the shapes of pity only reveal
Our frightened selves, distortions of our dreams.
Marooned in that discoloured wilderness,
Distractedly looking for the healing streams,
We hear the terrible chatter of those birds.
Their shadows blotting out the vacant sky
Remind us of our heritage of debt
And doubt, and the inexorable need to die.

The shapes of pity like bubbles elude us.
The storied animals of our nursery
Stalk monster-wise across our withered landscape.
Doom is despair; the dead not dead are we.
The skeleton sprawled across the desert rock
Is smiling in its empty staring eyes.
All metaphors are murder; death is human,
The one true pity, the undeceiving surprise.

The Erotic Season

Today the erotic season begins,
The coughing tide is tipsy in the veins,
The whaleback metaphors that murder truth
Are tumbling where the foundered mansions lie,
Green nightmares, hollow dreams
Of promised lands fantastic in the dawn.
The dancer in the blood puts on his mask
Of riot, and the insolent music flings
Its gaudy lies to the doubting air.
The coloured castles totter to the sky.

The small white bones, half-buried, lie
Tongueless, and cannot prophesy of ruin,
Nor foretell the waiting worms.

The Wounded Water

The wounded water lies like broken sleep,
Cold miracle of anger, the wild blade
Of history beating down our innocent myths,
Green fount and origin of our ambiguous truths,
Spun, fuelled oracle our voices made,
The lyric doom, the judgement of the deep.

Lost with Leviathan in that proud waste
The drowning men have frenzy in their eyes,
The deep is dark, is ruin; in that toil
Of waters the sick centuries are lost.
Oh! pride and courage are only seabirds' cries
Above that green original turmoil.

Plunge, plunge into the darkness of that doom,
Let the salt water wear away the flesh
And leave the outlined purity of the bone,

Dive to the mystery of that martyrdom
Where the wild tides no longer beat and lash
The clean, picked beauty of the skeleton.

All history is water, a green myth,
The wounded sleep of our despairing past,
The glaucous lyricism of our fate.
Pluck from those depths some vestige of truth,
Some symbol of an innocence not lost,
Miraculous knowledge under waters' weight.

Song

O who unribbed me where I lay
Sleeping like Adam that bright day?

The dancing light, the dancing blood,
Those images of clangorous love,
What were they to the death of pride
And what ambitious verse had said.

Rage and compassion I had known,
And the harsh smouldering to possess
Some intimacy deeper than
The touch of wavebright bone on bone –

But who unribbed me where I lay
Sleeping like Adam that bright day?

Song for Rachel

Stare, stare, said the soldier,
At ghosts in uniforms.
Peer in the deeps, said the sailor,
For those who died in storms.

And stare, said my evil love,
At the hole I made in the sky,
Or in the mirror look at
A man about to die.

I saw the uniformed ghosts,
And the bones on the bed of the sea,
And when I looked at the mirror,
My love murdered me.

Poem

Wild in the ambush and agony of love
I tread my days towards heaven.
Breath-cast, blood-suckled, from the ragged country
I dream my pastoral death.
Hunter to hunted cries. The discipline of pain
Lies hungrily upon the curious flesh and bone.

Urgent the morning in my pride of blood
Shudders its cry and clamour
Conscript to love. The lechery of death
Compels me to this knowledge.
O hidden in that face I have not seen
What answer waits of pity or derision?

Symbols are swords. Upon our wounded faces falls
The dazzle of their light.
Lost in the alien forest our articulate fathers
Prophesy ruin, wrestle
With visions. Angel and anarchy of love
Move with us like a shadow when we move.

The Country of Hurt

This is the country of hurt
Where, after an innocent hazard,
You and I must part,
Leave the immunity
Of love, our golden desert.

Here we are refugees
From dreams and created wonder.
Our private sympathies
Disperse among the crowds
Of untouched aliens, unloved faces.

There is no armour to wear
Against this loss of pride.
Move sullenly where
The anonymous crowds
May hide you like lovers' hair.

In this acrid country
Of inevitable hurt

We go separately,
Having come far from
The desert of our immunity.

Dishonour or delight
May lie along these streets,
But we have come too late
To the country of hurt
For joy by day or rest by night.

Aubade

The whinnying animals of sleep
Prance to ambition and the ache
Of morning, the bleak and sudden day.
We shudder at their echoes when we wake.

Daybreak is desperate, a cold moment
Burning our lethargy and lies.
The serpent blood is fearful of the light.
Lie close, beloved, and keep shut your eyes.

Turning for comfort in that cold moment
We see our faces featureless. The hurt remains.
Love and wonder are the iron forgeries
Of cunning tongues and lying brains.

Trust only then in that old serpent blood.
Daybreak, the cruel moment, has gone by,
Ignore the echoes of the mutual nightmare,
Beloved, now were it sweet to die.

Poem

Awkward or innocent
Or abandoned as saints
In the postures of love,
Prayer on the tipsy tide
May make our marriage
In a seabed grave.

If prodigal grief return
Where the burdened trees
Like priests imploring love

Lift their nailed arms
To the sultry weather,
Blood may suffer, spittle save.

The cry of the crossed woods,
The unsexed mystery,
Bid us to love.
Birdsong or blessing
Curfews us to marriage,
The seadeep grave.

Blood and spittle remain
In the water dances,
The livelong grief of love.
Laid low on that cold bed
The crossed woods cry our kiss.
Blood may suffer, spittle save.

Poem

Back to the loved sky and the humped hills,
The night-infested woods, the fish-cold brooks,
Pride of the fox and buzzard, all lonely terror
Of empty winds over Wales.
My fronded boyhood breaking like a tide
Flung up all contraries, the five gay kingdoms
Of sense, and, dominant as a cloud,
The obsolete map of chapels.
God, a crabbed shepherd on a misty path,
Whistled a thunderclap of truth.
The stammer of spring, the shout of summer
Drowned my husked prayers in the colours
Of time, and the jet of birth, the pain of growing,
The accident of death.
And rascal girls in the spilled calm of winter
In pews as warm as bed dreamed me to marriage.
Under a grassblade on the hill's lean rib
I found the bastard grief.
Bellmusic in the caverns of my sleep
Hymned my dark hope.

Orphaned by indolence and dreams,
Bridehaunted in that scriptural enchantment,
Lonely as priest or fox, I mouthed the seasons

And mourned undying time.
Lost in the quick and tangle of the groin
The dance and horror grew; the spit of God
Cracked the wild globe, his dirty tears
Made sea and slime.
I found the hangman's tree, the livid prayer,
The hot mercy of fear.

Sighed breath and seed in the ominous weathers
Sprouted in glory; in my green ruins
I sang like the rain; and the cold dogs
Of my fathers ran
Howling in the graveyard of my heart.
The careless charity of time
Nailed me with silver to the four, crossed hills;
A maggot murdered Eden.
Bird-droppings on the secret withered grass
Signalled where comfort was.

Rising like flower or the pressing bone
I broke and bloodied the holy circle,
And ran to the far, complaining seas
With a cloud round my head.
Now it is a long cry and a hard voyage
To that inheritance, that lost revolt,
The bell and candle in the fathered dark
Showing the tree of the dead.
Alone like a priest or a fox on the stubborn hills
I recall a child in Wales.

(In this blind time)

      In this blind time
   Some make a virtue of denying history
   Some seek the reassuring emblem
   Or the definite hero, Some have a pure concern
   For phrase, the lapidary or exotic
   Style, and some, half-shy, half-insolent,
   Parade their learning with ironic comment,
   Some fish the gutters with observant ear
   For voices incoherent and absurd.
   These are the toys and labours of our days,
   These are the peas that rattle in our bladders.

Poem in Absence

Absence is pride, the unforgiving warfare
Bawdy by day and night, the hopes of words,
The loud seas threatening the lonely tower

Riding the waves' pulse, hammered by the wind.
I press my knuckled longings to your heart,
The sensual anchor in the storm of days.

Never until the last wind shout
To crack the enormous ice shall envious mermen
Drown my long answers,
Nor the thunder of spring
Beat on your pale withdrawal
Before my whisper covers you for ever.

(Where my seafellow in a windless humour)

Where my seafellow in a windless humour
Ransomed my jackdaw heart
I heard the bone's thin voice.
Helpless and bloodless in that fallow light
Coiled hair and water
On my murdered face
Lay like petals or snow's annunciation.
My cold earthfellow in a narrow room
Lay on my sleep like heartburn.
I heard the seasoft murmur
Of blood falling from sky and ceiling
And my murdered head.
Under the flower patterns
A mouse gnawed patiently at time.

When my skyfellow on his blowcock ghost
Shaped my print on tides and days
My murder echoed
Among the rafters in the owlwise barn.
Helpless and heartless
I ran among the clouds
Weeping because he wore my murdered face.

Mediterranean: Wartime

Drinking in bars around the sunlit harbours
My randy ghosts, persistent as coral,
Are muted in a dream
Of sulky, reluctant seasons,
An innocent world, another time than this.

Their passionate questions are dimly answered
By forgotten girls in this perpetual summer.
Reading in classic albums,
Only the wine-reek bears
Time and the unregenerate dream away.

The patient erotic sea surrounds us always.
The tawny lands reject our wistfulness.
Sun's kiss and hammer
Press our memories
To dark corners, to elusive fields.

Neither heroic nor lucky we take our turn
In the corrupted patterns of the war.
The indifferent tides
Perhaps will heal or hurt
The already lost, the impatient drinkers.

I hold the middle sea in a glass of wine
And listen to the vowelled bawdiness
Hiding a world of longings.
Taut in the sunlight
I throw my dreams upon the public bar.

Mother and mistress the wine-dark enemy
Estranges us in time as well as space.
Persistent ghosts
In this perpetual summer
Dream of slow seasons in the sunlit harbours.

(When the bone cried)

When the bone cried
The lovely winds were still.
When the obsolete wishes died
The dancers went under the hill.
This was the end of suffering and pride.

When the blood slept
The obstinate seas were calm.
When desire wept
The poison turned to balm.
This was the end of loyalty and harm.

When that bitter peace
Lay on the aching earth,
When those cleansing seas
Spoiled the ripe earth,
This was the end of death, the second birth.

(Seeking to make a music of the myth)

Seeking to make a music of the myth,
Impose a pattern on the twisted days,
He stumbled through fantastic alleyways
And broke his head against the walls of truth.

Seeking a queen of innocence and light
His brothel haunting brought him little peace,
And when old age at last conveyed him ease
That vision still was urgent in the night.

His wisdom was the anarchy of stars,
His poems brooded on his heavy lust,
His age was poverty and bitterness.

But we have seen him in a royal dress,
And we have read him till our minds are dust,
And worn his language like the proudest scars.

Nostalgia

The gaudy summers of my youth
Betray their carols to the air,
Erect a gallows in my heart.
Buried beneath that flaunted chime
A boy's romantic violence
Disrupts the grammar of my art.

In the cool pilgrimage of time
Remote and passionate as queens

Dark girls dismay the present tense.
The bridal storm infects the will;
And drowned desires haunt again
The mouldy tapestries of sense.

The ballad fails me now, the dream
Is conqueror, the morbid heart
Turns eagerly to coloured days.
And where that broken boy remains
A gaudy summer carol makes
Memorial innocence and praise.

(Mirror and mask abound)

Mirror and mask abound
In the prophetic air.
A barren pomp of sound
Deceives the curious ear.
Clockwork dancers reel
In the whorls of nightmare.

Beyond the lying face,
Behind the rigid dance,
That music of disgrace,
What miracle of bronze
Redeems for us at last
The numbness of nightmare.

(Now let me circumambulate dead charms)

Now let me circumambulate dead charms,
Marmoreal witnesses,
The fragmentary heroism of days
Dispelled in the anarchic light
Where the immortal matrix still reclines
Indolently beneath bronze ardour of the sun.

Mermaiden wishes fold me with cool hands
And in a cobalt grave
Bury illusions and my dreamform face.
The sombre forests close about my guilt
And I am deep with that remembered mummery
Of fishes and the cold heroic gods.

And she, the Cyprian, foam-conceived
And light-engendered, will the flush
Illume again those limbs
To make a glory on a foreign shore?

Dead charms, and deader dreams.
The endless sea
Enfolds me, and the blue heroic light
And veriest images
Of remote anarchic days.

Deep on the shady bed of ocean
Far from the unrelenting ardour of the sun,
I dream
Cold heroes and the Cyprian queen.

Orestes

Obsessed by the colours of decay
This natural Orestes, an average lout,
Will cut his way to a more pleasing light,
Will murder darkness for a promised day.

Then in the hands of the inevitable police
Will murmur sadly, What have I done wrong?
I sought to end our suffering – we suffered long –
The black cap will pronounce his sentence of peace.

Lake Woman's Song

Young man, when you pasture
Your animals there
O bring me a tribute
As I comb my wet hair.

O bring me a tribute
A tribute of bread
And if I am satisfied
With you I will wed.

But if you don't please me
You will not see me where
I sit in the sunlight
And comb my wet hair.

Birth of Venus

Furious nativity,
Thrash of the sea,
Wind-whiplash,
Torn waves,
The dead fish turning
Red sides to the sky,
The pearl-fresh goddess
Smiling in the sudden calm.

Poem

The lying calendar of youth,
Remorseless and anarchic days,
Brought at last the sensual truth
In which the rant of dreams decays,
Brought that bitter, intricate love
Our weakness is the symbol of.

Our bodily passion could not make
The virtue that our hearts denied,
Nor from love's ignorance could take
Either our pity or our pride.
Caught in that brutal argument
We murdered love, and were content.

(Burning against the lyric dark)

Burning against the lyric dark
Your dance invites my praising eye,
And in this missed heartbeat of time
I watch my greedy intellect die.

The mountain like a silent wave
Towers behind you as you move,
I wait my drowning underneath
The stinging waters of your love.

The desolate promise of the wind
Invokes from me the heart's response.
Upon my broken altar lay
The timeless tribute of your dance.

(The small, indifferent birds)

The small, indifferent birds
Make madness in my heart.
The shy, reluctant words
Mock my laboured art.
And I am dumb as any wind
To tell your image in my mind.

Poem

Heart-madness and the labouring craft
Move me to dumbness like any wind
When I have looked upon your loveliness.
As if a cripple laboured to express
Some image formed in his befuddled mind
In dancing, and the people called him daft.

I remember only the small, indifferent birds
Being practical and impudent in the sun,
Or comically sheltering from the rain,
And no magnificent figure of passion or pain
Mirrors the eagerness with which bloods run.
I am helpless, and my words are empty words.

Poem

The animal sleep in winter
Foretold our luck in summer
Bewildered by hot seas,
Keeping the anniversaries.
To feel our history harden
To art we need not pardon.

Under the prayer of the sky
Our bland emotions lie.
We are not afraid
Of the sun or any god,
Merely wishing to look
Upon our summer luck.

Ode

To those who, keeping like ourselves
Private records of disappointment and loss,
Find in them later a thin happiness,

To those to whom all history is unforgiving,
God's finger without remorse,
To those for whom art is both
Less subtle and less noble than it seems,
Those who suffer much in dreams –

To them, and to the unpredictable others,
We dedicate this war.

For what is taken in the eclipses of ourselves
May be what after all abides –
The hope of children, the slow
Intricate chime of seasons, the well-kept garden,
Or any wilder ambition.
We have the bitter flavour.
Fear not to bite deep
If what is taken still abides.

Meanwhile, the war is ours.
And what we have still left to give,
Worn phrases, the futile dedication,
We give, and not less freely
Because we have no choice.

Let it be entered duly in the records.
One day the tired words may shine
With faint nostalgic light,
May even, misunderstood, or wrongly read,
Inspire.
Or simply they may be forgotten,
Or lose all significance, or even meaning.
But in any case, enter it duly in the records:

The war was theirs,
But all the rest they gave.

O Mariner, Return

O mariner, return, return
To where beneath the phallic sun
My empty body and the empty house
Wait for the enterprise of your bright limbs.

Return over the coldness of the seas
To lie upon my breast.
O mariner, return, return
To make me children before I grow old.

O mariner, o mariner,
What charm have the cold seas and the glittering waves
To keep you from your lover growing old?

Return, return.

(Not, where he lay)

Not, where he lay, the cool resilience of grass, the sure fertility
beneath, but under him there the hard shudder of the ship, and above
the sun, the sun. The sea was the mother of all; all must go back to the
sea, in time or out of time. His eyelids filtered the sunshine to darkness,
and in that darkness he was already sunk, already in the cool enduring
unfathomable depths. Yearning for grass, the comfort of earth, for
sounds and scents, he opened his eyes, but the glaucous vision clung for
moments in the bright air.

The ship drove on with its little methodical shudder. The sailors
cursed the sun, he cursed the ship, his comrades and himself, he cursed
the sea, the mother of all, and in his cursing he found only a little
comfort. He was reminded of prayers unwillingly made, from
compulsion not necessity, in the cruel days of childhood. And life was
still hard for him; instead of rain and religion he had now the sun and
the sea, instead of the barren farm the brutal ship; and always, always,
discipline without heart or imagination.

Easter Poem

Witness the paradise upon the mountain.

The two thieves make two attitudes to death,
Evocative of anger or compassion.
The wounded man between
In the descent of darkness and of blood
Blesses our failure and depravity.

In this enormous pause
Of history we taste the dregs
Of malice and hysteria, know
The miracle of truth.
The weeping blood asks its insistent question,
O *how attain*
The animal innocence or the rational good?

Looking upon this ritual of love,
We remember those others,
The wanderers on cold nostalgic waters,
Those who in pride worship the phallic sun,
Those who are ardent on mountains,
Or sentimental in meadows.
Or frightened and austere in the hearts of woods,
And we ask,
Do they need or deserve our forgiveness?

The wounded man is hung between two thieves.

And we ask,
Can we be ever nonchalant again,
Can we flirt with the forces of darkness,
Or callously under the hill
Lay siege to pain?

Can we win the desperate fight
With darkness and circumstance?
Can we really believe in the dawn
After this night?

Can we hope to be freed from error,
From the fatal consequence,
In the descent of the dove
See love, not terror?
Between two thieves our paradise is hung.

Mirror and mask abound
In the prophetic air.
A barren pomp of sound
Deceives the curious ear.
Clockwork dancers reel
In the whorls of nightmare.

Beyond the lying face,
Behind the rigid dance,
That music of disgrace,
What miracle of bronze
Redeems for us at last
The numbness of nightmare?

In the descent of darkness and of blood
A wounded paradise between two thieves
Blesses our weak intentions and our faults
In love, our failures of knowledge
And of understanding, our lack of peace.

Genesis

Sweat and the hot blood tell his genesis,
The plague to follow like the rain the wind
And in the nervy hollows of my brain
Love's maggot eats his secret food.
The waste dawn cools a ruffled sun.

The play of limbs foretells a following sweat,
Love's plague comes after as the rain the wind.
Along the riddling channels of my blood
The wizard sea is fed on secret flame.
The cold dawn ruffles the waste sea.

The hot limbs and the sweat of blood
Foretell the genesis of wind and rain,
Love's plague to eat the weathers of the heart.
There where the secret tyrant of my sex
Is cold and waste the dawn ruffles the sea.

(In my beginning)

In my beginning was the sweat of sleep,
The sung confusion, roaring in the veins,
The loud adultery of seas.

My father at his wedding smelt of Adam,
And all his virgin guilt could not release
My origin before the fall of blood.
In my beginning was the hymn of stars,
The bloodred rumours of the ragged skies,
The thunderclock of love.
My mother made a cross upon the bed
Where her wild innocence was murdering sleep
To nurture my dark seed.

(Not *in that drunken morning*)

Not in that drunken morning shall my dew
Be sacrificed to your triumphant priest
But my committed blasphemies shall take
Their blessing from the abstract dark
Where still those blinded choirs spill out their song
The apogee of prayer, the psalm of love.

O in that sweat what agony of breath
Shall urge this sweetness to its bloody end
What heated nerves prove impulse to this song?

The Midnight Words

Turn with the turning world, and hear
The midnight words, the oracle of sorrow.

'Explore this guilt
From the beginning in the sweat of sleep
Through all tentative and assured embraces
To the dove's descending on the ache of age.'

I have turned away from so many
Old terrors and defeated loves,
And now I hold this guilt and challenge
For you where the sea moves.
Turn with the turning world, and hear
The midnight words, the oracle of sorrow.

In stalwart pride, the ship leaving harbour,
Or a woman smiling for me with all her body –
And this guilt remains.
I keep it for you in my heart and hands.
Turn with the turning world, and hear
The midnight words, the oracle of sorrow.

(Lost on the floor)

Lost on the floor of darkness
The idioms of our love
Trample and thrash like horses
Or ruining towers of the sea.
Burial or bridal, our frenzy
Now counterfeits the love
Which once like daybreak
Showed us our naked selves.

Somewhere within this thunder
The seed of light remains,
Though on the floor of darkness
Our furious love lies lost.

(Though body on body press)

Though body on body press
After nightfall or winterfall
What cold kiss
Shall bind us after the last fall?

After firelight, fearlight
What shall warm
Or keep from harm
Our bodies in the last night?

(The contradiction of your images)

The contradiction of your images
Falls so insistently upon my sleep
I would come to you over the jealous seas
Though time and distance are wounds in my bright hope.

Lie then, beloved, in your foreign bed
And dream my coming and your proud surrender.
Here where the salt waves kiss the dead
Face of your lover such dreams are tender.

Wrapped from the sulky beauty of the day
I lie in dreams beneath the waves of pain.
O close your frantic mouth, your sensual eye –
Only in dreams will I come to you again.

All Passion Spent

Now wisdom comes after idolatry,
After the cold corruption of the tides.
A poignant singing in the bone abides
For love is more estranging than the sea.
Malevolent passion now has left us free
To muse upon the wildness of those hours
When all my songs a wilderness of flowers
Were yours to pick, to scatter, or let be.

I was that lyric fool, that cruel singer
Who trapped you dumbly in the folds of anger
And gave you gifts of my archaic pride.
What wanton ghost of hurt or of forgiving
Can still torment your loyalty of living
Since that bewilderment gave tongue and died.

The Nature of Love

After barbaric centuries and lands
Excess of music dazzles the weak sense;
The pattern blinds, the exactness of its glory
Lost in the colours of its violence.

Now in this centre, the cloud of innocence,
Clean of the dragonish tang of the old seas,
I walk, studying the pattern, and knowing
The body's wisdom and the intellect's ease.

Hiraeth

The landscape and the myth escape me now
In this archaic exile from my dreams,
Labouring by the harsh intolerant light
I only hear the incoherent fact
Of loud seas endlessly about the shore of Wales
Echoing the lonely tumult of my blood.

(In the demented wood)

In the demented wood
Pale virgins kneel and wait
For fabulous white beasts
To lean their glistening horns
Between their frenzied breasts.

These dolorous images
Break on the sensual heart
Between the night and the day.

(Beyond this murder)

Beyond this murder
A pagan praise
Breaks the monotony of ancient skies.
The anarchy of tears
Is far from that bright kingdom
Where the glad centaurs
Stamp their joy
And breathe exultantly beside the clamouring seas.

War Generation

From shabby towns or lucid pastures
Through dreams or deeds of violence
We came to this emotion in the desert,
The turbulent question in the storm of dust.

The lethargy and lust of boyhood
Rankling in the crouching desert-beast
Evades hysteria, but what rough, tawny ghost
Shall walk beside us down the future streets?

Small cloud of doubt, if not despairing,
Darkens our fierce exultance in the war,
The labyrinth of thought and action
Where Theseus like me makes our ethics death

And even while we joy in desert wildness
And the paradise of war
We know this problem means that never
Will the lucid pastures or the shabby towns

Be the same again to our bloodshot eyes
That somewhere in the future
We must supply an answer
To this question which will never again be simple.

Seascape

The listless waters
                    (deep blue of Mary's colour)
The agonizing sun
The span of memory

Across the shifting surface of the light
The intrepid eye
Sees a sour land under a colder heaven
The classic seascape fades

A humdrum ship
                    (no sirens sing to us)
Vibrates its melancholy way
Across the incredible colour
A sour land beckons

All ships are dreams
Dancing on gaudy floors of glass

All mariners
                    efficient, braggart, wild
Are travellers
Neither desiring nor intending
To return

Home
Is where the heart is
When the heart is dead

Ships dream monotonously
Across incredible seas
The sour lands beckon
                    in vain
We are blind in this fantastic light.

(Tomorrow is an island)

Tomorrow is an island
Where the tumult of the clock
Shall no more stir
A sulky conflagration in the heart.
Where banished metaphors
Consort at ease
Among the casual brilliance of the birds,
Where love and language
Are not separate,
Tomorrow is a dream
Across the dark estrangement of the waters.

(Beneath the surface of decay)

Beneath the surface of decay
Anarchy of the heart and head
Preoccupied with love and war
Are reconciled in time at last
To that wild kingdom of the sun,
Are put to sleep in that bronze glare.

Mechanical song and content,
The outer darkness of the mind,
The smile of ruined centuries,
Are persecuted by the light,
Are reconciled in time at last
To the wild music of the seas.

Song for a Time of Trouble

When the lion brings to the broken city
The dialectic of hate
When the bird screams across the heavens
Its anger and grace
Show your sulky hearts on your sleeves
Believe that grief is beautiful.

When you see beyond the ruined waters
Tall images of towers
Or when you quiver in the mountain grass
Like hares in their forms
Hide your vivid hearts in your hands
Understand grief is terrible.

Allegory

The sick poet in his tower,
His owled and bat-hung melancholy,
Observes the daft boy in the lane,
The shadow of an allegory.

The stabbing silence of the night
Beats on miasmic fields of pain;
The obsession of his images
Is murder in that hidden lane.

His savage fingers writhe and write,
His body dreams of healing seas,
The daft boy singing in the lane
Is all that he has known of peace.

He murmurs to his baring hands
Stifling his candle's sooty gleam:
I only choose to know
The bloods disorder and the dream.

The daft boy hangs upon a tree
His face a black distorted flower.
Across his scribbled pages lies
The dead poet in his dower.

Children in the Park

Assailed by various weathers and temptations
The bright heraldic children accuse our dreams.
Their dialectic in the echoing parks
Denies the force of our infallible language
Borne on the coloured breezes of despair
To loss and rupture in the bitter sea.
The bitter sea enfolds our loss and longing,
The careful serenades which a cracked moon
Elicited in fevered evenings from wry lips,
The awkwardly elaborated hymns
Of celebrations, the odes the children heard
And heard not, eating their unfaithful bread.

The faithless bread we scattered on the waters
Mocks now the casual delight of children.

The sea reminds us of our ancient terror,
The blind fear of forgetting. The bright shapes
Are scattered on the coloured grass. The wind
Bears their denial across the bitter sea.

(Utter the pangs of grass)

Utter the pangs of grass
Or tell the terror
Talking by night and day
In the tall untidy trees

Speak the sigh of the sea
Or whisper the wind's
Negation, the dry tones of dust,
The animal sermons.

Say, heart, or heartless voice,
These secret fears.
Or if you must be dumb
Be dumb, be dead.

(The miles of water)

The miles of water
Do not alas define
Our pity or our pain.
The limitless disorder
Of hurt and separation
Is only warning.
The unlucky miles
Of water smile,
Are our betrayal.

Sonnet for my Daughter's Childhood

In your great kingdom of uncertainties
May you be innocent and amorous;
Love flowers always; be courteous
In all the exacting ceremonies
Of loving and of hating; imagine seas
Exist for your crossing, and the mountainous
Lands for your climbing; and be to us
Always birdsong in sun-aroused trees.

Because there will always be time for you later
To accumulate bitter or romantic knowledge,
To find you love the theatre or bed,
To be a big girl, go to work or college,
Be scornful or admiring of the dead,
And acquire what now you lack, a guilty nature.

Poem for a Birthday

Now told by eight and twenty years
My natural anger and my antique pride
Remember what the desert voices cried
Admonishing my vanity of fears:
Intemperance of action and of thought
Wins the strong graces which cannot be bought.

Twenty eight years of wayward indolence
Alloyed with thoughts of that indifferent heaven
My fathers vanquished at such great expence
– What thorns reward me for the way I've striven?
At least I have the wild mouth and wild eye,
Can live with saint or drunkard, or can die.

A handful of unsatisfactory verse,
A certain reputation among friends,
Ambitious knowledge of my possible ends
With probable inclining to the worse –
I've learned one lesson in my ranting school,
'Twas ever folly to be beautiful.
And when the arteries harden, and the heart,
And the thorns crackle louder round the pot,
May my regret for having little art
Be tempered by no sorrow I've forgot
To kindle at a passing pretty face
Or with my friends to drink even to disgrace.

Twenty eight years: not nearly half enough
To learn to love or how to perfect art.
Meanwhile, I have the wild eye and sound heart,
And something of ancestral stubborn stuff.
Tell my proud fathers that I'm living yet
And will not waste my future in regret.

Annunciation

A clamour in the night
Falls on my listening ears,
I wait bewildering light
Huddled in hopes and fears.

Triumphant sounds that break
Upon my solitude
Of raucous crowds that make
A dancing in the wood

Snarling through the air
Their rhythmic cries declare
Have done, have done
With sneering at the moon.

The Anglo-Welsh

Remembering among the unlovely London voices
A man who said, out of enthusiasm and love,
'You live upon your grandparents' memories',
I am vexed and despondent; where my unruly heart rejoices
I am tongue-tied, having not gratitude enough
To speak in my own language or to hold my peace.

I hear uneasily in the racket of my dreams
Ancestral summonses to a more splendid cause
Than making poems in the beautiful alien tongue.
I remember the accusation. Endeavour seems
Barren unless I learn the ancient intricate laws,
And sing the defeats and triumphs my fathers sung.

I ask, born of the mountains, enamoured of the sea,
What am I doing where mechanic roadways run
To merit that ancestral piety and pride?
Why am I shackled in guilt and heresy
Who might have been the resonant laurelled son
Of those who fought and laboured and undoubting died?

This is the struggle of self with self; out of this war
What may emerge of richer rhetoric may seem
To justify this treason and this bitterness.
Even here I see the dragon's splendour in the air;

Even here a mighty singing breaks upon my dream.
What have my ancestors or I to do with peace?

So, from among the unlovely London voices
I send this poem to a keen scholarly man
Whose rebuke will always smoulder now for me,
And sometimes leap to fame when the heart rejoices
Remembering ancestral pride or present vision,
The music of discontent born of the hills and the sea.

(A man may feel)

A man may feel what Homer sung
Flow through his being intimately
Like the rich labour of the seas,
Yet all that young antiquity
Imprisoned in a vase or song
Grieves the barbaric centuries.

A man may dream that body, white
Beneath the power of the swan,
Or that on Troy's defeated walls,
But what our knowledge has put on
In the long interval of night
Imputes the vision it recalls.

But let the dream and dreamer blend
In one intense dramatic flare
Brightening the gap of centuries,
What intellect and heart see there
Burns for a moment without end
Upon the rich Homeric seas.

(Once in a time)

Once in a time of blossoming and air
My enemy bride delighted savagely
My warring innocence of blood.
That dance is stilled, but not her dancing hair,
Nor the wild froth and glitter of the sea,
Nor the dark clamour of the wood.

Amends

(for Aneirin Talfan Davies)

There were no gods among that bitten grass,
Those rocky challenges, those wind-torn trees,
Only the presence of the ancient thunderer
Cloudy with terror of his images.

Buzzard and carrion-crow controlled the air,
The weasel slinked bloodthirsty through the woods;
The fox and badger plundered and ran free
Where the grey winds made howling solitudes.

In that harsh landscape dreams were unconfined,
Dreams of hot sunlight and of older gods.
The coloured birds were singing in my head
When I set out to find the city roads.

Years after, in a thronged and barren parish,
I make old pictures of blackthorn and of pine,
The weasel and the crow, the mountain wastes,
And recall the only god that was ever mine.

Narcissus

Fascinated by murder and by mirrors
He hoped to bear brute witness to the fact
That self is independent of the others,
That law has no control over the act.

For him no searching for a willing girl
In whose spread nakedness might be discerned
The vision of the poets, no long toil
To find how long the candle might be burned.

Nothing except the one destructive leap
Into the clear reflecting element
And in the fatal moment no itch of hope
Appeared to make the cool embrace lament.

(With rags of honour)

With rags of honour
We dress the shade
Being desperate to believe
That the pale tower of grief
We live in with the dead
Shall not totter, fall,
Or break to dust at all.

Unfaithful

She had not strength enough to undergo
Long trial; her lively body could not know,
Crying for comfort in the dark,
The bitter passion of virginity.
Did she, I wonder, at all remember me
The day a stranger took her in the park?

The Oracle

The priestess writhes, breathes heavily,
Then, in the darkness, with unexpected coherence
The oracle gives mechanical utterance.
I hear and believe. This goddess knows not pity.

L'Invitation au Voyage

Beyond the promise and deceit of seasons,
Blurred yet precise upon the dark horizons,
An invitation to the sensual eye
Green and remote the fabled islands lie.

Abandoned in the labour of the sun
We might live there and let our fancies run
Unbroken colts upon the brilliant sands
Or hold the light forever in our hands.

We could have poems there not made with words
But sung by coloured and impassioned birds
Dancing at evening on the lulling sea
An art synonymous with liberty.

Free of the cares and pains of urban man
There we could be a cultured Caliban
Without the fear of watching Prospero
To inhibit us from all the loves we know.

Where is the waiting spread of eager sail
To carry us before the scented gale
To where, entreating to the sensual eye,
Green and remote the fabled islands lie?

An Old Story

Pleased with the green extravagance of ocean
He forgot that tall distracting lady
Waiting for him in a field of flowers,
Her, to whose readiness for such a passion
His pulse and ardour he had all displayed
Last summer to beguile some scented hours.
But she, so constant in her field of flowers,
Slept with his image, and refused to see
Her other suitors pleading for some grace.
His memory could not alter with the hours
Of clocks, nor could her future be
Until he reappeared in time and space.

A Wish for My Eldest Daughter

Let her remember in outrageous youth,
Let her remember in every dreaming bed,
The women poets praise are mostly dead,
Though some of them had stumbled on this truth,
That love is only a gift to loving eyes,
Before they listened to those rhythmic lies.

Let her not know extravagant despair
Because no poet finds her wholly fair.

Attainment

Vagrant through jewelled nights of Asia
Under the glimmering pressure of his dreams
He hoped to interrupt the mists of morning

And reveal the cold ambitious sea
Whose echo and whose image always shivered
Beyond the edge of sense like beaten gongs
In distant, exquisite, tormented temples.

That sea eluded all his mystic travels.
Only he came once to a broken line
Where the profusion of the darkness promised
To dissipate itself in callous light.
The promise was deceptive. When he listened
Only a sleepy clamour in his blood proclaimed
That darkness, rich with many gems and odours,
Would remain about him always, and the wild
Unclaimable promise of the sea and daybreak
Call him for ever on enchanted journeys.

Cursing, he shook his dreams and darkness from him,
The sea encompassed him. In the green light
His decomposing body fed the tides.

Pathetic Fallacy

Obsessed by the morbidity of time
He felt the rage and hunger of the sea
Tower in the narrow channels of his blood,
He felt the harsh eternity of mountains
Jutting obscurely within his flesh.

Song

Once, beneath a morbid sun,
My heart had grown indifferent,
Watching its various lovers run
To where the watchmen cried 'Repent!'
And the grass withered in the sun.

Obliterated in the rain
My lovers sang a song of praise
That the wild heart should beat again
As in my green forgotten days.
– The grass was singing in the rain.

The Place of Failure

And having come
    by many indifferent journeys
Continents, islands, seas
having been crossed and re-crossed
with little satisfaction to be had out of any of them
Having come thus
having been near to death
        not once only
death sometimes heroic, more often ignoble
Having wasted my life in endless journeys
to come thus at the end
to a steep cliff
running irrevocably down to a place
of bones and failure
All this explains why I sit here weeping
waiting the courage to jump.

Poem

O girl merry as apples
let not my vanity
prevent your singing
Keep my grey hairs
from brushing lightly
but fatally your smile.

Sickbed Fantasy

Diluted voices in the neighbouring room
Proclaim the imminence of doom
While here upon my bed I lie
Dreaming of cracks across the sky
Through which the angels flaming white
Dispel the shadows of the night.

(I have watched his pale hands shuffling money in the moonlight)

I have watched his pale hands shuffling money in the moonlight
I have heard his greasy prayers go up to heaven
Who had no time to find a girl in darkness
Or be idle in the merry, merry sun.

(All the torn and blistered fields)

All the torn and blistered fields
Where pastoral innocence once fed
Deny the white nostalgia of
A heart too dedicate to love
And noble musing on the dead
To hear their shrill and broken prayer
Vibrating in the livid air
Above those torn and blistered fields.

My Angel

My angel slept within my side
Lulled upon delirium's tide
Deaf to the voices of my power
Roaring to signify their hour
Blind to the gaudy caricatures
To which my eyes set signatures
Dumb to the knocking in my brain
That witnessed to an outer pain.
The angel slept within my side
Not knowing if I lived or died.
I hung my angel on a cross
To testify a bitter loss.

(Never that love shall languish)

Never that love shall languish
Never grow sour
That is caught and kept in a moment
Let go within the hour.

O the tribe of all my lovelies
In dim procession pass
Through the air like phantoms
Grow in the earth like grass.

And I am left to triumph
My love has not turned sour
I only knew by moments
And never kept an hour.

(Afraid of being converted like St Paul)

Afraid of being converted like St Paul,
Afraid of hearing oracles speak truth
That lays a wild command upon us all,
Afraid of recognizing in discarded myth
The certainties and visions we denied,
Afraid of action and of too much ease,
Afraid of meekness and afraid of pride,
Afraid of mountains and afraid of seas,
We face the daft procession of the years
Afraid, afraid, afraid of all of our fears.

Now the Expected Ambush

Now the expected ambush of spring
Again surprises our myopic faith
Again we shiver gladly with the thought
That winter is over
And with the winter death.

Reply

Reprove my contraband desires,
Burn them in autumn's dowdy fires,
Still in the stifle of their smoke
Your intellect shall cough and choke.

Difference

Under God's violent unsleeping eye
My fathers laboured for three hundred years
On the same farm, in the expected legend.
Their hymns were anodynes against defeat,
But sin, the original and withering worm,
Was always with them, whether they excelled
In prayers, made songs on winter nights,
Or slobbered in temptation, women, drink.

I inherit their long arms and mountain face,
The withering worm sleeps too within my blood
But I know loneliness unwatched by God.

The Princes of This World

The princes of this world
They roar and sweat and lie,
And reel in drunken splendour
Beneath the indifferent sky.

But when their dance is over
The princes of this world
Kneel before God in terror
And unto Hell are hurled.

Restlessly Seeking

Restlessly seeking the archaic sea
Whose waves are blood and rhythm of me

I am forever dissatisfied with land
Whose solidness I cannot understand

I am for ever lonely in the air
Whose brightness forces me to dumb despair

Restless through air and over earth I go
Seeking the only happiness I know

In the eternal rhythm of the sea
Whose waves are blood and rhythm of me.

Love Song

The nightingales of former lovers
Tell their tall legends to this night
Whose caul obscures us in its luck.
O, tears are wanton, flow and knock
Of blood assume that leaping song,
And all our powers conceive the light.

Dumb morning druid of your drowsy
Body I psalm and celebrate
The jealous passion of those antique birds
Whose music died in our unrivalled bloods.
All fabulous song now in your sleep
Is wisdom after blood's debate.

An Old Man Murmured

An old man murmured a country prayer,
O give me girls and give me wine
With a crazy glitter in his eyes,
As he slobbered his words to the frozen air:
I remember the merry days that were mine.

An old man clambered up the stair:
O give me girls and give me wine,
With fanatic words and staring eyes
And crazily dancing thin white hair:
I remember the merry days that were mine.

An old man's mouthings died in the air,
O give me girls and give me wine.
The light went out of his staring eyes,
The dancing stilled of his snowy hair:
I remember the merry days that were mine.

Rivers and Revolutions

Rivers and revolutions of my thought
Bring me at last to that cold sea
Where passion and intellect are set at naught
In the waters rocking me endlessly.

The World in the Mirror

The world in the mirror has a different life
Teased by no dialectic in thin air,
As unambiguous as a threatening knife
Breaking the spasm and the charm of prayer.

In that chilly and didactic scene
Our fates grow morbid as we realise
The unbecoming rectitude of eyes
That never saw the thing we might have been.

Fracture the light and break the mirror's spell,
Reclaim the vision to your anguished sight,
Plunge through the glass into a world of night –
That thin reflecting glass that shuts out hell,

Or shuts it in. Who knows behind the glass
If that austerity thus fashioned there
Mocking our taut entanglement in air
Is or is not? Our world is made of glass.

Image

Brutal comedian of my common act;
My uncommitted reason in the dark
Scorns the lucidity my hands assert.
Out of this warring of the passionate fact
With secular certainty an image comes:
A delicate lady in a pastoral scene
Nursing upon her uninvaded breast
The fabulous beauty of the unicorn.

Lines for a Play

Pressed in the throng of guilt
Heart hurries to look
Upon its vivid self,
Strains in the whirl, in the wind,
For momentary peace,
The still point where motion
Is rest, activity
Is rest, where all is rest.

Spring Sonnet

Now the ambitious season of the year
Mocks my ditchwater taste, bleared eyes,
My lack of passion, and the dulled surprise
That anguish could so rust away to fear.
Now the invisible lyrics to my ear
Present a fading challenge; smeared skies
Image the slums of heaven; my sloganed lies
Blunder into the ambush of the year.

I will not slander my grave going down
With trumpet of remorse nor urgent prayer
Nor sermon wrenched from water or from stone,
But in the anonymous silence of the town
Watch brightness supersede the winter air,
And praise the lovers and the proud alone.

My Daughter Asleep

Here is the feature and fashion knows not bruise
Nor strident mark. The venom of the years
In these young veins has not yet made carouse:
These bones are not yet strained, flesh trenched with cares.

This childgrace is a benediction of the blood,
Promise and resurrection: sleeping it signs
The argosy and ark its fathers made:
Denies, rewards heaven's anguish and earth's pains.

Here is the blossom and the laboured print
Not tempest-daunted yet, not by the beat and whirl
Of winds and waters strifesodden, savourspent,
Dragoned by days and nights to weary hell.

O morning miracle, O pride of peace,
When you have grown to stature and to guilt,
Look in the dance and agony of your days
Upon your child and learn how love is spelt.

Portrait of the Artist as a Young Man

Intimations of honour and of fear
Attended on my shy predicament,
I did not know what those brute questions meant,
Nor what the masked assertions of the year
In its disguise of purpose and of green.
I was a truant in the pastoral scene.

Although apprenticed to divinity
I had not then contrived a cunning tower
Wherein to question history and the hour,
Or listen to the uninvaded sea.
All my wild ambiguity of prayer
Beat up like smoke into the barren air.

But in the sullen provinces of my pride
The tribal myths made promise and despair,
Confusing metaphors and methods there
Where my ambition's urge had almost died.
This was my prologue to integrity
Torn from the hour and hurt from history.

Infirm, Infirm

Infirm, infirm, but all too passionate,
I tried to cultivate a violent eye
Watching old hopes and youthful habits die
Beside a sea that stayed immaculate.
And in the frantic stretches of the night
Mocked at the chaster outlines of the light.

Barnacled slowly by experience
I learned the murderous corrosive care
With which the callous unimagined air
Exploits the inevitable impotence
Of youth immersed in danger and delight.
I learned the uneasy wisdom of the night.

Slowly I learned the ultimate miracle
That love and language are our greatest needs.
The structural magnificence of deeds
Impresses, but is doomed to sway and crumble.
The artifice of language and of love
Keeps beasts and terrors at a safe remove.

Thus on the shore of the essential sea
I grew to something like a man's estate,
With still some sweating hope inviolate,
Ardour and anger of my ancestry.
I grew into my fable, and I grew
Into the artifice my first dream knew.

Pale Hands You Loved

The weather altered in your long delay:
Ten frozen fingers hanging from the sky
If they could not complain could testify
That absence is a kind of slow decay
Rotting all tenderness and rage away.
You did not think of this. Neither did I
When I heard your reasonable cry
For breath before you gave something away.

Now if you should come back, I think you'd find
The weather altered, the place no more the same,
Ten idiot fingers craftily together
Knitting, unknitting pieces of the mind
In an elaborate and bitter game:
Ten idiot fingers in the altered weather.

Dilemma

Having contrived a history of crisis
I live it all again in staring nights
When images of fabulous animals
Corrupt my knowledge with insistent changes,
Lapped in the sensual silence and the dark
I feel the urgent sweat and strain of loins
Caught in a wild engendering struggle,
And yet the morning brings but barrenness,
The sterile magnanimity of light.

Poem

I have gone walking in dishevelled fields
But have disdained to pick their obvious flowers
Because of some reluctance in my blood,
The flowers growing in disordered fields,
The dance and decoration of the mud.

I have gone walking in contrary winds
But have refused to feel against my face
The clarity and challenge of the air
The poise and brilliance of the crisscross winds
Blown to no purpose in my dusty hair.

I have gone walking in familiar woods
But have denied the message of the trees
Soughed in the branching fever of my veins,
The message of the dark impetuous woods
After the long carousal of the rains.

I will go walking on the ancient seas
With no refusal in my greening eyes
And no denial in my secret heart
To greet the ancient welcome of the seas
Whose tides already roar about my heart.

Speech for a Play

The assumption of convenient passion.
The mask suiting the moment,
The appropriate gesture, tragic or derisive,
Has wrought a terrible mobility
Where once I dreamed of being rockfast,
Bound by my own chains to my own endurance.
How can I tell
If my heroic dream
Has been translated into vivid action,
Or if it still remains
In that uncertain glory where I set it?
What if the actor grows his own interpreter,
The mask becomes the face?

There is a Country

There is a country of no suffering,
A country carved of stone
By the benevolent despairing hands
Of gods or godlike men.

In that stone country love and lust
Are indistinguishable and sad.

Advice from a Friend

This bitter friend would have me understand
Excess of intimacy can cut across
Lines on a map or on a sweating hand
To reach the poles on fingertips of loss:

Not cankered, but certainly no kindly man,
Would have me realize despite of him
We win what virtue or what worth we can
By lights despicably distraught and dim:

Would have me be but a poor patch indeed,
Not unafraid (his words) to look truth straight,
Distinguish undone thought from undone deed,
And thankfully decline to master fate.

The Nonconformist Hills

The nonconformist hills have kept
Their virtue and hypocrisy,
Their rant and rhetoric have not slept
While I was wandering on the sea.
The hills remain above the sea.

The Loitering Hounds

The loitering hounds of the sea
Babble about your way.
That dialect is sweet
In the bright room of day.

Here on the Atlas

Here on the atlas of my suffering
I mark the patterns of desire,
The looming masses of the continents
Estranged by seas, consumed by fire.

With nervous pencil on the map I mark
The stations of my pilgrimage,
A livid track that blossoms out
In torment from the glossy page.

Baptized in those devouring seas
What should I seek in any land?
Sick with the saltness of desire
I drop the pencil from my hand,

Crumple the atlas, face the night.
I hear the roaring of the tides, the hiss
Of surf, and plunge into the dark, and plunge
To the salt splendour of her kiss.

Out of Wales

(A Poem for my Daughter)

Remembering today the land from which
You come, the huddled nonconformist hills,
The short grass sweetening the mountain sheep,
The stubborn ponies proof against the weather,
A shepherd's hazel stick and favourite bitch,
(My best-loved image of remembered Wales)
I watch you in your curled exotic sleep,
Waywardly growing, already another stranger.

There is No Way

There is no way that does not lead to water,
No road that ultimately does not tumble down
Through green to black. Your feet may wander
Through cities or through deserts, in the end
You come to water as the final friend.

Martyrdom

This is authentic dark. Startling the air
Comes the beat, beat of the heart: the breath
Shivers unseen. Is there anything there?
How can we image the lonely moment of death?

Then suddenly all breaks, dissolves to light,
Such light as childhood only had adored.
Calm, he receives in the transfigured night,
Burning, the undesired arrows of the Lord.

For Sian

The ambushed and didactic years
In dismaying patience wait
To educate your innocence
With menacing and adult fears.
Oh, learn before it is too late
Love's unpredictable violence.

Know, in the treacherous calms and terrors
Time diminishes each grace;
Distorts your conscious happiness
With guilt, anxiety, and errors;
Edits the lyric of your face;–
Time is the pedant of distress.

There will be many days and nights
Of cold and dark, of tears and sorrow,
Failure of flesh, reluctant will,
Despair, and cloying of delights.
Hold in your hand against tomorrow
This bitter charm: be human still.

The Persuasion of Light

Now the persuasion of light
On the persistent sea
Moves to the moment of myth.
The hopes of the scattered night
Birdlike, dominant, free,
Ride the heavens of truth
Above time's ritual,
The waves' topple and fall.

In this ardent light
All voyages must seem
More than miraculous –
Voyages out of night
Out of the perilous dream,
The merely fabulous,
The dark and the despair,
Into the brilliant air.

The vision and the song,
The assumption of light,
Promise endless day.
Although the night was long,
Now the miraculous light
Breaks the heavens in play,
Reveals the moment of myth,
The brilliant, endless truth.

For Rachel

The moment has gone by
When I could have stared
Unwinking in your eye,
And with assurance dared
To love you till I die.

Whether it was a lie
Or not no longer matters.
Only you and I
Will know in what deep waters
We threw our love to die.

And only you and I
Will ever have to dream
Whether a lover's lie
Might not have made it seem
More difficult to die.

Prayer

For those who have been lost in innocent woods,
        Receive our prayer.
For those who chronically lost their places,
And those who do not believe in the power of words,
        Hear us, O Lord.
For those cheated by time,
And those who think evil is synonymous with crime,
        Hear us, we pray.

For those who are unable to dream of horses,
For those to whom the sea is always an enemy,
        Receive our prayer.

For those who inevitably inhabit narrow houses,
And those who sweeten with scandal their afternoon tea,
    Hear us, O Lord.
For those despairing of love,
And for those lucky ones who go together like hand and glove,
    Hear us, we pray.

For those to whom the darkness is always a threat,
For those whom mirrors irresistibly allure,
    Receive our prayer.
For those to whom tomorrow is never a treat,
And those whom the past is unable to assure,
    Hear us, O Lord.
For those in sickness, those in health,
And for those dismayed by too much or too little wealth,
    Hear us, we pray.

For all the pagans who might have been our fathers,
For all the members of the unnumbered sects,
    Receive our prayer.
For all good women who resemble our sainted mothers,
For all kings, and for all obedient and rebel subjects,
    Hear us, O Lord.
For all enchanted makers,
For all scientists, athletes, conjurers and fakers,
    Hear us, we pray.

And lastly, which is also firstly, and always,
For ourselves, for our lonely, and yet, we hope, significant selves,
    Receive our prayer.
For ourselves, in all the sweating nights and days,
Whether we are happy in connubial beds or parked on
unsatisfactory shelves,
    Hear us, O Lord.
O Lord, O Only One,
Before our prayer is done,
    Hear us, we pray.

(O Light, O Menace, our unlucky hearts)

O light, O menace, our unlucky hearts,
Still haunted by the possibilities
Our childhoods thought they recognised in arts,
– Those luscious islands in the human seas –
Fail in obedience of your stringent law.

How may our hunger for ordered images
Be reconciled with the wild things we saw
When gospel grew into authority,
The dark light on the overwhelming sea?

On the Death of Yeats

How should that famous man have come,
When neither lust nor rage could spur
Him more to quarrels or to verse,
To wisdom fatal as a curse
Upon his deathbed to confer
The sanction of an ordinary tomb?

Song

Commend we that prodigious grief
Which in the shadowed woods can walk
Listening to each wind-torn leaf
Across the wound of darkness talk;
Or on the glimmer of the seas
Beneath a cold, attractive moon
Hear in the whistle of the breeze
Only an old, seductive tune:
Commend that grief which is unmoved
By these sweet fictions, lost
In a trance with what it loved,
And unresponsive as a ghost.

Sestina for Sian Crossing the Seas

Under you now the enchanting waters foretell
The poems of another continent,
While, islanded in the ancestral myth,
I move my natural terrors into words
So that your dance and laughter shall not spill
Into the hungry playgrounds of the fish.

Darkness and concupiscence of the fish
In the unpenetrated cold foretell
The laughter and the blood that you will spill
After the landfall on that continent

Where the enormous agape of words
Becomes the real, the right, the only myth.
If in the bloody corridors of that myth
The glittering abstractions of the fish
Oppose, destroy, or disenchant the words
Which I have used thus darkly to foretell
Your exploration of that continent,
Be not afraid – the urgent angels spell

Their anger and compassion, spill
The tears they had before the myth
Began, before that continent
Rose in the innocent wanderings of the fish,
To interpret what I here and now foretell,
The hidden unction of my loving words.

Listen not too precisely to my words:
Their faith and future you shall not spill
As you will pour the lifeblood of the myth
I in absence inevitably foretell,
Fearing the cold attraction of the fish,
Into the sands of that bright continent.

Be not too certain of that continent.
Be not too certain of my power of words.
But know, O always know, you shall not spill
Into the greedy circuits of the fish
The happiness that I dare to foretell
For you, in this or in another myth.

O my beloved, you shall not spill
The happiness and hunger of my words
Into the frigid playgrounds of the fish.

To Madeleine

What I have found between your thighs,
The eager strain, the blessed rest,
I will not try to poetize.
Silence is best.

Portrait

By foreign calculation led to infer
That the absurdities in the mirror were
The very lineaments of pride,
He forswore abstraction, bargained for a kiss.
And this was virtue in him, this
Kept many foul shadows at bay until he died.

Had he for any reason done otherwise,
Insisted on the mirror's fantastic lies,
The self-spun, self-informed design,
Who could have reached him from across the border
In the other country of disorder
Where the will is stubborn and even loves decline?

But he made his choice, and this in him I praise:
However he remembered his mirror days,
He never allowed regret
To create more than a little fever in his blood.
He went about his work, ate solid food,
Got children. His memory has some fragrance yet.

Invented Seasons

Invented seasons, known by snakespit, cuckoocall,
Boy memories submerged, drowned innocence,
In what strange kingdom do the poets tell
I shall encounter you to learn at last
The burning miracle of ignorance,
The sapflow from the seasons of the past?
O in the alphabet of wind and wave
I learned to spell the ceremony of words,
In heartsick climates where heroic swords
Fostered the antique virtue. O I have
Invented seasons where all life shall know
Its time and signature. The singing birds
Create a final mystery of words.
O wind and wave go with me where I go.

The Ballad of Me

The wideawake sky went on for ever and ever
Over my boyhood, the eternal trees
Denied the fear of death, the flowers in their seasons
Were all immortal, and the birds sang
As everlastingly as the grass enchanted.

Tall men, tall women, went walking like trees
On my blue horizons, and catkin children
Swung in adventurous breezes to the tunes
Behind the chapels and cowsheds, the tunes
Of ferns and grasses, of druidic trees.

Slinked animals in water and on hillsides,
Weasel and badger, dandy fox and otter,
Fish were responsive to water-urges,
And birds hung and swung on the unseen edges of wind,
– And I among them walking and dreaming.

Near away sounded the sea, the ancestral summons,
But here in the hot pulse of the summer,
And vivid against the powdered skies of winter
Went on and on the preacher's sounding voice,
The word, the beginning, God's tremendous breath.

Can the buzzard escape from its nature, do other
Than kill from the depths of the sky?
Can the otter, sinuous, splashless, split
The murmur of water with no thought of death?
Shall a mountain pony be tamed by man or by weather?

Shall the voice of the preacher be silenced?
The poet hang like a gamekeeper's plunder
Nailed on a foreign street and an alien tongue?
The fox is still prancing the hillside, the hawk
Has always dominion of air.

The streets break on my feet and my heart,
But boyhood's immortal kingdom is still
In the words of the preacher, the weave
Of the otter, the pad of the badger, the slink
Of the fox, the circle and swoop of the buzzard.

Still and still immortal waters move
About me, that lovely sky goes on
To where all words are woven in one word,
The first, immortal breath, the living breath
Shadowed in trees and grass and poets' words.

Another Form of Farewell

Being thus analytical, no wilder ghost
Shall be companion to the wanderings
Your proud mind has set out on. Love once lost
Will not return with the returning springs,
Nor when the starved heart sings
At landfall on the long-familiar coast.

All the sung, empty winters through
I shall be musing by the secret fire,
Seeking in its deep heart the heart of you,
And waiting for the end of my desire.
But oh! what subtle choir
Could have convinced you only love is true?

(In the nightmare of the heart)

In the nightmare of the heart
What furious images
Trampled my dreams?
Now that wild music seems
The roaring of the seas
Still unsubdued by art.
Though I have found my voice,
Raised it above those screams,
Taken the bitter choice,
Still those foaming seas
Shatter and bruise my dreams,
And mock my art.

Lullaby

Low and low
Out of the swing
Of tides and history
Let your brave head
Lie on your bed
While I sing.

Sweet and sweet
Be your sleep.
While I sing
Of time and tears
Shut eyes and ears
And slumber deep.

Long and long
Keep all your charms
While I sing
Above your bed.
Until you are dead
Be safe from harm.

Words from Any Poet

My masters and colleagues will come riding by
In a splendid company presently,
Most reverend sirs, most learned, and most witty,
And all of them full of the honourable city,
While I for the sake of a hag-whelped bitch
Accept their pennies as I lie in the ditch.
Each of them riding after his dinner
To ease his belly and pity the sinner
– The devil take them, and me as well
– Which of us goes the surer to hell?

Love

Beggars snuffle in doorways,
Women offer their wares,
But I have seen the location
Of hell upon the stairs.

Dogs howl in the moonlight,
Stones cover the dead,
But I have heard the clamour
Of devils in the bed.

Time coughs and threatens,
Evil are the streets,
And love is murdered nightly
Between the loving sheets.

(Time wears and watches, dread is this)

Time wears and watches; dread is this,
Is doom, in the unchallengeable glass to see
That countenance become an enemy
That once smiled promise like a lover's kiss.
No remedy; uncoil the springs of blood
Can no man, nor the plod of time persuade
To stop, turn back, or slow. We are all betrayed
By the same vision, born from the same mud.

Yet if, flaring the sweat and agony of the night,
The angel should come down to our despair,
Making his glory round him in the air
A plenitude of love, of love and light,
Who would not be the victim helpless there
To welcome that destroyer in his might?

Words to Any Exile

Assassin, lover, from your exile
What words shall serve to recall
You to the country which your words
Once rescued from the ordinary?
Across the separation of the sea
What dream of beasts or birds,
Of trees, of hills, of stony farms,
Recall you to the once-familiar arms?

Apocalyptic

Emblems of blood and the bloodthirsty moon,
Dogs howling over every hollow death, –
If there is blessing it has come too late
To save this land from the downpour of blood,
Too late to ease the agony of breath.

If there is blessing, – but the pictures rave,
Animals sodden with the wine of blood,
And men more sodden than the animals
Lifting dog-voices underneath the moon
To celebrate their victories in the mud.

There is no blessing underneath this moon:
No blessing for the pain or painful voice
Of man or animal, naked in the mud,
Singing the victory that's also death;
No blessing for the blood that cries, Rejoice,

Rejoice, for we have found at last,
Beneath the barren emblem of the moon,
A barren virtue struggling in the mud.
Rejoice, for in the howling of our pain
We hear the filthy and remembered tune

That made the sunlight of our youth go mad.
No blessing on these pictures or this land,
Or on distortion of those human voices,
Those cries from animals and beast-tongued men.
There is no blessing ever on this land.

A Question

What I really meant was this –
In this mutual robbery,
Disguised by word and look and kiss,
Of our fond identity,
Did either for a moment break
The unformulated covenant,
Would the other ever grant,
Even for this love's own sake
The right, should lover feel the mood,
To shrink back into solitude?

The Anonymous Ghost

It was indeed its anonymity,
That ghost upon the turning of the stair,
Frightened me so. Had I but known that face,
Or recognised the sadness of that voice,
I had been reconciled to meet its challenge.
I might have lived to tell another story.

Love Lost and Found

The ravening of this ghost
Spilt on the draughty curtain of the night
Sudden as dropping hawk or meteorite
Plumb to the shaking centre,
Shall reveal the mystery we lost
When the door opened and we did not enter.

Listen. Be still. Be dumb.
This moment holds us helpless in its hand.
When the wild creature gives us its command,
Breaking the brittle air
With the dark force of that trite axiom,
Pray that our sins may be dissolved in prayer.

Anger is useless now,
And gone the alchemy of bitterness
Which once perhaps transmuted our distress
Into the wan nobility
Worn like a badge by other lovers. Bow
Your head. The ghost ordains humility.

And look. The ravening ghost
That terrified the pity of our night,
Dispelled in tumult of the morning light
Leaves us the deeper peace,
Restores us beyond everything we lost,
The light breaks on the rock of our release.

Epilogue

Yes, I have written my poem;
Have, from the thresh of words
And images and tunes,
Conjured the natural dance.
What if it all be chance?
I have paid my debt to the birds.

(Witch woman of small breasts
and sulky eyes)

Witch woman of small breasts and sulky eyes
You put your hands upon me, and I cried
That we were caught in that intolerant tide
Where the old bitterness of loving lies
Reminds us that the fairest honour dies
When the impenitent passions roar and ride
About the moonstruck earth. Your sobbing side
Implored me to forget I could be wise.

O in the sweat and enchantment of the bed,
Lost in the yellow rhythms of your hair,
I heard a ghost of love upon the stair
Reprove the musty virtue of the dead.
I felt the doom along my bloodstream where
The echo lasted of the words you said.

Poem

In the towns and centuries of youth,
A multitude of exiles, the long voyages,
The dream, the dream, had carried away
His heart and the poem's origin.

Waking on foreign pillows, he saw
His deepsea bride sail in a mist of loves
Away, away, and wept to be alone.
The dream had carried his heart away.

Turning and turning in his restless dark,
Interpreting the root of memory,
He made his shrill cry to the absent morning.
His fled bride did not interrupt his prayer.

After the exiles there was no returning.
Not till the mandrake poem break the silence
Should the departed bride be celebrated.
The dream had carried his heart away.

Poem on St David's Day, 1951

I have come far now from the kiss of frost,
Far from my mountain mornings, when the cold
Made visible the breath, and spring seemed lost.

Mine was an arduous country, and so old
That even boyhood withered, waiting spring,
Except when the miraculous tale was told

And the people lifted up their hearts to sing
With angel exultation and the pride,
The double pride, that God and mountains bring.

I have come far now from that mountain side,
But have kept something of that singing voice,
So that should even my memories have died,

My fathers listening should say, Rejoice.
The stubborn music still remains, and still
The fire of song illumines one Welsh hill.

Poem for Patricia

Before time began
For others more than you
My guilty tongue had told
Grief I found in the world,
Each sensual deceit,
The failure of prayer.

No casual defeat
Darkened my promised air,
The singing man
Between desert and seas
By time's blind images
Brought to unwilling knees.

Accept the involuntary
Gift, the customary
Offering of the blind:
Enter the kingdom of love,
And think it enough
A poet gave you words
Since like the flowers and birds
You had been kind.

(In the annunciation and surprise)

In the annunciation and surprise
Of your laid hands, your suppliant mouth,
I cherish my green vanity.
Smiling among the flowers of your kisses,
Drunken in the meadows of your breast,
Helpless with the delicacy of love,
I remember forgotten beauty.

In my undying arms a moment I hold
The first beauty to astonish the world,
And the last flower of loveliness.
Heart beats to heart a lifetime of pride,
And happy in the Eden of your eyes
My words are always singing for you.
The world ends in our kiss.

Such love, such lovers, never before were,
Nor shall be, except in legend.
Let my verse proclaim
The uniqueness that we found
Making two hearts beat one, making
Together our comfort and our pride,
But not disclose your name.

The Vocabulary of Promise

Nostalgic sailors in a dream of gardens
Have known a holy and immediate urge
To build upon the boredom of the sea
The city of invulnerable glass,
As poets, landfast in their private kingdoms
Of pain and beauty, see the lovers walking

Eternally two by two down the enchantment
Of children's smiles, lost in the dark forest.

Each takes from the vocabulary of promise
The little words like Love or Sesame
He seems to need, or would believe he needs.
Each feels in the contraction of his muscles
The world condense into infinity.
Each sees, or thinks he sees, the wild horizons
Rising above the ordinary phenomena
Of grief, bad luck, missed chances, or old age.

And all the time the treachery of blood
Revokes the casual promise of the dream,
The wasting bones prepare their wilderness,
The breath is tainted with its own decay.

The children in the enchanted wood explode
Into monsters, the lovers' contortions
And grimaces reveal the fear of death,
The sailors on the boredom of the seas
Forget the lovely city and their dream
Of gardens, and the helpless poets remain
Landfast within their private kingdoms
Of despair and pain, in terror making
Visions of love and beauty, and destroying
The value of each unenduring word
In the demoded vocabulary of promise.

Poem for Madeleine

An ocean or embrace away
The weeping of my love fulfils
The sensual vision and the prayer.
Lost in the clarity of day,
Bewildered in the hurt of air,
My words are rain her sorrow spills.

A century or kiss ago
The generations in her eyes
Answered my urgency of prayer.
Now with the words I do not know
The vision in the random air
Of absence casually dies.

O love upon the distant shore,
O love so absent from my nights,
O image of my ecstasies,
O love, grant pardon to me for
Estranging time, estranging seas,
And all refusal of delights.

And grant me pardon, love, for pride
Expert in disobedience.
Forgive me that I could not reach
You when your longing cried.
And grant me pardon, love, for each
Failure of will, deceit of sense.

A Saviour

Remote in all his casual brilliancies
He made his debonair impact on those
Romantic lovers whose assurance grows
Beneath the bleak enchantment of disease.
Victim and priest of his own mysteries
He wore ambition like a gathered nose,
But hinted always at inviolate snows
And deserts and the vast and virgin seas.
The deftness of this poor somnambulist
Led finally to bitter unsuccess.
The histories of solid folk he missed
Became the frontiers he could not transgress.
The features of the failures he had kissed
Remained to curse where they had come to bless.

(I dreamed when I was young)

I dreamed when I was young that I might make
Out of the blood and beauty of this life
An image as compelling as the light
On which all men should stare and be convinced.
O labour and necessity of right
Where unavailingly my dreams have danced
What comfort from your silence can I take
When my ambitions kiss the final knife?

I dreamed to be a great artificer
Who should transfigure by his making hands
The boredom and the sweat of common day.
I dreamed a passionate economy
Where every fellow artificer should say,
Our life is rich and infinite as the sea.
We do not fear the judge or executioner
Or conscience's revengeful skulking bands.

What solace can remain of that fond dream?
At midnight in the pale deserted town
I look into the mirror of my heart
And tremble at the image burning there.
O bitter treadmill of remorseless art
I want release into that pristine air,
I want again those images which seem
To raise man up while yet they beat him down.

(Elle a les jambes maigres)

Elle a les jambes maigres comme le remords,
Et les petits seins qui me séduisent, et son corps
Est une ombre effrayante de cette Vénus
Ou je me plonge a me noyer, aveugle et nu.

Les nuits que j'étais auprès d'elle, ses yeux
Me regardaient comme les flammes d'un grand feu
Au coeur duquel luisait une belle sorcière,
– Et je n'avais qu'un mot pour ma seule prière.

Dans la corruption fatale de ses yeux,
Et la lumière indolente de ses cheveux,
J'oubliais même la poésie et les baisers
D'autrui et le vin – les nuits de ses baisers.

Song

The sensual wind had blown away
– *O where is shelter from that wind?* –
The burden of identity.
Within each other's arms we lay
And did not hear the moaning sea
Whipped into sorrow by the wind.

The sensual wind that murdered dreams
– *O where is shelter from that wind?* –
Told to our unresponsive arms
That fidelity which seems
Enduring turns so soon to tears
Whipped into sorrow by the wind.

And when the sensual wind had blown,
– *O where is shelter from that wind?* –
We lay once more alone, apart,
And heard the unregarded moan
The blood makes in the telltale heart,
Whipped into sorrow by the wind.

The Poet

Rhetorician or somnambulist,
Deceiving others or himself, he moves
Always between an image and an image,
Between the thinning horror of the blood
And the abstraction of a verbal fame,
A victim, dedicate and arrogant.

Always he must make, remake a frenzy
Recurrent as the movement of the sea
Or ritual of seasons; must forgo
The triumphs and the comforts that relieve
The lives of other men; must emulate
A proud bird's loneliness, the lonely pride
Sustaining in his wisdom and his work
The sage, the doctor, and the executioner.

He does not know in what wild metaphors
His being is caught up; but in the night,
Alone as always with his questions,
Caught in that brutal strife without regret,
Waits for the brave delirium of dawn,
Waits without hope for his last disenchantment.

And the fools honour him into his grave.

(When the world was a wonder)

When the world was a wonder, the weather was gay,
On the pride of her breasts my pride I did lay,
And to my dear darling no words need I say.

But a cloud came up creeping and put out our sun.
Through all the world's cities in search do I run.
But girls like my darling I do not find one.

And if I should find her, what words should I say,
If on her proud bosom she'd again my pride lay?
My darling, I love you, but just for a day.

Song

There was a lady loved a bull,
Another had a swan for mate,
And one I knew that laughed at luck
Took thirteen sailors in a night.
Why should a man lie all alone
Because his love has turned to stone?

There was a queen in Sheba
Who delighted Solomon.
And I have heard of empresses
That slept with common men.
Why should a man lie all alone
Because his love has turned to stone?

There are girls in every village
And in every city street
Who will lie down and stretch their limbs
For money or the fun of it.
Why should a man lie all alone
Because his love has turned to stone?

And so I sing this ranting song,
This randy song, this leching song.
I will go out and get a girl,
And sing to her and make her sing
Why should a man lie all alone
Because his love has turned to stone?

Epigrams

I

The puritan, the profiteer, the pimp,
Are all descendants of a certain imp
Who, when expelled from heaven, made it his mission
To make man joyless even in coition.

II

A Government has fallen, with a crash
A little louder than a breaking cup.
When the last empire of the world goes smash,
Will there be charwomen to sweep it up?

III

In times of public strain and stress
It's good to know the freedom of the Press
Permits us to commit vicarious rape
Though enterprise is strangled by red tape.

IV

Now the position has been made quite clear,
The Englishman sips thoughtfully his beer.
Now that a Yankee rules Britannia's waves,
The English never, never shall be slaves.

V

The early Fathers of the Church were all
In principle opposed to birth control.
Marriage or burning was the choice to Paul.
They did not know that Stopes could save the soul.

VI. MACARTHUR'S RETURN

The great proconsul hurries home.
Unable to engage in war,
As generals did in ancient Rome
He'll give the democrats what for.

Poem in Several Moods

You told me, being violent in the extreme
And full of vanity, to beat those figures down,
Those images of poet and of king
And passionate lady which sanctioned all
My dreams, and those, more terrible, in which
I fell beneath the tread of horses,
Black horses on the white ones of the sea.
You said they were but figures of my own
Insistent wantonness and guilt,
And only the patience of refusal could achieve
The peace I needed, the love that needed me.

So I mouthed the improbable syllables,
And waited for the perfect word to fall,
The shooting star across the worded heavens,
The brightness, momentary love, and then
The dark, the silence, the annunciate peace.

But from the confession of mirrors and from
The dusty ashes and corners of memory
And from the leash of lust that holds us strained
To the coil of conception I have learned
The barren doubletalk of pain and failure,
The masturbation of confession
And the easy ceremonies by which God's spies
Become the ambassadors of casual sin.

Give me my nightmares back that I may know
Again the terror and the triumph
Of kings above the battle, and passionate ladies,
And fall again beneath the unpitying feet
Of horses, black horses, on white ones of the sea.

Death of a Poet

In the corruption of the distances
His poems like forgotten continents
Beyond the sad horizon's promises
Marry the grief and music of the seas.

He learns the vanity of craft and prayer,
The vanity of every offering.
Even the soundless image in the air
Betrays him – there is nothing there.

And so he waits for the impartial night
To cover him from every sin and blessing.
The last mercy never comes too late
To overcome the cheating of the light.
His empty hand he closes and uncloses
Vainly on the impotence of air.
His thoughts are ashes of a fire of roses.
And he is killed by what a dream discloses.

Deathbed

In the room of the curse and the web of prayer,
The room of the conversation in the dying head,
The flowers unfold and expand under the eyelid
Like confessions. A stained envelope of fear
Contains the little innocence and guilt
Which now become enormous and explosive.

Stifled faraway sounds only serve to enhance
The silence of his breathing. Time's erosion
Has suddenly stopped. He is back at the dark confusion
Where he bloodily broke on the world in a startled entrance.
Now we must parcel out his innocence and guilt
Among ourselves, but cannot make it any less explosive.

Reflections on Tragedy

The meaning of fear is not apparent
In the trapped smile;
The shriek and penetration of the truth
Evoke, perhaps, only a casual response
From the audience locked in its own distance.

Emblems and similitudes of fear
We know only
In the remembered lines and situations.
It is easy to identify with the pathos of the hero
The reconstruction of a private sorrow.

And with some tart reflections on despair
To imagine glibly
Incredible landscapes moulded by catharsis
To a resemblance of the needed city,
Free of the tax of guilt, restriction of pity.

It is better, then, to encounter the dilemma
In the stretched night
Alone, and not to expect the answer
To be as simple for us as the grief of Lear,
Or Hamlet borne off in the applauding air.

True tragedy may touch us, yes. What counts
Is the willingness
To recognize in the soul's desert
The one flower that holds the real meaning of fear
And to nourish it in every admonishing air.

The Definitions of Circumstance

Removed from the definitions of circumstance,
This love might prove to be the pure
Involvement in the holy ambience
Our vision coincides with now no more.

For now harsh vistas of regret and pain
Intrude upon the unaccomplished eye;
The gesture of our intricate design
Lacks something of conviction, suggests a day

Devoted to emotions not less brash
Than those that first conflicted in the hour
When the serpent confident in the lush
Though innocent garden, demonstrated power

To make distinction between good and good,
And separated with enduring art
The mutual compassions of our blood,
Writing the book of knowledge with that hurt.

No legendary comfort from this rock
Releases you, for my abortive mission
Only proves conclusively I lack
The purity of that heroic passion

Which might have visited your sacrifice
Immaculately armed to kill the beast,
And, deft and courteous on the baffled seas,
Encounter you in no disguise of lust.

Thus, hampered and defined by circumstance,
The limitations of this love can prove
Only what we guessed before by chance:
We can expect no more from human love.

Song

There is a country of disorder
Far away, near to us
Where tatters of our lives provoke
Neither homily nor joke,
And our spindrift dreams assume
Proportions of an ampler doom.
Every action is a kiss.

There is a country of disorder
Far away, near to us
Where sandy moments do not bite
Gradually at our delight,
And the erosion of the sea
Is only song continually.
Every action is a kiss.

There is a country of disorder
Far away, near to us.
Where is your passport? Where is mine?
Patrols of fear and chance decline
Although we have declared our sins
To show us where that land begins.
Every action is a kiss.

Sonnet to Pam

When I have paid my debt to time and terror,
And free at last of logic and of lust
Look for the first time in an unclouded mirror
Upon the image which a word released:

When I have had my days of rant and riot,
And have no longer enemies or friends,
Only the question in the eternal quiet
As ineluctable as mountain winds:

When I have reached my last apostasy,
And ceased either to charm or to betray
Or lose myself in any glittering ecstasy,
May there be one like you, my dear, to say:

Peace to the wildness which his wildness dreamed.
He was a little better than he seemed.

Poet

Gartered with love and gadded with ambition,
Tethered to a suicidal stake,
Noting the way waves break, hearts break,
The trapped man, ruttish in condition,
At the cavorting choruses of bells and birds
Stretches between the envy of his ears
A twist and torrent and thunder of words,
– His blood is fearful only of his fears.

Harnessed in lust and whipped by hope,
Dreaming of roses in suburban sun,
But watching lissom movements as they run,
He has to hang himself in his own rope,
Though he'd prefer at home to read his paper,
Back or tickle his fancy, paint a wall,
Cheat or assist or disavow his neighbour,
– And hear nothing, nothing at all.

But the thud and splendour of the stallion feet
Splash and spurn the waves of his blood;
He must find flowers erupting from the mud,
Measure and mortify his own heartbeat,
Poke and peer into every corner,
Put his burnt hand back in the fire.
– The worst is, he is already his own warner,
And dead already of his own desire.

A Song for You and Me

Who would want to pardon
The sunlight for infringing
The protocol of night,
Or disinfect the garden
Of the lithe, estranging
Serpent of delight?

Dispersal of our roses
On random, interloping
Breezes of despair
May, one half-supposes,
End our banal hoping
In the vanity of air.

After breeze and flower
We still may see remaining
The toughness of the briar;
Nor is it in our power
To meditate disdaining
The serpent of desire.

So we abjure pardon,
And concentrate on winning
From every chance and mood
The cherished secret garden
Where the serpent in his sinning
Knows not solitude.

Four

Four corners of the room I'm in
Betray possession of the face and gender
Of each disputed context of surrender
To the archaic images of sin.

Four images, each armed with blast and flame,
Contract the narrow story of this room
To slavering minutiae of doom
After a shoddy mimicry of fame.

Four murders, crouching with possessive haste,
Leer at the mirage of my fortitude,
Waiting to occupy the solitude
That was my heart before love laid it waste.

Four beasts will spring at me eventually
From dusty lairs in corners of the room
To tear me in the processes of doom
Already studied in love's nursery.

Prayer Against Old Age

A poem for my thirtieth birthday

I set a rage apart
In the marrow of a wish
Against the pride of wounds in age's dark
And slow drop on blood's bounty. Let tall
Dreams ambush then
The dumb, miraculous

Thrust of the heart like a caught bird sailing
    Its sorrow and song
    Up a heaven of blindness
    To the dazzle and dare
Of love God hovers over every day.

    Let me not celebrate
    Torn psalms and praise
Of driftwood in the luxury of sun
Reviewing pubic dreams. O may the sears of hate
    Itch in that night,
    And scurf of memories
Appal like falling snow upon the landscape
    Where the hurt bird limps
    To hungry death,
    The last, significant
Murder, silent assassin stifle of love.

    May my stilted dreams
    Knock against clouds
In the spindrift warring of my midnight
Sweat when the encountered reek of deeds
    Answers for no
    Dedication or gift
Of the unhallowed, kept-secret of the self
    Which in the groins
    And graves of youth
    Waited the impulse
Of the last flying trumpet's blast, the blaze of love.

    In the smug asylum
    Of comfort and care
Let me be always insolent and drunk,
Tuning accepting whispers to a scream
    Vain as a peacock's,
    Haunted as a hare's,
Disturbing as the needle of desire.
    Let seventy years
    Affront the angels
    With lusts dispersed,
Shifting and sudden as the multitudinous sands.

    Surround me O
    In that extremity
With fears and fables of my deliberate sins,

Chimera choirs to lilt and celebrate
    My many-voiced, deep,
    Dark delirium
To match God's fury and the pitying anger
    Of all his angels
    In their envied toil
    To make my trial
The proof and prophecy of his tremendous love.

II

    Now in my thirtieth
    Vision I set down
This prayer and promise to the obscure threat
Of forty futures: I will not turn
    To any death,
    Nor, carrion-witted,
Feed on the desperate drama of mere age
    Accomplishing
    Its run and ruin
    Among the armies
Of tears and desolations and the deceit of time.

    In my persistent
    Trade and trouble
I set a rage apart to anticipate
The last stampede of love when God,
    After the wrestle,
    After the horror
Crouched like a beast upon a naked pavement,
    Shows me time,
    The faithless, dying
    Of its own dream
Of Gone and Gone-For-Ever and Tomorrow.

    May each year's anguish
    Now define and clinch
My overdrawn bravado. Let the bawdy
Seeds of my gestures surely sprout
    To glory. Let
    The rank animal
Break the corral of regret, and caper
    Singing down the days
    Of forty futures
    To the last, forgiving
Spasm in the hidden, loving crotch of time.

A Plea against Armistice

After the bickering among the trophies,
Our almost banal internecine wars,
The casual intrusion of the stars
On our blurred vision of hostilities
Reminds us, not without a certain sneer,
Of concepts once held honourably dear.

Advantage of that momentary pause
May not be taken easily – not, at least,
Without some soft placating of the beast
Who lays upon the neck his cloying paws
Of reason, justifying every act
By irresistible appeal to fact.

Better then to shut the image out
Of old ideals still decorating heaven.
The beast is at our back. That is the given
Riddle in the core of every shout
With which the last ambition of despair
Attempts to crack the agony of air.

Better sustain among the tarnished trophies
This subtle vanity of bickering
Than hear again those ruined voices sing
That beckoned childhood over famous seas.
Let us, beneath the indifferent charm of stars,
Acquit us in our lost, inferior wars.

The Bridegroom

Impatient, debonair,
The bridegroom sits alone
In a sexy room
With his mirrored stare.

His unclenched love unfolds
A history of light
Which the improbable
Ceremony holds

Aloof from him. His eyes
Define a miracle
As, in the glass,
Identity dies.

And the room's ambience
Holds as a cunning vase
The nourished flower
That had been innocence.

Thanks

When this lust lies beyond geography
And only the old eyes
Flame at the proud fancy of a bride,
Take comfort that your thighs
Once made a poem of my vanity
And on your breast my swollen anguish died.

The Formulas

Distinguished and remote, the formulas arranged
Their uninvited discipline about the room
With all the deliberate neat gravity of doom
As if their mere portentousness of advent changed
Our inheritance of flurry and our neurotic fuss
To dignity of proper ends somehow exalting us.

This had not been expected; though the accusation
Frigidly made by the mirror's candour had earlier warned
That our love of freedom might more easily be suborned
Externally than by our timid hesitation
To refuse the careful propaganda of despair
That followed us each night up every guilty stair.

So now in the ultimate impotent disgrace
Our humble mouths and knees make at last the correct prayer,
While the formulas display their clever menacing flair
For rejoicing cynically at our loss of hope and face;
And all the hostility of their discipline
Contrives to make us repent of an unreal sin.

Address to My Face

My double darling, witty dismay
Of every mirror, morning disaster
To the equilibrist, Hope,
And hangover of every day,
Must you indefinitely stay?

Old obsession, favourite dream
Of my romantic ghost (stalking
Tiger among the flower ladies),
Are you, my discredited theme,
Ugly as you begin to seem?

Constant companion, friend or foe,
Inevitably you disguise
Somebody I might have been,
Though nobody can ever know
Whether or not it's better so.

I shrug my shoulders in the glass
And end the diatribe.
You cannot answer anyway,
And so we let the matter pass,
– Until I meet you in another glass.

Ballad

As I was going by the sweet legend
(Believing in roses and crossing my fingers)
A sudden woman waylaid and wed me
(O withered the roses, my fingers are stiff).

Where are you going in the sweet legend
(Believing in roses and crossing your fingers)
As if you don't know that all legends are doomed
(The roses will wither, your fingers grow stiff)?

I am just going in the sweet legend
(Believing in roses and crossing my fingers)
Because I am young and not yet done dreaming
(O withered the roses, my fingers are stiff).

Better for you in the sweet legend
(Believing in roses and crossing your fingers)
To linger with love while yet there is time
(The roses will wither, your fingers grow stiff).

Who will direct me in the sweet legend
(Believing in roses and crossing my fingers)
To find my true love or to dodge my true doom
(O withered the roses, my fingers are stiff)?

I will direct you in the sweet legend
(Believing in roses and crossing your fingers)
I'll be your true love, your darling, your doom
(The roses will wither, your fingers grow stiff).

Then I'll stay with you in the sweet legend
(Believing in roses and crossing my fingers)
Forgetting the end of all dreaming is doom
(O withered the roses, my fingers are stiff).

I lingered and rotted in the sweet legend
(Believing in roses and crossing my fingers)
With the woman who loved me and left me my doom
(O withered the roses, my fingers are stiff).

Still I am singing of the sweet legend
(Believing in roses and crossing my fingers)
Long, long ago my dreaming was over
(O withered the roses, my fingers are stiff).

Not Much Comfort

No convert even now to gentleness,
The limbs like holly discomfort any bed,
And dribbled memories and stale desires
Make puddles in the mind – this consolation
Can still evoke approximate peace:
Vehemence of my dreams and my daft words
Gave me one woman's summer.
Now I would prefer a little fire.

Dedicatory Poem

These disturbances now I dedicate
To you, the proud disturber
Of more than blood, deceiver
Of more than sense. No surrogate
Could ever satisfy
Lover or poet for his exquisite lie.

I do not ask you to remain content
With riddling ambiguities
To resolutions that may please

Your vanity or flatter my intent;
But ask you to believe
Poets and lovers are fated to deceive.

If there is any comfort for grey hairs
In proudly saying, *Look,*
A poet yesterday put in a book
His love for me, its triumphs and despairs –
That comfort's yours.
Do we regret love dies, while art endures?

Disturber, take with no reluctant hand
This offering; look with no cold eye
On each affectionate lie.
Only the certainty you understand
Gets you the gift. Be wise,
And listen to no other poet's lies.

Willy and Reality

Willy was a wishful thinker.
  Willy couldn't see
The awful appearance of things as they are,
  Drab reality.

Willy lived in a coloured kingdom,
  Coloured pink and gold,
Where all politicians were public-spirited,
  No lies told.

Willy's favourite food was candy,
  A rather monotonous diet.
Whenever a quack produced a panacea
  Willy would buy it.

Willy, of course, idolized women,
  He loved them one and all,
Though he preferred them to be golden-haired
  And not too tall.

Willy also believed in God,
  A kind of Santa Claus
Who rewarded the good and punished the wicked
  According to laws.

Willy eventually met a woman
    Who preyed on his mind.
She was golden-haired, and evidently
    Exactly his kind.

Willy insisted on a white wedding,
    And everything just so.
That the white was supposed to symbolize something
    He wouldn't know.

Willy lived in a dream of delight
    Longer than you'd suppose,
Because he couldn't see what was happening
    Under his nose.

Willy was called up for the Army.
    Though he had always believed
The Germans were thoroughly decent people,
    He was deceived.

Willy came home on leave one day,
    Earlier than expected.
He found a reality in his bed
    He'd not suspected.

Willy no longer believes in God,
    Or colours pink and gold.
Willy is, like the two he murdered,
    Much too cold.

Willy wouldn't have wanted a moral
    To end his little tale.
He heard too many from the chaplain
    While in jail.

Willy didn't learn from the chaplain
    What you may learn from him:
Life may be a coloured daydream;
    It can be grim.

Short Story

The woman supine on the bed
Scratches idly at her head.
Her lover, wild between her thighs,
Sees in her unguarded eyes
Lineaments of unworthy hire,
Not those of gratified desire.

Plaintive

The hairs on my belly are wet with your sweat,
My loins are empty since the need of yours;–
Can you so easily shake your head and forget,
Put on fresh powder, and walk out of doors?

Gorse Idyll

Her hair was like the sunlit gorse,
Her body like the gorse on fire,
And what we knew of souls we'd take
To any fair for hire.

I took her to the golden gorse
We made a gold to-do.
No deacon sighed with such content
As we, when we were through.

Deacons and gorse in any land
Would be so far apart –
And all the lands I walk through now
I have a double heart.

Love Poem

The imperception of your absences
Defines remoteness that exists
After denial and the tousled lists –
You still can keep important distances.

Matter it were indeed for a great wonder
If you had not that gift of going off.
Would it not make even the pious scoff
If what we'd joined we could not also sunder?

In love, it seems, our greatest need is this:
To let the other go, alone, apart
Into the farthest regions of the heart
Without the least disturbance of a kiss.

Data for Dr Kinsey

Discreet old age, I'd often said,
Will have one blessing at the least:
No fear of in a stranger's bed
Being caught as half a two-backed beast.
My youth, it seems, was fed on lies:
Age has had more than one surprise.

Adam

Walking alone in the garden of day
In the virgin weather,
Did he dream that sweat of intercourse
Or thought might stain and strain
His bright prophetic body?
Or that God's wrath would cloud
Over their agony together
And rob them of their innocent sleep?
That he and she
And all the unsullied skies would weep?

A Curse

My manhood, powdered by your lust,
Will, as a sick, determined ghost,
Crawl after your declining grace
Like spittle down your withering face,
And though its vengeance must be dumb,
Render your wanton longings numb.

A Lesson in Grammar

I never learned to say it properly,
To join two pronouns with an active verb,
– That's how I see it now with the acerb
Grammarian's somewhat faded faculty

For conjugation and analysis –
To say, I love you, with due emphasis.

For in my lesson-days I always found
This grammar much less needful than the rest
And never really put it to the test,
But tucked it in a footnote as unsound
And doubtful, lacking in authority
Except by hearsay and empirically.

Now, of course, I find it difficult
To say the sentence never properly learned
In youth when tongues may easily be turned
And twisted to obtain a glib result.
But pondering my lesson-book today,
I fear it will be harder to unsay.

The Way of the World

She that has sweated in my sweat
Must find this bitter knowledge yet:
Because one woman's true to me,
I must be true to two or three.

Song

Interlocked upon the bed
The lovers do what they must do,
But when it's done, they lie apart,
Knowing in the separate heart
That one is one and two is two,
Number is for ever so.

Sprawled upon the glittering plain
The armies at the end of day
Know that even the salty fight
Cannot their separates unite
In that long roar of interplay.
Number is for ever so.

Whatever words have sought to tell,
Lovers and armies sought to do,
Neither the one nor other fight
Can these poor separates unite,
For one is one and two is two,
Number is for ever so.

A Late Quarrel

All other quarrels being now forgotten,
When love that knew not time discovers age,
It is good we feed the remnant of our rage
Upon these trivialities. Love's rotten,
Maybe, but these flickerings of strife
Show that it still retains a little life.

Hard Luck

Mary Ann Evans went to bed,
Pulled the clothes right over her head,
Prayed to the Lord that only he
Might ever come near her virginity.

She needn't have bothered – no local rake,
However hard-up for a woman to make,
Could warmly consider the thought of bed,
With a woman already three quarters dead.

Epigrams

I

My neighbour, learning that I lacked for meat,
Thanked the Lord gravely he'd enough to eat.

II

Gardeners are Friendly People

My neighbour foolishly left me alone
Once with his most admired rose.
I did not notice it was overblown
Until I'd plucked it. I wonder if he knows?

III

A Contemporary

Aloysius stroked his finely-modelled head,
And preened himself among the nearly great.
Dear man, at least he's known before he's dead
The cosiness of being second-rate.

IV

Poppy, considering every man a beast,
Was always seeing sexual intent.
Now the poor virgin's dead without the least
Return of her one compliment.

V

Mother and Daughter

Millicent, having had her share of sin,
Is piously determined to begin
Ensuring that her daughter has no fun.
Too late, of course – the girl has long begun.

VI

My Mirror Loves Me, Anyway

She combs and combs her yellow hair,
Though there's no chance that on the stair
She'll hear the man who used to spread
Its glory on a double bed.
He, though he loved her in his fashion,
For black hair now reserves his passion.

The Pride of the Morning

As I walked out in the pride of the morning,
Too young to admire and too old to deride,
I saw the whole city was bonny with fire
And everyone else had suddenly died.

So I walked for a while in the pride of the morning,
Alone, with a strut, and a dandified smile,
The king of the fire, the lord of the city,
Flamboyant, alone, and proud for a while.

But alas for the dandy, alas for the king,
Alas for the pride that is nourished on fire,
The flames as I passed them were courteous with homage,
But my heart wanted someone to see and admire.

My heart shrivelled up in the pride of the morning,
Played traitor, alas, to the dandy and king,
Because I was walking alone in my splendour
And the fire was deaf to the song I could sing.

Voyages

In the mornings where my mercies were
The ballad in my breast
Hurt like a cough; ambition ripped
Like tidal ice
Across my voyages, my green unrest.

Authentic violence compelled
Those random voyages.
Love's big and blizzard clutch
Could daunt my song
To silence in the uproar of the seas.

Sometimes a lucky island held
My obstinate desire
And let the daunted song erupt
Out of its ache
And die in the exhaustion of its fire.
But always other landfalls promised:
The ballad in my breast
Persisted in its hurt, and drove
My green pursuit
Over the endless waters of unrest.

Two

Deadlocked and still indubitably two
This loyal pair now struggle to undo
The grapple each laid on the other's body
To obtain and hold impossible unity.

Each in the struggle lacks desired scope
For the bold acts commensurate with hope
That could effect the needed dissidence
And sanction each in his own difference.

Tangled among the loving and the lies
Each in the mirrors of the other's eyes
Reads the reluctance of his own admission
That nothing now can alter his condition.

Helplessly the struggle still goes on
Although each knows no victory can be won,
For each is nourished by the other's body,
Lockfast and lonely in duality.

And every twitch and writhe draws tighter yet
The scarifying and necessary net
That once promised impossible unity
To separateness of body and body.

Stare-in-the-Face

Stare-in-the-face said to me,
'Do not be capable of doubt.
If in the mirror you should see
The captive beast, perplexity,
Be brave and let it out.'

Stare-in-the-face admonished me,
'Out in the open factual air
The niggling animal you see
Will vanish in its liberty
And leave you honest there.'

Stare-in-the-face was kind to me,
He meant each word he said.
He did not know that liberty
Disposes not of doubt, but me.
He does not know I'm dead.

The Last Regret

(for Ted)

If you should come, a slack-loined ghost,
To trouble corners of my sleep
I shall remember that the most
Demanding lust, being dead,
Can do no more than creep
And ask for comfort in my bed.

And I shall press dried breasts and say,
What have I now for your delight?
Down on your bony knees and pray,
Old man, forgiveness of your sins.
Then, shrinking in the night,
Learn how the last regret begins.

Song of the Dandy Bones
(for Ted)

It was not in the lubber lands
Nor in the city made with hands
The windy weather made me go.
It was not anywhere you know,
Sang the dandy bones as they swung in the tides.

It was not woman's kindling heat
That made my roaring pulses beat
Or any trick that you may know,
Impelled me on my way to go,
Sang the dandy bones as they swung in the tides.

But wilder wishes made me ride
The mocking horses of the tide
And in the windy weather find
The peace unknown to lubber mind,
Sang the dandy bones as they swung in the tides.

Let lubber bones in graves forget
The windy weather rocks me yet,
But I am scavenged clean and free
To feed the harvest of the sea,
Sang the dandy bones as they swung in the tides.

Villanelle

Something there is not cured with a kiss.
To be distracted to a greater rage –
The need of the heart was never less than this.

It is a cry not apt for emphasis
Or slick manipulation on a page.
Something there is not cured with a kiss.

Nor is it cured when you hear the hiss
The expiring serpent makes in his old age.
The need of the heart was never less than this.

It is a cry you cannot hope to miss
Sometime on your ragged pilgrimage.
Something there is not cured with a kiss.

Nor is it cured when paralysis
Subtly invades your make-do equipage.
The need of the heart was never less than this.

And at the end of all experiences
We are distracted to a greater rage.
Something there is not cured with a kiss.
The need of the heart was never less than this.

Stanzas in a Mirror

Tomorrow round the corner,
The country through the mirror,
The man I may become,
These betray me daily,
These distract me wholly
From perfection of the dream.

Poems I am not writing,
Like love that may be waiting
For me to play my part,
Can give me grief and terror
Like any other error
Or self-inflicted hurt.

And staring in the mirror
At my own continued murder,
I see behind my eyes
The man I may become
Take possession of my dream
With his assured lies.

Tomorrow round the corner,
Says the liar in the mirror,
Will give you the command
Of art and love and living.
Dreaming is believing,
And easier in the end.

So daily in the mirror
I contemplate my murder
And listen to his lies.
Tomorrow round the corner
I may be older, wiser –
But when I die, he dies.

But when I die, the mirror,
Survivor of my murder
And witness of my dream,
Will it tell the coroner,
Tomorrow round the corner,
What I have become?

Workers of the World, Unite

(for Stanley)

On the worn and public grass
Underneath the bourgeois sky
Proletarian lovers lie
Careless of the crowds that pass
And cast an eye.

In the perfect, workers' state
They shall lie on beds of down
And their likings consummate
Unexposed to public frown.
And torch shone down.

Or should any lovers sigh
For a bit of love on grass,
The State will always let them lie
Underneath the workers' sky
If they've a pass.

Proletarian lovers know
In their own desired park
Only the keepers come and go
In a routine to-and-fro
After dark.

For the State must still ensure
Even in such lusts divine
That rutting comrades still make sure
That their passions keep the pure
Party line.

And that on the careless grass
They still remember that coition
Even with a government pass
Is not just fun for lad and lass –
It means fruition.

So the servants of the State
Severely look by night and day
That the lovers consummate
Their joys to benefit the State,
Not merely play.

But underneath the bourgeois sky
Where heartless crowds may pass,
The unenfranchised lovers lie
Exposed to every sneering eye
On the bourgeois grass.

Nursery Rhyme

Eve's first laughter shook the leaves
When that serpentine clown
Taught her the merriest words he knew,
All fall down.

When Adam failed to see the joke,
She smoothed away his frown
By whispering into his ear,
All fall down.

When Cain and Abel drove her mad,
Clutching at her gown,
She showed them the merriest game,
All fall down.

And you, my dear, had better learn
This game of great renown.
Be good, my dear, be careful, for –
All fall down.

Critical Encounter

This critic was too subtle is my guess.
I was dismayed at first, but later thought
His ambiguities concerned me less
Than the cold comfort that my poem brought.

Not that I'd trust entirely my own wit
To tell me what I mean by every word.
Doubtless he's right when he untangles it –
But then I have a sense of the absurd.

Would it have made any difference
If I'd disclaimed responsibility?
No. For the critic must have confidence –
The poet makes do with fallibility.

So we agreed at last to separate,
And go our ways, and try to understand.
We did not make our gestures desperate –
Just smiled, and shook each other by the hand.

And left. The poem still remains.
Now that I read it in a different light,
(How cunningly I picked the fellow's brains!)
I could so easily believe him right.

Invocation

Lady, the stilted bird who gave me love
Has vanished, and the land
Is suddenly forlorn. Between bare trees
I can see nothing but the nothing
That is sky, and the withered bed
Where once the bird drank freely.
O lady, will you send again the beat
Of wings, the drumming clangour,
The bird, and water for its sustenance
To this dry land?
Or must I watch the trees now slowly dying?

A New Song of Old Despair

The ballad's wormy eye
Glitters with hunger,
All history's malice
Shrivelled to metaphor.
Where is the lee of the gallows?
Asks the old sailor.

The sermon's bony shout
Is not of pardon,
Being too much aware

Of necessary sin.
Where is the lee of the gallows?
Asks the old sailor.

Bloodspattered tragedy
Pays no debt off,
No more than comedy's
Racking laugh.
Where is the lee of the gallows?
Asks the old sailor.

Nothing written or said
Dodges paradox.
There is shelter to be found
In the lee of all rocks.
Where is the lee of the gallows?
Asks the old sailor

Long-ago Love

My long-ago love goes lightly through the summer
As random as a dream, and the ruined boys
Forget their debt to time to see her smiling.
But I, marooned in winter, remember.

My long-ago love speaks in the old language
To listeners drowsy in her summer heat,
Forgetful of the turn, return of seasons.
But I, marooned in winter, remember.

O young men glad to see my long-ago love,
Do not remember in the smile of summer
That winter comes and the ruin of your joys.
Let me, marooned in winter, remember.

Let me, in memory of my long-ago love
Make one more dream of how she looked in summer,
And how I smiled in response to her smiling.
Let me, marooned in winter, remember.

Homage to Wallace Stevens

I

The crude constructions of fortuitous dream
Flare by, but in his coloured room
A clown lays on his colours in a rage.

It is a rage that pedantry or suave
Analysis cannot dissuade or touch.
It is a rage for colours as they are.

And colours as they are are tricksy things.
The clown is helped to find them as they are
By music he evokes from a guitar.

Suppose the colours of the original sea,
The sea of syllables at first and last,
Primal oh-ho and last ironic ha:

The clown, then, as he rides, rides on that sea,
The clown, then, as he sings, sings with that sea.
He matches the sea's rage with his rage.

II

Displacement of our dreams cannot provide
Per se for symbols of reality.
We have to recognize before we learn.

It is a tedious process for the weak.
The sure music that the clown evokes
Can help us as he lays his colours on.

It is the colour of ourselves we seek.
But how are we to know it when we see
Unless some angel plucks the plangent strings,

Unless the raging sea resolves itself
To order as the raging clown commands,
Like the responsive blue of his guitar?

The clown makes music of the raging sea,
Finding the ultimate of colour there
Which was before he spoke or lifted hand.

III

No other angel interposing here
With formula or ban can disappoint
Those who have listened to the blue guitar.

Rage, clown, among the colours of your room
And memories of the necessary sea,
Blue music of your ultimate guitar.

We have discarded other colourists,
And hope in time we can discard ourselves
Into the ordered raging of the sea.

Then we shall know the colour of ourselves.
Meanwhile we too are more or less aware
That colours in themselves are tricksy things.

We listen to the raging of the sea,
And to the raging of the clown who plucks
Blue secrets from his blue and plangent strings.

For the Marriage of Hugh and Barbara

Attended by multitudes of wishes
The princess in an ancient fairy tale
Traversed a continent's enormity
To reach an unknown harbour, and set sail
Across a foreign but imagined sea.

So long she voyaged, she almost forgot
The silken features of her native land,
The cherry-blossom, and the dappled fawn
She used to feed out of her lilied hand,
The peacocks screaming on her father's lawn.

A happy landfall came at last as promised,
And marriage to a prince. Long days
Of doubled happiness are briefly told
In the familiar 'ever after' phrase
Which ends those stories which are true and old.

Our wishes now make multitudes for you.
But even poets do not try to find
New worlds to bless you as you go together.
Only an old story in my mind
Is made a charm for you against the weather.

I Love Your Beautiful Mind, but I Love Especially Your Body

The augury of this am,
Under the sky's same,
Negatives another
Fond or of lover.

Moves through the this
An elsewhere yes,
And in the furies of doom
Again announces am.

Imply the body's but,
An answer to the that
Mind postulates.
Undo the dates.

Release the never
Gift to the lover,
Under the sky's same
A recompense for am.

Lady in a Garden

Penned in the garden of her own disaster
The lady feels the cold creep to her knees.
The taut and easy wit she has to master
The brilliant talking fellow is gone. The trees
Are suddenly tall.

The lady is alone with all her flowers.
(What was it that the grass refused to hide?)
His talk had charmed away the waiting hours,
And served to indulge her in a little pride
– But was that all?

The lady feels the curl and lash of cold
Imprison her in an attitude of shame.
She knows already how it will be told,
Regrets not asking for the fellow's name,
And sees night fall.

Problems of Language: Old Man, Young Girl

Language is always dogma, said the sage,
Who had not heard
Your one derisive word
Topple the tower of my presumptuous age.

The ruins of dead languages reveal,
The poet said,
Always that love is dead.
He had not seen the life my shards conceal.

I cannot find in poet or in sage,
In them or you,
Anything now to do
Except to put delusion in a cage

Of other words, and hope again that rhyme
Will deaden grief.
– But can I cheat belief,
Who failed so obviously at cheating time?

Debate

My love and I held long debate
With wild and cautious art.
The question moved was, Which could do
The other greater hurt?

Our double art was wasted
In that attempt to prove
Our dialectic could be used
To demonstrate our love.

Theorems end expectedly,
And so with our debate.
Each of us was the loser,
Each is alone tonight.

Intimations of Mortality

There on that hot, unlucky bed,
(Miles away, miles away)
Embarrassed but intrepid still
The boy who would be admiral
Went down beneath the ninth wave,
Hearing the laughter in the love –
You are unlucky, no one wins today.

Drained and warm upon that bed,
(Miles away, miles away)
Brave in recovery from his fever
The would-be lone explorer
Died in the tangles of the trees
Hearing the parrot mockeries –
You are unlucky, no one wins today.

Emptied on that unlucky bed,
(Miles away, miles away)
The boy who'd be a jaunty gambler
Careless what his fates uncover,
Died at the flicking of a card
To call a bluff he had not heard –
You are unlucky, no one wins today.

Wordless on that unlucky bed,
(Miles away, miles away)
The beardless poet proves his love
Who now will fill his paper grave
With words he heard before his fall,
The words the winner says to all –
You are unlucky, no one wins today.

Love Dies as a Tree Grows

What is it that begins, or ends, in this room at midnight?
A tree grows in the dark. So we easily say: but which of us
can conceive of the terrors and thrustings that ever-nocturnal
growing and stirring to grow involve? Who has heard the
scream of the tortured roots? Or felt himself drenched and
drowning in the torrent of the sap?
The wind brings us no answers.
Who has heard love dying in the dark?
It dies with the same soundless scream as the tree utters in its
    growing.

We are all deaf to that scream.

The night passes; and reluctant eyes see on waking that the tree is the same as on the day before, and the love is unaltered.

But, despite the sensual evidence, the tree has grown, as the love has died – only a little, but the growth and the death are both there, though we have not heard the scream of their process.

What is it that is beginning, or ending, in this midnight?

The wind brings no answer, for the answer is already known.

Love dies as a tree grows: in the dark, softly, and with a terrible scream.

Tribute

Strange things have happened in her ambient,
For signs been taken and misunderstood
By men in natural bewilderment,
Unused to such disturbing, timid
Of her contradictory demands.

This was inevitable. In what other way
Could she, the needed and divine,
Achieve her necessary and impossible ends?

A Song of the Days

On Monday it is the waking
Drenched in the light
And the cast dream.
On Monday it is beginning.

On Tuesday it is the drumming
Dazzle of words
And the hurt tongue.
On Tuesday it is the saying.

On Wednesday it is the bruising
Delight of hands,
The calloused fingers.
On Wednesday it is the touching.

On Thursday it is the rushing
Together of all
Sweet, sour savours.
On Thursday it is the tasting.

On Friday it is the burning
Of weed and incense,
Confusion of air.
On Friday it is the smelling.

On Saturday it is the bringing
Of five truants
Together. The five
On Saturday are ending.

On Sunday it is the praying
With the five and more.
Tomorrow it is Monday.
On Sunday it is everything.

Complaint

Why does the trouble of your sleep
Stir such reluctant ghosts
Whose ineffective pasts
You do not even pretend to weep?

And why, so late, do you call
To join that company
Of scaresleep imagery
The ghost of one you did not love at all?

A Young Man Reproves His Elders

Bald witnesses observant of my plight
May make bland comments as they shake their heads,
Or tell me that I'll learn another use for beds
When you no longer can invade my night
Nor I keep up love-tussling till the light.

These, as they shift upon their stringy thighs,
Can cough whatever wisdom they may please
Or mutter covetous prayers upon thin knees
That I may find conviction in their lies –
You controvert their meagre proof love dies.

So I am chosen by and choose this love,
Committed to its struggle and delight.
Bald witnesses, who lie awake at night,
Neither your aching joints nor theories prove
That you yourselves were never thus in love.

It Is Not Fear

It is not fear but knowing what to fear
Frightens you most, whatever you believe.
I ought to know: I bought the knowledge dear.

You will find out, this or some other year,
In saying this I don't mean to deceive:
It is not fear but knowing what to fear.

And when my meaning's made completely clear,
You will of course have further cause to grieve.
I ought to know: I bought the knowledge dear.

And then you shall regret the shrug and sneer
With which you take this warning I must give:
It is not fear but knowing what to fear.

I give the warning now because you're near
And I must try to tell you how to live –
I ought to know: I bought the knowledge dear.

And even though you still refuse to hear
The warning or claim your right to disbelieve:
It is not fear but knowing what to fear.
I ought to know: I bought the knowledge dear.

Old Man's Song

Children do not read the clock
Or stare in mirrors at their fate
Or care that dictionaries lack
The words to make their loving right
Said the old man as he took off his clothes.

Children do not need to think
Precisely on original sin
Nor have they urges to get drunk
Or from this foul world to be gone
Said the old man as he took off his clothes.

The child is father to the man
And if that man grow old enough
He may discover once again
The childish meaning of I love
Said the old man as he took off his clothes.

And cease to read the brutal clock
Or stare in mirrors at his fate
And find what dictionaries lack
The words to make his loving right
Said the old man as he took off his clothes.

Love's Tautology

All statements that I make may be defined
In philosophic terms as meaningful,
Tautologous, or nonsense; but I find
That, having got myself this bellyful
Of love (begging the question now what love may be),
All my statements easily reduce
To one, the random universe to unity;
And instantly my philosophic wits deduce:

To say *I love you* is not indeed to be
In any new or desperate category:
I love you is the first, and last, tautology.

Situation

Your eyes are telling the weather back
          In a summer still as stone.
Under the hot and innocent skies
          A backward wind has blown
          My love to be alone.

This was not told upon the chart
          You gave me for my own
To guide me to a green, green place
          My love had always known
          Was yours and mine alone.

Now I am withered in this wind
          Of summer like a stone.
Your eyes, the chart, the innocent weather
          Leave me here alone,
          In a green place alone.

Sailor

Easy now on a beach, he notes the sea
(An old bitch once, angry to bite and keep)
As over-emphatic in vulgarity;
And turns upon his side prepared to sleep.

Remembered tides at once roar in his ears
And ride him down beneath his frightened eyes.
Scrabble and gasp among the plunging fears
Betray the nonchalance with which he lies.

Easy on whatever harmless shore
The green ghost will not lightly let him be.
His blood cannot forget the salty roar,
The suck and gobble of the feeding sea.

Saltsick, seadriven, he abdicates his right
To be at ease with his old enemy.
Witness the longdrawn watches of the night
He drowns again in a remembered sea.

Remembrance

The time I expect was summer
Said the old man trying to remember
But I have completely forgotten the weather.

Her wishes were no doubt auspicious
Said the old man remembering his wishes
But I have forgotten if I gratified her wishes.

I expect it was a very happy season
Said the old man remembering the sun
But I have forgotten the affair's conclusion.

Poem Dedicated to the Memory
of Dylan Thomas

From gorse and cinder hills I Adamed out
To take to name to praise all things I breathe
Before I burn in other breath, before
The tall shout take me and the nameless
Name me luckily and the praise be praise
And name and breath and all the burning

Unparadised I found the spinning world
A noise in nothing and before a fall
I turned unribbed on the world's turning
To tread a morning name on printless days
And follow where it led the burning voice.

All else was accident, what errors fell
Or joys upshot as I moved out of grace
And five green seasons named the world for me.
Grained in the deep earth, lapped in the long water
I had lain who now moved tenderly
Towards a box of love and one last name.

The world is spinning and the world is named,
Adam unribbed and waking to his dream,
Five senses rule the world, and five
Are lucky in the last and burning name.

Merlin's lament

I knew those rigid kings
In their erected state,
And knew their supine queens,
Their lying fate.

I gave their nightmares names,
Answered their riddles;
Told them what the signs meant
On graves and cradles.

I told them how to hunt
The incredible animals
And return victorious
With the true symbols.

But for all my knowledge
The table cracked and broke;
Died all the young gallantry
In the battle smoke.

I'm left alone in my wisdom
With a careless love,
The broken land around me,
The birdless sky above.

A Lesson in Criticism

The poem reminded this one of a moth
Beating its fated wings into the light;
While that one thought the lines a pretty froth
On top of nothing half as solid as broth.
Poor teacher had to show neither was right.

Somewhere I expect the proper moral lies:
Either – do not expose your poems in school;
Or – pick on teachers who are poem-wise;
Or – think conflicting readings are a prize.
What hope from readers when the poet's a fool?

Innocent Song for Two Voices

SHE

Shafted body in the sun,
When your work or play is done,
What is left of you to me?

HE

Graingold body in the sun,
When my work or play is done,
Something of myself I leave.

SHE

Shall I laugh or shall I grieve
When you've done what must be done
With my body in the sun?

HE

Laughter and grief for you and me
And what we sunlocked two have done
Are gifts unto the child I leave.

BOTH

Then we both must laugh and grieve,
For this witness there shall be
To show the world what we have done,
The graingold and the shafted one,
Body on body in the sun.

One Song of a Mad Prince

I sent a letter to my love,
    Sent it late and early,
A letter to my love who lives
    In a distant country.

It was a letter written out
    In the heart's despairing,
Asking her who could not read
    Why love was disappearing.

I sent a letter to my love,
    But did not wait an answer.
In the middle of the night
    I dreamed of love and danger.

My letter came back from my love,
    Came back late and early,
Burning over mackerel fields
    And over seas of barley.

And my love who could not write
    Told to me who could not read
A story older than our love
    In a single word.

Now I swim in mackerel fields
    Or lie in seas of barley,
Writing a letter to my love,
    A letter late and early.

I post it to that distant country
    Where her single word
Murdered all the witness air
    And epitaphed my heart.

    Letter, letter that I write,
Burning to my love,
    Tell her if she learns to read
I'll rise out of my grave

And come to her in mackerel fields
    Over the seas of barley
To witness in the living air
    My love was late and early.

A Promise to My Old Age

Strut, arrogant frame, your pride of bones
Over this green stage while the sun is shining.
When the sag comes and your now so limber lines
Begin to blur and creak, and the complaining
Breath annoys the air your movements cumber,
Then you shall with no regret remember
How you, lordly, strode earth once
Like any rightful owner, and were pleased
To see tall trees reflect your arrogance,
And knew that nothing young could be despised.

Old age, my fatal friend I do not know,
Remember, when some young itch interferes
With your anticipated peace, I pray
You freedom from these terrors and desires
Of disobedient flesh, and promise pride
Only in glories that have long been dead.
Whatever song or madness your last lust
May farrow, blame or thank or curse or praise
This earlier brash hero if you must.
Only remember here his promise lies.

A Sonnet Instead of Theology

God, as we know him in a world of fact,
Said the philosopher[†], writing down a sum,
Is defining limit of his continuum.

This does not mean that God is mere abstract;
But, if God should irrupt into a state,
Then chaos would begin.

(*The Christian cried:*
'But I have seen my God, and know He died
For me.' And the devout Muslim: 'It is fate.'
The atheist stoutly said: 'God does not exist.')

While I, John Thomas on any faithful line,
Aware of many meanings I have missed,
Am obstinately uneager to resign
My right of disagreement or my hope
Even in hoping there may be no hope.

But know one thing: that chaos is a fact:
Therefore presume God guilty of one act.

†*cf. C. S. Pierce (sic)*

The Time of Love

The time, the time, the time of love
    Says the clock in the bed,
Is told by the creaking of your knees
    And the drumming in your head.

    The time of love you springily felt
Was a time not told by clocks;
    And you did not hear in the welcoming bed
The drummer who knocks and knocks,

The drummer who tells you the time of love,
    And measures it in your bed,
And announces its end with creaking knees
    And a knocking in your head,

By a clock that doesn't need face or hands
    To measure your despair
That the time, the time, the time of love
    Has vanished in the air,

The empty air, the air you hate,
    The air around your head,
The air that gives its resonance to
    The clock that shares your bed,
The air that feeds and echoes
    The drummer in your head.

Sunday on the Beach

(*for Rhiannon*)

The wind was clouting the beach
With proper motherly slaps
That did not hurt perhaps
Though it seemed they were meant to teach
Something how to behave
In the presence of wind and wave.

Among the knots of knees,
By right assuming ease
In the water's salt and blue,
A baby laughed and ran,

A blob with legs and arms,
A blonde hullabaloo,
Squealing for liberty,
To jump in inches of sea
And lie in the sucks and laps
Of the little waves.

Watching her nakedness
And bellylove of the water,
Though I know the harms of the sea,
Though I know the harms of the crowd
In their best brown Sunday suits
And their candy frocks, though I know
That, however unique, my daughter
Will behave as the crowd behaves
In certain essential pursuits –

Though I know all this, I dare
To make for her one prayer:
Though she may not escape
That last and lurking shape
By the transfigured sea,
May she assume a rage
Decrepitude or age
Or mere external stain
Are powerless to touch.
Let her, like the sea,
All her life retain
Grace of body and mind
No accident can smutch.
As even the winter bough
Recalls its glory of leaf,
Let her, in spite of grief,
Stay beautiful as now.

Sea Shanty

O randy and random I roamed through the town,
Sang the ghost of a sailor on a lee shore,
The prince of the pavements,
The toast of the taverns,
The guest of the girls who will know me no more
Since the cold winds, the old winds, blew this man down.

O randy and dandy I danced through the town,
Sang the ghost of a sailor on a lee shore,
The cock of the fo'c'sle,
The pride of the pubs,
The darling of girls who will know me no more
Since the sad winds, the bad winds, blew this man down.

O randy immortal and lord of that town,
Sang the ghost of a sailor on a lee shore,
Did you not hear the trumpets,
Did you not hear the drums,
And the voices of girls who will love you no more
Say a wind always comes that shall blow a man down?

> *Blow the man down*
> Be he randy and random
> The cock of the fo'c'sle
> *Blow the man down*
> Be he randy and dandy
> The pride of the pavements
> Be he randy and handsome

The voices of girls who will love him no more
Say a wind always comes that shall blow the man down.
Sang the ghost of a sailor on a lee shore.

The Child at Night

Locked in the green house of the dark,
Where flowers pulse about him as they grow,
He rides the fearful engines of his wishes
Into the distance and delay of morning.

Astride his terrors he must keep delicate stance,
Or fall into the soft devouring mouths
Of night, the tiger with a thousand heads
Whom promises placate and dreams sometimes.

Better are lucky words which make night's fur
Lie down as when you stroke a cat.
But it is hard to hear words properly
And say them out again to listening dark
When ears are full of flowers roaring
And the prowl of night and the thunder of his wishes.

If he can only cry just loud enough,
The house of dark will crack and morning come.

The Lady and the Fir-Tree

(for Mairit)

The storm without, the storm within,
To my true love how shall I win?
Sang the fair lady.

O ride the storm, ride the storm
Until your true love keep you warm,
Answered the fir-tree.

The wind is high, the sea is high.
How shall my true love hear me cry?
Asked the fair lady.

O raise your voice, raise your voice
Until your true love shall rejoice,
Answered the fir-tree.

My love is dead, my true love dead,
And his death upon my head,
Mourned the fair lady.

O no, my love, my lady, no,
True love and death you now shall know,
Sang the dark fir-tree.

Poetic Retrospect

I tried to keep the summer in my head,
　　Words, wishes, double weather,
But when I looked in the hiding-place
My heart had drowned that summer away
And nothing remained but the echoing bone
　　And a cold wind blowing.

I tried to put the summer in a poem,
　　Words, wishes, double weather,
But when I looked at the empty paper
My heart had wept that season away
And nothing remained but the echoing pen
　　In a cold wind blowing.

The summer will not stay in mind or poem,
    Words, wishes, double weather,
And what I seek in the hidden places
Drowned in the charity of my heart
And nothing remains but bits of paper
    In a cold wind blowing.

The Ring of Language

(for Hildie)

What we are aware of are concepts and representations. It is a world into which the speechless animals have no entry, but from which we humans, no doubt, have no exit.
    – W. J. Entwhistle, *Aspects of Language.*

And out of the ground the LORD God formed every beast of the field, and every fowl of the air; and brought them unto Adam to see what he would call them: and whatsoever Adam called every living creature, that was the name thereof.

And Adam gave names to all cattle, and to the fowl of the air, and to every beast of the field; but for Adam there was no found an help meet for him.
    – *Genesis.*

That morning Adam named the animals
And for the first time knew he was alone.

Fur, fin, and feather, tusk, and hoof
Paraded there for Adam as he stood
Alone among them with his gift and glory.

Each, as it stamped its pattern on the sunlight,
Looked at Adam and received its name,
And moving on left Adam all alone
To wait for the next one to be named.

And when the morning ceremony was done,
Adam look round and saw himself alone.

A ring of animals made round him a horizon,
But he was lonely in the middle of their names.
Adam had named the animals and now
The names themselves made Adam's loneliness.
The friendly animals were all outside

The ring of language where he stood alone.
They could not come within his ring of speech,
And he could not get out and go to them.
Their names themselves made Adam's loneliness.

Adam had named the animals and knew
His gift was also his despair for ever.
Adam and all the animals he'd named
Must live for ever separate and alone.

Adam had named the animals – Adam alone.

Christening Poem for Alison Morgan

Alison is now your name.
We have given what we can.
To help you further in the game
Is more than you may ask of man.

Except that, Alison, your name
Sounds so sweetly in our ears,
We pray that neither grief nor shame,
We pray that neither blood nor tears

May blot the virtue of this name,
This sweetly-sounding Alison,
Till death and life are both the same,
And you have lost the game – and won.

A Second Song of a Mad Prince

I saw my blood run down the stairs
        Like a river, all night.
My love danced on the landing
        In a red light.

I woke in the blue morning
        And saw the bloodless day
Wrap my love in a white sheet
        And carry her away.

My love was dancing in the air
        Gaily, gaily.
Look, she said, my steps are light,
        My heart is free.

But I stood on the landing
    In the red light,
And gave my bloodstained fingers
    A message to write:

O the blood, the blood is a river
    That runs away.
And love is a dance, a dance
    By night, by day.

The river of blood that ran from me
    Runs as I write.
But though you dance in the bloodless day,
    You shall not dance at night.

For I shall lie on the landing
    In the river of my blood,
And should you come to dance there,
    Drown you in that red flood.

Your delicate bones will make me pens.
    And on your skin I'll write
The song of the bloody river
    That runs all night.

I'll tie up the song with a loveknot
    Of your drowned and bloody hair.
I'll burn the song, my darling,
    In the red air.

Portsmouth at Night: 'Hostilities Only' Rating

Ghosted with sailors, the sleeping city
Waits by the water for an admiral
To take her out to sea. Down the long decks
That are her streets I hear the carol
Of dead marines and snotty midshipmen
Ruffle the rigging of the Victory.
The sea-wind carrying ecstasies of rum
Forbids me to indulge in idle pity
For those who've sailed from here to a long sleep
Where mermaids give them cold and coral welcome.
The Pompey chimes ring out over seven seas.
Portsmouth is pointed for a long commission.

I am a sailor and on watch again.
And as I walk these admiralty streets,
I make a prayer for Pompey's able seamen:
Lord, on the day when earth your judgement meets,
Remember that I once was one of these.

The Monster

When the sea-monster came to visit us,
Grey harbour-filling bulk with hungry head,
Although our shuddering hundreds ran to stare
In terror on his glaucous length, or pray
Where the sea boiled around him to the shore,
We were not properly prepared for such
An advent: no virgins could be found
Of the right age to satisfy the beast.

Although enthusiastic citizens
Threw fat babies, doddering grandparents,
Nubile non-virgins into the broth of sea
Around him, the monster snorted once
To show his great displeasure, and withdrew
The enormous serpentinings of his body
Over the horizon, leaving the town to mourn
Its inability to make a sacrifice,
And wonder what it is we want of monsters.

Grandparents

(for Knut Johansen)

This is a house inhabited by the young
Whose laughter gives the air a sprightliness
That charms our many guests; we are famous
For our hospitality; the house is full,
So people say, of love, of graciousness,
Sweetness and light, the classic recipe
For all we understand that's not barbarian.
Few people ever see our grandparents:
Grandfather sitting with his lidded eyes,
A trail of spittle down his fallen chin,
His fly undone, a squat, strong-smelling man;
Or grandmother shut up in the attic room
Screaming soundlessly at spiders
What she remembers of life's plague and damage.

Both are dead, of course; but all the same
We keep the old man tied firmly down
And grandma's attic room is always locked
In case he should destroy us or she warn.

For Louise Bogan

You call yourself 'old lady' and the phrase
Becomes a poem. We poets who have known
You also love you. May our love be shown
In many poems brightening out your days,
And may your tough New England charm
Be sheltered long from ordinary harm.

For Roberto Sanesi, il miglior fabbro

Intense, a fawn, hearing mad sounds,
Makes music out of words. His eyes
Perceive reality and make us real.
He burns the torch, the taste, the scent, the feel
Of love and language. O tears and wounds
Of words let his truth speak beyond the daily lies.

Third Song of a Mad Prince

I walked abroad in my kingdom
        With my lost daughter
To show her her heritage,
        Bright lands, blue water –
Lie down, lie down in peace, poor prince's daughter.

    I said, This land is ours,
     Tall trees, green grass, flowers,
    Fat valleys, burly mountains,
    Great rivers, cool fountains.
    This as you understand
    Is a rich, heroic land.
    Our fathers here did deeds
    Famous across far seas.
    Here is all man needs
    To feed him or to please.
Lie down, lie down in peace, poor prince's daughter.

As we walked boldly there
Jays mocked in my face,
Bats sneered at my hair,
Worms returned my stare.
Greasy rats in the grass
Slithered like snakes.
The fields were fenced about
With scrawny stakes
And sagging wires where hung
Bones that had once been birds,
Foxtails, staghorns.
An idiot's fumbling words
Lolled from his tongue
Where children dined on acorns.
Some wry and stunted trees
Scrawled gestures on the sky.
Weeds tangled our knees
Where springs were foul or dry.
We saw an old horse dying
In a dirty place;
A ravaged salmon lying
In the cold water.
We heard the wounded crying
Of deer in the mouldy wood.
Carrion birds were flying
Where the tall nettles stood.
Lie down, lie down in peace, poor prince's daughter.

My daughter said to me,
Father, in your kingdom
I would not be a princess
Nor a woodcutter's daughter.
Father, in your kingdom
Of bright lands, blue water,
There is blight and sadness,
No heritage for me.
Father, let me wander
Across the beckoning sea
To find another kingdom
And a prince who loves me.
Lie down, lie down in peace, poor prince's daughter.

I walk abroad in my kingdom
Without my daughter,
And look at her heritage,

Grey lands, cold water,
And all that's left to say
To comfort my daughter
Who has left and gone far away
Over the water
Is, lie down, lie down in peace, poor prince's daughter.

Failure of Narcissus

Ah, it was cold that water and a cheat.

After the first blue shock
It seemed that he was going down a street
Of water that would end in sand or rock
But not in any dream or any love.
He would have tried retreat
Into the air's familiarity above
But he could see no grace in such defeat.

And so he sank.
　　　His staring eyes
Mirrored the element and his surprise
That even water could not make him wise.

A Woman Who Loved to Look on Running Water

(for Elizabeth)

A woman who loved to look on running water
Tawny in sunlight or mottled by the moon –
It could not be we should forget her soon
Or confuse her with somebody else's sister or daughter.

I see her stand upon a bridge in starlight
And dream herself into the river's flow
Until it seemed the water ceased to go
And she was rippling with that dream's delight.

O woman who loved to look on water moving,
O dreamer on bridges and on the banks of streams,
If I can keep you for ever in my dreams,
I shall know much of water and more of loving.

The Crab

(*from the Italian of Roberto Sanesi*)

It was at the wave's foot the crab was scrabbling
With rusty pincers wet in the sand, the hidden
Labyrinths into the salt and August drowsiness of sun,
The quiet floss-sulking of the foams between
The sticks on the beach veined with small red grains.
He came back in a springing toil of movement,
The vault shook down each time the wave woke up,
With thrusts, with seaweeds, cyclones of sand.
Orpheus' wild beast has now transformed himself.
In the free yoke of the water, repetition, future,
He draws himself up; he arches himself
To orient and impel his vertix,
Pincers of living rust, to the heart of the iron

Horizon; he pierces the lighter element
With anguish, he shapes it, and wakes himself up in the blue.

Not Lack of Children Only

Not lack of children only
    Tethered these two apart
Where neither heard the knocking
    Of the other's heart.

A keener lack compelled them
    Not to cut the rope
They tautly stretched between them
    Without love, without hope.

Not lack of children only –
    What could not be denied
To these two lonely lovers
    Was the unsatisfied

Longing to be neither
    Together nor apart,
Not to hear the knocking
    Of either heart.

The Savage Balance

(from the Italian of Roberto Sanesi)

This black, this person, self-dissolving
In the black of pitch and wounds, black,
Under a sun that is black and round
Only because it was made by two broad hands
Into a cup compounded of bitumen,
Abomination, and the confusion of insects,
This black is a pillar of rock and moves unmoving
Towards a sky yellowed with smashed elytra,
Quick, unmoving, under a black sun.
And because that which follows its course
From eternity to eternity, and that which is moved
From one word to another in tourbillions of light
Marshals itself as it is thrust away
By that which moves it, the sun that sweats
The fat petrolic constellations, one will always
Move, the other be always moved
In the savage balance of black and black.

False Dedication

(to Anita)
(from the Italian of Roberto Sanesi)

It was your sign to believe in a future: a kingdom in which to distinguish
the purists of bulls and ghosts upon the unfinished green
of the wave on the wave, in the water sombred by fishes
from rivers pursued by the sea, white winding-sheet
over which to project wounding. But it was also
as a response to an adagio
of symbols and syllables, a liquid encounter
of Nothingness with the To-Be: and then the demiurge bird
could trace his signs of light between the wires of the grass, could,
whistling, reduce the time and space of you,
and the reason burning on your face. This was your kingdom.
       The darting impulse.
The idea of a rose or a pebble. And you, nobody, moving from the nothingness
of a thing that is casually born from a thing,
you balanced yourself in the ring's eternal centre:
rhymes and rocks and creatures endured in this kingdom.

Draw An Arch of Light at the Window

(*from the Italian of Roberto Sanesi*)

Draw, winter, an arch of light at the window,
a white flight of sparrows that never fly
from these walls, and a white flower, a hostile
still life made in our image. Refuse
the slender fire on the heights, God's
snowdrop, but live with objects, join
thread by thread the fable and the idea,
freedom's air created and recreated
with only one spring of your branches weighted with snow.
Listen how silence swarms at the shutters,
and pity moans in this cold. If Minerva
does not descend in the night with her sinister eyes
of intelligence, we shall accuse the heart
of its gravity leading us down to the earth's centre.

Statue of Salt and Wall of Hyacinth

(*from the Italian of Roberto Sanesi*)

In this poisonous intimacy of trees and wind
(hypothesis and procession) that confines thought
should a day of stars reveal and betray the world
and not express the void, a different
substance comes from our speech, a different
fable and memory, and should it happen,
now and for ever, that the earth also
refuses the cold breath of your heart,
then indeed it is for us to say,
you must not, you do not love, it is too late,
harp of the wind and the will, our fate
is to give a new meaning to truth, a new
embrace to your water-limbs
in an intimacy of dry consents and golden
denials against my sky's white background,
an epic vainly refused to needs and gestures,
statue of salt and wall of hyacinth,
born already keeping a vigil, anciently budded,
beyond the eyes of you become a person.

And Resolve Themselves

(*to Gio' Pomodoro*)
(*from the Italian of Roberto Sanesi*)

Flowers of stone and thorn in a
Sea of stone and thorn and between essence
And existence now of the shade
Does not fall but the light falls
Falls headlong, the sun, if you like,
But stone and thorn and not
On this stone, and wheels and signs
And sunflowers and faces
With little horns with savage
Eyes where the wind gives way to the only
Living act, the act
And the only act where the sounds
Of clear water meet in chorus and
The flowers of stone and thorn
Resolve themselves in one light En Clair.

Bewilderment

In a perhaps momentary confusion
I said I loved you; but I did not know,
Flushed as I was then with the warm contagion
Of your flesh, how love could grow
To these proportions of bewilderment.

Now that the flesh grows cautious some old rage
Works yeastily within me. I had thought
It might be possible in middle age
To be less constantly distraught
Because of you into bewilderment.

That moment of my luck becomes too late
This time now when we might have been at peace
If either of us knew how to create
From our poor weathers of unease
Climates of unbewilderment.

In the Light of Ordinary Evenings

In the light of ordinary evenings
We have seen revelation, and let it go
Without a comment, almost without wonder,
Conscious merely of a thin fear
It might insist upon the opening
Of our hearts in welcome to its presence,
Its unbearable white radiance,
So unlike the light of ordinary evenings.

The Ditch of Desire

In the ditch of desire your true man I lay
My bruises like badges adorning the mud.
You turned on your tall heels, walked proudly away
From where I lay tasting the salt of my blood.
Your beauty assaulted the light of the day.

In the ditch of desire I heard a voice say
'There are plenty of pebbles still left on the shore.
Why should a gay lad like you want to stay
Regretting the loss of a petulant whore?'
Your beauty assaulted the light of the day.

In the ditch of desire for a year and a day
I lay besotted and happily drunk.
Even now I remember when you walked away
The cords of my longing cut deep as they shrunk.
Your beauty assaulted the light of the day.

Not When I Came

Not when I came
With anger and tall drum
Ranger of seas
To pull down towns
Ravener of forests
Uprooter of mountains
Not when I came
Tall in my danger
Did your proud refuge
Fall to my storm.

But when at nightfall
Weary with wounds
Slashed drum trailing
War-cry silent
I sat down to weep
You opened your gates
To let me conquer
Your proud refusal.

Lucky Jonah

(for Ted)

IN MEMORIAM – FRIENDS KILLED ON ACTIVE SERVICE
'*A man born to be hanged cannot be drowned*' – Old Saying

Cold comfort when the blue yawn of the sea
Crimped men for the voyage even Admiralty charts
Have not yet marked.
                I saw a ship go down,
Quietly in the middle of the afternoon,
And thought, 'That's one man will never play cards again
With confident fingers and goalscoring eye.
He loved football and cards and girls – but had to die.'

And then to hear my name in a brazen bar
In Alexandria
           (sailors in white duck escaping
From the copper sun and memories)
My name spoken by a schoolfellow
Who had come so far and – 'Yes, sunk twice' –
And so was going home. And twelve months later
Killed by a motor car in Newfoundland.
O ships we dreamed of when we both were boys,
And saw the sea once annually when the Sunday School
Charabanced us chorally to the gold coast
Of Wales and all our longings.
                 You indeed went down
To the great waters – and came back again,
Not once, but twice, and so one would have thought
Had earned the right to go back home and garden,
And grow garrulous with memories over beer,
But the car got you, certain as a shark.

O ships, o seamen, – convoys, brawls, and rum,
And offered sisters – 'Nice girl, very clean' –
The mad, forgiven captains – 'Clear Lower Deck.
I have to tell you that we probably sha'n't

Set foot on land again. Men, I rely on you.'
The scalded stokers and the sick, singed smell.
Torpedoes – and the quick way down to hell.

Captain's Requestmen and Defaulters: *'Hang that man*
Like Billy Budd. He sees a submarine
In the undershadow of every blasted wave.
Permission to grow? Granted. We'll all
Wear beards in hell. Compassionate leave?
Not granted. Let the woman have her fun.'
Who hit the bo's'n in the pirate town?
In the nostalgia of our rum we drown.

Drown – *'Is it better in the warm and classic blue*
Than in the cold waste north where even the strongest
Cannot survive three minutes? Anyway, thank God
We're not poor bloody pongos in the sand.
At least we've water, rum, and cigarettes,
Almost enough to eat, and – Battle Stations!
Here the bastards come again.'
The bombs drop like a mockery of rain.

I have seen the proud ships sail – and, broken-backed,
Or gaping bows, or holes torn in the side,
Crawl back to harbour or go down, go down
To Davy Jones's Locker like broken toys.
One day we caught a submarine, trapped like a fish
In the relentless circle of sixteen ships.
She ran the white flag up, and still our gunners
Pressed their automatic fingers
To make her run with blood. Later, we laid
The wounded on our upper deck – one was dying –
'Like a butchered sheep,' I thought,
And though I tried for it, I had no pity.

Voices: *'Remember me, mate? Had a run ashore*
With you in Alex. once. We found a girl
And christened her the Nut-Brown Maid.'
'Remember me? I hit a gharri-driver once
Because he wouldn't let me have his whip.'
'Remember me? I fell out of the motor-boat.'
'Remember–' all the frantic runs ashore
With Jacks who are not jolly any more.
Alex., Benghazi, Tripoli, Algiers,
Beirut, Valetta, Famagusta, –
O ports and harbours of my sunken years.

And all of life a long survivor's leave
For lucky Jonah, spewed up from the maw
To wait and wait and wait for death.
The sea's a populous city – half my world
Is walking there, up home with mermaids,
Cold, picked clean to the white bones,
And braggarting to fish, 'The Navy's here.'

A small boy in a small Welsh school
Dreamed over books that he would go to sea,
Knew schooners, barques, and brigantines,
The names of sails and rigging,
Dreamed of being a captain, proud and almighty,
Pacing the quarterdeck, and taming
Weather and mutiny with eyes reflecting
Glitter of seas, the seas
Of all the world – he knew them all.
Dreams, dreams – and now these drowning memories,
Marine entanglements to dreams and five
Long years of waiting to be drowned.

'A man born to be hanged cannot be drowned.'
Maybe. But I can hear ships' bells
Strike the melancholy sound
Of dead men's names, of sunk ships' names,
The lullaby and catalogue of the drowned.

Excuse

(for Marlene)

I blame it all on those headhurting books:
        The dreams and journeys,
Destructions, idylls, time's ambiguous mercies,
        And whatever looks
Like my revenge on what I found in books.

I blame it on the novels and the plays:
        Murders and marriages,
Visions and sermons, symbols, images,
        Those heady days
I ranted like the heroes of the plays.

I blame it on the poems above all:
        From that contagion
Comes the paradox of my condition:
        When I have blamed it all
On poems, it is the poems save me after all.

Taut Rigidity of the Senses

(from the Italian of Roberto Sanesi)

Taut rigidity of the senses that strangle life, and you, labyrinthine body
where Gods hide their ears under seaweed hairs on the edge
of a dense, deep sea where garrulous objects, stones, and deliberate
gestures, and cries
whose existence is pure form . . .
    But the others, I mean the other Gods, wander in the baying
of stubborn desires (desires that are needs, daily needs, incautious
desires), they stray like dogs
after a scent, the scent of myself, witchcrafts, mirages, mirrors, using
what pitch
to hide the sounds of myself pressing the steeps of the upright horizons,
studying what arts in dull silence to make me a cave where the opposed
voices deny themselves at every new assault? Then, order
lacking disorder, trees where the wind does not resurrect the songs in
the leaves, it is true,
it is true, after all, that you are a substance, a divine egg, a body, which
cannot answer yes to such questions, or if you
can answer yes, the answer is meaningless? . . . they live in a pure form.
But when
I plunge into a violet clarity of words and waters freeing myself from
the graves
of anxiety that draw still clouds in the shallows and hollows of the
tongue,
the voice that talks of myself, solemn and smiling, has the likeness a
statue has to a man,
and Athikte dances, with her naked feet, naked,
in the eyes abandoned in a false sleep shut in by eyelashes and light.

The Colour of Cockcrowing

(for Robyn)

It was always the colour of cockcrowing. On the first morning
Of creation Leviathan lifted his mighty shoulders
Above the waves and saw the colour of the cockcrow.
And on the following mornings, bull, and stallion,
Roebuck, reindeer, rhinoceros, the timid mouse,
The moose, eland, okapi, kangaroo, jerboa,
Fox, badger, otter, seal, and all the birds,
Sun-daring eagle, vulture already aware of death,
The great sea-spanning albatross, swallow,
Lark, and nightingale, the murderous Christmas robin,

Brawling sparrow, and laughing kookaburra,
And the fish, the sainted herring, and the holy salmon,
Mackerel, bream, and bass, sardine, and shark,
Perch, pilchard, trout, and coelacanth,
Insects, flies, spiders, bees, wasps, hornets, locusts,
Reptiles, giant boas and the deadly mambas,
Great king cobras and black Papuan snakes,
Crocodiles, alligators, duck-billed platypi,
The natives and anomalies of the world,
They all looked out on their first morning
And knew at once the colour of cockcrowing.

And God made Adam, and after Adam, Eve.
And Adam knew, even as he delighted
In the world about him, the colour of cockcrowing.
And Eve knew too, and when she took the apple,
Gave it to Adam that they might share their knowledge.

The cock crew first when those two put on leaves.
The cock has crown in your hearts and in mine
Since Adam hid himself among the trees,
And Eve lay waiting for him somewhere.

Crow, cock, until this woman and this man
Return to dust, crow until their children
And their children's children too are dust,
Crow until God revoke his first decree
That earth and all the inhabitants thereof
Should wear forever the colour of cockcrowing.

In the world we know it was always the colour of the cockcrow.

A Christmas Poem

(for Audrey and Doug)

My world is upsidedown, and Christmas burns
Me now on a foreign continent.
But still Christ's blood streams through the firmament.
The axis of man's hunger turns and turns
Between the poles of longings and of loss.
And every kiss erects another cross.
My land puts on her petticoat of snow;
But even in this sunburnt continent
Mary of Magdalen can still repent;
And Joan dream of holly and mistletoe,
And take my friends with me wherever I go.
I lean my breast upon a bloody thorn

(Which austral friends say is pure metaphor).
Believing, unbelieving, this day the child is born
And I am here, meaning or metaphor.
And all I know is, facing various ends,
There ought to be a God to bless my friends.

Italian Baroque Music

(to Louise Bogan)
(from the Italian of Roberto Sanesi)

Just as the doors are closing, when the air darkens
under the swallows' flight, dark, and clenched like a pebble
scratched by the cry, by the burst of the wind pursuing its limits,
there was a man who related how this sky, enfolded, silver-haired,
will be one day like a copperplate.
                    Oh, to exercise time, to condemn it to a rhythm
whose stases the eye can glimpse and where poetry can cast
(in this age of transition) its aerial net, miraculous
draught of the dangerous truths of fact, rhetoric, epiphany
of what appears in time and space and does not live to itself alone
in this concreteness, and yet with undoubted weight.
                    You rascals,
surly-coloured hangings and arabesques which serve as your
background, and a head
of a Moon on the Rialto, and from that little calcined world
I seek to gain counsel, and I see *you* again – o speak – but what else
remains
of you: only leaves and scrolls frequent my spirit, Dorilla.

Famous knights and unhappy lovers with lute and sword, and now
Harri and Doctor Luck enter from the wings, and the strumpet cat
prowls in the library.
                    Invisible Oberon, in excelsis
be glory, and kyrie at the transformation, and praise for your merry
ambiguity: these volumes have been floating over the lake for centuries.
                    Every night. And at midsummer the moon drags herself along
like an animal, undulant, padding, and the wanton she-cat
mews in the library, and sank its claws, Dorilla.
                    Damned rascals,
painted there where still only birds dip their wings – and Robin too
comes in
in his wine-coloured sweater – birdwings spread to the wind
and into its bloodstained resurrection. But if the eyes deny reality and
    refuse
to understand in their choosing, then within its scratched pebble heart

reason cannot feed on what makes you true, and the dream hunts us
down from the world's edges, from the floating bed,
where incessant activity urges us to use
the body day after day, as we must, to survive.

There was a man who related how one day this sky, enfolded,
silver-haired,
will be like a copperplate, and you with your flowers at the windows,
with the voice and gesture
of the wooden knight on the stair, with the standing stones and the
busts of elves
under the walnut-tree in the park, o figure, o person, tidings of one
summer, you sang.

And then the last sound: in the dark
the hours of light begin. Oberon sleeps. Let us go out.

Rhiannon

My daughter of the Mabinogion name
Tells me Ayer's Rock is ten times higher than
A house, and she, being seven today,
Would like to see it, especially
To ride there on a camel from Alice Springs.
She also says she wants to be a poet –
Would the vision of that monolith
Stay in her mind and dominate her dreams
As in my mind and dreams these thirty years
There stays the small hill, Allt-y-clych,
The hill of bells, bedraggled with wet fern
And stained with sheep, and holding like a threat
The wild religion and the ancient tongue,
All the defeated centuries of Wales?

On a Painting, 'Sunk Lyonesse', by Rae Richards

Perform is a word of which we forget the singular beauty. Its
meaning is: to furnish forth, to complete, to finish, in a sense
which is influenced by the ideas clustered in the word *form*; so
that *performance* is an enlightening name for one of our richest
activities, rich with extra life.
    R. P. Blackmur

It was to make the words perform
I laboured, and it was to make the paint
Perform you toiled in sea-sunk Lyonesse.

And now we ride the ruffian storm
Of our distress, the world's distress,
By virtue of these words, this paint.

Recalcitrance of paint and words
Is now redeemed, and all the long
Submergence in the labouring seas.
Now we ride out the storm like birds
– Performance of consummate ease
At which we laboured hard and long!

Now we have made our work complete.
Now we have found the lovely form.
Under green arches once more drown
So that our labourings may meet
Where our two languages go down
To find and finish what we form.

The Same Story

(for Rupert Hart-Davis)

Always, it seems, I wanted to tell, compulsive
As that ancient mariner, the same story,
Careless of my listener's response
Or consideration of my own shame or glory.

The same story: the one of which I had intimations
In childhood when a cousin told a lie
And I was beaten for it. Another version
Was war and watching my betters die.

And there were other versions too – that girl,
And perhaps those others, most certainly
The one I loved and most betrayed
By my failure to be anything but me.

But if you know better stories, or truer ones,
I might tell them as fairy-tales for my grandsons.

Thinking to Write an Ode

Thinking to write an ode, to avoid elegy,
And to exceed for once the lyric impulse
As brief and long-lasting as last night's love-making,
To avoid also satire and the desire to tell

You what you already ought to know –
Thinking to write an ode, I thought of my country
Which has been for centuries an elegy,
And where everybody speaks always in lyrics,
And you have to be satirical to keep sane
As we tell each other what we already know –
And then, thinking to write an ode, I thought of love,
And of how the best of love is always somehow elegiac,
Though also brittle and enduring as lyrics,
And in defence against love we resort to satire,
And tell ourselves what we already know.

Thinking to write an ode, I thought of these things,
And thought – are odes impossible in these bloody days?
And told myself what I already know.

On Having My Portrait Painted

(to Rae)

I

I sit, trying to look nonchalant,
As if I'm used to being a painter's model,
As if I'm paid or famous or beautiful,
And as I sit, while your small skilled hands
Make only a painting out of me, I am
Abashed, not only at my own inept
Pickers and stealers, but at my indolence,
So often satisfied only to think of poems.
In the mirror I see a face
You have not seen in any place.

II

Another sitting: and now it's you complain,
'Your eyes aren't right. There's something wrong
About your mouth.'
                    My eyes were never right
To see the colour and happiness of the world;
My mouth was always twisted into wrongness.
Still your patient labouring hands transform
Them into something rich and strange.
But though I'd recognize it anywhere
In the mirror I see a face
You have not seen in any place.

III

Now I am hanging on the wall, the owl
Reminds me that our only wisdom
Is to know the labour and the love we put
Into our making. I have seen you work,
And now each day can see what you have made.
And this contents me. I do not need to ask
What does this portrait show of me to the world.
    In the mirror I see a face
    No one has seen in any place.

A Rule of Three Sum Wrong

(*for Ivor*)

' . . . a rule of three sum *wrong*, thus: As the sweet smell to those
kind people so the Welsh landscape is NOT to the Welsh.'

    – G. M. Hopkins on 'In the Valley of the Elwy'.

No, the landscape never sweetened us,
Nor all our mouthings brought us nearer God.
But where those windy generations trod,
Archaic fathers nearly anonymous,
Their poor paths chapelled and precarious
Between defeat and dogma, their old God
Was waiting with his necessary rod
To show them heaven is high and dangerous.

What waits now in the historic rain
For those who've left the language and the land?
Only the heart's willingness to understand
The centuries' inalienable refrain –
What God has spared you from his powerful hand
Is never yours to lose or find again.

Sea-faiths

'Till all our sea-faiths die'
                    – Dylan Thomas

In countries where no sea-faiths were
I would not wish to live,
Nor would I have my love
Walk in any but a spindrift air.

In countries where no rip of tides
Or battering of waves
Threatens, whatever moves
Moves behind dusty palisades

Where no sea-faiths exalt, exult
Mermaid and merryman
To salt devotion
In the waters' praise and lilt.

In countries where no sea-faiths were
My love would wither,
Death and the dust together
Take what came from glory and the water.

Let kiss be sacrifice and prayer
Now, that we never come
To any dusty doom
In countries where no sea-faiths are.

Money

The bauble and glint and glitter of it,
The tickle and slide and slime of it,
The greasiness and the glide of it,
The fingered coins, the crackling notes,
The guile and ghastliness of it,
The need and nastiness of it,
The suave seductiveness of it,
The way its name sticks in our throats –
How pleasant it is to have money, said Clough.
I'll settle for having merely enough.

Doubloons, moidores, guineas, pence,
Pecunia, half-crowns, guilders, cents,

Cowrie-shells, lire, or what-have-you?
I have nothing – give me bread.
Dollars and francs and gold réal,
Schillings and shillings and ten-bob notes,
Fivers and favours and – not allowed?
Will we need money when we are dead?
How pleasant it is to have money, said Clough.
I'll settle for having merely enough.

Lost Love, Unwritten Poems

Once I would have fretted, been ill at ease
To think that now your love and loving body
Of old devoted so tenderly to me
Were now another's to do with as he please.

Once I would have fretted in weak discontent
Before the blank despairing of a page
I'd sit and look at or scribble on an age
Unable to write the poem that I meant.

But, praise be, the withering into age
Brings some small mercies, and among them this:
Now an unwritten poem or unkissed kiss
Can stir no more to any sort of rage.

Once I would have fretted and soaked my brow
With sweat over such things.
                    As I do now.

Fall of an Empire

There were omens of course, but mostly unheeded,
And besides nearly always inscrutable
Even to those old mad mouthers who needed
Nothing to tell them that the implacable
Future is already here, was always here,
And that our only courage is our fear.

Now as we listen to the violent hooves
In the rain as intolerable as blood
Only the frailest certainty moves
Us to erect against that flood
A foolish doomed impossible barrier
That only serves to emphasize our fear.

Whatever it was that made us disregard
The omens or fail to read them properly,
The trampling hooves now bring us our reward.
In the smoky light of torches we can see
The axe and iron club swing nearer, near,
And our last comfort is articulate fear.

P is for Poetry

Predicaments of landscape, old despairs,
Roads not taken on for wrong reasons,
And the importunate belly of the sea
– Should these invoke a proper catalogue
Of your and mine lost and invented seasons?

Paradox of language and of love,
What speech had I before you gave me tongue?
Before that and before that was the sea.
The sea gave birth to you, and something else
Spoke from the waters before I was young.

Paragraphs of landscape, seascape, now
Elude me more than any original love.
Ghosts of my guesses flaunt and parade
Where once the possibility of the word
Lurked around, about, and treacherously above.

Paragraphs, paradox, predicaments
– But how should my inadequate language make
Even from landscapes or from love
The one poem to show poems unnecessary
– And that it was for your dear, sea-born sake?

Sonnets at Forty

I

Not bald or impotent yet – should one give thanks
For having come so far with such small loss?
Or whimper that it is a savage cross
To still be walking on such narrow shanks?
Is one proud to still be 'other ranks',
Or envious of those who in the pitch and toss
Have won the ambiguous status of 'the boss'?

Not fair, not fat, but forty – Christ! give thanks,
Boy, that you still can play these wordy games,
And still imagine that your future holds
Impossible girls and better poems and more
Luck than you've ever had before.
Whatever it is your future holds and moulds
You've still the privilege of calling names.

II

That, as Eliot says, was an unsatisfactory
Way of putting it; and after forty years
Of blood sweat toil nightmares and tears,
Of being delinquent and refractory,
Who would not welcome the idea of thirty
More years in which to grow adult,
Learn to write properly, and insult
Those who think only young men should be dirty.
'No, I am not Prince Hamlet' – nor am I Dante.
I'm only making a fuss about being forty.
No marvellous boy, but the only prayer I mean
Is Yeats's: may I wither into truth, be naughty,
Be riper at ninety than I dreamed of at nineteen,
And when I go, be kidnapped in flagrante.

Never Again

Never again I said shall that invader
Come to incite the mutinous provinces
Of my blood: now I can look on women undisturbed.
Never I said, and stammered into silence,
For suddenly I saw your candid eyes.

Country Sentiment

(for Marie)

In country sentiment I said I loved you,
And you were kind enough (if it be kind)
To take the words as literally true.
Now when the circumstance comes back to mind
I am not oversure what I meant
Except that love's my country sentiment.

A Different Idiom

I used to talk in quite a different idiom,
Uncouth but honest, smacking of the earth
And country matters. You could have called it rich
Or quaint or sneered at it as boorish.
Its only merit was it was my own.

Now, this long while in your jealous service
I speak the silken idiom of your court:
Polite, dishonest, smacking of nothing half so much
As wine adulterated or pills made palatable.
It does not call for notice or remark.
I should be thankful that it's not my own.

They Lie

(for Madeleine)

They lie, who tell me love is such
That nothing else would matter
If I could only touch
Her once and love her ever after,
They lie.

They lie, who tell me love is such
It's no more than a matter
Of near enough to touch
Her rightly and then leave her after,
They lie.

They lie – and yet our love is such
That it seems to matter.
And if we do not touch, or if we touch,
Whatever they say after,
They lie.

Not Young Any Longer

The definition of being young
Is not believing in death as something
Personal: death happens to others.
The first whisper, warning, welcome, of age
Is when one says, I too will die.
One gets used to the idea.
                Then suddenly
Your young breasts bring again
The illusion of immortality.

To Michelene

It was that great man Thomas Jefferson
Who said that every travelled man
Asked in which country he would rather live
Would have two answers: my own, and France.

Somehow, as the years went by, I'd twisted
This into the equal truth that every
Civilized man is native to two countries:
His own, and France. It was my boast
Until I wondered if I still believed it.

Then I met you. And know for ever after
That, like the English queen upon whose heart
You'd find engraved the name of a French town,
My heart shall wear for ever now the Welsh
Red dragon tangled in France's lilies.

The Poet Writes on the Imminent Death of His Mistress

Dear, stay a little while that I
May have a further taste of thee;
Tempt me once more, my dear, but not
Into necrophily.

Once more, and then I shall ensure
In verse your immortality,
And, left alone to live, find
Some body else for me.

Poem for My Daughters

Be dancers first: go gay
Through the great solitude
Of being human; do not brood
On those dark figures that intrude
On the bright pattern of your day.

Be lovers next: go free
Of that rich world of senses
Whose each munificence
Defeats the least pretence
That joy's impossibility.

Be human always: go
Through the bright days and the dark days
So that your going is a praise
For the bright ways and the dark ways
Your mother and your father know.

A Queen's Lover

Invested by you in that royal sleep
I woke to feel the old vexation
That even such love as we know cannot keep
The lineaments of love upon your face
When you go from me to another place.

But with such small things I must be content
After our royal hour of celebration:
What closed eyes, slightly parted lips, meant
In the uncertain morning's light and shade
To the naked victim of your accolade.

And how upon your body I have lain,
Upon your wild heart's perturbation,
Waking to know that I shall never again
Evoke from you that all too human cry
Or you from me that last triumphant sigh.

And when I go now in the common day,
Memory turning to imagination
Already as the passionate dark gives way
To dreaming light, my distant queen, you rise
To other lovers dawning in your eyes.

But this one gift you cannot take from me
As I cannot recover my oblation:
Whenever in the morning light I see
A woman's face beside me in the bed,
I shall remember you though you be dead.

She is Asleep

Sleep recomposes
Your features so that one would not guess
Now in your nude defencelessness
The terror your waking face imposes
Upon your lover:

Terror that he might lose
Through lack of tenderness, through lack of tact,
Through some importunate act,
His dreamed-of, undesired power to choose
Between lover and lover.

Macaronics for Marlene

Mädchen fach, du bist'ne Blume,
Et je t'adore. Black Rhondda hair,
Sliante, cariad, mon amour,
da mi mille basie, deinde centum,
and, Duw, girl, with those eyes,
d'ocche blau, eh, Mia,
come and make us happy in South Wales.

The Panther

In the Jardin des Plantes, Paris
– after Rilke
and for Marlene

So tired his eyes are grown from the bars passing
that they are empty. He feels as if
there were for him a thousand bars
and behind those bars, no world at all.

Pad, subtle pad of soft strong steps
turning, turning in the somnolent circles

at whose centre even purpose is benumbed
a dance of power tethered to a circle's centre.

From time to time the curtain of the pupil
lifts silently. Then an image enters,
travels the tense stillness of the limbs.
and comes to an end in the still point, the centre.

from Brin – Harri

Lovers' Colloquy

She said, 'I do not like my belly,
Too creased with having children.'
And he, 'But if I press my lips
There, see, the creases vanish.'
And she, 'But not my children.'
Then he asked, looming above her,
'Dear, what do you want?'
And hardly heard her answer Yes.

Are There any Modern Poets?

(*for Madeleine*)

Mimic, you called me, and said I had that comic
Gift, and I was pleased with what I took to be
A compliment, and all the while my heart –
Romantic property – was ill at ease
Feeling that it belonged to a tragic hero,
Doomed to a doomed love, – and so I said
'Heart, stop beating; a modern poet
Doesn't write that sort of poetry' – and my heart
Told me that I am an old-fashioned poet
Writing over and over again, My love.

You

Your small voice frightens me,
it has such power to shake
me out of whatever fit
of meanness or despondency
I've once again succumbed to.
Your small voice and your honest eyes
compel me to the writing of poems
because the only thing I want
is the enchanting comfort of your bed.

Lovers' Quarrel

It was bound to come; and I grew
Murderous, and your shouting broke in screams.
And then the shame and readjustment,
Body clinging to body, teaching
That this is love if there be love.

The Poet is a Bastard Just Like Other People

'I love my husband too.' How many wives
Have said so, plaintive, pathetic,
Or defiant. But I've learned
Not to speculate on people's lives
Or wonder too much who is being buried
When I make desperate efforts to be poetic.

A Question of Responsibility

You said, 'All those bloody poems
That somebody might misinterpret, make you seem
Cynical, despairing – oh I don't know
The words for what I want to say, but not
At all like the lost little boy I love.'
But, darling, how could I have written them
If I'd not seen you naked on our bed?

The Lover Shows How Conventional He Is

For I would give you
Parrots of memory, peacocks of desire,
The brawling sparrows of love,
Gulls in their grace, and hawks at height,
All birds of day and night,
A paradise of birds, for you, my bird,
To be uncaged in – that I might come
And snare you and put you in
My brand-new cage.

In love matters, country matters,
This is a very ancient rage.

Waiting for You

(to Madeleine)

Waiting for you
Was waiting only: in the stretch and stress
Of those long minutes, how could I guess
That now, impenitent,
I still should bless
The time I spent
Waiting for you?

A Love Poem, Perhaps

Under this sky, and this compulsion,
Bewildered, too late now, I lie
Revoking emblems or provoking signs
To show that, in spite of your compassion,
I am human enough to die,
– False end to all your true designs.

Does this mean anything? Does this mean
After all your pity and your passion
And the condescension of my art
There was some purpose in our usual scene?
That though we loved each other in our fashion
We did not guess how this could break the heart?

Under the compulsion of this sky
I put these questions, not to you, for you
Would answer in a different way,
And tell me, tell me, that I lie, I lie
Although my words are desperately true.
I hope you come to tell me so today.

Simply the Chance

Simply the chance
Of seeing you can so disturb me now
That I wonder how
I ever thought only the young can love
Or that I would never learn to dance.
Because of you I am again in love,
And you have taught me how to dance,
And the chance of seeing you disturbs me now,
Simply the chance.

Anniversary

An anniversary poem you said: what should
I celebrate except the simply astonishing fact
That you love me, that we have been in that dark wood
Where the dark dream's translated to bright fact
And even beggars know that this is good.

Beggars – that word – perhaps you would apply
It to me in other rhymes, but not, I hope,
To any other fool who'd rather die
At the end of his own sufficient rope
Than say, as I do, I want to lie, I lie.

It turns, as anniversaries usually do,
Into a strange fashion of forsaking.
I am yours, yours, to do or not to do
Whatever the pattern of our undertaking
To do or not do what we want to do.

And so what can I do but lie for you,
Lie, lie, hoping not to be forsaken,
Hoping that somehow I'll still be able to do
That which means love is not to be untaken
When there's nothing in the bed but me and you.

Sick with Requited Love

Whether upon his own dishevelled bed,
Waking to the sweat upon his pillow,
His flung arm encountering nobody there,
That loyal fever would have driven him then
To rise, take pen and paper, and write to you
Better poems in that hour of longing
Than will ever be provoked by the piety
He feels for the satisfying nightmare
He shares with you now as he shares your bed.

The Welshman in Exile Speaks

(for Brin)

Being a boy from the hills, brought up
Believing that fornication is a sin,
Adultery abomination, what should I do
But fornicate until I'm caught, and then
Commit adultery in my dreams. *My* dreams
– You have to plough the furrows I have ploughed,
Or pick the stones off the bitter fields
Before they're fit for ploughing, all day, all day,
Or lift potatoes until your back is breaking,
And then go home to the grudged candlelight
And the green bacon – you want your childhood
Spent like that – and with the compensations:
An old man's voice like something out of Daniel
Making the Belshazzars of the tractors tremble,
Hills, like Mam's breasts, homely and tremendous,
Schooled wildness of sheepdogs, ponies stubborn
As myself, and each winter's killing snow,
And the capel, God in a little bwthin
Once whitewashed – but God in the voices
Of the mean, the crippled, the green bacon eaters,
The lead me beside still waters buggers, the wild boys,
The sin-eaters, and the godly daughters,
All of them suddenly in unison
In the ugliest building I have ever seen
– Pisgah I shall never see again –
All suddenly bursting – not bursting,
All suddenly startled into song, to praise
The god of fornication and the world we lived in.

Boyo, if you come from a country like that
You can talk to me of sin and related matters.

Lines for Marion

On the Occasion of her Graduation and her Twentyfirst Birthday

I

There is, we say, nothing extraordinary
In being a bachelor of arts, a girl
Of twenty-one, nothing at all
To pay attention to – and then
We look at you, and we know that to be
A bachelor of arts and twenty-one
Is everything.
        You could call this sentimental
– But would even a sentimental lecturer write
A poem for his favourite student
If he didn't think that somehow she deserves it.

II

The swans are still there on that lake at Coole,
And the herons stalking under Sir John's Hill,
And the white whale spouting in tremendous seas.
Marion, my student, if you'll now take these
Remembrances from me for good or ill,
I'll be content to think that even a fool
Like me may be remembered by you still
When this lost traveller sleeps under the hill.

The Moods of the Sea

The moods of the sea I celebrate
Early, late, in all my sunken voices,
When the maw of the marrying wave rejoices,
Or when its treachery lies sedate,
All moods, all colours, blue, white, green, slate,
These are the matters of my celebration,
The moods and colours of all generation,
Fountain of birth and of man's glaucous fate.

Moods of the sea reveal our monstrous wish
To sleep forever to that lullaby
That rocks the whiteness of albatross and whale,
Desire fostered by the seabirds' cry
To admit that we are born of water and that we fail
Until we die and worship with the fish.

Illicit Colloquy

She: Thief.
He: But I would not steal
    Anything but your affections.
She: Do you not feel
    That your thievery casts reflections
    On both of us?
He: Oh, yes.
She: Then –
He: then, why do you allow
    Me to enjoy those sweets I am enjoying now?

Lines by a Not Too Dejected Lover

'Go home, and write poems,'
         – Flecker's *Hassan*.

So I went,
Frowning and muttering my discontent.

Had I stayed
And my body on your body laid,

Would you have missed
This, or any poem, as we kissed?

But you made
The order, and I foolishly obeyed.

Disconsolate
Now I sit and write; and you may wait

A long time now,
Creasing your once immaculate brow,

Before I grant
You poems or kisses or anything you want.

Easy to say
This while I am angry and you so far away.

But if you came
And touched me, murmuring my name,

You could not miss
To claim a poem from me or a kiss

Or whatever
Else you might lovingly endeavour

To obtain
Before you proudly sent me home again.

Tonight, in bed,
Remember me, and what we both have said.

She Bit Me, But Not In Anger

As malefactors once were branded, so
I hoped your bites would stay upon my body
That the whole envious world might know
This was my guerdon when I served you nightly.

But not even the deepest or the sharpest bite
Leaves marks that stay much longer than a day.
And those who know my body in the night
Are wilfully ignorant of our warring play.

And when, alone, I look at this forked thing
Which is my body, I can see the scars
Crisscrossing it, and call myself a king
Wounded and valiant in love's civil wars.

King, malefactor – so that you only bite
Me, brand me, love me as you did tonight.

Keeping Chooks

a Genuine Australian Folk-Song

I had a cock, and he was tall,
        My lady loved him dearly,
He'd rise to answer to her call
        Either late or early
With a Cockadoodle, how d'you do,
You love this, and I love you.

I had a cock, and he was red,
        My lady liked the colour,
She often thought when in her bed
        That life would be much duller
Without a Cockadoodle doo,
And she loved this, and I did too.

I had a cock, and he would stand
    At any hour of day or night
Proudly in my lady's hand
    Or even in her sight
For she would cockadoodle doo
With him or me or even you.

I had a cock, I have him still,
    My lady loves him even more,
She cannot find the heart to kill
    The cock – but she'd adore
Another Cockadoodle doo
To cherish dearly – wouldn't you?

Self-Criticism

Accused of, praised for, being an erotic poet,
I have my moments of self-questioning:
Even if we grant that all versifying
Is trivial and unnecessary, still
Shouldn't the poet occupy his time and ours
With serious matters? Then I recall
An old Mesopotamian scandal –
If Adam hadn't been erotic with Eve's
Connivance there'd be no need to write
Poems of any sort. Perhaps I'm serious
After all in writing always on this simple theme:
You, me, and what we do at night.

Love, Poetry, and Middle Age

Poets have written much about love's madness,
And much of this was mere convention, granted,
But still convention can embody truth,
And what sane man has ever wanted
His age to duplicate the joy and sadness
Love brought him in his youth?

But it happens, and it's not much use to blame
The poets – some of them have suffered too.
All this I tell you in an offhand way.
Perhaps it's lust, I add – then you:
'I am indifferent to the choice of name;
I'm glad you're here today.'

And I am helpless as any antic lover
In a conventional sonnet, mad again,
Only it's worse now than it was before
Because now there's the additional pain
That though you can me back to life recover
I haven't all of life again

In which to be as happily tormented.
I can expect now only a few scant kisses
Compared with even twenty years ago.
But the man who's not in love so – what he misses,
However much he thinks himself contented,
Lovers and poets know.

Recovering From You

Recovering from you, taking
My bitter medicine, I said,
No, not again that fever and that fret,
And then remembered that love brings
Not only fever but also
This unimaginable peace.

Two Coffee Cups

Two coffee cups as paradigm
Of two who would be one in bed –
We were oblivious of the time
And hardly conscious what we said.
The machine's contrapuntal hiss
Seethed in the cauldron of our kiss.

That kiss that like the coffee cups
We could not take but looked instead
With unintended downs and ups
Into our eyes which spelled out bed.
And felt the table melt away
Till there was nothing left to say.

Nothing to say, or do, about
Two coffee cups upon a table.
We paid our money and went out,
Willing and utterly unable
To reach love's right true end,
Scorning to call each other friend.

And now two coffee cups can seem
More than two cups, even more
Than what we hardly dared to dream
When we walked through the swinging door.
Coffee itself can symbolise
The desperate urgency of eyes.

Two cups, the same, and yet apart,
Together and terribly alone,
So obviously your heart, my heart,
Your flesh, my flesh, your bone, my bone.
Now I have nothing but this word
Which only you have overheard.

Tribute to Rae Richards' Painting of Leda and the Swan

I

Our Greek imaginations kept the story
For centuries until we saw or heard
The coupling of the woman and the bird
As the beginning of whatever glory
May blaze out sometimes from our sorry
Bodies in love or war – the poet's word,
The painter's line and colour, had so stirred
Us, Leda was our loveliest memory.

But that was in the North: here in the South
I have seen the black swan stalled above
Leda's surrendered body, and his mouth
Holding her helpless for the impulse of love.
Now that my other images are gone
I would be only that black swan.

Disorganized

Disorganized,
And by a woman again,
I try to bring myself
To concentrate on something proper,
Work, family, or even poems,
Only to find that all I am doing
Is murmuring, murmuring your name.

Love is Different From What You Think it is

Love should have been as harsh and challenging
As the landscape of my childhood, rough
With winds, worn away with rain,
Haunted by ghosts of old defeat, livid
With language and a wild religion,
Confident only in a sense of sin.

And love turned out to be
This tender landscape under this blue sky.

Homage to Robert Graves

(after reading his 'Symptoms of Love')

Long dedicated to the service of the goddess
In whatever womanly guise she came to me,
I spent many sleepless nights complaining
That, despite my loyalty,
My poems still seemed rough, inadequate.
Now the example of your long servitude
Rewards me with the hope
That one day she will smite me too.
So I turn urgently towards this woman.

Epigram

Girls were betrayed by men in the old stories,
– Except the oldest one of all.
Can we count it one of our modern glories
We're back to the procedure of the Fall?

Acceptance of Fate

To have been content with ordinary things,
A garden, say, and quiet love –
Sometimes one sighs for such an impossible fate.

Then the exhilaration of your storm,
Its following exhaustion –
I can only live and die
Thus discontented on your furious breast.

Can It Be So Long?

Can it be so long – twenty four hours
Since you touched me last, and your touch
Established in me such a madness
That I swore that this was truly love
For the first time – how can it be so long
When I can still taste on my bitten tongue
Nothing but you, and see here on my shoulder
Bruises, bite-marks on my breast?

Surely it was only moments ago
You put your clothes on, laughed goodbye,
And left me – only moments ago
Or a whole lifetime.

Restless

Restless, I rose
And walked out at some shivery hour
After midnight, hoping to exorcize
Whatever it was that would not let me sleep.

The silent streets, the sleeping houses,
Soothed me, and the distant sea.

Then insolently from behind a cloud
The moon appeared.
               Helpless, I turned
Back to my restless bed, knowing
That while you rule me and I wait
For your inevitable stroke
I cannot even hope to wish for peace.

Love in the Antipodes
(for Stephanie)

And this preposterous inversion
Of seasons – at Christmas I was burned,
And now in May I think of lighting fires.
But there's something to be said
From the confusion that's a consequence

Of crossing the equator – living half
In the ancestral hemisphere, and half
In this incredible one, even a poet
May be forgiven for assuming
That there's one season only:
Bittersweet spring, the season of love.

In Love

(for Stephanie and Ivor)

To be in love – this is to suffer
Pains of absence, strains of being together,
To wake alone and sweating with a sense of loss,
To be subject to sudden startles
When you see in a crowded street
A curl, a shoulder's movement,
Or a way of walking, that you think
Might be hers – though it never is.

To be in love is to be given
Keys to kingdoms of delight and terror,
To be other than your ordinary self,
To be always in amazement.

To be in love is a hard thing to bear,
A wrench, a dislocation of your life,
– And the inevitable desired fate
Of a man like you meeting a woman like her.

No Name But Love

And you invite me to your bed.
How should I react? With terror,
Delight, mere animal expectancy?
– No, none of these, or all of these,
Adding up in love's arithmetic
To something more than all of these,
Something for which we have no name but love.

From the French of Pemette de Guillet

To content him who thus torments me,
I wish no remedy for my tormenting:
Seeing that my ill-fate contents him,
I am content in his contenting.

The Ship Sonnet

(after Petrarch)

My ship goes, laden with forgetfulness,
On a winter midnight through the rough sea
Between Scylla and Charybdis; and he who steers
Her is my lord, but more my enemy.
At every oar's a cruel thought and ready
To tempest-toss her to end in mockery.
A sighing wind of hope and of desire,
A wet wind, rips her sails unceasingly.
Rainfall of tears in disdaining clouds
Washes and slacks already tired shrouds
Twisted from yarn of ignorance and error.
Both my sweet seamarks, my reason and my skill,
Are hidden, dead to me, in the waves' terror:
Despair of harbour already infects my will.

Tribute to Rae Richards' Painting of Leda and the Swan, II

When that great girl lies down to cool her thighs
On the expectant riverbank, her breasts
Uptilted to the sky, while her bottom rests
On the cold earth that comforts as she lies,
What image in those greedy, half-shut eyes
Twitches and tickles her lithe contours till
She feels it is impossible to lie still,
And does not see the bird as down he flies.

And when his blackness spreads apart her knees,
His sharp bill holds her helpless under the thrash
Of his impetuous wings while he invades
Her as she sobs and stammers Please,
Responding to his plumed and rhythmic lash
Till even the sun into swan's darkness fades.

In Despite of John Milton, or,
What Adam Probably Said to Eve

Pluck me an apple, darling,
    Off that special tree,
And when you've plucked it, pare it
    Before you share with me.
And when you share, be sure
    I get the bigger half,
Or else I'll have to teach you
    Whipped bottoms do not laugh.

Pick now some fig-leaves, darling,
    And cover up that part
Which but a little while ago
    Made me stand and start,
But now looks so disgusting
    I think I'll found a church
Purely to make nakedness
    Liable to the birch.

Take off my fig-leaves, darling,
    Now we are in bed,
And wrap your loving fingers
    Round your dear pride instead.
Now that we are married
    And wear our clothes by day,
At night we may be naked
    Whatever He may say.

And share our loving apples
    As we share our bed,
So long as you remember
    That I alone am head
And ruler of this family.
    Open now your knees
To let your master enter.
    – Damn you, darling, please.

Wales-New South Wales. May 1961

Autumn was always cold, and so was spring,
In the country that I remember for ever
Despite this sun and despite whatever

Landfall luckily after my voyaging.
In that land it was always a hard faring
For men contracted to a brute endeavour
By their great taskmaster to what would never
Be more than a thin and bitter harvesting.

But here the sun is warm on belly and back
As I indulge in wine and memories
And hear above the long Pacific swell
Stern voices of my fathers saying I lack
Their faith, their courage, their black certainties,
And everything they knew of Heaven and Hell.

If This Is Love

If this is love, to feel in absence
The terrible necessity of being together,
To feel in togetherness the more
Terrible hopelessness of being apart;
To shudder shamefully at the thought
Of anyone else touching you even innocently;
To be envious of your mirror that looks back
So often into your eyes; envious of your bed
That so often takes the impress of your softness;
To be tremulous walking down any street
In case those hips disappearing round
A corner should be yours; to jump
When the telephone rings because
It might bring your voice; to wake
Alone in the middle of the night
Crying your name: if this is love
Then I suppose I am in love indeed.
And what more could you want from me?
If this is love, then I am your lover.

Gratuitous Advice to Aging Poets

You have to be forty and half impotent
Before you can believe in glorifying
That sweet act with which you were content
Before the need arose of magnifying.

A Sort of Love Poem

Boasting merely of the bodily contact
He made the thump and slump of his body seem
An incorrigible animal act
Which never really measured to his dream.

This other, boasting of finer attitudes,
The delicate way he had of cherishing,
Made women only mirrors of his moods,
While for the act itself he was not perishing.

I would be neither of these men – I mean
I would be both of them: give you my body
Willingly when you choose, or wean
Me when you like to love you abstractly.

But let me boast in either case, that I
Loved you too much to boast of loving you.
Bodies or not, I only want to lie
And do whatever it is you want to do.

Adam, Thoughtfully, To Eve

Half awake, I heard you murmur to my side,
And half awake I turned to you, and then
All the great trumpets sounded, and you sighed
Your dear command to do the deed again.
And if my upright passion had not died
In you, how could there have been other men
For other women to turn to half awake
To love them so, as I do for your sake?

Chambermaid's Song

They were tidy and unrumpled,
The beds I never made
In the days when I was dreaming
Of the game that we have played.
And now untidy sheets
And crumpled pillows make
Me sick with longing
– And all for your sake.

Fireworks Night

A rocket soars, explodes, and dies away
And I turn helplessly to you to say
Something, as usual inadequate,
And, as usual too, I am too late,
For you are watching in the bonfire's glow
Somebody else who might have loved you so.

Any Husband to any Wife

Waiting for you in coffee-rooms, in bars,
In public libraries or art galleries,
At bus stops, or on always windy corners;
Waiting with rising impatience in bed
While you fiddle with your hair, put powder on,
Or think about some problem of tomorrow;
Or even waiting for you to leave the bathroom,
Or to choose between two identical cabbages,
Or for your next inevitable change of mind:

Some statistician doubtless could compute
The percentage of my allotted span so far
That I have spent waiting for you:

But only I can tell you, and I can not,
How well spent I've spent the time
Waiting for you.

Nightmare

Terror: nightmare: and my crawling skin,
My risen hackles and my sweating hands
To remind me that I can never
Be truly unafraid or innocent.
I shudder into waking: what unjust goddess
Pursues and persecutes me so? Groaning,
I open my reluctant, gummy eyes,
And see only the usual untidy bedroom
And the reassurance of your sleeping presence,
And calm myself into the day's decisions.
But in the night, though you lay by my side
And slept your beautiful contented sleep,

The hag was riding me, as she will do
Until, dissatisfied with my paltry offerings
Of poems and terrors like these, she'll come,
Naked, insatiable, to ask for her last tribute,
And I shall shudder to her and my death.

Jealousy

No, I am not jealous, I said
In our disdain of being ordinary;
Then saw, between us in the bed,
Merely in the way you turned your head,
That rigid interloper between you and me.

Not jealous, because you've shown
Me over and over again
That you love me and me alone.
But still I see that other, prone
Beside us as you claim me for your own.

Jealousy would be a terrible thing
I think as I invite your arms.
Then, even as the tremendous anvils ring,
I hear another ride and sing,
And jealously I turn to you from jealousy's harms.

Perplexed

Perplexed as always by your absence
I evoke the transitory triumph
Of your smile, and my blood cataracts
For a naked and impossible vision.
Woman, asleep in your contented bed,
Do you, safe in your beauty, know or care
That because of you I spend these sleepless nights,
By your absence continually perplexed?

Urgency

Urgency was what I always felt with you,
The importunate need of being closer together,
The impossible demand to defeat mere

Momentariness, to enjoy for ever
The pulsing richness of your summer season.
Even my ghost will go urgently
Across the pallid pastures to meet your ghost,
And in an echo trembling with impatience
Make again impossible demands, urging
That love be not a matter of seasons, nor
Subject to limits, especially them,
Bound to our incorporeality.

Between Nightmare and Nightmare

Walking between nightmare and nightmare
I have grown accustomed to being tense
Against what unexpected violence
Love or not-love may demand I bear.
And though you make of me your nightly care,
Your arms around me as loving evidence
That such proximity is our best defence
Against the terrors of nightmare and nightmare,
My guilt is closer to me even than you.
Witness this startled hair, these shaking hands,
That when I am incautious and relax
In sleep, I am taken by treacherous bands
And in just flames am melted down like wax
– Between nightmare and nightmare I am tense with you.

There Are Some Connections Between
Life and Literature

Once I read Donne to you, and was undone.
And now we only read when we have done.

Heloise, being read to by Abelard,
Suddenly felt even learning could be hard.

How do I love thee? asked Elizabeth.
And Robert answered her, Unto the death.

Pope, being polite, couldn't really hunt
A rhyme for his dear friend, Miss Martha Blount.

Byron had to admit about his sister
That even in other women's beds he missed her.

Wordsworth abjured his French frivolity,
And lived – somehow – with sister Dorothy.

John Keats with a venereal affection
Thought about Fanny with a dear dejection.

Yeats, unable to endure the amorous cries,
Found some content between somebody's thighs.

Oscar, reaching the bottom of a page,
Reminded Oscar of the Athenian sage.

And, rolling in the heather, Robert Burns
Found bonnie lassies lying down in turns.

I ask you, what's the point of poetry,
If poets are the same as you and me.

Now That I Love You Truly

Now that I love you truly, I can tell
You, or confess or boast I tell, the half-truths
Which were sufficient until I loved you truly.

Such as these: wilful retreat into nightmare,
Remembered horrors of remembered seas;
Or by contrast a legendary landscape
Contoured by language and by love;
Or the abandon of being one's own Circe.

But now I can be content in being – not
Myself, but what you take to be myself,
Abandon nightmare as I abandon hope
Surrendering at last to your insistence
That I do not love you until I love you truly.

Ruth Myfanwy

Being the youngest of a poet's three daughters
You have this much luck, that you are nearly seven
Before your father turns his verses on you.
Will you, when you are seventeen, say, or twenty-seven,
Be resentful of your sisters who had more poems?

Will you say, 'Thank God, he left me alone'?
Or, 'Poor father, he really couldn't help It'?
Or even perhaps turn poet yourself,
And write impossible stuff like this
Called On being the daughter of a poet?
Or merely invert Ben Jonson's phrase
And boast, 'I am my father's best poem'?

At least I wrote a poem when I named you
Ruth Myfanwy out of the Bible and Wales.

Ulysses in Ithaca

Debts, sick children, your own morning cough,
Penelope still faithful, as you have to be:
Do these justify the sudden sulkiness
That takes you because when you are shaving
You see in the mist over the mirror
The islands of ten good years, the girls
Who would not want to play with you now?

In This Degenerate Age

To have this at least in common with Solomon:
Not wisdom certainly, but to be prone
To this disturbance when a virgin,
Probable or improbable, sidles
That look at my hoary and distinguished
Hairs.
        But times have changed. No doubt
We are less mighty men now in the bed.
A mere half-dozen women last any of us moderns
More than a lifetime.
                I console myself
That even Solomon had but the one Sheba,
And in that at least I do as well as he did.

Who'd Be an Erotic Poet, Anyway?

Waking with the taste still of your nipples
In my mouth, I groan and stretch my empty arms,
Remembering too well I have a member,
And rise reluctantly to write a poem.

Mr Jones As The Transported Poet
(*for Gwen*)

'And how do you react to exile?' Politely
They ask; and remnants of my country courtesy
Make me answer politely, meaninglessly.

I say, 'Of course, a poet is in exile
Anyway, always.' And that 'of course' disarms,
Undoes them. They are politely satisfied
There was something they always knew about poets.

Or I say, putting on a bit more accent,
And of course prefacing what I have to say
With that disarming and dishonest 'of course',
I say, 'Of course, we Welshmen are exiles
Just as much in England as Australia.'
And they nod understandingly and smile politely,
And think I didn't really understand the question.

How could I tell them, politely or impolitely,
That the only exile is from her bed,
From that visionary and impossible moment
When our customary involvement made
A sudden meaning we had not known before?

Exile, like love, is a word not to be lightly said.

Outrageous

Outrageous – I didn't even use the word,
Nor would have used it had I not met
Somebody who was more outrageous yet
Than I who didn't dare to use the word.

Drunk on Duty

Drunk on duty, not for the first time,
Private Ianto stands limply at attention,
Thankful that though being unable's a crime
At least it can't be punished by detention.

A Confusion of Bright Women

It was a confusion of bright women troubled
Me this morning between sleeping and waking,
The jargon of their names making a twittering
In my head and their too well remembered bodies
Making in mine the usual disturbance.

Olwen, and Blodwen, Mary, Jane, and Anne,
Megan and Deborah and Marguerite,
Came back like ghosts to stir my ghostly blood.
All honest housewives now, or maybe dead,
Though still for me causing this bright confusion.

And some indeed were daughters of the swan,
And others, though not beautiful, were merry girls.
Their hair of different colours, and their eyes.
Go from me now, trilling your tender names,
Forgotten girls I once was glad to know.

One had a mole like Imogen, and one
Was witty even in the morning, and one
Would sulk for hours, rejecting kisses.
How am I tangled still in those endearments
Murmured to your sweet and bygone names.

Comfort myself against this bright confusion
In this uncertain time between sleeping and waking.
If I should call you by some other name,
What matter so that I hold you rightly
And make this poem for you, only for you?

Llanafan Unrevisited

I took for emblem the upland moors and the rocky
Slopes above them, bitter parishes
Of the buzzard striking from lonely circles
And the ragged fox hunting the lean
Rabbits, and the starved preacher nourishing
A little heat from a hell that once had meaning.
I had thought to be a proud man and isolated,
Inviolate as my hills even in defeat,
Not easily marked even by the incessant
Savagery of weather, God, and my relations.

Small, maybe, but tough I thought and unendearing
As feg and able to endure weather
That smashes the great oaks and makes mud
Of the good meadows and destroys good men.

And now I live in the good meadows, and I have
No emblem except your body, and I am
Still a member of a narrow chapel, and a boy
From a hungry parish, a spoiled preacher,
Greedily taking the surplus of your sunshine,
And still afraid of hell because I've been there.

Adam's Song After Paradise

(to A. D. Hope)

And I remember how I named
The innocent beasts that came to me
And God said what I did was good
And for reward created thee
Torn from my side and fashioned fair
To be my hope and my despair.

How I have lapsed from innocence
Since first we lay and were as one
So that we now do furtively
The deed in open joy begun
And beg the favour of the night
To cover us from our delight.

And shall I blame thee? Shall I blame
Seductiveness of hair and eyes
The promised welcome of your breasts
The long allurements of your thighs,
Say are these blazons of my shame
And know the heartbreak of your name?

I take again your guilty hand
I look into your candid eyes
And am content that I have lost
That half-regretted Paradise
To win your human smiles and tears
To comfort my declining years.

The Mirror of Herself

(for Jill)

'And Eve made air a mirror of herself' – Wallace Stevens
'Notes towards a Supreme Fiction'

We are descended in more senses than one
From that bright mirror-making myth,
Comic inheritors of a tragic fault,
And the air is blue about us everywhere.
How fair she was whose daughters are so fair.

This you might think is the merest allegory
For some casual encounter of the flesh,
A sharpening of my wits on some bright bone
To disentangle images from hair
And praise her darkly whom I find most fair.

And yet – the blue mirror is a very fact,
And I am conscious of her dear descent
Reflected in my serio-comic eyes
As well as in the circumambient air
Informing us and her that she is fair.

And so give thanks for the original
Making the air a mirror of herself
And carelessly preparing our descent.
Praise be for fallen beauty everywhere,
Daughters and rivals of that original fair.

Exile

'And all his years of exile fell away' – A. D. Hope, 'Man Friday'

He had been long away; too long, too long
For breasts to be maternal any more;
Or for that repeated shuddering on the shore
To be the source now of his practised song.
He could let the old artificer beat his gong,
And shut his own ears; let the old whore
In through the discretion of the deacons' door,
– And recognize he'd been away too long.

But then you came, to brighten the bright day,
And he forgot about exile and being lonely,

And thought on the generosity of your breast,
Where he had at last found proper rest,
That he had been away a short time only,
And all his years of exile fell away.

I Gave You Roses Once

I gave you roses once – do you remember
How they were more than roses? do you remember
How you watched them wilt, as later you watched
Me walk or wither out of your life?

One can be sentimental after all
– Especially as that self-conscious line's designed
To show, sentimental in the tough,
Ironic manner, sentimentally
Mocking one's own sentimentality.

Still – I remember that I gave you roses
Once, and you were more than usually pleased
With me, as I am more than usually pleased
Now to remember that once I gave you roses.

Verbalist

It is the verbalist in me concedes
That love is not to be destroyed by words
Despite the impediments that we admit,
Being not so single-purposed as those birds
That mate in the blue emptiness of air.
Lacking in pride, we must make do with wit
To salvage from the bedwreck of our deeds
Whatever unity we hope to share
From this compounding of passion and despair.

Let me then remain part verbalist
At least, if only enough to indicate
To interested parties that we would not love
At any lesser or less dangerous rate,
Our virtue being in our infirmity.
We may not couple in that heaven above,
We may not have there for antagonist
These words which lend a little dignity
To our bedreckoned, bedfound duality.

Nor would there seem to be necessity
To keep the verbalist in me apart
From the swaggering funambulist
Swaying above the plaudits of your heart
And only sorry when the act is done.
You did not ask for words when first we kissed
Though since you've had some superfluity.
Our war of words and love is lost and won
In the same bed where it has just begun.

A Woodland Walk

Lost in the curls and tendrils of your forest
I erect a tangible monument
To all such walking trees who trembled too
On realising what the impulse meant
That sent them to stumble or tremble in the end
In demonstrating even tall trees bend
At last and lie completely overthrown
Until you rear them once more for your own.

A Thought

I said I did not mean to make you jealous.
– But how could I be sure of your love unless
You could be so provoked to jealousy?
Now we are equal too in this – we both
Itch where we both can scratch. Perhaps
This means we really love each other.

The Gold Clarity Of This Moment

Observe the gold clarity of this moment,
And ask, inveterate questioner, how much
Of this is sheerly there, how much is
The impact of the external on five
Uncertain receptors – is that colour there,
That gold invitation of her hair?
Or the astonishing blue welcome of her eyes?
This tenderness I touch, does it exist?
Or those low sounds I hear, this heady
Inhalation, or this tang I taste?

Ask in the gold clarity of this moment
– If you dare – how far these things exist,
How far they are created – if that's the word –
By your own impossible longing.

Epistemology was never my strong point.
Observing the gold clarity of this moment
I know there is only one way in which I want
To know you and know we know each other.

A Birthday Poem for Madeleine

It was at first merely the inconvenience
– Children, we thought, would interrupt our love,
Our lovemaking, thwart our careers,
Interfere with plans for foreign travel,
Leave us less money for drink and cigarettes,
And generally be a bloody nuisance.

Then, almost without our noticing it,
There the three enchanters were, and we
Were more in love than ever, and we told
Childless friends to follow our example.

But now – three tall daughters growing taller
Every day – who am I to boast I bear
Such tall and triple responsibility?
I should be frightened, I should run away
To sea, or to some childless woman's arms,
Or to writing poems in a lonely room.

Then I see your smile upon the pillow,
And, forgetting inconvenience, responsibility,
I answer as I can to your sweet asking,
And only hope these girls deserve their mother.

Mr Pope

Mr Pope, full of pain and fine feeling,
Walked down the ordered alleys of his verse,
In precise anguish as he went revealing
Writing and morals go from bad to worse.

He turned in a neat fury of indignation
His wit upon the dunces and their crimes,
Measuring the justice of his commination
In the balanced complexity of his rhymes.

How we could use now his pain and his perfection
When the stupid army's swollen even more,
And literacy has become a means of rejection
Of everything by which Mr Pope set store.

But Mr Pope today would be a personality,
And to the rigid harness of his pain,
Would have, for celebration of his mockery,
To add one monstrous insult, though in vain.

We should rejoice before the curtain falls
That once the ordered walks of Twickenham
Witnessed, despite the slobberings and catcalls
Of the mob, the meditations of this gentleman
Who knew about chaos in his little world,
And stoutly strove as he might against the powers
That have always darkness on darkness hurled
To obliterate Mr Pope's bright vision and ours.

A Birthday Wish for a Painter

Poems about paintings – after Leda, who?
Obscure beginnings lead to – God knows where.
This is intended as a wish for you,
The painter, and the woman, and the fair.

Best Wishes, Happy Birthday, Many Happy Returns,
How they sound trite in verse even more than prose.
But this true wish at least your true art earns,
Let me see many paintings as good as those.

Dear painter, how I stammer after all.
Accept this snobbish substitute for a card.
Paint some more paintings – hang one on my wall
Saying what I wish for you is far too hard.

Except, I wish you simply happiness.
You may want more, but you deserve no less.

Obviously for Somebody

Sprawlheels again, easily on your back,
Darling, you are willing to admit
The penetration of my ready wit,
And although regretting that perhaps I lack
Some qualities, you won't for that attack
Me as inadequate. A litle bit
Of loving – how my metaphors fit
You closely when you lie upon your back.

Spread knees, I come, helpless and standfast,
To where you lie to listen to my lies.
Hold tight, my darling. I am seldom here.
But, in the beckon and challenge of your eyes,
Or even in the feeling that you are near,
This witness stands for you, heart fast, stonefast.

Tutor

(*for Marie*)

Insulting people is so easy, insulting
Persons so difficult; no wonder a mere
– What have you? – tutor, mountebank,
Friend, (this hopefully) – faced again
With twenty partly anonymous faces,
And hopings, after ten years happy
Desperation, somehow, somebody, there
In the uncomfortable seats before me,
Listening to what I fear is only
The gab, the fluent nonsense, given again
With the histrionic gestures, the preacher's
Manufactured *hwyl* – that somebody
Will begin to understand – just hoping
Somebody understands what I mean
By that wild word – and suddenly
I don't have to justify poetry any longer,
Because, out of the corner of my cornered
Eye, I see a face, and talking to that face
Means poetry, and I know, and glow
In the glowing of that face, there are
A few people it is worth insulting.

Lines for the Early Stages of a Love Affair

Not even wanting to be Hercules,
Contented with a tithe of all those girls,
(I wouldn't quibble about the technical term)
– Why do I thrash my bed like this
Because I haven't had *you* fifty times?

You come tomorrow: already I know
How I shall greet you, concealing, or rather
Revealing, my bedward mind in banter,
Stammered welcome and adoration,
And even – God help you – promises of rhymes.

And I will love you for ever and a day
– But please don't ask me to be specific
About next Tuesday – I might feel then,
Twentyfour hours after your return,
It might have been better to be Hercules.

But I am not, and not Don Juan either,
Only a man, in love with you, addicted
To poems, in debt, and fond of drink,
Made, in part, to a classic formula,
– Ovid knew girls like you and nights like these.

Come, darling, listen to my rhymes,
Anticipate tomorrow and prevent
One poem about our Herculean times.
I swear, especially on nights like these,
In loving you I could be Hercules.

Doublecross

'And doublecrossed my mother's womb' – Dylan Thomas

Not only hers: crisscross from the light
That leaped out of my father's eyes
I came to cross you, cross my heart.
A kiss betrays, and in the double night
Doubly, because of you, I die
– And call this doublecrossing art.
Would it have been your, or anybody's, loss
Had you not crossed me to this doublecross?

On the Banks of Some River or Other

I heard the water talking like a woman.
It made me into a tall tree.
Go from me, from us, little fish and birds;
Reach for your own sky, flow to your own sea.

Now that I am a tall tree above this water,
Gone the little fish and birds,
I would give anything if I could only
Understand this woman's words.

An Affair

Devoted – the word was yours. I had said
Distracted. What does the word matter?
Since we both mean we only smile and chatter
Thus because we cannot go to bed
To prove to our mutual satisfaction
From this devotion there is no distraction.

Surprising and Inevitable

Sometimes, when one has almost given up
Trying, the words come suddenly right,
Surprising and inevitable as love,
And to be thankful would be an insult
– Who would dare to say Thank you for the gift
Of breasts, the benediction of your thighs,
Or that surprising and inevitable moment
When the words come suddenly right,
When everything comes suddenly right,
And one will never be lonely or wordless any more?

A Poem for Flowers, Perhaps

Rose uprose, magnificent above
The garden of her love,
Forget-me-not entangled in the thick
Hairs where she is quick,
Foxglove, aromatic, flushed
As we were the first time that we blushed.
Only flowers – not her flowering breasts
Where my love of flowers comes and rests.

Scansion

Persuaded was one way of putting it,
Bullied another – even a poet couldn't
Care about the choice of words, so long
As he could come to where you lay, wordless
And welcoming, to persuade or bully
Him into believing that for a long time
And a quick death he had no need of words
While he scanned, correctly, the rhythm of your breast.

For a Painting of Clea

A girl against a background, holding
In her ignorant curves such promise
Of delight, I am proud to know
Her mother and her painter, and I hope
I live long enough to know this beauty.

Entire

(dedicated to some horsewoman or other)

Touching your flesh, or merely dreaming
Of touching your flesh, I learn the meaning,
Learn it the hard way, of resurrection,
And I stand before you, yours and entire,
Waiting to touch and be touched, to do
That deed for which we have no adequate
Words, but which gives a meaning
To all words, and leaves me entire,
And entirely yours, speaking my words
From there, only from there, and only from you.

Even Fathers Can Be Honest

I had always thought it right and proper
Other men should have beautiful daughters
For men like me to enjoy, and now I look
At my three beautiful ones, and hate
All young men for my selfish sake.

Portrait Gallery

See Davies, who hates his wife because
At least once a week she makes him forget
He is a deacon; see Tomos
Who is married to the old language,
And resentful of everything English, especially
Money, which he needs; see Isaac
Who seems to have an orgasm when he sings;
John Pritchard, the blue-eyed, who looks
As if he takes every woman in the parish;
Bill Beynon, with the accent dropping thick
From his lips as he denies that he is Welsh.

Turn to the women: see Mary Jane, tiny
And eighty, who's had ten children, and milked
The cows immediately before and after
Each birth; see Sarah, who got lost once
On a mountain, and noted for her good works
Ever since; and Megan, who has three children,
Two she thinks may be her husband's, little
Ifor she knows is not; and Miriam,
Who has been going properly to chapel
For fifty years and never understood a word.

Look on this gallery, boy, and wonder
What these, your ancestors, would think of you.

From Whence Cometh My Help

Cloudburst, sunblast, tiderip, bedwrack,
I knew on holy hills, long, long ago.
If I had known then what now I unholily know,
Would I have followed the worn and sheepdropped track
To which I now nostalgically look back
As once in deserts I was starved for snow?
Or would I still say to that lumper, Go,
Boy, out, and down, so, possibly, back?

Improper question. I am what I may be.
I went, out, and down, and here, at last,
To suffer, suffer, over and over again,
That hillborn appetency for pain,
Tiderip, bedwrack, cloudburst, sunblast,
And whatever else is mine ineluctably.

Advertisement

(for Marie)

Fairflesh, used, still wanted. Not for sale,
At least it's credible. Who would believe
Me if I advertised another Eve
Or told some other equally improbable tale?
Then let's be factual: flesh, female,
Made to make a man rejoice and grieve
– Already we are back again with Eve,
And the advertiser's self-condemned as male.

Had we but world enough and time – then, madam,
I could do you justice even in rhyme
Without mocking at myself as Adam
Seeing bewilderedly his wife put on
The lineaments of the approaching time
When Eve and Adam, you and I, are gone.

Glory Be

The disappearance of old honesty
Between us means a new beginning
As we crawl crookedly to maturity,
Learning our lessons as we can from sinning.

A new beginning means a new end.
And there is still for me the promise of glory
When I refuse, refuse to call you friend
And re-enact a very ancient story.

The promise of glory is perhaps as much
As any man can hope for, but I have known
With you, and on you, and for you, such
Love as baffles the mere bright bone.

And now, as I mumble to you this old story,
My new honesty declares your glory.

In Memoriam Ernest Hemingway

A good whisky, a good girl, a good
Shoot on life, a clear prose style –
These were your criteria; would
It matter much to you that we file
You in such and such a category?
Discuss dead Pappa and live Hemingway
As if we cared, or you cared, for the story
That said you couldn't help it anyway?
Why should we blame you for your imitations?
Paris was liberated – if that's the word
By one expatriate – & no gyrations
Have since made English prose a sweeter turd.

Pappa, old gunman, you could write as if
You were a poet: we take our poems stiff.

Country Matters

'Do you think I meant country matters?' – *Hamlet*

And if I did mean country matters,
Could these not include that courtesy
That goes with being just a country boy?
Can I not show the unurban ability
To say Goodmorning or Goodevening
To you, even though these courtesies mean
I want you – courtesy apart,
I recognize you as belonging to my
Country, and I say Goodmorning
Or Goodevening to you, even Goodnight,
And courteously and clumsily,
Talking of country matters, give you my heart.

Land of My Fathers

Some frosty farmers fathered me to fare
Where their dreams never led, the sunned and blue
Salt acres where Menelaus once made ado
Because Paris also thought Helen was fair;
And now this ancient sunburnt country where
Everything's impossibly bright and new
Except what happens between me and you
When I ransack your bright and ravished hair.

Always I feel the cold and cutting blast
Of winds that blow about my native hills,
And know that I can never be content
In this or any other continent
Until with my frosty fathers I am at last
Back in the old country that sings and kills.

Owl and Echo

'I am the owl and the echo' – Dylan Thomas

Night is transparent, and the mousing sounds
Blade its black meaning: undertake me now
You overpowers as these branches tent
Me where I hover wising for the strike.

Soundstruck, I leave the toppled branches,
Mousing down all the wordy heavens
To lap me at the bottom of my plummet
Beneath her naked and re-echoing stroke.

Listen: for in the branches I had wisdom,
And I am wise now only in my echo.

Wordless

Wilt, wanton, if you will;
I am no weeper. Leave,
Love, grieving for the lost
Impossible moments.
Cry, darling, for the dear
Departure of our love.

I had this triad
Ready to greet you,
Had only to pick
The appropriate one.

And then you came,
And I was wordless.

Storms Etc

Storms I had been through before, heaved
My heart up into the sick and towering green;
And storms I could survive, however obscene
The way in which I grieve for them, and through them grieved.

Storms are one thing, but this is not a storm:
Merely your incredible cool saying
That you no longer feel the need for weighing
How much I am now worth your keeping warm.

The only answer to a tempest is a kiss:
But how can I, creeping into middle age,
Evoke the proper and very loving rage
To say, Leave it if you must, but not like this?

Come, darling, make me sick again in storms;
At least permit the grapple of my hands
To show you once more where your true love stands
As witness how your blood his blood still warms.

And then I can face any storm again,
Blinded with your spindrift, sick, heartsick,
But with the knowledge quickening in my quick
We share each other in our separate pain.

The Different Skies

Under different skies: the loved and rainy
One watching over poets and preaching
Herons and their dear, damned fathers;
The classic and incredible one
Still smiling on Helen,
Her limbs, and all her havoc;
And this one, antipodean, playing
Tricks with light which only
A painter could, not describe
Or represent, but luckily evoke:

For ever, under different skies,
The poet lies for somebody, and lies.

Unknown to Lexicologists

Is there such a word as gnatchen?
Why isn't there such a word as gnatchen?
There ought to be a word like gnatchen
– I would use it about you.

Between you and me, gnatchen would mean
A terribly common phenomenon,
Thank God, or the White Goddess
Rather – I speak privately.

A gnatchen is obviously somebody
Who gnaws my roots in absence
At the same time that she snatches
Them with my full permission.

It seems that I misspent my youth
– Not in billiards, but in the wrong
Academy – any proper
Institutions would have long ago

Compiled a dictionary commencing
With the important letter G
So that I could have used the word gnatchen
About you authoritatively.

Never an Armistice

Now in midwinter and still at war:
Though frozen into attrition, we are numbly
Waiting for the cruel coming of flowers
And the hurt of sap beginning to move
To announce to us that we are again free
To grapple each other's bodies, die once more
Upon each other still more bloodily.
Not even midwinter brings us peace, only
This temporary lull and preparation
For renewal of combat to perpetuity
– Never an armistice between you and me.

They Also Serve

Inadequate but still importunate,
I beg, while I am storming at your gate,
To be your bedfellow – you turn your head,
And I upon my pillow storm instead
That after years of begging at your gate
I still impatiently must stand and wait.

Veteran

I

Young veteran, and still presumptuous,
Hoping still to win on the rough field
If not some silk or golden trophy to grace
My hard accustomed bed, at least
Some honourable scars – but routed
Even before the encounter – I would be ashamed
Were it not for the terrible kindness
Of your eyes as you forbade me even
To think of fighting, and sent me home
To sulk among the tents in glossy meadows
While the true champions killed each other
With fine disregard because of you.

II

Why do you summon me now the fight
Is over and all the champions dead? Lady,
Was it for this you saved me? Save your breath.
I am a soldier still, and I will take you
As a soldier, not a pavilioned skulker,
Take you as spoils, as plunder to be taken
And then thrown away. Despite your commands
I owe a loyalty to my dead comrades.

III

Ah lady, I am an old veteran now,
Without presumption, and need not be commanded
To stay thus, in this pavilion, with you, for ever.

On Seeing an Australian Play

(Alan Seymour's *The One Day of the Year*)

The one day of the year – but every day
We, defeated long before Gallipoli,
Get drunk, one way or another: beer,
Cunt, religion, the class war – it's all the same,
– Or is it? Now you fright me, boy.
Dammo, was that business of the apple
Serious after all? Boy, you could
Play for Wales after your fashion
And still wonder did those tricksy patterns
In which you cut the Saesneg to bloody
Ribbons give the same answers as the bloody
Sermons which made you so much in love
With sin you can't even enjoy your wife
Unless you think it's wicked. The one day
Of the year – destroy me now
I am drunken with the thought of fighting
You, smelling your armpits, and feeling
Your breasts emerge into my hands
Like mountains – dammo, even in defeat,
The one day of the year for me is the day
When I forget my wars in fucking you.

Rain Forest

(*to Rae*)

Flowers, forest, in the downing rain.
Tall trees, stretch like women, reach
Up to the sky or God; tendrils teach
Us how to cling and cling again.

Rain forest, rise, proliferate
Richly before my bushed and bushy eyes
To tell me that the small cry the rain cries
Does not downpour my poor heart too late.

How my woody wishes wander – in the rain
I remember, as always, another country,
And the bare hills and raging of the sea,
And the rain forest takes me home again
To loud and holy Wales I never leave
Even when rain forests witness for me and grieve.

There Is Something In What The Psychologists Say
(to Madeleine)

Ride, horseman, confidently astride
Your mount – the mountains wait,
The distances, and the flesh you ride
With the offhand skill of having come too late.

Sail, seaman, the tossed and offering seas,
On sealegs beautifully balanced, while
You long for lubber landscapes, and for these
Women waiting for you in single file.

Ride, sail, on, man, extend a finger,
– Horses, seas, or those ecstatic thighs,
– How a man's memory can stand and linger
Where he told or made his truest lies.

Horseman, sailor, I shall ride tonight
The sea, the mare, I've always chosen right.

My Grandmother Died in the Early Hours of the Morning

It was cold in that room, after the cold hours
Of keeping company with a big, shrunk man
Who had been her husband, my father's father.
Her sallow face seemed peaceful as ever,
Her straggle of hair blanched into the pillow
– You would not have guessed at a body under the bedclothes.
Past tiredness, I was a boy, incurious.
A little woman was dead, a little old woman
Who had long confused me with her youngest son.
I did not even think, How small she looks.
And certainly had no thoughts for her life of labour,
Nor wondered how she who had always been old to me
Had once been whatever beauty the world has
To the old man I now led out of the room,
Out of the house, up the narrow road,
In the dawn he could not see for tears, taking
My hand in his as he'd done when I was small,
Both of us wordless against the dawn and death.

Memories of a Country Childhood

The bull upon the cow: in those rough days
I had not heard of Pasiphae, nor dreamed
Of you for mounting as I must do now.

The nervous horse urgent upon the mare
Would be a better image of what I feel
When I dream of burning Troy for your bright hair.

The boar grunting upon the sow, not that
My sensibility's appalled even as I grunt
And grant you what we've both been aiming at.

The other animals deserted Paradise:
We were expelled, but in each other's eyes
We saw the better promise of this one rise:
Man has the luck that more than once he dies.

A Christmas Poem for Michelene

Once I wrote you a simple poem,
And now I know I can do nothing better
Than imagine a poem beautiful as you
In two languages or three, each
Inadequate to tell you how you speak
The one language of the heart.

Poet at Night

(for Barbara)

As the night rains away,
In a discordant room
My witness fingers take
A lying pencil, and make
Signals against the day,
Charms against doom.

As my bloodtide recedes,
Leaving the heartless bone,
The sensual messengers
In small scurries and stirs
Depart, leave me alone
With my lost needs.

As the night, as the heart
– This signal pencil writes
What may not be said:
Against the living, the dead,
Against the days, the nights
– You cannot choose your part.

This Wedded Gentleman

This wedded gentleman now for a long time bound
Has carolled loudly enough in his day
And once stepped out as springily as you
To face the challenge of flowers in the dusk,
With the young maidens could make harmless play.
Why should we remember his careless days
Before he was gravely bound in this cold ring?
He is married for ever and would in no way thank us
For recollecting old gaiety and so on,
How trippingly he could dance, how catchingly sing.

And yet – it is, I suppose, ourselves we remember
As we drink a toast to this wedded gentleman.
We too could carol once, play pretty games,
Challenge the flowers, even be charming to girls.
We have not long to wait for our weddings, gentlemen.

Once

(for Madeleine)

Once

It was the hay sloped above the house,
Or a fox upon the snow – and sky-line
On Christmas day, or an otter
Killed at last after the fine chasing.

Once

It was other boys and girls being
Dirty and exciting among the ferns.

Once

It was my grandfather carrying
Me home the long miles from the fair
And, drunk as usual, falling with me
Against the mountainside, then in the brook
Where he always washed his boots, and both of us
Bawling in unison against our womenfolk
Who wanted to separate us.

    Once

I lived in another country.

    Once

I saw a woman for the first time
And knew then why I'd always made
So many mistakes in mental arithmetic
For sometimes two ones make so much more
Than two, and some onces are much more
Than twice – some onces, against odds, are

    For ever.

A Poem Which is Better Without a Title

Sweet cheat – if I sound like a bloody bird
It's not because I have been plucked – my dear,
You have not anything from me to fear –
Plucked birds taste sweetest, so I've heard.
And you are biped and implumis, furred
Exactly to my taste, and every year
That greys you makes you even more dear
To me, because when you cried I heard.

Taliesin Broods Upon the Founder of Harvard

New Englands of the mind: and such choice grain
As God has sifted; borne in the teeth of winds
We would not have believed in in our windy home;
And over such brute seas, to heave at last
Our fearing and God sickened hearts on such
A rocky strand: the prayers, the psalms, the thanks
Flowed from our mouths like honey: we were persuaded,

And witnessed, and went on witnessing. The Lord
Looked on our work at first and found it good:
The New Jerusalem in the Wilderness.
New England, New Holland, New Jerusalem:
How old they all are now, eternal Sodom
And Gomorrah: and His face withdrawn from us
These centuries, even His bright Backside.
What else could we have lost by staying at home?

At home? Whose home? It was neither God's nor mine.
Banished our beautiful barbarity, and forbid
The solace of the sweet religion. So we went,
Sulking, with the aliens over the alien
And annihilating seas to reap this fat
And bitter harvest. The bright has vanished
And the thunder is not His any more.
This footnote will not get me a doctorate.

The Hunger of This Love

The hunger of this love
Picks on its own bonefeast,
Wanting the one guest
To spill the wedding salt,
Asperge this married guilt,
Return this love.

Your unborn children cry
That I have been afraid;
Words that I have said
Wound my intending mouth
As my wishes gutter forth
To you, today.

Banquet me not, nor give
Me supper to assuage
This want with which I rage.
Bring only bread and wine
So, when at last we dine,
You give, forgive.

Not Blessed

If I were blessed, my rage would praise
Now in a loud season the innocent
Wilderness of love and the fallen,
Nourishing armies of the dead, the holy,
Hanging trees, and the old
Incontinence of waters.

If I were blessed, my song should burn
Through silence, the darkling hurt
Be soothed, and the sweet welcome
Laid and arrayed like a bridebed
Everywhere, and dominion
Be no more.

I am not blessed, and have been hurt by silence
Now for a long sorrow, and I would not praise
This lack, but utter only
The raging words I know
To ease this unblessed and this silent time,
If only now.

Late Spring in Wales

(for Pat)

It was a cuckooed land going gravely
About green business, and the lambs unbound
From snow and terror bounced high and bravely
On the moving, holy, and always dying ground.

A wind blew, warm as loving, from the west
And the girls came out like berries. The old hedgerows
Were sprung and blossomed to life, and could not rest
Till the hawthorn was subdued by one torn rose.

It was a curt cuckooing and the wind
Soon turned and all the girls were gone,
But a good time in which we should have sinned
When the eloquent and searocked skeleton

Of Wales put on a sensual covering
Briefly to preach the dogma of late spring.

In the Tremble of the Year

In the tremble of the year, the uncertain moment
Before the coming of summer, I stood in a fair field
Or parable, holding your hand, reluctant
To let you go or let the summer come.

Now that you have gone and summer has overcome
Me, I tremble as I remember that moment
And know that I would still be reluctant
To let you go from parable or field.

In the tremble of the year, in a fair field,
I was reluctant, and the summer came.

Ever

All night in the ready fields
      My love went running,
Looking for a likely man
      With all her cunning
To play catch her who can.

All night it was gay for her
      In the compliant grass.
Tall men tried helplessly
      To stop her pass
As she ran so ingeniously.

But in the cold morning
      As she tasted the dew
My love was caught for ever
      By you know who.
My one word now is never.

Ancestor, Old Lady

You know that old and angry look of hers,
The one that disinherits you but compels
You to remember you must share her hells
As she shares with your unforgiven fathers.

Now at ninety, in her ignorance
Of any torments but the ones that burned
Her as she saw a true love torn and turned
To otherness, she lacks no assurance

That you, the small boy tautened at her knee,
Will too grow up to beast and learn to break
Whatever good things you clumsily make or take;
From you, too, takes refuge in her piety.

And you are wordless for her as you must be,
And know that even could you loose the words
That whirr and chatter in your mind like birds,
You would not. You regard her wordlessly.

Now, after her dead years, you are still not free
From her assumption and her angry look.
You can put down your fathers in a book,
But only stammer for her, unwillingly.

A Little Elegy

These are your mourners, now your world is cast
In corners, webbed and dusty, sharded
Empire of your once and sure brightness.

These are your mourners, fallen themselves
Now that no longer the glittering of your going
Upholds them as it were all in a gay dance.

These are your mourners: whoever turned
His head to be thankful at the wonder
Of your passing by; whoever said
That you were always beautiful; and whoever
Doubted that you too could die.

These are your mourners: these many,
And these few inadequate lines.

And in the Woods to Walk

In the indeed and always countries
My love, among the close and other trees,
    Was walking, and her fallen leaves
    Were whispers of whatever grieves
If I should study new anatomies.

May that once and with me forest stand
As long and fair as I try to understand
    That all her lovely leaving, unleaving
    Was no more than yes to this grieving
Unless I give her back what she had in hand.

And in the woods to walk: how the tall
Trees would comfort us, the soft leaves fall,
    And all the bright and brown birds sing
    For us, who'd not want anything
Since there we would have each and ever and all.

Only

(to Madeleine)

Once I wanted to be a vegetable,
And I went through the usual madness
Of wanting to be God. I stopped
Wanting to turn and live with animals
When I knew I was one. Now I look
At you, and touch you, and hope only
That you find my only virtue
Is, like your wisdom, that I am only human.

The Beast at the Door

(to Brin)

When the beast came to the door,
Amiably slavering, his paw
Uplifted as in salute,
I noted the burrs on his coat,
And the small thorns that clung
To the wilful clots of dung
He wore like medals, felt

The sweat reek from his pelt,
His friendly stinking breath,
My knees bent therewith;
For all his looming size,
And his incongruous eyes
Small as a pig's, or mine,
I would have him as my own,
Blatantly in my house,
Bald-rumped, big-pilled, wise
To smell out my tricks
As he sniffed around for sex
Or murdered meat,
Mauled what he would not eat.
When the beast came to the door,
Ambiguous visitor,
Expected and casual,
Despite his grin and scowl
I was ready to welcome it
Until I knew those white
Fangs were for me, and shut
The door, too late, too late.

Reluctant

'Yet heaven, since time began,
Loves a reluctant man.' – Vernon Watkins

I would make a sullen claim
To sit in those harsh pews,
Stretching the dry sinews
Of wit to learn a name
And slowly spell my shame.

Tardy indeed, and loth
To admit I could admire
Such a consuming fire
In which the one was both
Desired and desire.

Pulpit and pew forgot,
The only sermon heard
Mine upon the word
That is my own like snot
Or the sweetness of my turd:

I find in another land
Another poet say
The words I dare not pray:
God, take me by the hand,
And let me understand.

Soil

Under the burn and toil
The savage breathing soil
Opens itself and breaks
For the keen air that aches
Above it and around
Soundlessly like sound
Of waking leaf or slow
Sift of sand. We also
Know this toil and burn
Time's grief and spurn
And the keen ache
To open ourselves and break
Into love's air awake.

The Pendulum

What will come
Quick to the window
Where I lie
Beneath the tall
Tick-tock, tick-tock
Of the ready clock?
What will come
To tell me I die?

What will come,
Angel or troll,
To catch and stop
The pendulum
And my quick,
Angel or troll
To lift me to the sky
Or let me drop
To that old hell?
Troll or angel,
What will come?

What will come?
I see its shadow
Lean on the sill
But cannot tell
If it be angel
Or sulky troll.
The shadow stays
A hand licks out
I hear the last
Tick-tock, tick-tock
Of quick and clock.
The pendulum
Is caught, is caught,
And what has come?

Bronwen

What should we blame
For Bronwen welcoming her shame?

Listen – you know as well as I do
Bronwen had been too often
Under the hedge or in the hay
At the lively but always too short play
For any likely lumper to fear to admit
That with Bronwen fach he had done it.
And now, who shall we blame
For Bronwen welcoming her shame
Once before – you ought to remember
How the women's tongues hissed, clacked,
And gobbled that particular November –
Bronwen went for a month's holiday
To her auntie somewhere in the Rhondda.
Who ever heard of a girl of twenty
Having a month's holiday from those hills
Even on a honeymoon?

We know what she went for.
It might have been any of us.
She came back without it.

And that was all right.
But now Bronwen,
Bronwen of the big breasts and dark eyes

Who has made so often a long merriment
For us of a short night,
Bronwen sweeter than honey,
Bronwen is marrying Old Tomos,
Tomos Tymawr, his big farm and his lies,
And his money.

And all the boys, those who lay
With her and those who dreamed of it,
Hate old Tomos and what we have to blame
For Bronwen welcoming her shame.
What should we blame? What can we blame?

The hard life of these hills, where a girl
Is lucky if she's had a few kisses
Before she's twenty, and then is either married
To somebody older and stinking of sheep,
And an old woman in five years, but with
At least another five children to come,
Or left to grow dryer and more virginal,
Working harder at home and for the chapel,
Carrying a growing pain around quietly,
And hoping somebody will remember
To put up a nice stone when the time comes?

That, which is life here, or the chapel doctrine
That makes every little pleasure a big sin?
Or what we knew and did not care we knew
To be, like any other tup's, our lust
To cover Bronwen, though we also knew,
Farm lumpers ploughing fields for fathers
Who'd leave their money to the chapel out of spite,
We couldn't marry even if we wanted or had to?

There was nobody sweeter, nobody,
Neither in the hay and honeysuckle,
The short meadows of summer,
Nor under a cold thorn hedge
In winter when even the owls
Were quiet and our breathing rang
Along the woodlands like bells,
Nobody sweeter to us starved boys
Who'd fight but not begrudge each other
Bronwen and all her joys.

There were fights after fairs over Bronwen.
The parish is seared with her. But which
Of us could fight an old bugger like that,
Or clout and kick him to lie or die in a ditch
Even to mount again that sweet and handy bitch.

Tomos is old, you say, and he'll not satisfy
Bronwen of the deacon-defying eye.
But who'll want Bronwen, though it's true what you've said,
After she's shared that rich and stinking bed?
Ach y fi! But what is there to blame
For Bronwen moithering into shame?

Head in the Clouds

Head in the clouds to you is a worn phrase
Weakly used to indicate disapproval
Of somebody else's ability to evade
Or ignore the day's burden and trial.

But to us who were born above Pencarreg
Head in the clouds is true, is simply true.
Nor all the brazen comfort of the sun
Can dissipate the clouds upon Penrhiw.

And if you say, as other friends have said,
That I walk always with my head in a cloud,
I am wilful enough to take you literally
And let your saying make me homesick and proud.

Homesick for clouded hills that never lose
The loom and shape they had when I,
My head in other clouds, trod their old paths
Too proud then to know that I too would die.

Proud now to know that when I have to die
My head has always been in clouds: first those
That still hang low over Pencarreg and Penrhiw,
And then the ones in which you shroud me close.

For Miranda

(*born 9 March 1962*)

Miranda, may
Your advent be
A portent of
The lucky sea
That will bring to you
On a happy strand
Your own and only
Ferdinand.

From grace to grace
As you grow
Let me be
Your Prospero
Whose magic shall
You safely keep
From all night harms,
Harms of the deep.

Miranda, be
Miranda always,
To be admired,
To welcome praise.
Miranda, may
You always be
A happy wave
Of the lucky sea.

Cwmchwefri

I have been walking above Cwmchwefri
Where the hills slant sharply into rock
And nothing, not even a kite, hopes to live.

Up there, above even the last sheepdroppings
And bits of rabbitfur and peewit feathers,
I could see sickeningly below me
The sideland farms precariously
Clinging among the bracken to an old
And often defeated hope.
                    You must believe
In some impossibly glorious promise

To mow meadows and milk cows in such
Unlikely places.
                    What will happen now
When they listen to the six o'clock news
Instead of bawling Alleluia
To their beautifully unjust God?

To Helen

(in a very proper spirit)

Helen, thy beauty is to me
Etc. etc.
Iambically I would with thee
Etc. etc.
Rejoice, rejoice, it's only me
Who's after your
Etc.

I would I were where Helen
Etc. etc.
For her sake I'd lie down and
Etc. etc.
Only an old man on the walls
Admiring Helen's
Etc.

I'd burn a Troy or two for her
Etc. etc.
Warming my old bones at her
Etc. etc.
I would thy beauty would I were
To me with thy
Etc.

by Bushmills
out of Harri

Worthy is the Lamb

Up there, in Cwmuchaf, Glyn
Whistles between the few black stumps
He has of teeth, and Fan, his bitch,
Performs beautifully and accurately

For him. And then he walks ten miles
To conduct an indifferent rehearsal
Of The Messiah; and then another six
To have, just before going home in time
For milking, what Blodwen said
Over and over again
She was keeping until she was married.

Thou Shalt Not

(to women, from the base of the scrum)

Thou shalt not: little Howells
Pitches his voice a squeak higher, and Bas
Davies eases his fourteen stone and groans
Amen, resolutely not remembering
What he was up to yesterday with Megan.

Thou shalt not: especially with sheep,
Their warm and ever present temptation.
Isaac moans Amen as he tries to forget
Whatever it was that Jesus bach said
About the one sheep in a hundred.

Thou shalt not: Howells bach B.A.
Is sending his little voice up and up
In a fervent fever of exhortation,
And the Amens are rising like clouds
From the neighbours telling each other
          Thou shalt not.

That Impossible She

(to Ialene)

She was, and is,
She is, I stop
And cannot stop,
She is, she was,
She will be, stop.

She comes and goes,
I go, I come,
I cannot stay,
She goes, I come,
I won't, I stay.

She is, and is,
And I am not,
Going, coming
Without her, with
Her, stop, stop.

Stay me within
This stop, and stop
With her, without
Her, I can come
And go, or can I?

Stop, stay, with me,
Coming or going
Not, or not being
What might have been
Complete going, coming

A New Ballad of Old Ireland

I was on me way to Ringsend
To live with a redheaded whore
When I saw that blackguard Joyce
Coming out of her door.

So I turned away from Ringsend,
Vowed I'd go there no more
When I found that bloody Beckett
Had made the same vow before.

By Brian Boru it would tear
A dacent man apart
After all that to have both of them
Ringsended by the Hart.

Stormy Night in Newcastle, N.S.W.

Rain thrashes the house, and I am back
Where such a ruffian night would lullaby
Me to a drunken sleep. I lie
And listen to the wind's threat and crack,

And cry, I am not homesick, am not sick
For hills so sodden with such rain

And wind their absence is a pain,
A calm day makes us wish a storm come quick.

No, it is too easy to remember, now
When just a harmless lash of rain
Can keep me from my sleep, that then
I could have slept as sound as other men
Through better storms than this, nor wondered how
A sleeper in such storms would wake again.

For Vanessa Stowell, Born 6 April 1962

Vanessa, heiress of an honoured name,
And, more important, daughter of two
(How difficult you make it for me to avoid
Clichés), two (why should I not use clichés?)
Nice people: darling, I am glad
That you are here. I am obviously not
A fairy godmother, but if a minor poet
May, without harming you, wish you something
And point his old bones at you: may you
Grow into loveliness like your mother's,
And when you too have a beautiful daughter
Remember that I wrote this for you, Vanessa.

For An Unborn Daughter

Darling, you would have floated in your hair,
And I would have been submissive to it,
And your name would have been a music in the air.

You cannot now forgive, nor even admit
A sort of father whom you'd rather not
Admire as what your mother once found fit.

O beautiful unborn, my luck or lot
Was not to have you, and I have to turn
Now to rhymes for what I might have begot.

But from these rhymes I hope in time to learn
As from your beautiful almost existence
That even poets have at last to burn
To the wilful ash of your resistance.

Improbable Land

The lineaments of my improbable land
Show no contrition that an old excess
Is now economy when hate grows less.
As conquering others still misunderstand
How can we, dangling always from God's hand,
Sullenly careless whether he curse or bless,
Absorb from stone and rain the rage to express
What long ago from paradise we banned.

Far from that stone and rain I try to say
How that incessant fall falls through my veins
And how my bones are hewn from that sad rock.
I give no keys to anybody to unlock
Mine or my land's heart. Some strains and stains
Are seen more plainly in this sunbright day.

The Poet Meditates Upon Byzantium

(for Doug Muecke)

Lousy Byzantiums of the mind
Bruise the ambitions of the flesh.
It is the wind that takes, the wind
That leaves us nothing but this,
All the brutality of love.

And we, marooned, always
Marooned on those moronic isles,
Whimpering out our residue
Of days, persistently recall
Byzantiums that we made, and lost.

It is a scratching signal
In the mind's foul armpit,
And we itch in pubic ecstasy,
Writhing to make Byzantium
The one town that we laid for ever.

It is an old, repeated song.
We have not any gong to strike
Or conch to blow, to startle
Old men marching in monotony
To that ejaculated memory

To any event, I am, I am
An heir of that Byzantium.

Three Verses for a Twentyfirst Birthday

I

Comedians are born, they say, not made:
Rough luck on some apprentices, but still,
Our boy is learning fast his proper trade.
For that there comes this message from the Hill:
To Julian – make of it what you will.

II

'Rough Johnson, the great moralist'
Once, on a similar occasion,
'Long expected one and twenty', gave
Obliquely good advice: I wouldn't dare.
But if upon majority you insist,
I hope that all your minor preparation
Has left you something which you need not save
Even from the queen of darkness and of air.

And, lest you overrate being twentyone,
We love the mother while we toast the son.

III

Now Julian's grown to man's estate,
        Love me early,
Who is waiting at the gate?
        Leave me late.

Now the boy is twentyone,
        Love me early,
What do you think he may have done?
        Leave me late.

With wine and with merrymaking,
        Love me early,
What the hell is Croft forsaking?
        Leave me late.

Julian, all the assembled throng
        Loved, and early:
After this unseemly song
        Will leave, too late.

But now you come into your own,
    Love me early.
Goodness, how the boy has grown,
    Leave me late.

We only need another drink,
    Love me early,
To tell you what we really think,
    Leave me late.

So Julian, here's a health to you,
    Love us early,
You may do as you may do,
    But leave us late.

Impeccable Strategy Let Down By Fallible Tactics (But Not Irreparably)

Our strategy was simple and, I thought,
Sound in its simplicity: attack
In force where the enemy was weakest, or where
Attack was least expected.
              In order to get
Required information and achieve
Necessary surprise, preliminary
Subtlety was also needed – mutter
About spies and so forth if you want to –
The one thing that we knew was that the enemy,
Our enemy, lies.
           We were defeated.
I still maintain our strategy was good
– I admit our tactics failed somewhere,
Or, more likely, counterintelligence
Misled us about important changes
In the enemy's disposition.
             We lost
That battle, granted, but the striving pattern
Rearranges, redisposes itself for the next war
And for that we are more than ready,
Careless who wins so that there is a fight.

The Green Tree

Caught young, I grew to be a pretty boy,
Fondled and dandled on many a lovely lap,
Called precious and a pet as well as pretty,
But the green tree keeps on growing,
Those ladies did not tell me of old age,
Of how reticulate wrinkles would creep
To cover their faces, lips grow dry
While the green tree keeps on growing.

Lissom ladies who were fond of me
I praise your unstrained quality of kindness
And all your wanton and your merry ways
While the green tree kept on growing.
Now that your limbs are grown rheumatic
Look at me out of your vague and clouded eyes
And assert I was indeed a pretty boy
But the green tree kept on growing.

Old Compulsions

Old compulsions, insistent as rain,
Distort our language so that we speak
In fashions mannerdly askew, oblique
About the nurtured marrow of our pain,
Are scornful of the kingdoms we would gain,
Admit, mock-modestly, we have technique
But not there is a love for which we seek
On hills we mourn we shall not walk again.

The bittersweet of exile intoxicates
Us with a still more savage grief
Than when we abdicated from belief
And all the imperative ancestral hates.
And yet with bitter competence of tongue
We crow the hymns our fathers proudly sung.

The Minstrel Boy

Out of invented countries, comic scenes,
Wearing a few real tatters of some antic
Dreams and passions, and a honed-down knife

Grandfather used for killing pigs or kings,
A pocketful of sermons, sixpennyworth
Of sins, the minstrel boy emerges into
The world, half-frightened, half-contemptuous,
And alone. Behind him lag his leman
And his faithfully sluttish bitch, ready
To run or lie at his uncertain whistle,
To bark or sigh in speechless admiration
Of his unharped and incredible songs.

Love's Overtones

It is a terrible thing to be young, young
With that vitality unaware
Of the secure depredations of age. Only
The old know the civility of death.

We are all subjects of sea-change, and change.
Tall columns lie and crumble in undergrowth.
Imperial bones moulder as surely
As your beautiful ones or the always rotten.

It is a terrible thing to be young, but more
Terrible to be aware of growing old
Simultaneously with the shock of you,
Your ignorant hair clouding the calm sky.

A conscious terror, therefore more terrible.
Meanwhile I keep my shudder in my bones,
And look at you in lust and wonderment.
Terror and death are but love's overtones.

Useless Advice to a Young Man Hopelessly in Love

If not of this, then of some other despair
Grow fat and sleek. Be sure there are enough.
I made a memorandum once of hair
And filed it irrevocably somewhere.

Seek not green pastures, be content with stone.
Their virtue is they cannot make you sick.
And meditate once daily on the bone:
It's almost permanent, and it's your own.

Do not expect even wise men to be wise.
Wisdom, at best, is incommunicable.
Look greedily into her greedy eyes,
And try to tell only convincing lies.

Put not your trust in words or anything.
Put not your trust in really saying enough.
Birds in the hand can't be compelled to sing.
Despair suffices. Love's something else . . . . some thing.

Prothalamion

(for Robyn)

Now is the news good, and our hearts high
For our beloved: I would pour
You many flagons, would recite
The many ways in which you cause delight,
O woman whom we all adore:
O sweet, be happy, now and ever, is our cry.

You will be always beautiful, but I,
Abashed at the new beauty of your face,
Find a new hope for living in the hope
That now you enter on your proper scope
You will perpetuate your wit and grace.
O sweet, be happy, now and ever, is our cry.

And under any harsh or alien sky,
I shall always, having known you, boast
Doubly: I knew you, once and ever, and
I praised your marriage. I hope you understand
This small voice speaks for a great host.
O sweet, be happy, now and ever, is our cry.

A Celebratory Poem for Robyn and Rod

There are old stories, some declare,
In which the true things happen. We,
With wit and wine and courtesy
Greet the deserving and the fair
Who walk into their proper story
  – That they're our friends is our glory.
Dolphin and swan, attend them as they go.

One and one is more than two
All the ancient stories say,
And what we celebrate today
Is insufficient I and You
Entering the blessed mystery
Of ever after being We.
Dolphin and swan, attend them as they go.

Happiness is not a grace,
But always fought for, sometimes won.
What can never be undone
In what we have of time and space
Are true stories, and we know
That yours will be always so.
Dolphin and swan, attend you as you go.

Simply to Write

To be magical, and yet direct.
To be sensuous as a girl's body, and pure.
To write, simply.

To use the one inevitable word.
To have a natural rhythm.
To write simply.

To pay homage, to exact
A proper modicum of praise
For writing, simply.

To not disgrace her, not
Offend one's fellow-sufferers,
But write simply.

If only in the blurred beginning
I had been warned how difficult
To write simply,

I would have gone on wilfully
For your sake trying
To write, simply.

Demand of me no more than that
For your sweet sake I learn
To write simply.

Reciprocal magic then, sensuous
And direct, shall teach us both
To love, simply.

A Dog Speaks To His Mistress

Do not despond: some over-obvious tricks
Attempt to show the old dog is still young,
And if he barks he's barking about sex.
Old dogs cannot be happily taught new tricks.

But old dogs can be faithful, even though
They're liable to succumb to patting. Still
Old dogs will try to be young dogs, so
You have to put up with the dog you know.

That I didn't mean to put that way
– Barking defensively is out of character,
And difficult – but I knew again today
That you and I are hopelessly this way.

So, do not despond, do not be too severe
On a semi-educated dog who's learned
To love you wholly: if my alphabet spells dear
It is because I love you far and near.

Lines for a Double Christening

Miranda Tietze and Vanessa Stowell, 30 June, 1962

For nine moons cradled in grace,
You and you have assumed
Your bright and proper place
Among the doomed, undoomed
Crowd of humanity.
May we have charity
To pray for you and you, that so
Angels speak always for you as you grow.

Love's Mythology

I have played so many rôles – swan, dolphin, lion –
In covering you, and still you can reduce
Me to this mere outraged despair
Simply at the thought of you lying naked there.

And this, no doubt, is love's mythology
And ours, but I did not want to turn
Your naked truth to words, not even mine,
Even though from myths poets cannot resign.

Turn for me then upon your naked bed
Warm shoulders waiting for me to declare
I am dolphin, swan, or lion, at command
Of your imperative caressing hand.

And thus we shall outdo mythology
By being nothing but our naked selves.
Think of me as lion or dolphin or as swan
So long as you are what I lie upon.

In Memoriam

'. . . where you may see how God blessed husbandry in this land.'
Francis Higginson. *New Englands Plantation, 1629*

But not in mine. See Daniel wear the sky
Like a sodden overcoat, the earth weighing down
His feet, as he wrestles with an old text
And wonders why his sheep are so obstinate about dying.
Sometimes, picking stones off an old, thin field,
Or riding, wet to the waist, through the bracken
In search of old, thin sheep scarce worth the saving,
His mind would be lifted from perverse sons and daughters,
His head kestrelled in space towards Allt-y-clych,
And he felt he could prophesy like Isaiah.
Or he would see somewhere towards Abergwesyn
The city that had no need of the sun, neither
Of the moon, to shine in it.
                              But always
He had to go back to the cramped house, to too many
Sons and daughters, unprofitable husbandry.
He would not have welcomed a more blessed land.
You can be terribly close to God in these places,
But what can he dream or prophesy in the jasper city?

I do not hope that he would approve of these lines
Written in the new language, but I hope
That when I am an old man, as he when last
I saw him, I too can continue picking the hostile
Stones off my sour fields, and riding wet to the waist
Through the recurrent bracken, and still
Lift my head to sudden visions and prophesyings,
And thank God that He never blessed husbandry
In his own land – Daniel's and mine.

Traditional

It was spring, we were in the country, we were together,
And the flowers around us all of a foam and a lather.
Now is another time and now is another weather.

A look or a laugh or a kiss were more than enough
To assert and approve and emphasize our love.
Now it is other things we ought to be thinking of.

But I wish I were back in the country with you once more.
It may not have been what we were intended for.
But now we are both of us lonely on opposite sides of the door.

Pastoral

An old ram, slithering along the feg,
Obeying a familiar, difficult command,
See, how he snuffles now and comes to stand
For what they used to importunately beg.

He is too old. As he lets his shrunken knees
Sink regretfully to earth again, his ewes
Maternally gossip of how he would use
Them in the old days, how he could please.

Young rams horn in; and old rams must retreat.
Young ewes become old ewes in one sharp spring
(Young lambs they tell us make the sweetest meat.)
This old ram, had they done this one swift thing
To him, would not now need to grudge the young
Rams mount the ewes he once was lord among.

A Birthday Sonnet

(for Rae)

That tribute should be annual does not mean
I celebrate the hastening years that wear
You to a final brightness fallen from air
– O long delay that darkening of the scene –
But that I throw a pattern on a screen,
Demonstrative of what is passing fair
As long as you are memorably there
To guess the words my silence falls between.

Accept then from this alien in the spring
His simple gratitude for knowing you.
In colder climates I was taught to sing
Where skies could never approximate to blue,
But now I send you these auspicious words
In lieu of golden and of singing birds.

Lines for the Death of an Alcoholic

No more stale rinsings of the sun
Shall cool and whet his pampered lust,
Nor the abasement of his tongue
Swell with accumulated dust.
A thirstier river drinks him now
Than all our licensings allow.

Morning shall not torment and parch
Him, fearful to sleep or wake,
Nor ambiguity of nerves betray
By wilful and beseeching shake
He burns with the consuming fire
That's fuel to its own desire.

Lapped now by deeper waves he lies,
An ague stilled, untwitching bones,
Taut tongue unswollen and relaxed,
And silent all hysteric moans.
Only the stink around his grave
Says, Here was one we could not save.

Cwmchwefri Rocks

(for Madeleine)

In the cold splendour of that rocky place
I killed a rabbit with a stick, and stood,
Exultant, virile, dominant,
And ten years old. Next day I crept
To worship with a washed and Sunday face
The God who killed me like that rabbit. Sick
Now with longing, I wonder what I've kept
These thirty learning years, or understood
No rocky god can ever again supplant
The goddess who is nourished by my blood.

Apollo had never shown his face up there,
So far above the brown and troubled brook
Its fretting hardly broke the insidious mist
That was closer and colder to you than your bones,
And when you avoided her in masculine prayer
It was the buzzard Jahveh swooped and struck
So that your verse has murderous undertones
Like rocky faces where you dare not look
Now, for the bloody thorn with which he missed
Might mark you if you dared to read his book.

I killed a rabbit once, and once allowed
A proud demanding woman to ache and take
Me to her bed, and once I hope to write
On pages savage as Cwmchwefri's rocks,
A few lines triumphing and loud
That show that neither Jahveh nor Apollo
Are responsible for these intermittent shocks
That kill me over and over, and make me take
Her hand in my hand in the stormy night
– What the gods kill, my breasted goddess mocks.

Ceridwen, in your arms I can forget
Cwmchwefri rocks and the stern face of God
So that you come to me by night and night,
Blot out those images and stricken cries,
And promise, promise that I may be yet
A poet worthy not to be refused
When you demand a proper sacrifice
Of running blood, of understanding blood.
Assure me Jahveh's nor Apollo's might
Assault your poet when for you he dies.

Swansea

Landor in Italy longed for an old bay
That even holidayers cannot spoil,
Smutch, litter, peekaboo it as they may,
Or violently rest there from their toil.

I would not walk now in that memoried town
In case I met the all too affable
Ghost of the wave's son, and with him drown
Happily saying life is terrible.

Drown in mixtures thinner than Mallarmé
Dreamed for Poe, but blacker in their way.
St. Helen's, Sketty, and Cwmdonkin Park –
O Iesu, what's there left for me to say?

Only that that old bay and that old park
Are there, as Dylan still is there for me.
No bloody air-raids ever rubbed away
The birdridden and sea-assaulted country

That belled our Dylan out over the bay.
Voice of the sea, and murmur of the land,
Bayvoice, seavoice, birdvoice, o silent voice,
Where you belong is all I understand.

The Nightmare of King Theseus

Blind days I ravelled unforgettable
Threads of unreason, stumbling down tunnels
Nearer and nearer to some urgent breath
Anticipatory of the moment when,
Dazed in the sudden light, I should stand helpless,
My dropped sword clanging on the stony floor,
Useless against pervading nothingness.

Heart, Mind, and Body

HEART

Patience, you counselled: when you look for it least
That love will come to take you unawares
So that you know then you have known it always.

MIND

Was I not right to counsel thus? Did not
Love come and take you unawares
So that you know now you have known him always?

BODY

You never counselled me that love would come
Repeatedly to take me unawares
Though what I knew cannot be known for always.

I let you hear this internecine
Conversation so that you know that for you only
I am this unequal triumvirate,
Aware now that I am yours for always.

With the Sea's Volubility

Young man, lover, poet; how easy to foretell
That for all of them the body will grow old.
Especially for the poet, conscious of other rôles
He must have played once, easy to imagine
He knows that he will savagely welcome the time
When in his old rage he will assault
The inevitable cliffs though helplessly.

But how hard to tell any of them, or yourself
In any of these rôles, that when you are middle-aged
You must storm helplessly against young beauty
With the sea's volubility but not its salt.

Dark Rival

Twin, dark rival, supplanter,
How I hate you in the morning mirror,
Punctual as midnight sweat,
All for the bright recurrence of her hair.

Though I can scrawl good verses yet,
You are as close to me as murder,
And I greet you every night in nightmare,
Every morning in the surly mirror,
Heedless so long as her bright hair falls.
It will fall so for my executioner,
My twin, my dark and doomed supplanter,
Companion of my sweat, face in my mirror,
Victim of her cool implacable eyes.

Midnight and morning I only prepare
In the intolerable shadow of her hair
Your usurpation and my sacrifice,
Of equal worth to her impartial eyes.

'But if it be a Boy You Shall Put Him to the Sea' – Traditional

The lecherous and griefless sea
Was always more beckoning than gardens
To a boy from bare, exciting mountains
Who would have been all green thumbs in gardens
And was so used to being bullied by mountains
He thought he did not fear the sea's oblivion.

The books did not tell me, nor your griefless flesh,
That oblivion can also be found in gardens,
Nor that my fear and clumsiness on mountains
Sought the sea's obvious oblivion
Because of some salt lecheries
Older than any mountains or gardens

I could know of, with only my green thumbs,
So clumsy in well-kept gardens and useless on mountains,
Itching for the griefless hills of the sea,
Glaucous and absolute mountains,
Only these fractures and twitchings to guide me
To oblivion, the last and salt oblivion.

Poem for the Winter Solstice

Prepared for the dark obliteration,
You may evoke now for the last time
The way it was in spring, how laughingly
She made a triumph of her invitation,
Baring her breasts for you as if you were
Indeed her unique conqueror.
And now you die, but you die gratefully
In this inevitable time.

Ready for the long obliviousness,
You can afford to recall a last time
Her imperious beckon and how gallantly
You showed then your more than readiness
To prove upon her insurrected breast
A puissant king can come to rest.
And now you die, but you die thankfully
Because of that brief time.

Now, at last, the longest night of all,
And you go willingly to sleep,

Careless on the abandon of her breasts,
In the stilled storm of her rich hairfall,
That you will never again look on the light
After the long recompense of tonight.
But where you die, your poor heart proudly rests,
And you go eagerly to sleep.

The Kingdom of Terror

You'd think you'd easily recognize
The kingdom of terror: a boundary
Of patient skulls or disembowelled
Babies, partless men, or women
With their breasts precisely lopped:
Such things, or tall walls of fire,
Or rampant horses seeking to devour,
Or the inexorable smash of seas.

Any old dream you've had over and over,
Or thing you've grown accustomed to:
Murder, rapine, and so on:
Any of these you thought would make
The kingdom of terror easy
To recognise – you even thought
You'd been there.
                    Nobody told you
That the kingdom of terror
Is outposted by a torn corner
Of a sheet, a mouse coldly nibbling
Crumbs, or these grey and greasy
Hairs from a once loved head
In this comb that should have been thrown
Away long ago.

To Ted Richards

Askew a bar, aslant
With your tall charm, you asked
'Don't you feel afraid
To see all your faults
Assault you in your children?'

Then, my one child only
Had temper. Now, I know
What you meant, and try
To keep quiet as they trample
Thoughtfully on my grave.

By God, we live, boy,
In some short memories,
Tall children, and some
Writings that are not
Better than they should be.

Belated Welcome for Mary

Hiraeth is a word that costs
A bit more than nostalgia, and a lot
More than homesickness; so, my dear,
You may forgive the poet who accosts
You now, homesick and bloody hot,
That he has always held you dear, and dear.

Letter Writing is a Lost Art

'I have a lot of things to say but will say nothing.'
– W. B. Yeats to Katharine Tynan, December 1889

I sent a letter to my love – wrote it in the wrong language,
Forgot to post it,
            and now regret it.
God, I have better things to do with her than writing letters.

Nevertheless, it was an interesting way of saying nothing.
I would try it again if somebody would teach me to write properly,
And fall assertively on my bed to be my love.

Meanwhile – that is, today, and all the long tomorrows –
I write too much,
Forget too little, and am confused for ever
Between the crookedness of my calligraphy
And the felicitously postlapsarian curls of her hair.

I remind myself that really I must write to her next year
When there will be more nothing
And anyway my amanuensis can do it.
Meanwhile –
            I sent a letter to my love
            And in her way she lost it.

To My Mother

A finch sang in the hazels
Thin above the thorn.
My scythe hissed drily
Through the headland corn
I moved alone.

Seagulls made clamour
About my leaning plough
Bickering for worms
I turned up now and now
Ploughing alone.

A woman seemed a woman
In wood or meadow
In the hard young days
When with my shadow
I moved alone.

And God was a loud voice
More urgent than thorn
There in the stoned acres
Shouting to warn
Me, me alone.

No finch now, no hazel,
Only the thorn,
God's shout a whisper,
One woman alone
          Cries I was born.

Australian Christmas

(for Rae)

Now in a season of heat and oddly holly
I remember snow and Christmases deep buried.
Perhaps in a minor key, but not that wholly
Because I too have been ecstatically ferried
By flakes of snow and falls of hair to believe
In something more than what I usually grieve.

So in a season of heat and oddly love
I remember Christmases buried deep in snow
And try to tell you how I watch you live
More richly than in snow-bound fields I know.
And beyond all my metaphors of despair
Am thankful that I know one woman's fair.

On Re-reading Old Myths

So you sit down, lean and slippered, expecting
A pleasant hour or two, more interesting
Because more reminiscent, than the latest fiction
Whether Who-done-it? or I-won-the-war.
Certainly – you've dined today, and your mind
Is easily random, picking up pebbles here
And there on the edge of the great ocean –
Certainly you don't expect or want
A shock like that young Keats sustained from reading
Chapman's Homer, you have no desire at all
To feel like stout whoever it was
Silent upon a peak with wild surmise.
You only want this lapping silence (family asleep)
And these old stories to read instead of new ones.

Then how forgive her for this startled hair,
This sweat and shake, this more than hopeless
Recourse to the hidden bottle, this rabid
Ingurgitation of barbiturates.

How can you forgive her that you cannot
Tell her what you cannot tell yourself?
It was your grandam straddled in that wooden
And accommodating cow: it was your daughter
Languished naked on the water's brim
For the swan's glory: your mother
Who drove that man to tear his eyeballs out:
Your wife for whom they waged those bloody wars,
Uselessly on the windy plains, and burned the town.

So you sit down, forget psychology,
Reach for the bottle, take too many
Barbiturates, and sweat a few more hours,
Recusant, remembering favourite stories.

On Re-reading the Twenty Third Psalm

No uncompanionable divinity
Comforts me now beside these unstill waters,
Nor in this shadow do I want to shout green praises.
All the days of my life, goodness and mercy
Are what I believe of the parables and thunder,

But what I remember, under this rod, unprepared
At the table, what I remember, is a dead sheep
Stinking in what we called a meadow, a pastor
Gutsily taking more than a proper tithe,
And three crows, indolently flapping
Back to a rotten, thunder-riven oak
When I disturbed their happy rotten luncheon.

In barren or fallow moods, I am tempted to make
Poems out of such obvious materials: a god
Renounced, but not forgotten, maggotty sheep,
Dumb insolence of crows, a half-dead tree,
A family sprawling and brawling back
Through pub and capel for three centuries
And more, the family lie, the pastor's lie,
And all the lies that I have told myself.

But beside these unstill waters, as I walk
In the valley of the shadow and am not comforted,
I ask, What have maggotty sheep and pastors
To do with my daughters, who never knew my God?

Marriage a la Mode

She believes in manners, I believe in sin.
Whatever she does, is done with a beautiful rightness.
Whatever I do, I am conscious of doing wrongly.

When she was young, words were personal matters.
Now they are very important to society,
But she hasn't changed a bit in her manners.

Whereas when I was young I was terribly troubled
About the relationship of morals to society,
And now that I couldn't care less, my manners are still pretty bad.

Nevertheless, we manage, between her sense
Of manners, of what is done, what not done,
And my sense of sin, what ought to be done,

And what not done, and what in fact is done,
– Between us we manage to live somehow together
Pretty comfortably unbalanced on a blunt edge

In what she would call sin if she believed in sin,
And I would probably recognize as bad manners
If bad manners had ever been a passport to hell.

To Miranda On Her First Birthday

To you, unequalled, unimpaired,
    What can I say
That won't sound strange, from
    Over the hills and far away?

You are fair, my dear,
    And you're one today.
But I brought my darkness long ago from
    Over the hills and far away.

Now for all my words
    I have little to say
But listen, listen to song that comes from
    Over the hills and far away.

And as you grow and are fairer still,
    Remember the day
When a dark man sang to you from
    Over the hills and far away.

Letter to a Dead Friend

Get fucked, is what I remember you saying.
You had an affectionate, unrancorous way of saying it.
I hope there are ghosts where you are to whom you can say
Get fucked.

I know if I let this letter become sentimental
And say I hope there are girls, or the ghosts of girls,
Where you are, your ghost will coolly reprove me,
Get fucked.

So, you old bastard, I'm damned if I'm going to write
To you, though you can't prevent me remembering
The affectionate way in which you used to tell people,
Get fucked.

And I know you wouldn't believe this, but I hope,
Wherever you are, and whatever you have to do,
And whatever companions you have, I hope you still
Get fucked.

Prayer to the Steep Atlantick Stream

(for the natives of Borth)

Rhymes, ships, and winter – all a western sea
Howls that it holds them far, far away
While here the golden blackmail of the day
Holds me in winterless security.

How can I stop that shouting in my ears
Of the cold waves that batter on the rocks
Of Wales with the sound to which my own heart knocks
And all my fathers howling down the years?

O ships, o winter, o remorseless rhymes,
Let me still howl against that western sea
The old cry of the defeated and the free
For all my fathers' eloquent times and crimes.

And, despite my surrender to the sun,
Despite my squandered lust, o western sea
Whose howl is in my head continually,
Permit me only do what they have done.

And so I may at last find a kind of peace,
And lie down with my fathers, safe from rhymes
And ships and winter and their storied times,
And even your knock and howl may still and cease.

Not That I Don't Like Kingsley Amis

(to Jill and John)

Yes, Evans was all right, decent type
For a Welshman; you know, went to
WEA classes, had read Kafka, Mann,
John Wain, and me; cultured sort of chap,
Terribly keen on football, thought cricket
A silly game except that marvellous year
Glamorgan were county champions – as a matter of fact
This odd aboriginal was also very much
Addicted to sex – he preferred it to beer.

I wonder sometimes if I could have written
Poems like this if I'd stayed the other side
Of the border – I mean, away from Evans.

To the Keeper of the Welsh Kitchen

You'd remember that summer when the barbarians
Really descended on us – and we were prepared –
No obvious weapons – our knuckledusters
Were merely mental – anyway, not being Romans,
We were prepared for the Huns and the Goths and the Vandals
From Birmingham and its suburbs – our hands were open.
O shit! – it's a nice thought over the long miles
That while I remember you and a few other proper
People, I've forgotten the names of all those Birmingham bastards.

To Rupert Hart-Davis

(on the receipt of The Letters of Oscar Wilde)

Scholar, friend, and gentleman – how good to use
These good old terms and know that they are true.
I am one of those the Muses too readily bemuse,
But there are some things I have learned from you;
Scholarship, friendliness, and gentleness
Are virtues which we cannot do without.
So I, too conscious of my worthlessness,
Whisper this praise and thanks I ought to shout,
To tell you, scholar, gentleman, and friend,
My admiration really has no end.

The couplets come too pat, perhaps, but still,
As far as meaning goes, I really mean
These words from under, under the hill
Where the rare light is occasionally seen,
And thank you, friend, scholar and gentleman,
In these poor rhymes which are the best I can.

One Memory

The delicate and reluctant deer
Stepped and stopped a moment in our garden,
Nibbled at a frosthard cabbage, and then departed
With the same hungry dignity with which she came

There were no hounds after her; only winter,
Remorseless as God or parents; and I was sick
For her boned beauty only for a little while,
And still do not dare to think of how she died.

But I know she died: the quick mouths of hounds
Would have been more merciful, some grace
Among that slaver and baying she could not find
In the slow sleep in the last drift she stumbled into.

And there, where houndtooth could not reach
Nor cabbagetop entice, there the bone of her beauty
Still whitens against the offwhite of bogcotton, as you
Still intrude with a bony gleam into my life.

Have You Ever Been Frightened?

Of course I've been frightened; by such
Obvious things as Stukas screaming down
While I repeated mechanically, meaninglessly,
'Get the bastards, get the bastards,' for once
En rapport with our gunners – I was trapped
In a box with dot-dash dash-dot hammering
My head – what could I pray except that bloody prayer?
There were also, if you want to know, E-boats
And submarines – both mean torpedoes.

Oh yes I've been frightened enough in my time.
That was all right in a way – at least you knew
If you went, a lot of good blokes went with you
It's odd to think now that that was a comforting thought.

But the brawls – the moment when you stood up
To an enormous Texan, or were simply involved
In one of those beautiful goes on behalf of the Allies
Or western civilization or some such sort of shit
And you fought like some sort of legend
Because you couldn't bear the thought that if
You were killed, as you were sure you would be,
Nobody who knew you would believe
That in fact you were coldly bloody sober –
Oh, yes, I've been frightened too in my time.

But have you ever tried crossing a field at night
Where a weasel has her young? That was the time
That I sidestepped, circuited, in cold blood.

Hwyl Fawr, Brin

Hwyl fawr, bach – the words must have been said
Often enough to ring factitiously in your head.
But who last said, and meant it as I do,
Hwyl fawr, bachgen? – except your Mam, who
Last called you bachgen, anyway. But take
This bastard way of saying Hwyl fawr, take
It as well meant for your Mam's, and your, and her sake.

Ambivalent Poem in the Old Manner

(To Whom Else)

O western winde, when shalt thou – Christ.
          Merely expletive – I'm at it again,
Rhyming about the girls I might have kissed
          Or those I would not dare to kiss again.

But you are not in either category,
          Kissed or unkissed, when I think
About you, darling, you wear for ever
          The green 'rags of the sea'.

A Man Without Eyelids

A man without eyelids – I call him a man
Now, though then I called him a bloody Arab.
Nothing else has ever frightened me so.

One day in school, Mr – whom I worshipped –
Caught me opening my eyes in morning prayers.
(I know now why I wanted to know how the others looked.)

But Mr caught the enquiry of my eyes, and whipped me
Only with words – I could have borne the cane –
And he said how useless I was with my hands,

And therefore how much I relied on my eyes.
And now that I know my eyes see only one thing,
I am very frightened to remember, as I do,

That flagrant man in the sun without eyelids,
Not even begging, merely without eyelids.
Even in nightmares now I close my eyes.

Salute to Marlene From Down in the Valleys
(Welsh accent obligatory)

M.A. now, and First Class Honours too.
I always said nothing but the best would do
For that girl, so it's no surprize.
But Christ, mun, wouldn't it make your hackles rise
A bit of a girl like that could take the prize
For learning as for teaching – Duw,
And she's got those beautiful blue eyes.

Thanks to Jean and Norman for Coming Here

Dear Jean, wife of a poet and occasion of poetry,
Your husband may not like occasional
Or dedicated poems, but you are woman enough
To welcome even these rough lines.

The occasion is simply your arrival
Here, the dedication simply to you.

And the verse is simple enough; it's only meant
To say that you, and yours, are more
Than welcome, and blessings on you all.

And – now I know what every poet knows,
Praising the beauty of an English rose.

The Second Critical Encounter
(to Marlene)

You said, looking at some poems, 'These are good',
And while I liked that, I discounted the friendly
Warmth of your voice – ('Bloody liar', a voice says,
My voice, – 'All right, boy, I see what you mean',
I meanly reply in the same voice, almost.)
But you went on, 'Because here I do not see
The poet watching himself write a poem'.
And I realised that this is perhaps the thing
I've been trying to do these 'prentice decades,
To stop that, simply to write poems
That are good enough to be anonymous,
And failing always, because on the touchlines

There has been the too obvious figure
Of the boy who once wrote a beautiful poem
And has ever since watched himself do it again.

And though I've failed again in this effort,
And can see myself watching myself looking
– In optics there is no end to the series – I hope
You believe, as I do, I really mean
These mumbled thanks are for showing me the way,
Or at least for telling me there is a way.

One Reason for Disliking Englishmen

'Balls, old boy,' he said, and he spread
His handlebar all over his face,
And I had some very hirsute doubts about him.

But, 'Balls, old chappie,' he went on saying,
Both ends of his enormous twirl quivering
As he kept on repeating to me, 'Balls, old boy.'

Poor bastard, he was, I believe, a Wing-Co,
And dropped the appropriate weight of bomb,
And now can only twiddle his moustache,

And say, over and over again, 'Balls,
Old boy,' while his handlebar flutters
And uncurls against his violent face.

To, And For, Caroline

You walked into our lives, beautifully,
And we feel that you have come to stay.
A rough old poet pens these rough old lines
To say, inadequately, we like
You both, and may
Your marriage be a true one, may
There be children for whom I can pray.

But anyway, Ivor and Caroline,
God bless! – I'm running short of rhyme,
But I wouldn't want any other sort of time
To say Hwyl fawr to Ivor and Caroline.

Sawmill Incident

(to Alan Mullard, Timberman)

Look, I tell you he let that bloody saw
Take his finger off. I was there,
I witnessed it. Accident? Keep that talk for the compo.
Boy, I saw him let that saw go
Just one burr – like that – and him there then
Holding up his hand, and the blood
Was everywhere. We all felt pretty sick,
Applying a tourniquet, ringing the ambulance,
Ringing his wife – I had to do that.
Fingers, of course, are often lost in sawmills.
I felt pretty sick about his, though.
Oh, he'd always been impetuous, but who'd have thought
He believed in sin enough to make the saw
Take away the finger that started the trouble?
You don't believe me? I had to tell his wife.
Pretty difficult to get that finger caught on a saw.
And the silly bugger's trouble still remains,
As all three of them know. Watch your hand there, boy,
These saws sometimes reach out and get you.
Don't you want any more fingers left than I've got?

Infidelity

I could not bear
              not in that unsustaining air
Your brutal absence, so I made,
Breathless and afraid,
A sort of image of you.
              I didn't think you'd care
That for a moment she was passing fair,
Or dare to believe that I would dare.

Welsh Pastoral Elegy

You could, I suppose, make some parable
About Dai, stone and story him in a way,
What the Lord giveth, and so on, but I
Don't believe in these sermons which I love.

The trouble is, I worked with Dai, year
After year: milk bottles round the town,
Torn timber lugged down cold and bleeding hillsides,
Wet, ravaged barley ripping the skin beneath the skin,
Kale and turnips cold gifts for fingers
Without feeling, cold and mudded rods of potatoes,
Maggotty sheep in August which you had to dress
Smartly in as long as you could hold your breath.

And Dai and me, through all the calendar,
Through all the bloody and the bloodless months,
Wordless antagonists, sweating against each other,
And still surprised we have never been charged
With that murder, when we quietly killed each other,
Slicing the tops off swedes with frozen fingers.

Adrift

Over there there are timid coasts
And the tamed land behind.
I walk the sea with ghosts.

Even the sun is brave
Over the tumble and haste
Of my populous grave.

I shun the foreign land,
Content to share the waves
With the ghosts I understand.

Companioned so by ghosts
I ride this burial sea
Away from the living coasts.

And so remain dumbfound
With the sound of the sea, and the sea
Of the sound I sound.

Lower Deck Attitude Illustrated

(Persons with O.L.Q. requested not to read)

Fuck me, said the Admiral's wife, and the Able
Seaman promptly showed how able he was,
And the Flag Lieutenant – tell it not in the Wardroom –
Flew a bloody fine flag – though not as good
As the bunting the bunting-tosser tossed –
Asdic would have it too – what became of the bo's'n?
The Gunner's Mate? and the gunners? Like the Cox'n
And the Chief – Chief Stoker I mean (and forget about golden rivets) –
The Cox'n, the Chief, and the other Chief, – E.R.A. –
Erect. Responsible – I forget what A stands for –
And don't omit the Cook and the Steward
– I suppose there ought to be a Leatherneck in somewhere –
Look, son, I don't want to boast about what
Or whom I did in the war, but you're old enough,
To understand what I mean when I say
You'd understand if you were old enough,
And you'd met the Admiral's wife, why the Army
Was always so happy to say The Navy's here.

In The Shadow Of Your Hair

A stammering repetition of your name
Can jerk me out of any waking nightmare,
So that I can believe your eyes still shine the same
And your hair is unequivocally your hair.

Permit me stammer with my voice and hands
A little longer: homage, thanks, and prayer:
So that your listening body understands
This is my curse and cure and care
By lamplight and starlight and moonlight
It is your bright hair's shadow by which I write.

And, writing in the shadow of that hair,
I say old sayings over and over again
Without much reference to here or there
Or now and then, still less to loss or gain
– I only hope that you can read me right
When I remember that even your shadow is bright.

Spoiled Preacher

(to many contemporaries, and some in especial)

Sometimes in the sweaty and stained night
The thought comes to you, thick in your mother's
Flannel nightgown and the drunken sweat
Of your father's dirthard shirt: Suppose,
You think, you had gone through with it,
Suppose a war hadn't come conveniently,
Suppose – this is the moment when your scream
Awakes you to your own sweat and dirt – suppose
You had let yourself be dipped in the Chwefru
(Below where the trout were, and where they washed the sheep),
Suppose you had learned from the ghosts of Christmas Evans
And Evan Jones 'the man from Eglwyswrw',
And you lived now in a meagre manse –
How beautifully you would have been able to thunder
Against sin (meaning only one thing, that thing)
To your thin and sinning congregation.

Pastor you would have been, as stained with sheep
As your grandfather – but without his little book
Of identifying notches, or the means to make them –
Or your uncle (McTurk's man) – he had thousands –
Or your cousin who was properly called Cutter.

Pastor you would have been – and what a hypocrite
You would have been in the glory of the pulpit –
Hair flowing all over the place, and hellfire texts
All endlessly against fornication
To a few thin and avaricious buggers
Of both sexes heedfully laying up their treasure
In the bank and whatever they thought was heaven.

But now you are emancipated – suppose
Any of them should look upon you now –
You could stand their contempt for your Sunday drinking,
And your tenderness for girl students and secretaries –
They took Sunday School in their time, and for their reasons.

But suppose, suppose,
You had to preach a sermon on a thin belly,
Hoping the big farmer would spare you an egg or two.

I suppose
I would have been a pretty good preacher,
Getting properly hot against fornication,
And getting my eggs.

Rape

A Footnote by Satan to Paradise Lost . . .

Rape is an old-fashioned sort of joke.
I mean, you've read all the reports, and all
Your girlfriends have laughingly repeated
The saying attributed to Confucius
About lying back and enjoying it when it's
Inevitable.
           Why now between these willing
And enjoying legs are you reluctant?
Do you remember the woman whose head
You held under water until it didn't matter
If she said Yes or not? Do you think
Rape isn't really fun if she insists
On enjoying it too? Do you?
                And you can't.

Rape is so much easier for women.
If I were not a snake, I think I'd like
To be a man, and to be raped again.

For A Good Marriage

(to *Valerie and Brin*)

Wishes are cheap, and life is ruinous
As we know to our own dear cost.
But let not from this happy day be lost
One wish from any of your friends
Such good beginning may have better ends.
We gain from you what you have taken from us,
Two separate friends now one and more than one
More than deserve our wish that what's begun
Today will bring
You all the happiness I want to sing
That all your friends may answer, and their echoes ring.

With Love, For Love

(*to Valerie and Brin*)

On the mutual bed assume
    Your proper form, and take
Great riches in a little room,
    Assured that the love you make
    Is no mistake.

The roaring of your friends around
    Dies away while now you make
Your proper love – the only sound
    The eloquent breath you take
    Is no mistake.

Love assumes its proper form,
    Love is what you give and take.
Be sheltered from the living storm
    While you mutually make
    No love's mistake.

Eyes, Hair, Sea, Fall

Having in mind that ambuscade of hair,
I averted my eyes, but to a blank avail.
Spindrift of your approach assailed me there
To fall before I felt myself to fail.

Argosies I ransacked then, astride
The bright main of the fallen world, to seize
O buccaneering looks into your wide
And unforeboding eyes, salt promises

To deny sere leaves and all that fall
Into the deeper and the greener deeps
Where my fault could answer to your call
To sleep satisfied so where your fault sleeps.

Now I inherit my kingdom, the bonestrewn
Bottom of the sea my bones knew before
The green sounds out of which they were hewn
Or dreamed of lying safe on some dry shore.

Eyesockets bequeath this upturned stare
To the ambush of your hair, your drowning eyes.
O queen of darkness and the falling air
Look on your ambushed lover where he lies.

Not that you should know anything of despair
Or care he is so fallen from your eyes
But that the tides and ambush of your hair
Ripple in triumph over one who lies.

On A Daughter

(for James McAuley)

My father's scowl, grandfather's scowl,
Just as I have transmitted it,
On this face now
Evokes a likelier kind of grace
Than was to be expected from
Such a filial deviation.

Do lovelier lineaments disguise
In her the long-nursed guilt
The family scowl
Is signature of, the carried shame
We could not do without nor felt
At home if we were lacking it?

What sort of hope I cannot help
Then makes me want to see that scowl
On the otherwise innocent
Face of a boy whose accusing eyes
Will call me grandfather and deviate
Perhaps into a path I left too late?

With Hunger, With Anger

With hunger, with anger, I shouted for images.
But they eluded me like charities.

There were trees, there were flowers, waiting to be used.
I stumbled on them, remained crazed.

Am still hungry, am still angry, am still
Hunting my forfeit images. I spell

My future, rooting hungrily and angrily
To find an image.
          Then you show me.

A Small Vision of Hell

Lipless, breastless, they importuned me with
Their tiny minds, huge hearts, tenderly
Telling me this was true love, I could forgive
The blind denial of their hairy parts.

Don Juan-like I stood as at command,
Slavering at navels, armpits, nipples,
Welcomed the cold rejection of a hand,
And sweated out my sentence.
                                        Apples,
Red and gold, rottenly promised to fall.
The girls lisped sweetly this is true love we make.
The last thing I remember before waking,
I'd turned aside to eat the hairless snake.

Welsh Childhood

Eating the bread of the world
In the thin rain of time
The child ignores the crow,
The stoat, and worm who know
What bread and child will come
To, crumble to at last.

In comfort on harsh rock
Or lacerated pine,
Never out of the wind
Or the thin nails of rain,
He thinks that wind the breath
Of the world he knows is truth.

A bible in his mind,
A pulpit for his mouth,
Should he seek further for
The absence of the wind
Or accommodating truth,
Life's wound without a scar?

The crow, the stoat, the worm
Wait because they know
He will never be out of the wind,
As long as he has breath,
That breath is the truth
He crumbles to in the end.

Instructions To A Painter: For Her Birthday

The year returns, turns
                    – but gold hair not yet grey
You have no need as yet to make me say
Remember I have put you in a book.
I would, though, say, remembering
Lyonesse, Tintagel, and King Arthur's Keep –
'Kynge Arthur Ys Nat Dede', you know,
But sleeps, his gold outbraving grey –
I would, outfacing troubadours, say, Look,
Except the advice is the merest superfluity,
I would say, Look upon, and paint, the sea.

Not simply that: o gold hair long from grey,
Let me untroubadourly say,
Paint me,
If not the glory of King Arthur's Keep
Where Gawain and Gwenhwyfar equally sleep,
If not the snarled and endless seas
Haunted by all the perjured sails,
Paint me one day
The gongs and dolphins of that tormented sea
From which I say,
Crying for knowledge of the gold and grey,
It is your vision that I praise today.

With A Distant Bow To Mrs Hemans

(I. M. Tomos Jones Crogau)

I've never cried
Because I had not bulk enough to fill the chair
Grandfather left me when he died.

Though all his care
Notched for keeping in the ledger of his mind
Leaves only bum's and elbows' greasemarks there

On his own chair
He left me when he died. And still I do not mind
That even then I never cried.

If he'd been unkind,
I could church out from this chair's emptiness
To show how much I do not mind,

Kick again those bars
Heels high off the floor, holding just legs together,
Or mark straight arms with famous scars,

Nicks of my name,
Old preachers, ungot girls, served cows, the always weather,
Or other testamented blame.

Grandfather, our predicaments we share:
We have the nicked involvement of our name.
I try to fill your chair with all my shame.

With Thanks

It was against the custom of the country,
So, the second time, she gave me her command,
Inflexible and smiling, a fair No
More dear to me than many darker Yeses.

Taffy Was Transported

Over there, the hills of Sion
        Tempt with their peculiar light,
Eternal beacons to the pilgrim
        Stumbling in this southern night.

With his eyes on heavenly mansions
        Treading where his fathers trod,
Knowing that he's even further
        From the comfort of his God.

But the pilgrim, stoutly faring,
        Keeps his eye upon the height.
He whom Jahveh once has blinded
        Never more shall lack for light.

And the way into Salvation
        Underneath the Southern Cross
Is no harder than the pathways
        Where his fathers found their loss.

Eyes uplifted unto Sion,
    Hands astray upon a fleece –
HE is surely a good shepherd
    Who will bring us to his peace,

And fold us in HIS glorious mansions,
    Safe from Satan, that old fox,
Singing, singing Hallelujah,
    Sweetly in HIS pious flocks.

See, from here the hills of Sion
    Shine more brightly from afar,
And the lost sheep find salvation
    Underneath a crooked star.

Recriminations Over

Recriminations over, what's to do
Except what we have always done,
Tear at the unhurt flesh and leave
The mind, some minutes, alone
As will be, after all our thrash and grieve
The unrecriminating bone?

Christmas Once More

Christmas once more, and once more I accept
The challenge of a poem to a reader. Dear,
Did you think the mere recurrence of the year
Would render me less willing or adept
At telling secrets that are worser kept?
Such as: I know a painter: who would think that here
Lies some enormous truth? I lie, my dear,
As much as, but no more than, tears I have wept.
Wept – there's a word for you to paint
– But you don't paint words – you'd better not.
And if I ever write a painting down,
Whether you call me sinner or swear me saint,
You can paint me as I take too long to rot,
But sonnet me as at least your best-drawn clown.

Instead of a Christmas Card

(for Jill and Marie)

As if it weren't enough
I should lay my words upon your daughters,
Crumbled upon your swanned and willing waters
Here is some more stuff
From the original Jones,
Mere pen and ink, or inky blood and bones.
I've daughters of my own,
And so can say
I love you for your own sake, not for theirs,
And mean it, too.
Darlings, whatever your daughters do
May they wing always in the loving airs
Their mothers make for me even as I pray
Their mothers may forgive this pen and bone.

A Sailor Who Reads Books Sends a Christmas Card to His Dead Sweetheart

(for Anna)

Christmas again – shall I decline?
(Do I decline?) I do declare
Those voices in the springing air
Are always harder to define
When once again the shuddering whirl
Defies me to announce
Anything else that happened once.

O hang me on the Christmas tree
Anything's better than going to sea.

Once and once alone beneath
A still and perfect toy-hung tree
I was you and you were me
Until we died for lack of breath.
But now with any other girl
I keep on breathing to the end
And think about my sailor friend.

O hang me on the Christmas tree
Anything's better than going to sea.

Darling, in that private place,
Do you hang toys upon the trees
As you used to hang your breasts to please
My unaccommodating face
And what you only saw behind
My sea-washed and Platonic mind?

O hang me on the Christmas tree
Anything's better than going to sea.

I take again my Christmas leave
– Of you, and Christ, and everything –
And all the bloody bones that sing
About me as I reel and heave
My guts up in the gutters of this town
Say, Sailor, go to sea and drown.

O hang me on the Christmas tree
Anything's better than going to sea.

No Regrets

But no regrets: upon the lithe response
Of your body, your beauty, I learned a little
More about writing poems, and still more
About the importance of being man and woman.
And, since we are not responsible for that,
It is as important as trying to write poems
That we should end that poem with no regrets.

My Country, My Grief

Anguish is my country.
　　I would not recognize
A land where only fair winds blow
　　And the sun shines.

But the land where every wind
　　Is the breath of guilt
Is home, and let the loud seas lash
　　Wherever I have slept.

My paradise will be despair
　　And the cold winds that blow
About the rocks, about your hair
　　And the grief I know.

Back?

(to R. S.Thomas)

Back is the question
Carried to me on the curlew's wing,
And the strong sides of the salmon.

Should I go back then
To the narrow path, the sheep turds,
And the birded language?

Back to an old, thin bitch
Fawning on my spit, writhing
Her lank belly with memories:

Back to the chapel, and a charade
Of the word of God made by a preacher
Without a tongue:

Back to the ingrowing quarrels,
The family where you have to remember
Who is not speaking to whom:

Back to the shamed memories of Glyn Dwr
And Saunders Lewis's aerodrome
And a match at Swansea?

Of course I'd go back if somebody'd pay me
To live in my own country
Like a bloody Englishman.

But for now, lacking the money,
I must be content with the curlew's cry
And the salmon's taut belly

And the waves, of water and of fern
And words, that beat unendingly
On the rocks of my mind's country.

Welsh Bastard

(*to David Jones*)

I was always defeated
My dad died at Camlann
And *his* dad at Catraeth

But I walked Sarn Elen
And helped to make Blodeuedd
And was Nest's lover

I was not absent from Glyn Dwr
Or the last Llewelyn
Or the bloody-minded Tudor

Look for me in the annals of defeat
Or now and again a bloody victory
Places like Agincourt

And always in the dark hall of Cynddylan
Where the eagle of Pengwern
Lifts his talon

And always before her bright face
Defeated, like my dads
Who died at Camlann and at Catraeth
For her bright sake.

Anoeth bid Bedd I Arthur

'A grave for March, a grave for Gwythur
A grave for Gwgan Red-sword
A hidden thing is the grave of Arthur'
　　　　　Old Welsh, *The Stanzas of the Graves*

'Anoeth ... refers to something difficult to acquire, hidden,
　　precious, a wonder.'
　　　　　David Jones, *Epoch and Artist*

And my grave, when you make it,
Will be hidden too,
Because, although a common man,
I married a princess,
Precious, a wonder.

So I would have my tomb unknown
But wherever it is,
Quondam and *futurus*
Written on it
So I may hope when Arthur comes again
I may recover my lost princess.

The Hedgeschoolmaster Talks To Himself

I walked with a bare mind
Between the rich hedgerows.
My urgent skin was prickled
By an insistent rose
While a rapid field-mouse
Mocked my lack of a house.

Harboured in twigs a bird
Stirred up a song
My deaf ear almost heard
As I lurched along
Between the thick hedgerows
Intent on a rose.

A rose, a bird, a mouse:
The thick skin of my mind
Twitched in that hedgehouse
To know that I, though blind
And deaf and dumb and worse,
Could still know the curse:

To walk with a bare mind
Between a hedge and a hedge
And breathe like a mouse the wind
Of the bird's knowledge
That even the rose's song
Is not for long.

Petrarch Did Not Write Like This

I stayed too late: my waiting was too slow.
You came, but could not wait my coming late,
And when I came could only bid me go.

I came too late: for you who could not wait
To tell me that sometimes I am too slow
To come to tell you that I cannot wait.

Now I am always waiting, waiting so
I may not be with you again too late
To come to you as only your hopes know.

Let me then, stay and wait too late, too late
To stop you coming to me in the way we know.
I stay for you, my dear, I stay and wait

For you to bid me to get up and go.
For you I come and make my coming slow.

On Being Asked To Contribute To A 'Theatre And Drama' Issue Of Meanjin

I thought I'd come upon the scene too late
To write one of those modern, dry,
And English poems with a title like
On First Reading Nahum Tate.

I was deceived; *Meanjin* opens with
Theoric arms and brazenly invites
A poem – provided that it has to do with
Sceneshifters and playwrights.

I'm honoured, naturally – but in a fix:
Shall I write dialogues between me and Kate,
Burtoned off-colour, or be witty on
Refusing to read Nahum Tate?

Keats did King Lear: what would you have *me* do –
A modern Browning, or an early Pound,
Dramatic lyric, idyll, monologue,
Or a stagey Dylan's sound?

Or what about a terribly clever poem
– I do want to be published after all –
A clever poem – Gautier could have done it:
First Night: Watching The Flats Fall?

But I must reluctantly renege,
Decline Meanjin's offer – too late, Cock,
You called to me:- I must put on my gown
And not read Nahum Tate.

The Solitary Wanderer

Walking, alone with sentiment, his twisted stick,
He can knock bravely off this thistle's threat
Or sideswipe this frog for its reminding face,
And stride on, meditate, and not be sick,
Though all his history is with him yet.

He takes his ruminative path, stoutly armed.
The mountains are subdued beneath his boots,
And the lakes are open to his eye, and shimmer.
It is a landscape he has wholly charmed.
The earth he tramps on snarls with all its roots.

He will arrive at, and look on, tarn and tor,
And make appropriate remarks on rhymes,
Preening himself on his ability to scan,
Even spare a thought for the jostled corridor
Where the slipshod shuffle through their crimes,

The slum were mere people scrabble, scratch
At what they have of life; he will stale and wait
More implacably than lakes or mountains
For what torn cloud of joy he can catch
As railways, people, intrude, intimidate

His stalwart hiking out against the thistle,
The evil eye of the toad, the thorns and burrs,
All those small and inappropriate
Enemies, owl's hoot, finches' whistle,
Or the drawn, hinged grinding of a gate

That warns him in the dialect of men
Stout sticks and boots tread, thrash, earth, air, in vain:
Thistles and toads dislike poetic men.

Builth Wells

A picture of a town beside a river:
Schoolcaps, girls' knickers, French letters,
And French teachers, beside the sylvan Wye:
How beautifully my memories lie.

Builth, Buallt, spa of no renown,
But sprawled about the grassy Groe,
Along the brawling reaches of the Wye,
Where I'll go home to die:

Small town, home of a great footballer
And of a greater choir, o Builth.
Stay small beside my memoried Wye
Where all my poems lie.

But That Was In Another Country

Love, that old, notorious country
I have wandered far from,
Said the old beachcomber,
Is still, you know, a proper land
Where such as you and I may learn
Between the downing of the sun
And its uprising
What the bloody world is for.

Love, that new and fabulous country
I am pressing on for,
Said the brash explorer,
Is bound to be, you know, a land
Where such as you and I may learn
Between the rising of the sun
And (I'm afraid) its downing
What this brightest world is for.

Love, that oldest, newest country
I have said so much about,
Said the young grandfather,
Is, I suppose, a bounden land
Where such as you and I must learn
Between the downing of one sun
And the downing of another
What these women want us for.

Not on this Continent

It's no good: not on this continent
Shall I get rid of my chains
Said the old poet
And the old convict agreed.

I thought here, now,
Said the old poet
To get rid of my chains.
There's no hope, son, said the old convict.

But you don't wear yours any more,
The poet said to the convict.
And the convict said to the poet,
You haven't noticed the way I walk.

And the convict said to the poet,
You never had any chains, son.
And the poet replied,
You haven't noticed the way I write.

And they both agreed
It isn't any good on this continent,
And decided over a beer
To emigrate to Australia or somewhere.

Treatment

(*To W. S., the Drunkard's Friend, Saviour of Souls, Contraceptive
    par excellence*)

I knew a doctor
          (as a matter of fact
I've known several)
           This one, however,
Was special
        he'd read some books
And he'd read what Freud said about the poets

So when he heard
          what my trouble was
He settled down to be sympathetic
(Looking more and more like a tourist's idea
Of Buddha

Or the way I'd imagine an up-to-date
Semyon Yaklovevich)*
And he asked me leading questions
                         About my sex-life
And my parents
And I gave him some good answers
Because, after all,
             I was a poet
And I'd read some books too
And then he said
         Go, with my blessing,
(Not forgetting his fee)
                   You are cured
And I think he spoke truly.
At least I've stopped writing poems.

Perhaps
         (it's not very late)
I'll become a doctor
There's money in that
         And you can't do too much harm:
There are too many poems anyway.

* in *The Possessed*

For David Jonathan Power

May David be a big boy who
         Will be the biggest joy unto
His mother and his father, especially
         His Mam, who'll be
         Always the reason he
Will know what's what and who is who.

May he like proper things, and women most,
And have words to say his liking in.
So when he meets his old similar ghost,
We can together put our two words in:
His mother and my sister. But no host
Of bad things can stand against our good word.

David, I hope sometime you'll say,
Though mother's brother could not pray,
He said some words for me: those words I heard,
And tell my Mam my love today.

Another Love

I straddled the world
And was not welcome.
I recoiled, curled up,
And was at home.
But who unleashed those singing stars
That bound me for my holy wars.

I strutted up and down,
Nobody flaunter.
I played, I displayed,
I was a bold venture.
But who called off those startling hounds
That licked and lapped my singing wounds?

I lay still as a mouse.
I breathed my own grave.
Not a woman nor seed could rouse
Me. I did not love.
What worm, what seed, what love was it that sang
To make these risen bones together clang?

I died into another grave,
Another love.

Unsuccessful Attempt at Suicide

A flat sea smugs in.
I look at it dully.
There's some honesty
In leaping, raging seas.

Smooth seas surround me.
I dive for a word.
These seas don't accost or assault
– They do me down.

Down. I nearly drown.
I come up for the third time,
Gasping a question:
Who sought me out?

Then I am breathed into.
In that smother to sea
Somebody breathed the flat verse
Of my limp body awake.

And a smug sea oiled in
Over acquiescent stones
To promise tomorrow I will make
A kind of storm for your storm's sake.

'Here is the peace of the fathers' – Hart Crane

Drowned meadows, submarine
Shadows, lapsed bones in the swell,
Old talkers who now talk ghostlily well
Between one green and another green,
How my bones feel that your bones do well.

Peace, fathers, peace.
Talk, and may the peace where your bones dwell
Requite in all green undertows
The bitter overtones
Of my unpeaceful bones.

After the Quarrel

Ignore, ignore. Forget, and sidle out.
The unforgiving door
Will greet you on your soused return
With as much ungraciousness as you can meet
Down any neighbourly street.

Or, if you prefer, sit in in sober sulks.
The difference to her
Is minimal. Your presence or your absence
To her are merely animal.

On pavement or in chair, you may adopt
The same indifferent air.
But you know who is the wounded one,
And why it is that so
Out of these quarrels grow
New fidelities. In the waste of the bed
You hug your celibate knees
And pray, ignore, forget, forgive
The hurt you did yourself today.

Disorderly Spring

Disorderly spring once more
Beats its loud drum
And lewdly we have come
To the taut stretch of welcome
With our bloods' roar.
Borne on the genial tide
We abdicate our sense
Of pride and diffidence,
Roiled in the nonsense
Of the warm flood we ride.

The riot of this newcomer
Blurs and blots out all
Foreboding we shall fall
Soon to the beat and maul
The dry bruise of summer.

Disorderly days deny
And the unsleeping nights
Hysteria of delights,
Pleasure of gasps and bites,
Come to winter to die.

A Failed Marriage

I crumple under the hurt hump of marriage,
Burden too hard, the bound sticks
Writhing, together and hostile, the belly empty,
Sucked dry, wrinkled flat back to
The back bone.
          Disowned now that original glory,
Dishevelled hair upon a procreant pillow.

Not even the ignominy of love,
Only unspeaking bodies that do not touch,
And shivering minds huddled in separateness.

An Apology of a Sort

(to Rae)

When a rhymer forgets to rhyme
    And lets your birthday pass
Without a word of a lie
    Do you frown in your looking-glass
And wish the poor devil would die?

When a poet forgets his pride
    In making you birthday rhymes
Without a word of a lie
    He has fallen on evil times
And he'd better amend or die.

But he hopes he is not too late
    Though your birthday has gone by
Without a word of a lie
    To be forgiven again
Till all things mortal die

And poems and beauty both
    In the broken looking-glass
Without a word of a lie
    Are gone for ever, gone
And nothing is left to die.

Cotton Mather Remembers the Trial of Elizabeth How: Salem, Massachusetts, 30 June 1692

Mather's righteous indignation that such things could be was unconsciously submerged in the thrill of having been present as spectator at a collision between heaven and hell . . . So far as he was concerned, the delirium might begin again with full force tomorrow.
    – Marion L. Starkey, *The Devil in Massachusetts*

I

My duty to set down, to propagate,
Assisted by its author, its holy author,
And by truth's conscience as the truth requires,
The wonders and the wonderful displays
His infinite power, wisdom, faithfulness,

And goodness hath irradiated this
Indian wilderness with, the wonders
Of Christ's religion fled old Europe's
Deprivations, to raise the New
Jerusalem on a barren strand,
And in the wilderness to reap choice grain.

So many memorable occurrences, so many
Amazing judgements and amazing mercies
Upon particular persons in New England,
My pen blazes its trail upon the paper,
A blinding witness of light towards Christ.
My bent's for praise – I hate those folio-writers,
Bigots for whom a contrary religion
Suffices to defame, condemn, pursue
With thousand calumnies – I hate with all
My heart such foul bias to obloquy.
And how commend what is commendable
Without commending?
                    But I would be
Impartial too, accounting of events
With praise or blame according; agreeing
With Tacitus despite Tertullian who called
Him the lyingest historian: the chief task
Of history is to record, as I have done,
Men's Christ-given virtues, and instil
The fear of sin and infamy, of evil
Words and deeds.
                    Even in the best of men,
Even in my friends, are many censurable
Things. I cannot forbear to censure,
Though I keep my censure sparing, more easy
Than my commendation. I have no wish
Vices and villainies to commemorate;
So some unuseful things have properly
Left to oblivion, while I praise all good.

II

Back in the spring I preached a sermon
Upon Temptations. Summer was doleful:
My poor country wholly entered into
Temptations; Heaven's dreadful judgement,
Here in Salem and in adjacent places,
Allowing the Devils bodily possession
Of many people, so that there seemed to be

An execrable witchcraft abroad,
And many were accused.
                    I can hear
The horrid cries from houses of poor people.

For my own part, I always was afraid
Of condemnation on feeble evidence
Of spectral representings, and testified so
In public and in private, and urged the Judges,
And wrote the Ministers' Advice, that they
Should by no means admit such evidence.
But I also knew the Judges, most of them,
Admired their patience, prudence, piety,
And saw the agony of soul with which they sought
Heaven's direction; compared them with
Those others whom the increase of distress
Enchanted to rail and rage, to a scandalous,
Unreasonable disposition.
Though I could not allow some principles
Some of the Judges had espoused, their persons
I could only honour, and said so;
Could only compassionate their difficulties,
And said so, here in Salem, the chief seat
Of these vexations from the Devil; wherefore
The mad people through the country
Reviled me as a doer of hard things,
A prosecutor in the time of witchcraft,
Though in the beginning of the Evil-Time
I had offered (none of my revilers
So courageous or so charitable),
To try without more bitter methods prayer
And fasting to end these heavy trials
Of these possessed people, scattered from each other.

III

That June day in the court at Salem I saw
The conflict and collision of Heaven and Hell,
The Indictment of Witchcraft against Goody How.

The depositions first of those afflicted
By sensible and evident witchcrafts laid
To the prisoner's charge. Some were not able
To bear her looks, and in their greatest swoons
Could tell her touch from that of others. Some
Testified the shape of How gave trouble to them

Ten yeas before. Others were visited
By ghostly apparitions that pretended
They had been murdered by this witch, this How.

At Ipswich, upon suspicion of witchcraft,
She was denied admission to the Church,
And preternatural mischiefs followed.
There was Joseph Safford's wife. When How took her hand,
And talked of scandal and of evil report,
Even like one enchanted, immediately,
Unreasonably, and unpersuadably,
She took this woman's part, saying 'Though men
Condemn you, before God you are justified'.
Thinking that How was a precious saint of God,
Raved, raged, cried out, being taken frantic
In strange manner. But afterwards she fell
Into a trance, and coming to herself
Cried out she was mistaken, bewitched by How,
Afflicted by the shape of How, enduring
Many miseries from that, not to be well again
Till there was testimony for How to take her
Into the Church, sorry to see her husband at that meeting.

Others told of cattle bewitched; of an ox
Choked with a turnip in his throat
At How's desire; of cattle leaping three
Or four feet high in the air, turning about,
Squeaking, falling, dying, as How wished;
A horse preternaturally abused;
Of Goody Sherwin's difference with How,
Upon her deathbed charging How's hand in her death;
And others told of unaccountable
Spoilings and spillings of their barrels of drink;
Another of being taken with a very strange
Kind of a maze from eating of How's apples.
And Isaac Cummings, who had refused to lend
His mare to How, found the beast much abused,
Being bruised as from much running over rocks,
And marked as if she'd worn a red-hot bridle;
And when one went with a tobacco pipe
To cure her, a blue flame spread and burnt on her,
Flew upwards to the barn roof, and was like
To have had the barn on fire; and the mare died.
Perley and his wife had differences with How:
Their cattle suffered; their daughter was struck down

Whenever How was spoken of. She charged
How to the very death, and said she might
Afflict, torment her body, but could not hurt
Her soul; the truth of all this matter
Would appear when she was dead and gone.
And penitent witches came to affirm that How
Was baptized with them by the Devil
At Newbery-Falls, having before been made
To kneel on the river's bank and worship him.

IV

These things in themselves were trivial, God knows,
But there being such a course of them,
The more they were considered. For the great
Part of the Summer, every week I spent
A day in fasting, alone with God. I cried
The Lord for preservation from the power
And malice of those bad angels, and the good
Issue of those calamities wherein
The miserable country was ensnared
With His permission by those evil angels.
I besought the Lord, I cried unto Him
To please to accept, direct, and prosper me
In publishing such proper Testimonies
As would be serviceable to His Interest.
I went unto the prison and preached therein
To those committed there upon suspicion,
Preached a sermon on a text from Acts,
Reasoning of righteousness and temperance
And coming judgement, helped by the Lord's Spirit.

That a right use be made of these stupendous,
These prodigious things, I have committed
Them to a book and published it, announcing
These wonders of the invisible world, and how
We fought the Devil here in Massachusetts.

V

The horns that sounded across Essex County
At midnight, the unaccountable mazes
In which men and women and beasts were wildered,
All the afflictions and torments, the agony
Of those who judged those who were only tried,
God's guidance for which I so strongly cried –

Were these things here in Salem? Did help come?
Is God's good wilderness now purified?
Or must we fear and go in constant sorrow
That we are still afflicted, that tomorrow
May bring back to Salem that delirium?

Note: I have taken some liberty with Mather's language (see
The Wonders of the Invisible World, 1693, and his *Diary*) and
have anachronistically used some phrases from the *Magnalia Christi
Americana*, 1702.

[How was executed 19 July]

Towards a Homage to Norman Talbot

A gentle man in a long wind
– Think of him as tall
To the accost of eyes,
Demure measure.
The fat wind wraps its rhymes around him.

He would go gravely.
But his far legs frolic
Between grassblades, and his tilted ears
Encourage madrigals and hymns
From skylost birds.
His back admires heaven.

As, in a long wind, I would admire him,
Hearing the grass speak,
Enlisting in the blue and dance of birds,
Welcome to eyes that harvest home,
Sharp to glints and goings
Of all this windwhirled.

But am as quiet as a stilled sea,
The almost silent lap, lapse of null
Waves void of hurt, untopped of foam;
No more than a fallible lisp,
Or a slurring out of a decrepit beard
Of a praise, an unkempt praise
Unheeded in the tall whisper of the grass

Where the birds decline from heaven
In an admiration of decrescent volutes
To fold their songs about him as he goes
In the hope and hurrying of his alation
Among the urge and listen of women,
Loud in the measure of their careful eyes.

I would praise him with my words in the long wind,
With the women and birds and the discrete grassblades.

The birds have sung to him and the grass heard.

Bird on a Jaunt

Hours ago he woke up the sky,
Has eaten well, now walks about
The kingdom of his confidence,
Feels good, his strong legs
Spur the ground, his neck
Tenses, and he crows again,
A cheer, a challenge,
Just for the hell of it, the gold
Cry vibrant to the horizon,
To the top of the sky, is conscious
Of the sheen of his wings, feels good
This blue morning he has called
Into being, now blesses,
And suddenly purposeful
Strides, pounces, jerks
His mien and mastery
Into the nearest compliant,
Inoffensive brown novice
Of his service, dismounts,
And walks away in the disdain
Of feeling really good this morning.

My Grandfather Going Blind

When the cataracts came down, he remembered
Verses, grew grumpier, but did not cry or break.
His bulk sagged, shrunk a little; he would have liked
The comforting presence of Mari, even as she was
Those last years, tiny woman in a big chair,
Talking mostly to her small boy sons, though
Sometimes she came back to this world for a moment.

When the cataracts came down, he remembered.
Was sometimes peevish, liked to talk in Welsh,
Was for the most part content with his old dog,
Blind, deaf, rheumatic, and pretty daft,
His firm stick, strong pipe, his memories – and me:
His grandson who could not speak his language,
Lacked his mountain skills, but in whom
He had a thorny faith not to be beaten
Down by any wind or language.
When the cataracts came down, creeping
Curtains over his shepherd eyes,
He talked to me.
                    The old names still resound
For me of farms, men, ponies, dogs,
The old names that are all that I possess
Of my own language, proud then
And prouder now to call myself only
Young Crogau, Old Crogau's grandson.

I remember when the cataracts came down.

Word Is All

I slur through the dingle, cwm,
To home in the wind,
A bare pine twisted above
A stumbled wall.
A word is all.

I try a bare poem, old
Like pine against winds,
Poem like where the cwm ends
Out on the hill
And word is all.

Could I make that bare poem,
True as home,
I could sing through the cwm,
Not slur, not fall,
Word being all.

But: twisted, winded, slur
All words, stumble the cwm
Wordbeat to home,
Slur and fall
The word is all.

A Welsh Poet Finds a Proper Story

The story told in the beginning garden
He breathes now, wants to shout it on
His ruined, cuddled paper, crying back
To the longago tree he climbed in Wales,
And asks for pardon.

On this loud paper he says I make that fable,
The woman in the tree, the grounded serpent,
And the treed paper is a white covenant
Damn-Adaming him to be his proper marker,
Initial syllable.

He will be humble to the paper serpent,
Cry down the woman and begin the garden
Over, crossed in an old grave story
A climbed tree told him guilty as promised.
Paper nor words relent.

In a garden beginning he finds a proper story
And lets the paper bellow, bark and build it
For him while he cradles in the treetop in Wales
His silence and the serpent and the woman
And all that glory.

You Can Have More Than One Breakdown If You Try Hard Enough

You've had, broken, enough. The watchful, kind,
Other bastard who postures, postures in my mind,
My moralist, defence against the dead,
Says, as he keeps hitting me in the head.

Shut up, to him my rational voter's voice says,
Driven to what booths by whose whips what knows?
And, on patrol, in a desperately clean purse
I demand my literate brother, perhaps friend,
Where do you think all this will end?
I bite my answer to that dear hypocrite, that –
O my dear, bully my refrain to say
My dear, I would not have had this other one
If you hadn't put in your temperate head again.

Then I wake up again
To the pill and prick refrain
I wake up in the usual word once more,
Wordier but more helpless than before.

But after two days' drying out
I am no more inclined to shout,
I do not even whisper poetry
Except inside the quiet of my head,
Not loud enough to disturb the other dead.

It seems
– Or perhaps my muse has funny dreams –
I went home and split open wide my wife
And gobbled up my children in a stew.
Stranger, my brother, what do *you* do
When you've had enough?

They tell me this I only dreamed.
But brother, stranger, you know
As well as I do dreams are dangerous.
Witness, beloved, these
Avoiding actions of my family,
This inaccessible muse.

Daily, I tie up my pyjama cord
Waiting to be released
Upon the always unsuspecting world.

Perennial Complaint of a Writer

Around me, my books leer, lour,
Insist, make an academic stink.
You, they say, like our
Authors have paper, pen and ink.
Why don't you use the bloody things?

I regard them timidly, and say
But if I did commit a book
O which of you would pray
That at least I ought to look
Before I use the bloody things?

You fright me, books, as other things do,
Only more so. Write, or not write,
When I face the readers too
It seems wrong or not right
Whatever I do
With paper, pen and ink – those bloody things.

Advice to a Knight

Wear modest armour; and walk quietly
In woods, where any noise is treacherous.
Avoid dragons and deceptive maidens.

Be polite to other men in armour,
Especially the fierce ones, who are often strong.
Treat all old men as they might be magicians.

So you may come back from your wanderings,
Clink proud and stiff into the queen's court
To doff your helmet and expect her thanks.

The young queen is amused at your white hair,
Asks you to show your notched and rusty sword,
And orders extra straw for your bedding.

Tomorrow put on your oldest clothes,
Take a stout stick and set off again,
It's safer that way if no more rewarding.

To Miranda Crossing the Seas

It would be a hard, a bitter man
Who would carelessly let
Two girls abscond without a word.
May the waves carry you lightly.
I am only an old godfather
Wishing you well, and your mother
Because she bore you, and for other reasons
Let all be well.

Enjoy the countries, my dear, enjoy
Whatever dish you are offered
And the words that praise.
May the waves carry you lightly.
Stay beautiful, my blonde,
So you grow to be like your mother
Who is kind even to poets.
Let all be well.

For now, enjoy the voyage. The sea
Is the mother of beauty, the mother

Of your mother, of you.
May the waves carry you lightly.
And a sea-soaked poet waits
For your return, beautiful
Christened daughter of sea-poems.
Let all be well.

Come back so that I shall be alarmed
By your young beauty, take refuge
In the snarl and stutter of poems –
May the waves carry you lightly
And write a refrain for you
And the waves that brought your mother
To wish me wish you always
Let all be well.

Small Protest from a Native

It is easy to grow up
On the edges of Brecon and Radnor
Thinking the Welsh
Are your peculiar cousins
From Llangammarch and Abergwesyn.
Even so, you know you are not English.

Today, a native, I write in exile
Passionate poems about Wales
I never knew until I left it.
I am a B.A. from Aber, and M.A., too
And proud of it.
But I am prouder still those letters
Come from the university
Of my country. I am M.A. (Wales).
Will they take that away from me, too?

I shall continue to write poems about Wales.

On Taking Part in a Recital of Baroque Music and Poetry at Newcastle Cathedral, Sunday, 4 October 1964

The lectern firms me; the Book's ever a strong prop
In whatever pit: an upright man resounds
The passion, sweat, of poets who perhaps
Are dead: but rhymed so to, for, an old wound,
Dead then in paradox or oxymoron,
Dying to life, erect for resurrection.

I am troubled by my own old poems:
Own poems: would, judas, do better not to:
What he or I made in what garden do
Could be kissed away, turned by, into, rhymes.
I weed the garden for my metaphors,
Desert into, from, the legion of the curse.

Here, propped by the unrotting timber of the Lord,
I, helpless, bellow his uproarious word
Up, off pillars, roofbeams, that not shake
Even to, from, this lectern's loud manquake.
And am the poem that He makes me make.

Death, I sermon, shout Easter: rafters ring
To double doubt of echo, of commanding
Sing, you poor, you unblessed in your begetting,
Hosanna His and your poor begetting!

Upon this slow cross He is nailed for us;
Some blood, much thirst, stretched, dried Him glorious
Like the timbers of this lectern that stand and sing,
Nail up this vault where prayed beams hold and ring,
Rafter the sing and pus of me: of us.

I nail you as He nailed you with a word,
Words not mine although my belly's flame,
His torn side, burns and tears you, as you sit
O in the Sabbath of clean underclothes.
I cry unto His Dove to shit, to shit
Upon the approve and smile of each your face
There pious for me to show crossed disgrace
It is nails, young gracenipped bustler who falls
When angels wrestle with him, savage his balls,
And leave him nothing but a raftered word
With which to acclaim, condemn, what else? Whose Lord?

For My Grandfather

Ballad the idiom of my ancestry,
The beginning men on the hills of speech,
Old pulpitwalkers, pathtakers in every
Wind that brought a weather from God,
And brought me out of Brecon to this talking.

Sermoned among their troubled consonants
On Allt-y-clych the dictionary of vowels
Is always open at Alpha and Omega,
The tongued wind turns the pages of a Bible
To mark my birthday in Llanafanfawr.

No fire spoke to me out of a thornbush,
No true Book preached or pleached me on the hills,
I went down to the sea, the great waters,
Rhymed in the antipodes of language,
But talk with a shepherd in the winds above Cwmcrogau.

Girl Reading John Donne

Her arms bare, and her eyes naked,
She tells her borrowed book, *I am in love*,
And the fierce poem jumps about under her skin.

Mr, the almost anonymous lecturer
Who prescribed this text for her undoing,
When he said *Goodmorrow* to his shaving self,
Remembered how she crossed her legs in class,
Thought vaguely of writing a poem, a declaration,
But after breakfast went on marking assignments.
The girl sits blazing in the Library,
Alight over the poem to which she says
I am in love, I am in love. And the poem's
Words flame up to her unseeing eyes.
She does not need to read, only remember
The poem says *I love* to her exposed
And wanted flesh.
                    She reads naked in the Library.

Mr every now and again is deflected
From his marking, boredom, marking time,

To wonder momentarily if he was right
To ask of vulnerable innocence
What it thinks about the imprisonment
Of a great Prince.
                    His automatic pencil,
Cancelling an ampersand, dismisses
The futile question. He feels morally secure
Because he didn't interrogate them,
Her, about her, his favourite Elegie.
At that minding of bed's America
He resolutely goes on marking.
                              It's marking time.
And the naked girl in the Library
Reads a naked poem to herself, and says
I am in love, I am in love, over and over
Until the poem's canicule and sear
Become unbearable, when she burns out
To dissertate over a coke or coffee
On anything, anything except this poem,
This love, bare longing, that bed, this poem.

And elsewhere a great Prince in prison lies.

Adam and Eve Hear the Thunder

All their bravado in that grove
Was dissipated like the light,
And their prerogative of love
Was cancelled from the bitter date

When, lying on slack limbs, they heard
About their shamed and burrowing heads,
Not the charmed descant of the bird
Who'd blessed them on their previous beds,

But from the skies reverberate
And make resound the clammy sod
The ineluctable and irate
Brag of the artillery of God.

Mountain Death

An old reticence of mountains
Stripped and maculate
Reassures late
More than gauzy fountains
That tinselly sung
To us when we were young.

It keeps in the wind residual
Faith that to be born
Is to wear a keen thorn
Without any renewal
Of bone or sinew
Until death is due.

Death is good on the taciturn
Mountain, in the wind
More close than a friend;
Under a familiar thorn,
Pay for your birth
On unrequiting earth.

Adam Wonders About Eve

She writhes so
In her hair's ambiguous clouds
How should I know the truth of this temptation?

I could believe
Easily she taught the serpent how to speak,
My fluent Eve, nurse of my indecision.

Or did she make
The story up? invent behind her eyes
The talking snake as one more pet illusion

With which to drown
Me as I drown between her palpable breasts,
Her lord, her clown, twitched at her animation.

Lord, I eat.
I do not know if eating's right or wrong.
But Lord I eat careless at her instruction.

Against Wantonness

Grandfather Adam, who first tried
The use of a divining-rod,
Found such pleasure when Eve cried
He no longer envied God.

So God chastised him in the bushes,
Made it divinely plain,
Though Eve looked charming in her blushes
They must not take such joy again.

But sweat and labour in the night
Only for procreative duty
And not for mutual delight.
And kiss the rod of sterner beauty.

After Divorce

Caught by the glory of her sensual head,
I forgot for a hectic second that a shade
Should have good manners and not invade
Again her ransomed thoughts or bed.
So I had this unmannerly wish instead
That, if she too had the courtesy to fade
Into the desolation I had made
Out of the sensuality of my head,

I could sleep at last.
                    But at that word,
As at my earlier denials, I heard
My pities and angers under the severe sky
Take once again their destinationless road,
Humbugged and stumbling with their barren load
Of merely obstinate refusals to die.

For Robyn Going Abroad

Dear departer, I do not wish
Only kind seas as you traverse
The expansive province of the fish,

But just such seas as are not worse
Than those that I have safely crossed;
For you, when you depart, this verse:

A sort of prayer you'll not be lost
On any seas, in any weather,
Or even by my verses crossed.

And may we be again together
Despite my rhymes, despite the seas,
Neither I hope more rough than these.

A Storm in Childhood

We had taken the long way home, a mile
Or two further than any of us had to walk,
But it meant being together longer, and home later.

The storm broke on us – broke is a cliché,
But us isn't – that storm was loosed for us, on us.
My cousin Blodwen, oldest and wisest of us,
Said in a voice we'd never heard her use before:
'The lightning kills you when it strikes the trees.'
If we were in anything besides a storm, it was trees.
On our left, the valley bottom was nothing but trees,
And on our right the trees went half way up
The hill. We ran, between the trees and the trees,
Five children hand-in-hand, afraid of God,
Afraid of being among the lightning-fetching
Trees, soaked, soaked with rain, with sweat, with tears,
Frightened, if that's the adequate word, frightened
By the loud voice and the lambent threat,
Frightened certainly of whippings for being late,
Five children, ages six to eleven, stumbling
After a bit of running through trees from God.
Even my cousin who was eleven – I can't remember
If she was crying, too – I suppose I hope so.
But I do remember the younger ones when the stumbling

Got worse as the older terror of trees got worse
Adding their tears' irritation to the loud world of wet
And tall trees waiting to be struck by the flash, and us
With them – that running stumble, hand-in-hand – five
Children aware of our sins as we ran stumblingly:
Our sins which seemed such pointless things to talk
About to mild Miss Davies on the hard Sunday benches.

The lightning struck no trees, nor any of us.
I think we all got beaten; some of us got colds.

It was the longest race I ever ran,
A race against God's voice sounding from the hills
And his blaze aimed at the trees and at us,
A race in the unfriendly rain, with only the other
Children, hand-in-hand, to comfort me to know
They too were frightened, all of us miserable sinners.

Thorn

The thorn is punished by the October wind
And by the wind of March,
Companion for a bitter mind
And the blood's dark.

The thorn through all its punishment
In March and in October
Would not have any wind relent,
No mercy ever.

This is the prayer of the bitter mind
In the bloody dark:
May I be relentless in the wind
As the thorn, as harsh

As the punished thorn,
The thrashed and lonely thorn.

Notes on the poems

The following abbreviations are used for published volumes:

E.H. – *The Enemy in the Heart* (Hart-Davis, 1957)
S.M.P. – *Songs of a Mad Prince* (Hart-Davis, 1960)
B.D. – *The Beast at the Door* (Hart-Davis, 1963)
C.C. – *The Colour of Cockcrowing* (Hart-Davis, 1966), posthumously
C.P. – Croft & Dale-Jones *The Collected Poems of T. Harri Jones* (Gomer Press, 1977) (applies only to twenty-nine poems selected from the 'Black Book' by Julian Croft for the 'Uncollected Poems' section).

Literary magazines and other publications in which individual poems were printed:

> *The Dragon* (Y Ddraig), Magazine of the University College of Wales, Aberystwyth
> *The Welsh Review*
> *Life and Letters*
> *The Dublin Magazine*
> *The Western Mail*
> *John o'London's Weekly*
> *Review Fifty*
> *The Glass*
> *Poetry New York*
> *The New Statesman and Nation*
> *Poetry* (Chicago)
> *Time and Tide*
> *Botteghe Oscure*
> *The Times Literary Supplement*
> *New Poems*, 1958
> *New Helios*
> *Hot Dog*
> *Nimrod International Journal of Prose and Poetry*
> *Poetry Wales*
> *Wales*
> *Dock Leaves/The Anglo-Welsh Review*
> *Australian Letters*
> *Meanjin*
> *Quadrant*
> *The Bulletin*
> *Australian Highway*
> *Poetry Magazine*

Whatever the state of his private life, T. H. Jones was highly professional about his craft. His schoolboy poems are preserved in typed versions in the archive deposited by his family at the National Library of Wales, Aberystwyth, in October 2004, and from 1943 until 12 April 1949, poems and drafts were entered into a series of exercise books and dated either individually or in batches. In May 1950, he acquired the 'Black Book', a leather-bound octavo volume, made specially for him by a friend, Delia Glanville, into which he now entered and dated *completed poems only*. The final poem in the 'Black Book', 'Cotton Mather Remembers the Trial of Elizabeth How', was entered in September 1964, so that the small number of poems completed between then and his death on 29 January 1965, exist as individual drafts and fair copies (also carefully preserved).

Many of the poems are entitled simply 'Poem' or 'Song'. In the Notes these will be identified by the addition of the first line *in brackets*. Many more are *untitled*. In the *text* these will be identified by employing *the first line*, IN BRACKETS, as a title; in the *Notes* they will be identified by the first line in brackets. *More than half* of the poems in this collection are published here *for the first time*; this is indicated, *in the Notes*, by two asterisks ** immediately following the title/first line.

PAGE

1939–41: Llanafanfawr and U.C.W. Aberystwyth, 1

1.   'Sonnet on a Lost Mistress' ** 1939. Eisteddfod entry on unlined, cream-laid notepaper with 'submitted by Henry Jones, Trefelin, Newbridge-on-Wye, Radnor' in pencil on reverse. A Petrarchan sonnet (see also pp. 12, 36, 41, 61, 80, 86, 91, 108, 119, 124, 138, 140, 156, 234, 254, 255, 260, 266, 276, 282, 302, 305, 311, 339).
        'The Pacifist' ** January–March 1940, on Central Welsh Examination Board paper. 'old heads bowed in shame' – cf. 'Bald heads forgetful of their sins', W. B. Yeats (see also pp. 15, 49, 50, 51, 65, 66, 75, 77, 87, 89, 90, 92, 99, 120, 147, 158, 182, 198, 234, 245, 250, 260, 264, 302, 307, 318, 337), 'The Scholars'; 'hare's collar-bone' – cf. 'I would find . . . The collar-bone of a hare . . . And pierce it through with a gimlet, and stare . . . And laugh over the untroubled water', Yeats, 'The Collar-bone of a Hare'; 'lipless grin' – cf. 'breastless creatures under ground/Leaned backwards with a lipless grin', T. S. Eliot, 'Whispers of Immortality'. (See also pp. 3, 9, 17, 18, 33, 107, 121, 137, 214, 234, 336, 345.)

2.   'Acrobat' ** January–March 1940, on reverse of same sheet.

1941–6: Naval Service, Mediterranean and UK

Exercise Book 1: 1943–November 1944

2.   (Calling within us the spring) ** On Naval Message sheet, *c*.1942. 'nescient' – ignorant; 'bacchanal dancer' – the Bacchae (Maenads or Thyiades) were priestesses of Bacchus (Dionysus) (see also pp. 26, 90) who worked themselves up to a frenzy at Dionysiac festivals; 'susurrus' – murmuring.
        (In the duality of man) ** On Naval Message sheet, *c*.1942. 'Janus' – Roman god of, amongst other things, the New Year, represented with two faces, the one looking back, the other forward.

3.   (Cool pity covers us) ** On Naval Message sheet, *c*.1943. Reminiscent of John Pudney, (1909–77). 'sorrow of the amorous nightingale' – Philomela, daughter of Pandion, King of Attica, bigamously married by her sister's

husband, Tereus, King of Thrace, had her tongue cut out to prevent her betraying him. She was transformed into a nightingale.

(Why should I be afraid?) ** On Naval Message sheet, *c*.1943. 'walked with Merlin . . . and sat among the dead' (see also p. 202) cf. 'walked among the lowest of the dead', 'The Waste Land', T. S. Eliot. (See also pp. 1, 9, 17, 18, 33, 107, 121, 137, 214, 234, 336, 345.)

(No more for you and I, my love) ** 'Tripoli, 11 March 1943'. Inspired by Clara (Claire) Jones (see also pp. 4, 8, 10, 12), Jones's girlfriend during his first year at the University College of Wales, Aberystwyth before volunteering for naval service. She terminated the relationship some time after 9 July 1944.

4.   'Landward' ** 'Alexandria, April 1943'. Inspired by Clara Jones (see also pp. 3, 8, 10, 12). Echoes Dylan Thomas's 'The Force that through the Green Fuse Drives the Flower' ('I am dumb to tell . . . how time has ticked a heaven round the stars.') (see also pp. 20, 30, 33, 40, 52, 53, 54, 57, 58, 64, 87, 96, 104, 106, 112, 116, 117, 119, 158, 170, 186, 201, 225, 232, 234, 245, 272, 278, 279, 284, 292, 313, 345); 'edge of the sea', 'mile of beach' etc. recall Aberystwyth, where she was continuing her studies and he would resume his in 1946.

(Reaching towards the light) ** On sheet of cheap exercise-book paper, 1943. Sent to, and returned by 'Horizon', the literary magazine founded in 1939 by Cyril Connolly, Stephen Spender and Peter Watson. Connolly edited it until it ceased publication in 1950. Used as the final six lines of 'Contemplation' (1946). See also p. 6, 8, 13.

'Epitaphs' ** April/June 1943. 'They shall not be forgotten' – typical inscription on a war-memorial; 'leaded over' – obscured as in early windows where small panes of glass are held together by strips of lead; 'bird that dazzles' – kingfisher.

5.   'No songs or sonnets' ** April/June 1943. 'King's shilling' – in earlier times recruits to the Army were given a shilling to confirm their enlistment; 'montaged' – a montage is a picture made in part by sticking objects on the canvas. Here he imagines the woman's face against the 'canvas' of the moonlit sky; 'die like Marlowe' – Christopher Marlowe (1564–93), brilliant, intemperate playwright with criminal tendencies killed in a Deptford tavern after a quarrel over the bill (see also p. 226); 'city in the plain' – the 'Cities in the Plain' were Sodom and Gomorrah, supposedly destroyed by God because of the exceptional immorality of their inhabitants; 'linked sweetness' – cf. 'linked sweetness long drawn out' in 'Lycidas', the famous poem by John Milton (1608–74) (see also pp. 17, 49, 255, 281, 323, 333, 367).

6.   'Contemplation' ** April/June 1943. Contrasts the Mediterranean climate and landscape with that of Llanafan (see also pp. 23, 94, 104, 138, 142, 222, 226, 228, 244, 261, 264, 275, 283, 296, 297, 302, 310, 311, 319, 324, 332, 336, 342, 343, 346, 359, 364, 366). Vigorous growth of brambles is a characteristic of that upland landscape and symbolises the poet's youth. The last six lines of this poem were sent as a complete lyric to 'Horizon' (see also p. 4, 8, 13).

7.   (Fear not the pettiness of time) ** 'Malta, August 1943'. The optimistic
      tone of the poem reflects the relief of Malta the previous year from the
      German/Italian siege.
          (Waiting the onslaught of the light) 'Malta, 13 August 1943'.

8.   (Before the bright bird write his epitaph) ** 'Augusta, 3 September 1943'.
      Augusta, an important port in Sicily, was bombarded during the Allied
      invasion and occupation of the island between 9 July and 17 August 1943.
      Jones's vessel, HMS *Seaham*, participated with distinction in this episode.
      'principalities and powers' – cf. Ephesians 6: 12, 'For we wrestle . . .
      against principalities, against powers, against the rulers of the darkness of
      this world'.
          (Oh! you who have been there) ** 'October 1943'.
          'Similes in Exile' ** *c.*October 1943. A copy exists on cheap exercise-
      book paper bearing the return address 'from T. H. Jones, P/J X 279998,
      HMS Seaham (crossed out) Hannibal, c/o G.P.O. London'. Jones was
      transferred from HMS *Seaham* to the Algiers shore-base, Hannibal, in
      October 1943. Sent to, and returned by 'Horizon' (see also pp. 4, 6, 13),
      the literary magazine founded in 1939 by Cyril Connolly, Stephen Spender
      and Peter Watson. Connolly edited it until it ceased publication in 1950.
      Inspired by Clara Jones (see also pp. 3, 4, 10, 12) and influenced by (in
      particular) W. H. Auden (1907–73) (see also pp. 12, 13, 17, 20, 23, 26, 33,
      48, 58, 64, 76, 78, 79, 80, 108, 147, 169, 175, 177, 181, 183, 186, 195,
      204, 233, 271, 316).

9.   (I remember the house) ** *c.*December 1943. Echoes the later work of T. S.
      Eliot (see also pp. 1, 3, 17, 18, 33, 107, 121, 137, 214, 234, 336, 345), in
      particular the 'Four Quartets'.
          'The singing wonder of the stars' ** 'Algiers, Xmas 1943'.

10.   'Winter Beeches'. ** 'Algiers, January 1944'.
          'Love Song'. ** January 1944. Inspired by Clara Jones (see also pp. 3,
      4, 8, 12).
          'Salvationist's Dream'. ** 'Algiers, January 1944'. A member of the
      Salvation Army has a vision of universal salvation. The poem's imagery is
      typical of such Salvationist hymns as 'Washed in the Blood of the Lamb'.
      'lamb' – Jesus Christ; 'dragon' – the devil; 'everlasting fires' – hell;
      'Gomorrah' – companion city to Sodom, destroyed by God as punishment
      for the immorality of its inhabitants; 'Sion' – (Zion) holy hill upon which
      the Temple of Jerusalem stands.

11.   (Jack Christ was kind to me) ** January 1944. 'poor thief' – Christians
      believe that Jesus Christ blesses repentant sinners; 'nails' – and, taking the
      burden of the world's sins upon himself, was nailed to the Cross to redeem
      mankind.
          (In this white courtyard) ** 'Algiers January 1944'. A serviceman's
      denunciation of complacent non-combatants back home. 'butter your mind
      to' – gloss over; 'well-spring' – fountain.

12. (Moondappled memories) ** Algiers, January 1944.
    'When we were young we felt the tortured cities'. ** *c.*January1944. A Petrarchan sonnet (see also pp. 1, 36, 41, 61, 80, 86, 91, 108, 119, 124, 138, 140, 156, 234, 254, 255, 260, 266, 276, 282, 302, 305, 311, 339), influenced by Thirties poets, especially W. H. Auden, of whose work it is virtually a pastiche. (See also pp. 8, 13, 17, 20, 23, 26, 33, 48, 58, 64, 76, 78, 79, 80, 108, 147, 169, 175, 177, 181, 183, 186, 195, 204, 233, 271, 316.) 'Austria' – because of Hitler's annexation of that country; 'Spain' – because of the Civil War initiated by Franco; 'China' – because of the Japanese invasion and atrocities.
    'Journey from a War' ** On Naval Message sheet, *c.*January 1944. Title after Auden and Isherwood's 'Journey to a War' (1939), inspired by their visit to China. 'runic' – mysterious or secret: the runic alphabet, invented by Gothic tribes of northern Europe, is the earliest one known; 'she' – Clara Jones (see also pp. 3, 4, 8, 10).

13. 'This Hero Now' Before 2 February 1944. Air letter, February 1944. Sent to 'Horizon' (see also pp. 4, 6, 8), but not accepted for publication, perhaps because (again) too reminiscent of Auden. (See also pp. 8, 12, 17, 20, 23, 26, 33, 48, 58, 64, 76, 78, 79, 80, 108, 147, 169, 175, 177, 181, 183, 186, 195, 204, 233, 271, 316.) 'The Dragon', Lent 1947. Founded in 1878, this was the magazine of the University College of Wales, Aberystwyth. 'seas incarnadined' – *Macbeth*, II. i. 61, 'this my hand will rather/The multitudinous seas incarnadine/Making the green one red'.

14. (It was a lovely lady) *c.*June 1944. A literary ballad with a twist in its tail. 'paramour' – lover; 'aestheticism' – the cult of the beautiful; 'muse' – in Greek mythology the Muses (see also p. 26) were the patronesses of art and science.
    'Exercise in Blank Verse: the Dancing Girl'. 'Algiers, June '44'. Another example of the poet developing his technique. The blank verse is significantly irregular. 'Cino' – Cino da Pistoia, *c.*1270–*c.*1337, a friend of Dante. Italy in their time was a collection of city-states.

15. (But that was yesterday) June–October 1944. The quotation is from 'Coole Park and Ballylee' by W. B. Yeats (1865–1939) (see also pp. 1, 49, 50, 51, 65, 66, 75, 77, 87, 89, 90, 92, 99, 120, 147, 158, 182, 198, 234, 245, 250, 260, 264, 302, 307, 318, 337). 'yesterday' – i.e. before the cataclysm of the Second World War destroyed all 'sanctity and loveliness'; 'Holy Grail' – allegedly the cup used by Jesus Christ at the last supper, in which Joseph of Arimathea collected some of Christ's blood. He brought it to England, where it disappeared and was sought by the Knights of the Round Table. As only a person of perfect purity can approach it, it has never been found.
    'Mountain Scene' June–October 1944. 'golgothic' – Golgotha – the place outside Jerusalem where Christ was crucified. The word is Aramaic for 'skull'.

16. 'Nostalgia' ** On sheet from cheap writing-pad. Dated 'Naples Oct '44'. Written, presumably, as its subject matter suggests, on voyage back to Britain. The only poem by Jones to make reference to his mother's country, the Valleys of South Wales.

Exercise Book 2: November 1944–September 1946

16. 'Sailor's Return' ** *c.*January 1945, on a sheet of large, good quality, blue notepaper headed 'HMS WESTMINSTER, c/o G.P.O., LONDON'. Jones had returned to England on 7 October, 1944 and in January 1945 joined 'Westminster', a destroyer which had seen service in the First World War and was at this time running the courier-service to Norway.

'Desertion' ** *c.*July 1945. Germany had capitulated on 7 May, bringing to an end the war in Europe. The poem is a brief retrospect on Jones's service in the Mediterranean. 'Arcadian' – simple/innocent: from Arcadia, a district in Greece where the people were primitive and thought to be unspoiled.

17. 'Invocation' 2 September 1945, 'The Dragon', Lent 1947.

'Dear Lady' ** 2 September 1945. A virtuoso piece influenced by Auden's (see also pp. 8, 12, 13, 20, 23, 26, 33, 48, 58, 64, 76, 78, 79, 80, 108, 147, 169, 175, 177, 181, 183, 186, 195, 204, 233, 271, 316) verse-letters, and designed to impress the object of a brief 'grand passion'. 'sonnets, jewelled things' – characteristic of the 'age' of Shakespeare (1564–1616) (see also pp. 33, 55, 56, 58, 79, 81, 89, 129, 138, 158, 229, 235, 261, 264, 270, 276, 288, 297, 311, 344, 345); 'gifts of kings' – gold, frankincense and myrrh, brought by the Magi as symbolic gifts to the Christ-child; 'evening star' – according to Milton (1608–74) (see also pp. 5, 49, 255, 281, 323, 333, 367), in 'Paradise Lost', where he associates it with the 'amorous bird of night', 'love's harbinger'; 'Great Virgil . . . of man and arms' – the subject of Virgil's (see also p. 95) epic poem, the 'Aeneid', which opens with the line 'arma virumque cano' ('I sing of arms and the man'; 'Milton of God . . . ' – Milton declared that the object of his epic, 'Paradise Lost', was to 'justify the ways of God to Men'; 'Eliot . . . Showed us the waste and desolate land' – in 'The Waste Land' (1922) T. S. Eliot (1888–1965) exposes the emptiness of contemporary life; (see also pp. 1, 3, 9, 18, 33, 107, 121, 137, 214, 234, 336, 345). 'Spenser' – Edmund Spenser's (*c.*1552–99) (see also pp. 46, 307) great allegorical poem, 'The Faerie Queene' (1589), evokes many 'enchanted' places; 'Shakespeare . . . of all the world' – (see also pp. 33, 55, 56, 58, 79, 81, 89, 129, 138, 158, 229, 235, 261, 264, 270, 276, 288, 297, 311, 344, 345) an allusion to the famous speech (*As You Like It*, II. vii. 139) which begins 'All the world's a stage . . . '; 'as Tennyson said' – 'Come down, O maid, from yonder mountain height:/What pleasure lives in height? . . . For Love is of the valley (*sic*) . . . come thou down/And (*sic*) find him', in 'The Princess' (see also p. 100).

18. (I have been one that loved) ** 7 September 1945. 'fragments shored against my ruins' – cf. T. S. Eliot, 'The Waste Land' – 'These fragments have I shored against my ruins.' (see also pp. 1, 3, 9, 17, 33, 107, 121, 137, 214, 234, 336, 345). 'laurel/palm' Greek/Roman symbols of victory.

(Sweet sleeper, do not wake) ** 7 September 1945. 'brightness gone from the air' – cf. Thomas Nashe (1567–1601), 'Brightness falls from the air' (from 'In Time of Pestilence'); 'sapper' – one who undermines.

19. (It was a voice serene) 7 September 1945.
     'Inaccessibility' ** 31 October 1945. Unsuccessful courtship imaged in
     nautical terms.

20. 'Love Gone' 31 October 1945 'Portsmouth'. At this time Jones was
     stationed at HMS *Collingwood*, a shore-establishment at Fareham,
     Hampshire. 'love's map' – allusion to Dylan Thomas's (see also pp. 4, 30,
     33, 40, 52, 53, 54, 57, 58, 64, 87, 96, 104, 106, 112, 116, 117, 119, 158,
     170, 186, 201, 225, 232, 234, 245, 272, 278, 279, 284, 292, 313, 345)
     The Map of Love (1939), a volume of sixteen poems and seven stories
        'Lament' ** 2 December 1945. The poet contrasts his wartime with his
     peacetime self. Influenced by W. H. Auden. (See also pp. 8, 12, 13, 17, 23,
     26, 33, 48, 58, 64, 76, 78, 79, 80, 108, 147, 169, 175, 177, 181, 183, 186,
     195, 204, 233, 271, 316.) 'fat' = swell.

21. 'Requiescat' ** 2 December 1945. The poem's title means 'may s/he rest in
     peace'.
        (Darlings) ** 28 December 1945. Verse-letter to the poet's sisters,
     Brenda, Myra, Valerie and Patricia from HMS *Collingwood*, a shore-base
     at Fareham, Hants. 'star-captains' – cf. James Elroy Flecker (1884–1915)
     (see also p. 246), 'the fleet of stars is anchored and the young star-captains
     glow' ('The Gates of Damascus. West Gate'); 'star/For guide' – like the
     Magi en route to Bethlehem; 'Wye' – river which runs through Builth Wells
     (see also pp. 64, 143, 157, 294, 297, 326, 343, 346), where Jones went to
     school; 'Val' – Valerie, the third of Jones's four sisters; 'little Pat' – Patricia,
     his youngest sister (see also pp. 157, 288, 349); 'Jerusalem' – a letter home
     (15 December 1942) records a visit to the city; 'Alexandria' – Jones was
     based there from 10 April 1942 to 7 October 1943; 'Algiers' – his base
     from 8 October 1943–26 July 1944.

1946–9: Aberystwyth, 2, and Borth

23. 'Poem for Wales' 3–20 January 1946. 'The Dragon' ('Y Ddraig'), Easter
     1946. 'Chemic' – chemical: the suggestion appears to be that the hills are
     a part of him, he shares their substance; 'neural treason' – an echo of
     Auden's (see also pp. 8, 12, 13, 17, 20, 26, 33, 48, 58, 64, 76, 78, 79, 80,
     108, 147, 169, 175, 177, 181, 183, 186, 195, 204, 233, 271, 316) 'neural
     itch' – to betray Wales would be to go against his innermost nature. The
     poem is the formal commitment, in the bardic tradition, of a Welsh poet to
     his native land, a commitment that would remain central to his writing in
     England from 1949–59 and Australia from 1959 until his death in 1965:
     'Thorn' (*c*.December 1964), the last poem he preserved, evokes yet again
     the harsh landscape of Llanafanfawr.

26. 'Song of Hope' ** *c*.3 February 1946. Celebration of the end of the war
     and his release from naval service. Heavily influenced by Auden (see also
     pp. 8, 12, 13, 17, 20, 23, 33, 48, 58, 64, 76, 78, 79, 80, 108, 147, 169, 175,
     177, 181, 183, 186, 195, 204, 233, 271, 316) and Thirties poetry. 'dogs of
     war' – *Julius Caesar*, III. i. 270; 'calyx' – the cup-shaped outer covering of

a flower; 'bacchic dance' – Bacchus (see also pp. 2, 90), god of wine, and his followers were noted for their wild, drunken dancing; 'satyrs' – goat-like lecherous forest gods; 'Grand Central' – New York's railway station; 'Parnassus' – mountain of Apollo (see also pp. 28, 217, 312) and the Muses (see also p. 14), sacred to poetry.

27.   'For a Proud Beauty' ** 3 February 1946.
     'Sea Voices' ** 22 February 1946. 'amorphous' – with no regular shape; 'languorous' – dreamy; 'glaucous' – sea-green.

28.   'Homage' ** 22 February 1946. According to one Greek legend, the soul of Apollo (see also pp. 28, 217, 312), god of poetry and poets, passed into a swan.

29.   'You' 6 March 1946. 'The Dragon', Summer 1947.
     'The Enemy in the Heart' 7 March 1946. 'The Welsh Review', V, 3, Autumn 1946; Nimrod 3, 1, Summer 1965. E.H., p. 30, first poem to be accepted by a literary magazine. T. H. Jones studied English in the department at Aberystwyth of which the magazine's founder/editor, 'Prof. Gwyn' (Gwyn Jones, 1907–99) was Professor. Published monthly between February and November 1939 and as a quarterly from March 1944 until December 1948. The poem's first line is an allusion to I Corinthians 15: 26, 'The last enemy that shall be destroyed is death'.

30.   'Found Love' 7 March 1946. The imagery of this poem is noticeably similar to that of 'The Enemy in the Heart' above. 'agate' – semi-precious stone, a variety of chalcedony.
     'Metamorphosis' ** March 1946. The poem's title means 'change/transformation'; 'sullen pride of craft' cf. Dylan Thomas's (see also pp. 4, 20, 33, 40, 52, 53, 54, 57, 58, 64, 87, 96, 104, 106, 112, 116, 117, 119, 158, 170, 186, 201, 225, 232, 234, 245, 272, 278, 279, 284, 292, 313, 345) poem 'In my craft or sullen art'; 'epitomised' – were the perfect example of.

31.   'Aberystwyth, March 1946' ** March 1946. 'coming/Home' – Jones had broken off his studies at the University College in 1941 to volunteer for war service.

32.   (Pay no more adulation) ** March 1946. 'adulation' – exaggerated respect.
     (What original or rare) ** March 1946.
     (He had a certain seagreen speech) ** March 1944. 'glaucous' – sea-green; 'He' – Death.

33.   (My heart is now an unlocked lucky room) ** March 1946. Shakespearean sonnet (see also pp. 17, 55, 56, 58, 79, 81, 89, 129, 138, 158, 229, 235, 261, 264, 270, 276, 288, 297, 311, 344, 345). 'little room . . . everywhere' – quoted from John Donne's (1571?–1631) 'the Good-Morrow' – 'And makes one little room, an everywhere.' (See also pp. 36, 60, 257, 260, 266, 334, 366.)
     'Builth' ** 'April 46'. Builth Wells, Powys, (formerly Breconshire) (see also pp. 21, 64, 143, 157, 294, 297, 326, 343, 346) is the nearest town to

Jones's birthplace. He attended secondary school there and wrote a more specific poem about the town, 'Builth Wells', p. 346) near the end of his life. 'his grief' – war service in the Mediterranean; 'quiet in the stony places' – cf. 'the agony in stony places' (T. S. Eliot, 'The Waste Land') (see also pp. 1, 3, 9, 17, 18, 107, 121, 137, 214, 234, 336, 345). 'sharded' – broken into fragments; 'annunciate' – joyful (as was the Virgin Mary at The annunciation, when an angel told her that she would give birth to Christ).

'In My Returning' 4 May 1946. 'The Welsh Review', VI, 4, Winter 1947. E.H. p. 16. The poem echoes both Dylan Thomas (see also pp. 4, 20, 30, 40, 52, 53, 54, 57, 58, 64, 87, 96, 104, 106, 112, 116, 117, 119, 158, 170, 186, 201, 225, 232, 234, 245, 272, 278, 279, 284, 292, 313, 345) and W. H. Auden (see also pp. 8, 12, 13, 17, 20, 23, 26, 48, 58, 64, 76, 78, 79, 80, 108, 147, 169, 175, 177, 181, 183, 186, 195, 204, 233, 271, 316). A distinctly postmodernist combination. 'cwms' – valleys.

34. (Now after many journeys) ** 22 May 1946. 'you' is presumably Madeleine Scott, whom Jones married on 14 December 1946. See also pp. 45, 64, 77, 143, 147, 148, 156, 159, 169, 218, 224, 234, 236, 240, 242, 266, 269, 283, 285, 291, 312, 343. The 'journeys' are emotional here, rather than geographical.

35. 'Poem' (I am the poet walking in the wind) 22 May 1946. 'The Dragon', Lent 1948.
    (No pity nor prophylactic) ** 24 May 1946. 'prophylactic' – protection (probably with a hint at 'contraceptive'); 'didactic' – instructive.

36. 'Idyll' ** 15 June 1946. An 'idyll' is both a picturesque poem and an experience of happy innocence.
    (From my singing sullenness) ** 19 June 1946.
    (We are in love) ** 19 June 1946. Petrarchan sonnet (see also pp. 1, 12, 36, 41, 61, 80, 86, 91, 108, 119, 124, 138, 140, 156, 234, 254, 255, 260, 266, 276, 282, 302, 305, 311, 339). Early example of the influence of John Donne (1571?–1631). cf. especially, 'Girl Reading John Donne'. (See also pp. 33, 60, 257, 260, 266, 334, 366.)

37. (Once I wanted to make) ** 19 June 1946.
    'First Kiss' ** 19 June 1946. Sonnet. 'immutably' – not capable of being changed (forever).
    (And I would send you argosies of words) ** 19 June 1946. Sonnet. 'argosies' – boatloads (an 'argosy' was a large Venetian merchant-ship); 'lapidary' – jewelled (beautiful); 'Venus rising' – Venus Anadyomene, a famous painting by Botticelli of Venus rising from the sea-foam accompanied by dolphins (see also pp. 38, 42, 46, 56, 86, 109, 111, 234, 307, 363); 'made from the spring's flowers' – in the 'Mabinogion' (see also pp. 228, 337, 343), Blodeuwedd, beautiful wife of Lleu Llawgyffes, was created from the flowers of oak, broom and meadowsweet.

38. (Were I that cold commemorative ghost) ** 19 June 1946. A kind of sonnet. 'commemorative' – almost untranslatable: he means 'if I still cared

for that woman who rejected me'; 'jade' – (worthless horse) a perverse, untrustworthy woman; 'tirade' – a lengthy declaration.

(Legends ago) ** 19 June 1946. 'Rose . . . seas' – see also pp. 37, 42, 46, 56, 86, 109, 111, 234, 307, 36; 'exultance' – delight; 'catalyst' – a substance which, unchanged itself, causes a change in another. Incorporated in 'The Weasel at the Heart' (see also pp. 66, 74, 145) (7–14 October 1947).

39.   (Grief's unscarred wounds) ** 24 June 1946. 'unscarred' – not yet healed.

'Prayer' ** 24 June 1946. 'idol days' – time spent in foolish worship of wrong things; 'uncreated commerce of delight' – trivial pleasures; 'prayers of mere profanity' – superficiality. (Jones feels the need to lead a more serious and worthwhile existence).

40.   'Epithalamion' 26 June 1946. The title means 'song for a marriage'; 'never until the meeting making' – cf. 'Never until the mankind making . . . ' the first line of Dylan Thomas's (1914–53) 'A Refusal to Mourn the Death by Fire of a Child in London' (see also pp. 4, 20, 30, 33, 52, 53, 54, 57, 58, 64, 87, 96, 104, 106, 112, 116, 117, 119, 158, 170, 186, 201, 225, 232, 234, 245, 272, 278, 279, 284, 292, 313, 345); 'waking . . . with a kiss' – as the Prince awakens Sleeping Beauty; 'auras' – cooing; 'benignant' – kindly.

(Bodies are poems) ** 26 June 1946.

'That Other I . . . ' ** 26 June 1946. 'time-belled' – preoccupied with the past.

41.   'Two Poems, I and II' 26 June 1946. 'The Dragon', Michaelmas 1946. I is a Petrarchan sonnet (see also pp. 1, 12, 36, 61, 80, 86, 91, 108, 119, 124, 138, 140, 156, 234, 254, 255, 260, 266, 276, 282, 302, 305, 311, 339), II is a sonnet-like lyric of four triplets and a couplet.

42.   'The Enemies' ** 27 June 1946. The poem is about the disabling effect of unpleasant memories (e.g. of the 1939–45 war, which haunted T. H. Jones for the rest of his life) upon present happiness. 'vowelled towers' – lovers' talk/poetry; 'succour' – help.

(I would send you words) ** 3 July 1946. Venus rising from the foam (see also pp. 37, 38, 46, 56, 86, 109, 111, 234, 307, 363).

(It was always easy) ** 3 July 1946. 'idylls' – delightful experiences; 'inanition' – exhaustion; 'this enduring summer' – 1946 was Jones's first peacetime summer for five years; 'translated' – heavenly.

43.   'Renunciation' ** 4 July 1946.

44.   'Benghazi, Christmas 1942' ** 4 July 1946. Benghazi, a city and port in north-eastern Libya, was fought over and destroyed in the Desert Campaign of the Second World War. It was finally secured after the Battle of El Alamein earlier in 1942. At that time Jones was serving aboard the minesweeper, HMS *Seaham*. 'Tintagel' – picturesque ruined castle in Cornwall associated, justifiably it now appears, with the era of King Arthur (see also pp. 203, 229, 337, 343); 'Troy' – historic city destroyed by the Greeks during the Trojan War.

(From what high heaven) ** 11 July 1946.

(Djinn-master Solomon) ** 11 July 1946. 'djinn' – spirits of Mohammedan mythology, in which, as in everything else, King Solomon (see also pp. 62, 262) was wiser than anyone else. He had a whole harem of wives.

45.   (Images of adventure and desire) ** 11 July 1946. 'faring' – travelling; 'paragon' – perfect example; 'tourbillion' – vortex; 'Ulysses . . . Penelope' – in Homer's 'Odyssey', Ulysses (Odysseus) (see also pp. 46, 261, 262) was separated from his wife, Penelope, for ten years by the siege of Troy.

'A Wish' ** 11 July 1946. 'dark women' – Madeleine, Jones's wife, was dark-haired. See also pp. 34, 64, 77, 143, 147, 148, 156, 159, 169, 218, 224, 234, 236, 240, 242, 266, 269, 283, 285, 291, 312, 343.

'Portrait' ** 11 July 1946.

46.   'Ulysses' ** 16 July 1946. Ulysses (see also pp. 45, 261, 262) was famous for his resourcefulness, especially in tight corners.

'Late Love' ** 16 July 1946. 'Squire of Dames' – a cavalier devoted to ladies. The original appears in the 'The Faerie Queene' of Edmund Spenser, bk.III, canto vii, l. 51; (see also pp. 17, 307) 'Venus and the trampling boar' – (see also pp. 37, 38, 42, 56, 86, 109, 111, 234, 307, 363) the Calydonian Boar was sent by Artemis (Diana), goddess of chastity, to ravage the lands of King Oeneus, who had failed to make suitable sacrifices to her. Jones means that he was neither (particularly) promiscuous nor (particularly) chaste.

(O broken by bright eyes) ** 17 July 1946. The form of the poem is terza rima, the verse-form of Dante's (1265–1321) (see also pp. 14, 234) 'Divina Commedia' – aba bcb cdc efe feff, the final quatrain being a slight variation. 'crusoe mind' – the eponymous hero of Defoe's 'Robinson Crusoe', shipwrecked on a desert island, longed for company (which he eventually found in the form of his Man Friday); 'estranging' – cutting off/separating cf. 'The unplumb'd, salt, estranging sea' (Matthew Arnold, 1822–88, 'To Marguerite') (see also pp. 107, 119).

47.   (I see the sad cities) ** 26 July 1946. The towns and cities devastated during the Second World War. (cf. 'Benghazi, Christmas 1942' above p. 44).

(Across the unresponsive oceans) ** 26 July 1946; 'pampas' – the treeless plain of southern South America.

(Traced on the dark skies) ** 26 July 1946.

(The young men who admired themselves) ** 26 July 1946. The poem is full of sexual innuendo, the most obvious example being 'field . . . plough'.

48.   (I would not have you otherwise) ** 30 July 1946. 'love engendered' – being in love has increased the woman's beauty.

(Now is the time to remember) ** 30 July 1946. Influenced by such earlier poems of W. H. Auden (1907–73) as 'Paysage Moralisé', in which landscape is used symbolically. (See also pp. 8, 12, 13, 17, 20, 23, 26, 33, 58, 64, 76, 78, 79, 80, 108, 147, 169, 175, 177, 181, 183, 186, 195, 204, 233, 271, 316.)

(Surrender) ** 30 July 1946.

(Agony is not to be encountered) ** 30 July 1946. The suffering of the Jews of Europe under Hitler's regime did not end with the war, but was followed by their displacement all over Europe and then by the further struggle to found the state of Israel. 'rhetoric garlands' – a satirical reference to people (politicians in particular) who congratulate themselves on their humanity, but whose only assistance to those in desperate need is to talk about it.

49.   (Who dealt in dogmas) ** 19 August 1946. 'dogma' – an opinion so settled that it is not to be argued about; 'Leda' – Zeus, king of the gods, took the form of a swan to rape Leda, wife of Tyndareus (see also pp. 127, 250, 254, 264, 309, 320). She gave birth to two eggs, out of one of which was born Helen of Troy (see also pp. 127, 250, 254, 264, 277, 279, 284, 298, 320). Subject of a fine poem by W. B. Yeats, another influence on these early poems. (See also pp. 1, 15, 50, 51, 65, 66, 75, 77, 87, 89, 90, 92, 99, 120, 147, 158, 182, 198, 234, 245, 250, 260, 264, 302, 307, 318, 337.)
      (Because of that great company) ** 19 August 1946.
      (Refusing now to sing) ** 19 August 1946. 'to be without art' – the writing of poetry, especially lyric poetry, can be a painful process, but however much the poet may wish to be relieved of his burden, it is even more painful not to write. John Milton (1608–74) (see also pp. 5, 17, 255, 281, 323, 333, 367) described poetry as the 'talent which is death to hide'.

50.   (Do not look for me) ** 19 August 1946. 'foreign place' – grave.
      (Of course that was no country) ** 19 August 1946. Again influenced by W. B. Yeats (see also pp. 1, 15, 49, 51, 65, 66, 75, 77, 87, 89, 90, 92, 99, 120, 147, 158, 182, 198, 234, 245, 250, 260, 264, 302, 307, 318, 337), this time his 'Sailing to Byzantium', which begins 'That is no country for old men. The young/In one another's arms . . . ' Jones's 'country' here is the Middle East, where he served aboard the minesweeper HMS *Seaham* during the Second World War.
      (Winter's shadowed hour) ** 22 August 1946.

51.   (Seeking the last deformity) ** 22 August 1946. The quotation is from 'The Phases of the Moon' in W. B. Yeats's (1865–1939) volume, *The Wild Swans at Coole* (1919), one of a number of poems featuring the symbolic figures, Hunchback, Saint and Fool. All three are, like the Poet, 'deformed' physically, mentally or spiritually and through their suffering have a particular insight. (See also pp. 1, 15, 49, 50, 65, 66, 75, 77, 87, 89, 90, 92, 99, 120, 147, 158, 182, 198, 234, 245, 250, 260, 264, 302, 307, 318, 337.) 'Lethean' – in Greek legend, the souls of the dead are obliged to taste the waters of Lethe, a river of Hades, so as to forget everything they have said or done in life.
      (Winter can be deceitful) ** 22 August 1946.

52.   'After the Funeral' ** 22 August 1946. Title from Dylan Thomas's (1914–1953) poem in memory of Ann Jones, which begins 'After the funeral, mule praises, brays . . . '. (See also pp. 4, 20, 30, 33, 40, 53, 54, 57, 58, 64, 87, 96, 104, 106, 112, 116, 117, 119, 158, 170, 186, 201, 225, 232, 234, 245, 272, 278, 279, 284, 292, 313, 345.) A kind of sonnet, rhyming aba bab aba bab cc. 'anodyne' – pain-reliever.

(Hot summer in the blood) ** September 1946. 'dumb to tell' borrowed from Dylan Thomas's 'The Force that throught the Green Fuse Drives the Flower'.

(It is not death I fear) ** September 1946.

53.   (Where no light breaks) ** September 1946. Virtual pastiche of Dylan Thomas. Title from his 'Light Breaks where no Sun Shines'. (See also pp. 4, 20, 30, 33, 40, 52, 54, 57, 58, 64, 87, 96, 104, 106, 112, 116, 117, 119, 158, 170, 186, 201, 225, 232, 234, 245, 272, 278, 279, 284, 292, 313, 345.) 'hands' commerce' – caresses.

Exercise Book 3: October 1946–13 December 1947

53.   (Oh! who would follow) ** *c.*October 1946. In 1940, Jones chose to leave the 'peaceful fertile fields and happy home' for war service in the Mediterranean. As a child he had been fascinated by the sea – 'A small boy in a small Welsh school/Dreamed . . . that he would go to sea' ('Lucky Jonah', p. 222 and see also p. 185); as a man, ironically, he met his death in it. 'siren song' – the Sirens of Greek legend were monsters, half woman, half bird, whose sweet song lured sailors to their death.

54.   (The limbs of summer) ** October 1946.
    (If I should lyrically lament) ** October 1946.
    (The separated limbs) ** October 1946. 'have their dominion' is an ironical allusion to Dylan Thomas's 'And death shall have no dominion'. (See also pp. 4, 20, 30, 33, 40, 52, 53, 57, 58, 64, 87, 96, 104, 106, 112, 116, 117, 119, 158, 170, 186, 201, 225, 232, 234, 245, 272, 278, 279, 284, 292, 313, 345.)
    (Love's weather changed) ** 15 October 1946.

55.   (So I was ruined) ** October 1946.
    (So I beget you) ** October 1946. Shakespearean (see also pp. 17, 33, 56, 58, 79, 81, 89, 129, 138, 158, 229, 235, 261, 264, 270, 276, 288, 297, 311, 344, 345) sonnet with something of an Elizabethan flavour.

56.   (From brooding on the possible event) ** October 1946.
    (I would have you remain) ** October 1946. 'venust' – adjective coined by the poet from 'Venus'. The Venus here is the Venus Anadyomene (rising from the Foam with Dolphins) – see also pp. 37, 38, 42, 46, 86, 109, 111, 234, 307, 363).
    (Prince Hamlet) October 1946. In Shakespeare's play, set at the Castle of Elsinore, Hamlet had a great deal to say, but, urged by the ghost of the King, his father, eventually managed to kill his uncle, Claudius, who had married Gertrude, the Queen. The play is set in the Castle of Elsinore. Osric is the affected courtier who presides at the fencing-match in which Hamlet is killed. (See also pp. 17, 33, 55, 58, 79, 81, 89, 129, 138, 158, 229, 235, 261, 264, 270, 276, 288, 297, 311, 344, 345.)

57.   (The lone mister) ** 31 October 1946. Inspired by Dylan Thomas's 'The Hunchback in the Park' ('A solitary mister'). (See also pp. 4, 20, 30, 33,

40, 52, 53, 54, 58, 64, 87, 96, 104, 106, 112, 116, 117, 119, 158, 170, 186, 201, 225, 232, 234, 245, 272, 278, 279, 284, 292, 313, 345.)

(A summer of birds) ** 18 January 1947. Strongly influenced by Dylan Thomas's 'Poem in October' (e.g. 'walked abroad in a shower of all my days').

'Alone' ** 18 January 1947.

58. 'For a Dead Sailor' ** 18 January 1947. A poignant tribute to seaman killed in the Second World War. 'Refusal to mourn . . . Deep with the dead' – postmodernist deliberate echo of Dylan Thomas's 'A Refusal to Mourn the Death by Fire of a Child in London', one line of which reads 'Deep with the first dead lies London's daughter'. (See also pp. 4, 20, 30, 33, 40, 52, 53, 54, 57, 64, 87, 96, 104, 106, 112, 116, 117, 119, 158, 170, 186, 201, 225, 232, 234, 245, 272, 278, 279, 284, 292, 313, 345.)

'Ferdinand to Miranda' ** 18 January 1947. Ferdinand and Miranda (see also pp. 129, 297) are the hero and heroine of Shakespeare's 'The Tempest'. (See also pp. 17, 33, 55, 56, 79, 81, 89, 129, 138, 158, 229, 235, 261, 264, 270, 276, 288, 297, 311, 344, 345.) The poem is influenced by the sonnet addressed to Miranda by Ferdinand in W. H. Auden's (1907–73) 'The Sea and the Mirror' published in *For the Time Being* (1945). (See also pp. 8, 12, 13, 17, 20, 23, 26, 33, 48, 64, 76, 78, 79, 80, 108, 147, 169, 175, 177, 181, 183, 186, 195, 204, 233, 271, 316.) 'kind tyrant' – Prospero.

59. 'War Widow' ** 18 January 1947. There were, of course, very many women widowed by the Second World War.

60. (When in the tousled bed) ** 18 January 1947. 'die' has the sexual sense cf. Donne's 'If . . . none doe slacken, none can die.' ('The Good Morrow'). (See also pp. 33, 36, 257, 260, 266, 334, 366.)

(It was a winter night) ** 7 February 1947.

(Let me make you a poem) ** 7 February 1947. 'ode'/'elegy'/'lyric' – various kinds of poem: an ode is a poem addressed to some person or thing, an elegy mourns a death and a lyric (this is one) is a song-like poem.

61. (The greenness of the heart) ** 7 February 1947.

(The mind alone) ** 7 February 1947. Petrarchan sonnet (see also pp. 1, 12, 36, 41, 80, 86, 91, 108, 119, 124, 138, 140, 156, 234, 254, 255, 260, 266, 276, 282, 302, 305, 311, 339).

(Though we lie now) ** 25 February 1947.

62. (At the close of a winter day) ** 25 February 1947.

'Song' (Were I as wise as Solomon) ** 9 March 1947. (See also pp. 44, 262.)

63. 'Poems in Separation, I' ** 9 March 1947.

'Poems in Separation, II' ** 9 March 1947. 'unrib' – tear away, as God took away one of Adam's ribs to create Eve (Genesis 3: 20 ff.) (see also pp. 93, 99, 101, 116, 167, 180, 210, 225, 251, 255, 257, 265, 266, 284, 318, 361, 367, 368).

64. 'Poem' (The hand that dreams of poems at my side) ** 18 July 1947, 'Ajaccio'. There is a gap of four months between this poem and the previous one. It seems likely that Jones devoted the time to preparation for his Final Examination, in which he achieved First Class Honours (academic achievement seems always to have been almost as important to him as becoming a successful poet, and from the time of his appointment to the University of New South Wales he very successfully combined the two). He and Madeleine (see also pp. 34, 45, 77, 143, 147, 148, 156, 159, 169, 218, 224, 234, 236, 240, 242, 266, 269, 283, 285, 291, 312, 343) celebrated his 'First' with a holiday at Marseilles and in Corsica. A carbon copy of this poem, signed 'Harri Jones', was discovered by Meic Stephens at Aberystwyth in Roy H. Evans" copy of 'The Beast at the Door', June 2001. Evans, an old boy of Builth County School (see also pp. 33 143, 157, 294, 297, 326, 343, 346), senior to Jones, became a close friend. A Marxist, he was President of the Labour Club at U.C. Aberystwyth when Jones began his course in 1939. Echoes of both Auden (see also pp. 8, 12, 13, 17, 20, 23, 26, 33, 48, 58, 76, 78, 79, 80, 108, 147, 169, 175, 177, 181, 183, 186, 195, 204, 233, 271, 316) and Dylan Thomas (see also pp. 4, 20, 30, 33, 40, 52, 53, 54, 57, 58, 87, 96, 104, 106, 112, 116, 117, 119, 158, 170, 186, 201, 225, 232, 234, 245, 272, 278, 279, 284, 292, 313, 345).

    'Apologia pro Carmina Sua' (Apology for his Poems) 3 August 1947. 'The Dragon', Lent 1948. The title is an allusion to John Henry Newman's (1801–90) famous autobiography, *Apologia pro Vita Sua* (1864).

65. (This circling dancer) ** 7 October 1947. 'some old painter' – a distinctly Yeatsian phrase (see also pp. 1, 15, 49, 50, 51, 66, 75, 77, 87, 89, 90, 92, 99, 120, 147, 158, 182, 198, 234, 245, 250, 260, 264, 302, 307, 318, 337); 'wave of the sea' – Jones may be thinking of 'The Great Wave', the famous painting by the Japanese artist, Katsushika Hokusai (1760–1849).

66. 'The Weasel at the Heart' ** 7–14 October 1947. Yeatsian verse-play written for the actress, then a student, Rachel (Ray) Roberts (1927–80) (see also pp. 101, 145), and performed with sensational success at Aberystwyth in the summer of 1948 with Rachel in the starring role. She was the poet's 'Muse' then (and Jones would have been aware that Yeats (see also pp. 1, 15, 49, 50, 51, 65, 75, 77, 87, 89, 90, 92, 99, 120, 147, 158, 182, 198, 234, 245, 250, 260, 264, 302, 307, 318, 337) had written 'Cathleen ni Houlihan' for his own 'Muse', Maud Gonne) and for some time thereafter (see 'Song for Rachel', p. 101) and this work relates to 'The Enemy in the Heart' (p. 29 above), 'Two Poems' (p. 41 above) and the three love poems, 'Invocation' (p. 70), 'You' (p. 29) and 'A Wish' (p. 45). 'weasel' – small, vicious animal with sharp teeth, symbolic here of female frustration; 'fabulous' (p. 70) – originally 'mythical/celebrated in story', but now a vague expression of pleasure of virtually any kind or degree; 'elder-branches' (p. 71) – among the many popular traditions associated with the elder tree are that Christ's cross was made from its wood and that Judas hanged himself from an elder. Jones wrote two further short verse-plays, 'The Walking Devil' (1947) and 'The Night Time Was Poured Out' (c.1948)

and a longer one, 'The Birds of Rhiannon', *A Comedy in Three Acts* (1951), but none of these has yet been performed.

74. 'Poet' ** 29 November 1947. Speech by the character, Poet, in 'The Weasel at the Heart' (see also pp. 38, 66, 145), preserved separately under this title.
    (Death is within us) ** 29 November 1947. 'leaping moment' – the *birth* of *death*, a striking oxymoron.
    'A Woman and Some Men' ** 29 November 1947. Male high-mindedness ('intellect') humiliated by female emotion ('passion').

75. 'The Sailor Speaks' ** 29 November 1947. 'elusive light' – the higher significance of life. Returning from war service at sea to the 'hills and little farms' of rural Breconshire, the poet finds his idealistic expectations disappointed.
    'Love is Like the Lion's Tooth' ** 29 November 1947. The quotation is from Yeats's 'Words for Music Perhaps, VII, Crazy Jane Grown Old Looks at the Dancers' where, out of the experience of a long life, she reflects that sexual love is powerful, sharp and potentially fatal. (See also pp. 1, 15, 49, 50, 51, 65, 66, 77, 87, 89, 90, 92, 99, 120, 147, 158, 182, 198, 234, 245, 250, 260, 264, 302, 307, 318, 337.)

76. 'Prologue to "Love for Love"' ** 30 November 1947. Written for a University College of Wales, Aberystwyth production of William Congreve's (1670–1729) Restoration comedy.

Exercise Book 4: 14 December 1947–12 April 1949

76. 'Poem' (In the mean parishes of my desire) ** 14 December 1947. Influenced by W. H. Auden's (1907–73) use, in his early poetry, of 'symbolic landscape'. (See also pp. 8, 12, 13, 17, 20, 23, 26, 33, 48, 58, 64, 78, 79, 80, 108, 147, 169, 175, 177, 181, 183, 186, 195, 204, 233, 271, 316.)

77. 'For My Unborn Child' ** 18 December 1947. At this time Madeleine Jones (see also pp. 34, 45, 64, 143, 147, 148, 156, 159, 169, 218, 224, 234, 236, 240, 242, 266, 269, 283, 285, 291, 312, 343) was pregnant with their first daughter, Sian; 'mixed bloods' – Welsh on his side and a mixture of French and Scots on hers. (See also pp. 124, 130, 138, 143, 144, 147, 169, 206, 218, 228, 238, 261, 269, 274, 301, 335.) Influenced by W. B. Yeats (1865–1939). (See also pp. 1, 15, 49, 50, 51, 65, 66, 75, 87, 89, 90, 92, 99, 120, 147, 158, 182, 198, 234, 245, 250, 260, 264, 302, 307, 318, 337.)
    'Song' (By violent, ambiguous ways) ** 3/4 January 1948.

78. 'The Heart of the Winter' 9 January 1948. 'The Dragon', Michaelmas 1948. A celebration of the poet's safe return from the dangers of war-service in the Mediterranean. 'pastures of the dolphin' – the sea (imitating Auden's (see also pp. 8, 12, 13, 17, 20, 23, 26, 33, 48, 58, 64, 76, 79, 80, 108, 147, 169, 175, 177, 181, 183, 186, 195, 204, 233, 271, 316) use of imagery from Norse Sagas); 'pastoral' – poem about rural life; 'idyll' – short pictorial poem; 'fabulous' – like something in a story; 'fabulous of' – tells wonderful stories about.

79. (Tonight I see an image) ** 9 January 1948.
     'Poem' (The innocent frenzy of the wind) 9 January 1948. 'The Dragon',
     Summer 1949. 'doldrum' – calm; 'This lust' – the true poet's irresistible
     compulsion to write (cf. Shakespeare's 'poet's eye in a fine frenzy rolling' –
     A Midsummer Night's Dream, v. i. 7). (See also pp. 17, 33, 55, 56, 58, 81,
     89, 129, 138, 158, 229, 235, 261, 264, 270, 276, 288, 297, 311, 344, 345.)
     'The Conquest of the West' ** 16 March 1948. Cf. such of Auden's
     early 'leadership' poems and such 'character' poems as 'Who's Who'
     (1934). (See also pp. 8, 12, 13, 17, 20, 23, 26, 33, 48, 58, 64, 76, 78, 80,
     108, 147, 169, 175, 177, 181, 183, 186, 195, 204, 233, 271, 316.) A
     characterisation of Imperialism appropriate after a war against that of
     Nazi Germany and Japan. 'hieroglyphics' – Egyptian writing: the idea that
     the heat of the sun is 'making impressions' upon the brain of the 'hero;
     'Cathay' – poetical name for China.

80. 'Biography' ** 17 March 1948. Cf. Auden again (see also pp. 8, 12, 13,
     17, 20, 23, 26, 33, 48, 58, 64, 76, 78, 79, 108, 147, 169, 175, 177, 181,
     183, 186, 195, 204, 233, 271, 316). A Petrarchan sonnet (see also pp. 1,
     12, 36, 41, 61, 86, 91, 108, 119, 124, 138, 140, 156, 234, 254, 255, 260,
     266, 276, 282, 302, 305, 311, 339). 'eclectic' – wide-ranging; 'manna' –
     miraculous substance provided by God to feed the Israelites in the
     wilderness; see Exodus 16: 15.
     'Peace' ** 17 March 1948. An irregular sonnet.

81. 'History' ** 17 March 1948. Shakespearean sonnet. (See also pp. 17, 33,
     55, 56, 58, 79, 89, 129, 138, 158, 229, 235, 261, 264, 270, 276, 288, 297,
     311, 344, 345.) 'imperium' – sovereignty.
     'Legends'. 26 March 1948. Shakespearean sonnet. (See above.)

82. 'Poem' (The sensual landscape in his mind) 26 March 1948. E.H., p. 31.
     'cathartic' – purifying.
     'Morning over the Valleys' ** 26 March 1948. These valleys appear to
     be those of Jones's Breconshire (now Powys) homeland, rather than 'The
     Valleys' of industrial South Wales.
     'Stanzas in Dejection' ** 28 March 1948. Cf. (Prince Hamlet) above p.
     56. 'autumnal' – gloomy/near death; 'Ophelia' – loved Hamlet, went mad
     and drowned herself; 'adultery' – Claudius committed adultery with
     Hamlet's mother, Gertrude; 'players' – travelling actors used by Hamlet to
     'catch the conscience of the king (Claudius)' – *Hamlet*, II. ii. 641.

83. 'Song' (Ten weathers at my finger-tips) 'Easter Sunday (*c*.2 April) 1948'.
     'Life and Letters Today', 58, 133, September 1948. This monthly
     magazine, founded in London in 1928 by Desmond MacCarthy
     (1877–1952), published a great deal of work by Welsh writers. It ceased
     publication in 1950. E.H. p. 64.

84. 'Poem' (In that rich dark) 6/7 April 1948. 'Life and Letters Today', 58,
     133, September 1948. 'ravelled' – tangled; 'platonic dissidence' – loving
     dispute; 'panic' – Pan was the god of woods; 'baroque' – flamboyant.
     'Poem' (Mortal, miraculous) 8 April 1948. 'The Dragon', Summer 1949.

85. 'Ennui, Mediterranean' 13 April 1948. 'Wales', November 1948. This
     magazine, founded in 1937 by Keidrych Rees (William Ronald Rees Jones,
     1915–87), was published in Carmarthen until 1940 and later in London
     (1943–9 and 1958–60). Another reminiscence of war-service which created
     neuroses that plagued Jones for the rest of his short life. 'suave' – relaxed;
     'avid indolence' – determined idleness.

86. 'Elegy' ** 'harboured' – safe; 'articulate urgency' – ability to put powerful
     feelings into suitable words (a good description of poems like this one in
     which it might be argued there are more complex words than there is
     complicated meaning); 'spelled configuration of impatience' – strong
     feelings put into words suitably arranged to 'spell them out' and make them
     additionally memorable by the poetry's form; 'conflagration' – heat (as in
     e.g. 'my blood boiled'); 'predicate' – predict.
         'Venus Anadyomene' ** 19 April 1948. Petrarchan sonnet (see also pp.
     1, 12, 36, 41, 61, 80, 91, 108, 119, 124, 138, 140, 156, 234, 254, 255, 260,
     266, 276, 282, 302, 305, 311, 339). The meaning of the title is 'Venus rising
     from the sea, accompanied by dolphins'. (See also pp. 37, 38, 42, 46, 56,
     109, 111, 234, 307, 363 9.) The famous lost painting by Apelles and the
     extant one by Botticelli in the Academia delle Belle Arte, Florence, bear that
     name. Jones was interested in art and artists: the Australia painter, Rae
     Richards (see also pp. 228, 230, 250, 254, 270, 274, 282, 311, 319, 337,
     339, 353), his 'Muse' for a time at the Newcastle College of the University
     of New South Wales (see also pp. 143, 214, 218, 224, 225, 226, 237, 239,
     244, 252, 284, 291, 299, 300, 301, 302, 303, 309, 312, 326, 327, 328, 333,
     343, 353, 358, 365, 370) and the inspiration for his 'Eve' poems (see also
     pp. 63, 93, 99, 101, 116, 167, 180, 210, 225, 251, 255, 257, 265, 266, 284,
     318, 361, 367, 368), painted the only extant portrait of him.

87. 'Stages to a Modern Prelude: "The Uncreated Conscience"' ** 20 April
     1948. 'Prelude' – Wordsworth's (1770–1850) (see also pp. 196, 199, 234,
     260, 346, 370) autobiographical poem in blank verse, 'The Prelude or
     Growth of a Poet's Mind', begun in 1798–9. The young Wordsworth was
     an enthusiastic supporter of the French Revolution (1789), the young Jones
     a fervent Communist. This 'Modern Prelude' is in iambic couplets whose
     lines vary from ten to sixteen or more syllables, an irregularity which
     reflects the poet's very strong feelings. 'The Weasel at the Heart' (see p. 66),
     a sensational success, was also a cause of controversy, which Jones was
     never reluctant to court. He was a postgraduate student in 1948, leading an
     irregular and defiant existence, in spite of his marriage. He presents himself
     here as very much the Romantic poet, revolutionary, misunderstood, reviled
     but resolute as W. B. Yeats (see also pp. 1, 15, 49, 50, 51, 65, 66, 75, 77,
     89, 90, 92, 99, 120, 147, 158, 182, 198, 234, 245, 250, 260, 264, 302, 307,
     318, 337), whom he greatly admired, had been. The poem's final line, 'In
     the wisdom of my artifice ('sullen craft and art' as Dylan Thomas (see also
     pp. 4, 20, 30, 33, 40, 52, 53, 54, 57, 58, 64, 96, 104, 106, 112, 116, 117,
     119, 158, 170, 186, 201, 225, 232, 234, 245, 272, 278, 279, 284, 292, 313,
     345) called it) I am prepared to die' remained true of Jones's idea of the
     poet's function to the end of his too-short life.

88. (The beauty lies with the fool) ** 20 April 1948. 'narrow beds' – graves.

89. 'Nightmare' ** 20/21 April 1948. 'drunken soldiery' cf. Yeats's (1865–1939) 'Byzantium'; (see also pp. 1, 15, 49, 50, 51, 65, 66, 75, 77, 87, 90, 92, 99, 120, 147, 158, 182, 198, 234, 245, 250, 260, 264, 302, 307, 318, 337). 'ceremony of evil' cf. 'ceremony of innocence' in Yeats's 'The Second Coming'. 'raddled' – coarsely rouged; 'lech' – fornicate.
    'Sonnet' (No rich complexity of flower or woman) 29 April 1948. E.H., p. 36. A Shakespearean sonnet. (See also pp. 17, 33, 55, 56, 58, 79, 81, 129, 138, 158, 229, 235, 261, 264, 270, 276, 288, 297, 311, 344, 345.) 'inhuman Zodiac' – hard life: the Zodiacal signs mark out, approximately, the months of the year; being represented as animals, they are, of course, 'inhuman'.

90. 'From a Play?' ** May 1948.
    'Brothel in Algiers: Wartime' 27 May 1948. 'Poetry Wales', 34/4 April 1999. 'Ithyphallic' – the 'Ithyphallus' was a representation of the erect penis carried in processions in honour of Dionysus (Bacchus) (see also pp. 2, 26). 'Ithyphallic' refers to the hymns sung on such occasions; 'gyres' – circular movements in the dance of the 'daughters' and perhaps also an allusion to W. B. Yeats's (1865–1939) cyclic view of history as expressed in such poems as 'The Second Coming'. (See also pp. 1, 15, 49, 50, 51, 65, 66, 75, 77, 87, 89, 92, 99, 120, 147, 158, 182, 198, 234, 245, 250, 260, 264, 302, 307, 318, 337.)

91. 'The Need for Pardon' 27 May 1948.. E.H., p. 37. Variation (ABBA BCCB EFG EFG) on Petrarchan Sonnet. 'formalism' – narrowing effect.

92. 'Judgement Day' ** 27 May 1948.
    'Art Poetique' (The Art of Poetry) ** 30 May 1948. The 'art' of this poem produces a fine pastiche of W. B. Yeats (1865–1939) (see also pp. 1, 15, 49, 50, 51, 65, 66, 75, 77, 87, 89, 90, 99, 120, 147, 158, 182, 198, 234, 245, 250, 260, 264, 302, 307, 318, 337) and is based on his fine poem, 'Byzantium'.

93. 'Garden of Eden' ** 30 May 1948. See Genesis 2 (where Adam names the animals) and Genesis 3 (where Satan in the form of a snake – 'cold ecstatic snake' – tempts Eve – 'innocent sensual woman' to eat the fruit of the Forbidden Tree). (See also pp. 63, 86, 99, 101, 116, 167, 180, 210, 225, 251, 255, 257, 265, 266, 284, 318, 361, 367, 368.) The behaviour of the animals and the nature of the language suggests that the poem takes place after the Fall, but before Adam and Eve were expelled from Paradise.

94. 'The Country Drunkard' ** 28 August 1948. Since his marriage in December 1946, Jones, the native of rural Breconshire, had been living, when not at Aberystwyth, in London, which was uncongenial. 'vocative' – calling up.
    'Orpheus' ** 28 August 1948. Orpheus, poet and musician (see also p. 217), was said to be able to move even stones by the power of his music.

When his wife, Eurydice, died, he went to Hades and charmed Pluto into releasing her. The God of the Underworld made the condition, however, that she walk behind her husband on the way out of hell and that if he looked back before they emerged, she would be taken back. His love for her was so strong that he could not help doing so, and thus lost her for the second time. 'hyperbolic' – curved.

'Ancestral' 30 August 1948. E.H., p. 15. The third Llanafanfawr poem (see also pp. 6, 23, 104, 138, 142, 222, 226, 228, 244, 261, 264, 275, 283, 296, 297, 302, 310, 311, 319, 324, 332, 336, 342, 343, 346, 359, 364, 366).

95.   'Eclogue' 30 September 1948. S.M.P., p. 9. An eclogue is a dialogue in verse about country life, in particular that of poetical shepherds: the Roman poet, Virgil (70–19 BC) (see also p. 17) is noted for such poems. Jones's grandfather (see also pp. 244, 283, 332, 337, 359, 366) was a shepherd and his uncle a 'Bardd Gwlad' (local poet).

96.   (I am the spindrift ghost) ** 30 October 1948. Jones's first prose-poem (see also pp. 114, 196). 'spindrift' – made of sea-spray; 'watches' – time spent on duty; 'restless crews' – drowned men. Another poem deriving from the poet's war-service.

'The Prisoner' ** 30 October 1948. The poet is a 'prisoner' to his inspiration, a gift from God. Angels are the servants of God. 'like an angel' – sweetly; 'angel madness' – poetic inspiration; 'sang in my prison' cf. Dylan Thomas, 'sang in my chains like the sea' ('Fern Hill'). (See also pp. 4, 20, 30, 33, 40, 52, 53, 54, 57, 58, 64, 87, 104, 106, 112, 116, 117, 119, 158, 170, 186, 201, 225, 232, 234, 245, 272, 278, 279, 284, 292, 313, 345.)

'Lost Love' 30 October 1948. E.H., p. 34.

97.   (At midnight) ** 9 November 1948. 'pastoral' – countryman.

'For a Play (Chorus for the Undefeated)' ** 9 November 1948. Though Britain was 'undefeated' in the Second World War, the country had many problems at this time. 'omens' – signs of future events.

98.   (In love's outrageous slums) ** 24 November 1948. 'tiger' – savage pain; 'angry breasts . . . murder' – billowing waves (which drown sailors); 'star-crossed' – cursed/doomed; 'goosegirl' – in medieval times, a girl who looked after a flock of geese.

'Poem' (From these five witnesses) 27 December 1948. 'The Dragon', Summer 1949. 'five witnesses' – the five senses; 'concupiscence' – the appetite of Death for its victims.

99.   'Winter' ** 28 December 1948. The awakening of unhappy feelings in the countryside.

'The Shapes of Pity' 1 January 1949. 'The Dublin Magazine', XXIV, 4, December 1949. E.H., p. 35. Adam (see also pp. 63, 86, 93, 101, 116, 167, 180, 210, 225, 251, 255, 257, 265, 266, 284, 318, 361, 367, 368) ('the sweating Adam') would in later poems be a favourite alter ego of T. H. Jones, a highly-sexed lapsed Nonconformist who never lost his Bible-knowledge or Calvinistic sense of sin. 'Across the desert wing the hideous birds' – an echo of W. B. Yeats's (1865–1939) 'The Second Coming: shadows of the indignant desert birds'. (See also pp. 1, 15, 49, 50, 51, 65, 66, 75, 77, 87, 89, 90, 92, 120, 147, 158, 182, 198, 234, 245, 250, 260, 264, 302, 307, 318, 337.)

100. 'The Erotic Season' ** 1 January 1949. Not Spring, when, according to Tennyson (see also p. 17), 'a young man's fancy lightly turns to thoughts of love', but New Year.
    'The Wounded Water' ** 2–15 January 1949. 'Leviathan' – sea-monster; 'original turmoil' – life originated in the sea; 'glaucous' – sea-green.

101. 'Song, O who unribbed me where I lay . . . ' 15 January 1949. 'The Glass' c.1950. E.H., p. 65. 'unribbed' – according to the Bible ('Genesis'), God took one of Adam's ribs in order to create Eve (see also pp. 63, 86, 93, 99, 116, 167, 180, 210, 225, 251, 255, 257, 265, 266, 284, 318, 361, 367, 368).
    'Song for Rachel' ** 21 January 1949. For Rachel Roberts. (See also pp. 66, 145.)

102. 'Poem' (Wild in the ambush and agony of love) ** 25 January 1949.
    'The Country of Hurt' ** 5 February 1949.

103. 'Aubade' ** 14 February 1949. 'aubade' – song for sunrise ('aube', french = dawn).
    'Poem' (Awkward or innocent) ** 17 February 1949. 'curfews' – restricts/binds; 'spittle save' – Greeks and Romans believed that spitting was a protection against evil.

104. 'Poem' (Back to the loved sky and the humped hills) 18 February 1949. 'Life and Letters Today', 64, 151, January 1950. E.H., p. 19. Heavily influenced by Dylan Thomas ('Fern Hill'), (see also pp. 4, 20, 30, 33, 40, 52, 53, 54, 57, 58, 64, 87, 96, 106, 112, 116, 117, 119, 158, 170, 186, 201, 225, 232, 234, 245, 272, 278, 279, 284, 292, 313, 345), this is among the first of Jones's poems relating to the Llanafanfawr landscape (see also pp. 6, 23, 94, 138, 142, 222, 226, 228, 244, 261, 264, 275, 283, 296, 297, 302, 310, 311, 319, 324, 332, 336, 342, 343, 346, 359, 364, 366) central to his mature work.

105. (In this blind time) ** 18 February 1949. 'lapidary' – (literally 'jewelled') – elaborate; 'peas . . . ' – he means that 'we' are fools: a pig's bladder rattle was part of the equipment of the Jester.

106. 'Poem in Absence' ** 18 February 1949.
    (Where my seafellow in a windless humour) ** 19 February 1949. So derivative from the work of Dylan Thomas as to be little more than pastiche. (See also pp. 4, 20, 30, 33, 40, 52, 53, 54, 57, 58, 64, 87, 96, 104, 112, 116, 117, 119, 158, 170, 186, 201, 225, 232, 234, 245, 272, 278, 279, 284, 292, 313, 345.)

107. 'Mediterranean: Wartime' 12 March 1949. Between June 1942 and October 1945, Jones, trained as a signals telegraphist, was stationed in the Mediterranean. 'middle sea' – Mediterranean; 'glass of wine' – Homer's favourite description of the Mediterranean is 'wine-dark'; 'estranges' – an allusion to 'the unplumb'd, salt, estranging sea' (Matthew Arnold's (1822–1888) poem, 'Isolation. To Marguerite' – see also pp. 46, 119).

    (When the bone cried) ** 28 March 1949. 'The dancers went under the hill' – cf. T. S. Eliot, 'East Coker II', 'The dancers are all gone under the hill.' (See also pp. 1, 3, 9, 17, 18, 33, 121, 137, 214, 234, 336, 345.)

108. (Seeking to make a music of the myth) ** 28 March 1949. Petrarchan Sonnet (see also pp. 1, 12, 36, 41, 61, 80, 86, 91, 119, 124, 138, 140, 156, 234, 254, 255, 260, 266, 276, 282, 302, 305, 311, 339). A 'biography' or 'portrait' poem, cf. W. H. Auden (1907–73). (See also pp. 8, 12, 13, 17, 20, 23, 26, 33, 48, 58, 64, 76, 78, 79, 80, 147, 169, 175, 177, 181, 183, 186, 195, 204, 233, 271, 316.)

    'Nostalgia' ** 28 March 1949.

109. (Mirror and mask abound) ** 31 March 1949.

    (Now let me circumambulate) ** 3 April 1949. 'marmoreal' – like marble; 'mummery' – foolish ceremonial; 'Cyprian queen' – Aphrodite/ Venus, who was associated with Cyprus (see also pp. 37, 38, 42, 46, 56, 86, 111, 234, 307, 363).

110. 'Orestes' ** 3 April 1949. Orestes, the son, and Pylades, the nephew of Agammemnon, took vengeance upon Aegisthus and Clytemnestra for the murder of Agammemnon.

    'Lake Woman's Song' ** 11 April 1949. Based on the Welsh folk-tale about the son of Blaen Sawdde farm, not far from Llyn y Fan Fach, Carmarthenshire, who fell in love with a beautiful maiden who lived in the lake. After being offered three kinds of bread, she agreed to marry him, but warned that she would leave him if he mistreated her.

111. 'Birth of Venus' ** 11 April 1949. According to legend, Aphrodite/Venus was born from the sea. (See also pp. 37, 38, 42, 46, 56, 86, 109, 234, 307, 363.)

    'Poem' (The lying calendar of youth) ** 11 April 1949. 'rant' – raving.

    (Burning against the lyric dark) ** 12 April 1949.

112. (The small, indifferent birds) ** 12 April 1945. 'I am dumb . . . To tell' – cf. Dylan Thomas, 'The Force that through the Green Fuse Drives the Flower'. (See also pp. 4, 20, 30, 33, 40, 52, 53, 54, 57, 58, 64, 87, 96, 104, 106, 116, 117, 119, 158, 170, 186, 201, 225, 232, 234, 245, 272, 278, 279, 284, 292, 313, 345.)

    'Poem' (Heart-madness and the labouring craft) ** 12 April 1949.

1949–51: London

Exercise Book 5: 13 April 1949–19 May 1950

(This was the first exercise book to be re-discovered, by T. H. Jones's widow, Madeleine, in October 2003.)

112. 'Poem' (The animal sleep in winter) ** 13 April 1949.

113. 'Ode' ** 13 April 1949.

114. 'O Mariner, Return' ** 19–20 April 1949. 'phallic' – creating sexual desire.
     (Not where he lay) ** 19–20 April 1949. Prose-poem (see also pp. 96,
     196). 'glaucous' – sea-green.

115. 'Easter Poem' ** 19–20 April 1949.

116. 'Genesis' ** 24 April 1949.
     (In my beginning) ** 20–21 May 1949. A poem obviously influenced by
     the work of Dylan Thomas. (See also pp. 4, 20, 30, 33, 40, 52, 53, 54, 57,
     58, 64, 87, 96, 104, 106, 112, 117, 119, 158, 170, 186, 201, 225, 232,
     234, 245, 272, 278, 279, 284, 292, 313, 345.) 'smelt of Adam' – shared
     Adam's original sin (see also pp. 63, 86, 93, 99, 101, 167, 180, 210, 225,
     251, 255, 257, 265, 266, 284, 318, 361, 367, 368); 'fall of blood' – loss of
     virginity; 'murdered sleep' – *Macbeth*, II. i. 37, 'Macbeth hath murdered
     sleep' – Macbeth's guilt after the murder of the sleeping King Duncan.

117. (Not in that drunken morning) ** 20–21 May 1949. Influence of Dylan
     Thomas (see also pp. 4, 20, 30, 33, 40, 52, 53, 54, 57, 58, 64, 87, 96, 104,
     106, 112, 116, 119, 158, 170, 186, 201, 225, 232, 234, 245, 272, 278,
     279, 284, 292, 313, 345). 'apogee' – climax.
     'The Midnight Words' ** 20–21 May 1949. 'dove' – symbol of peace
     and of the Holy Spirit.

118. (Lost on the floor) ** 21 May 1949.
     (Though body on body press) ** 27 May 1949.
     (The contradiction of your images) ** 27 May 1949.

119. 'All Passion Spent' ** 30 June 1949. Slightly modified Petrarchan sonnet
     (see also pp. 1, 12, 36, 41, 61, 80, 86, 91, 108, 124, 138, 140, 156, 234,
     254, 255, 260, 266, 276, 282, 302, 305, 311, 339); 'estranging sea' – cf.
     Matthew Arnold (1822–88') (see also pp. 46, 107), 'The unplumbed, salt,
     estranging sea' in 'Isolation. To Marguerite'.
     'The Nature of Love' ** 13 July 1949. 'dragonish tang of the old seas'
     – wartime experience in the Mediterranean.
     'Hiraeth' ** 13 July 1949. 'hiraeth' – nostalgia'; 'Labouring . . . light' –
     cf. Dylan Thomas, 'I labour by singing light' ('In My Craft or Sullen Art').
     (See also pp. 4, 20, 30, 33, 40, 52, 53, 54, 57, 58, 64, 87, 96, 104, 106,
     112, 116, 117, 158, 170, 186, 201, 225, 232, 234, 245, 272, 278, 279,
     284, 292, 313, 345.)

120. (In the demented wood) ** 14 July 1949. 'fabulous white beasts' – unicorns: according to legend the unicorn reverences young virgins and can be captured by placing one in its haunts.

(Beyond this murder) * 22 July 1949. 'centaurs' – mythological beasts, half man, half horse, said to have lived in Thessaly.

'War Generation' ** 22 July 1949. 'emotion in the desert' – during the Second World War Jones was based initially at Alexandria, not far from the site of the Battle of El Alamein; 'desert beast . . . what rough tawny ghost' – cf. W. B. Yeats (see also pp. 1, 15, 49, 50, 51, 65, 66, 75, 77, 87, 89, 90, 92, 99, 147, 158, 182, 198, 234, 245, 250, 260, 264, 302, 307, 318, 337) 'The Second Coming': 'somewhere in sands of the desert/A shape with lion body and the head of a man . . . what rough beast . . . slouches towards Bethlehem to be born'; the 'beast' is the Sphinx; 'labyrinth' – the maze at Knossos on the island of Crete. At the centre of the labyrinth was the monstrous Minotaur for which Athens had to provide each year seven youths and seven maidens. Theseus (see also p. 314) killed the monster with the assistance of King Minos' daughter, Ariadne, who supplied him with the necessary 'clue', a ball of thread which he secured and paid out as he advanced so that he should be able to find his way out again.

121. 'Seascape' ** 25 July 1949. The absence of end-of-line punctuation, apart from the final full stop, is deliberate; 'blue of Mary's colour' – see T. S. Eliot, (see also pp. 1, 3, 9, 17, 18, 33, 107, 137, 214, 234, 336, 345) 'Ash Wednesday': 'Made cool the dry rock and made firm the sand/In blue of larkspur, blue of Mary's colour . . . '; 'no sirens sing to us' – cf. 'The Love Song of J. Alfred Prufrock': 'I have heard the mermaids singing . . . I do not think that they will sing to me'; 'sirens' – sea-nymphs who, by their singing, charmed all who heard them; 'home is where the heart is' – proverbial expression.

122. (Tomorrow is an island) ** 6 August 1949.

(Beneath the surface of decay) ** 6 August 1949.

'Song for a Time of Trouble'. 10 August 1949. E.H., p. 63.

123. 'Allegory' ** 16 August 1949. The poem explored two sides to the poet's personality: the innocent boy and the experienced man. 'miasmic' – misty.

'Children in the Park' ** 25 August 1949.

124. (Utter the pangs of grass) ** 25 August 1949.

(The miles of water) ** 30 August 1949.

'Sonnet for my Daughter's Childhood' ** 30 August 1949. Petrarchan sonnet (see also pp. 1, 12, 36, 41, 61, 80, 86, 91, 108, 119, 138, 140, 156, 234, 254, 255, 260, 266, 276, 282, 302, 305, 311, 339). Sian, born in May 1948, was 15 months old. (See also pp. 77, 130, 138, 143, 144, 147, 169, 206, 218, 228, 238, 261, 269, 274, 301, 335.)

125. 'Poem for a Birthday' ** 30 August–12 September 1949. Jones would not, in fact, be twenty-eight until 21 December; 'expence' – *sic* in manuscript.

126. 'Annunciation'. ** 4–7 October 1949. THE Annunciation (*Luke I*, 26–38) was the Angel Gabriel's announcement to the Virgin Mary that she would give birth to the Messiah.

    'The Anglo-Welsh' 4–7 October 1949. Dock Leaves, 4.11, Summer 1953. Addressed to Aneirin Talfan Davies (Aneirin ap Talfan, 1909–80) (see also p. 128), critic, poet, broadcaster, founder of the Welsh magazine, 'Heddiw', and, with his brother, Alun, of the Welsh Publishing House, Christopher Davies. Davies recalled, in 'Passing of a Prince' ('The Welsh Outlook', 2 May 1965), entering 'the bar of a pub in Cardiganshire' where a 'loud debate' was going on 'about the Welsh language'. Ted Richards (see also pp. 168, 185, 214, 222, 298, 317, 323, 324), antique dealer and short story writer, a friend of them both, introduced him to 'the young man, T. H. Jones', and Jones and Davies engaged in a 'fierce argument' in which Jones denied 'the need for the survival of the Welsh language to ensure the survival of Welshness . . . The argument was carried on until stop tap', and during the course of it Davies told Jones that he was 'destined to live on your grandmother's memories'. Months later, Jones sent Davies 'Amends' (see below, p. 128) and this poem. 'I am proud to think that he came to consider me as one of his friends', wrote Davies.

127. (A man may feel) ** 9 October 1949. 'young antiquity' – the culture of ancient Greece; 'vase or song' – Grecian urns (cf. Keats's 'Ode') (see also pp. 260, 320, 345), like Homer's poems, conveyed myths and stories such as that of the Trojan War; 'swan' – Zeus, in the form of a swan, raped Leda (see also pp. 49, 250, 254, 264, 309, 320), who gave birth to Helen (see also pp. 49, 250, 254, 264, 277, 279, 284, 298, 320), cause of the Trojan War.

    (Once in a time) ** 20 October 1949.

128. 'Amends' 20–21 October 1949. 'The Dublin Magazine', XXV, 3, September 1950. 'The Dublin Magazine', founded by Seamus O'Sullivan (Starkey), was published from 1923–5 and 1926–58. It was friendly to Anglo-Welsh writers: Jones wrote to O'Sullivan in 1949, 'You, and your magazine, will always be remembered by us, the Welsh who write in English, because of Alun Lewis.' O'Sullivan published Jones's short stories as well as his poems. E.H., p. 18. Addressed to Aneirin Talfan Davies (see above p. 126).

    'Narcissus' ** 10 November 1949. The nymph, Echo, died of grief when Narcissus rejected her love. Nemesis punished him by causing him to see his own image in water and fall in love with that, so that he pined away until changed into the flower that bears his name; for 'Failure of Narcissus', published in S.M.P. (p. 54) – see p. 216 below.

129. (With rags of honour) ** 10 November 1949.

    'Unfaithful' ** 10 November 1949.

    'The Oracle' ** 10 November 1949.

    'L'invitation au Voyage' (Invitation to Travel) ** 23 November 1949. Caliban is the deformed, half-human servant of the magician, Prospero, in Shakespeare's (see also pp. 17, 33, 55, 56, 58, 79, 81, 89, 138, 158, 229, 235, 261, 264, 270, 276, 288, 297, 311, 344, 345) play, *The Tempest*; 'inhibit' – Caliban was prevented by Prospero from raping Miranda (see also pp. 58, 297).

130. 'An Old Story' ** December 1949.
   'A Wish for My Daughter' 25 December 1949. E.H., p. 78, where 'Eldest'
   was added, Jones's second daughter, Rhiannon, having been born in February
   1953, and his third, Ruth Myfanwy, in October 1954. (See also pp. 77, 124,
   138, 143, 144, 147, 169, 206, 218, 228, 238, 261, 269, 274, 301, 335.)
   'Attainment' ** 4 January 1950.

131. 'Pathetic Fallacy' ** 10 January 1950. 'Pathetic Fallacy' – John Ruskin's
   (1819–1900) phrase for the erroneous belief that nature shares human
   feelings.
   'Song' (Once, beneath a morbid sun) ** 10 January 1950.

132. 'The Place of Failure' ** January 1950. absence of punctuation is deliberate.
   'Poem' (O girl merry as apples) ** 28 January 1950.
   'Sickbed Fantasy' ** 28 January 1950.

133. (I have watched his pale hands shuffling money in the moonlight' **
   28 January 1950.
   (All the torn and blistered fields) ** 28 January 1950.
   'My Angel' 28 January 1950. E.H., p. 45. Untitled in 'Exercise Book'.
   (Never That Love Shall Languish) ** 28 January 1950.

134. (Afraid of Being Converted Like St Paul) ** 30 January 1950. 'like St Paul'
   – under his original name of Saul, a persecutor of Christ's Disciples, he was
   miraculously converted to Christianity on the road to Damascus and
   changed his name to Paul.
   'Now the Expected Ambush' ** 30 January 1950. 'myopic' – weak.
   'Reply' ** 30 January 1950.

135. 'Difference' 31 January–1 February 1950. 'The Dublin Magazine', XXV,
   3 September 1950 E.H., p. 17. 'anodynes' – painkillers.
   'The Princes of This World' ** 3 February 1950. In both its sentiments
   and its neat quatrains, this poem resembles the work of Idris Davies
   (1905–53).
   'Restlessly Seeking' ** 3 February 1950. The complete absence of
   punctuation here is intended to cause the poem to revolve endlessly, like
   the poet's mood.

136. 'Love Song' ** 7 February 1950. 'caul' – membrane sometimes covering
   the head of a newly born baby. Once thought to have magical properties.
   'An Old Man Murmured' ** 15 February 1950.
   'Rivers and Revolutions' ** 15 February 1950.

137. 'The World in the Mirror' ** 15 February 1950. The image of the mirror
   is common in Jones's poetry, especially his early work. Discontent with the
   world in which he is obliged to live and in which ambitions are frustrated
   and love never ideal, he finds comfort and uncertainty in the idea that, like
   Alice, he might be able to escape into a world both exciting and dangerous.
   See also 'My Mirror Loves Me Anyway' (p. 183), 'Stanzas in a Mirror' (p.
   187) and 'The Mirror of Herself' (p. 266).

'Image' ** 18 February 1950. 'uninvaded . . . unicorn' – according to legend, a unicorn can be captured only by placing a young virgin in its haunts.

'Lines for a Play' ** 18 February 1950. 'still point' – cf. T. S. Eliot, 'Burnt Norton': 'At the still point of the turning world'. (See also pp. 1, 3, 9, 17, 18, 33, 107, 121, 214, 234, 336, 345.)

138. 'Spring Sonnet' ** 18 February 1950. A Petrarchan sonnet (see also pp. 1, 12, 36, 41, 61, 80, 86, 91, 108, 119, 124, 140, 156, 234, 254, 255, 260, 266, 276, 282, 302, 305, 311, 339). 'sermon wrenched from water or from stones' cf. Shakespeare *As You Like It*, II. i. 11–12: 'books in the running brooks,/Sermons in stones . . . ' (see also pp. 17, 33, 55, 56, 58, 79, 81, 89, 129, 158, 229, 235, 261, 264, 270, 276, 288, 297, 311, 344, 345).

'My Daughter Asleep' 18–19 February 1950. E.H., p. 27. Sian was now twenty months old. (See also pp. 77, 124, 130, 143, 144, 147, 169, 206, 218, 228, 238, 261, 269, 274, 301, 335.) The contrast between the style of this poem (heavy influence of Shakespeare and G. M. Hopkins (see also pp. 141, 231)) and the following one, with its Llanafan landscape (see also pp. 6, 23, 94, 104, 142, 222, 226, 228, 244, 261, 264, 275, 283, 296, 297, 302, 310, 311, 319, 324, 332, 336, 342, 343, 346, 359, 364, 366) and anticipation of the mature style is notable.

139. 'Portrait of the Artist as a Young Man' ** 23 February 1950. The title is that of James Joyce's (1882–1941) (see also p. 300) first novel (1914–5).

'Infirm, Infirm' ** 23 February 1950.

140. 'Pale Hands You Loved' ** 27–28 February 1950. Petrarchan sonnet (see also pp. 1, 12, 36, 41, 61, 80, 86, 91, 108, 119, 124, 138, 156, 234, 254, 255, 260, 266, 276, 282, 302, 305, 311, 339). Title from 'Pale Hands I Loved' in *India's Love Lyrics* (1919) by 'Laurence Hope' (pen-name of Florence Nicolson, 1865–1904).

'Dilemma' ** 3 March 1950.

'Poem' (I have gone walking in dishevelled fields) ** 7 March 1950.

141. 'Speech for a Play' ** May 1950. 'rockfast . . . chains' – Prometheus was chained to a rock for stealing fire from the gods and giving it to human beings.

'There Is a Country' ** May 1950. 'poor patch' – cf. G. M. Hopkins (1844–89) (see also pp. 138, 231): 'This Jack, joke, poor potsherd, patch . . . ' ('That Nature Is a Heraclitean Fire').

142. 'Advice from a Friend' ** May 1950.

'The Nonconformist Hills' ** May 1950. 'nonconformist' – refers to the religion of the people who live in or near the Welsh hills, especially those of Llanafanfawr (see also pp. 6, 23, 94, 104, 138, 222, 226, 228, 244, 261, 264, 275, 283, 296, 297, 302, 310, 311, 319, 324, 332, 336, 342, 343, 346, 359, 364, 366).

'The Loitering Hounds' ** May 1950.

'Here on the Atlas' ** May 1950. The poem recalls Jones's frightening war experiences – 'stations of my pilgrimage' cf. Stations of the Cross, those points at which the pilgrim pauses to offer a prayer in memory of Christ's suffering and death.

143. 'Out of Wales' 18 May 1950. E.H.. p. 28. For Sian, the Jones's first child, now aged two. (See also pp. 77, 124, 130, 138, 144, 147, 169, 206, 218, 228, 238, 261, 269, 274, 301, 335.)

    'There is No Way' ** 19 May 1950.

    'Martyrdom' 19 May 1950. S.M.P., p. 11. 'undesired arrows' – St Sebastian was martyred by being shot with arrows, then beaten to death.

'The Black Book': 20 May 1950–26 September 1964

The 'Black Book' (see also pp. 145, 159, 167, 195, 203, 204, 210, 211, 214, 217, 220, 239, 255, 261, 303, 353) is the leather-bound octavo volume presented to Jones in November 1949 by Delia Glanville. Delia and her husband, John, became friends of the Joneses after Madeleine (see also pp. 34, 45, 64, 77, 147, 148, 156, 159, 169, 218, 224, 234, 236, 240, 242, 266, 269, 283, 285, 291, 312, 343) met them at the Camberwell School of Art, where she was studying Ceramics. John was the sculptor who created the bronze head of the poet now in the custody of Builth Wells High School (see also pp. 33, 64, 157, 294, 297, 326, 343, 346); Delia was studying bookbinding. In the summer of 2003, Jones's eldest daughter, Sian, presented the Book to the National Library of Wales.

    Into this book Jones entered, between 20 May 1950 ('For Sian') and 26 September 1964 ('Cotton Mather Remembers the Trial of Elizabeth How: Salem, Massachusetts, 30 June 1692') all of the poems he considered worthy of preservation. It differs from the 'Exercise Books' in that it contains completed poems only.

    Its first page bears the inscription 'London, May 1950–Portsmouth, June 1951'. In May 1950 the Joneses were living at Asylum Road, Camberwell; by June 1951 they had moved to Portsmouth, where he taught at the Dockyard School. After 'Cotton Mather', no further space remained in the Book. The poem is followed by a further inscription: 'Newcastle, N.S.W., September 1964' (see also pp. 86, 214, 218, 224, 225, 226, 237, 239, 244, 252, 284, 291, 299, 300, 301, 302, 303, 309, 312, 326, 327, 328, 333, 343, 353, 358, 365, 370). Between then and his tragic death in January 1965, Jones composed at least twenty more poems, among them several of his finest.

    The 'Black Book' contains more than 400 poems, handwritten and dated either individually or in groups of two or more. At least half of these are published for the first time in this Collection. With the five exercise books it comprises a detailed chronological record of the ebb and flow of a significant poet's inspiration and of his development to maturity over a period of more than twenty years. Such a day-to-day record of creative activity is, we believe, unique.

144. 'For Sian' ** 20 May 1950. Marking his daughter's second birthday. (See also pp. 77, 124, 130, 138, 143, 147, 169, 206, 218, 228, 238, 261, 269, 274, 301, 335.)

    'The Persuasion of Light' 14 June 1950. Dock Leaves, 2, 5. May 1951. This magazine was founded in 1949 by a literary circle at Pembroke Dock, among them Raymond Garlick, its first editor, who taught English at the Grammar School, and Roland Mathias, at that time head teacher at the school, who edited it from 1961–76. In 1961 it became 'The Anglo-Welsh Review'. It ceased publication, after eighty-eight numbers, in 1988, when the Arts Council of Wales withdrew the subsidy essential to its existence. The magazine was an important influence in bridging the gap and easing the animosity between Welsh writers in the English language and those in the Welsh.

145. 'For Rachel' ('To Rachel Roberts' in the 'Black Book' (see also pp. 143, 159, 167, 195, 203, 204, 210, 211, 214, 217, 220, 239, 255, 261, 303, 353)) 15 June 1950. E.H., p. 32. The friendship between the Joneses and Rachel Roberts, begun at Aberystwyth, where she took the leading role in his verse-play, 'The Weasel at the Heart' (1947), had continued during their time in London, where she was beginning her career as an actress, and thereafter. When a number of his poems were broadcast by the BBC in 1954, Jones suggested to Ludovic Kennedy that Rachel (see also pp. 66, 101) should be involved in the performance of 'Song of the Dandy Bones' (p. 186) because 'Miss Roberts has broadcast frequently and is familiar with my poetry'.
      'Prayer' ** 15 June 1950.

146. (O light, O menace, our unlucky hearts) ** 25 June 1950.

147. 'On the Death of Yeats' ** 25 June 1950. Yeats died in 1939. (See also pp. 1, 15, 49, 50, 51, 65, 66, 75, 77, 87, 89, 90, 92, 99, 120, 158, 182, 198, 234, 245, 250, 260, 264, 302, 307, 318, 337.)
      'Song' (Commend we that prodigious grief) ** 14 July 1950.

In August 1950, Madeleine and Sian travelled to Rio de Janeiro where her sister, Peg, needed help with her young family. They did not return until September 1951.

147. 'Sestina for Sian Crossing the Seas' ** 17–22 August 1950. (See also pp. 77, 124, 130, 138, 143, 144, 169, 206, 218, 228, 238, 261, 269, 274, 301, 335.) Sestina: a poem of six six-line stanzas (with an envoy) in which the line-endings of the first stanza are repeated, but in a different order, in the other five. W. H. Auden favoured this form. (See also pp. 8, 12, 13, 17, 20, 23, 26, 33, 48, 58, 64, 76, 78, 79, 80, 108, 169, 175, 177, 181, 183, 186, 195, 204, 233, 271, 316.)

148. 'To Madeleine' ** 22 August 1950. See also pp. 34, 45, 64, 77, 143, 147, 156, 159, 169, 218, 224, 234, 236, 240, 242, 266, 269, 283, 285, 291, 312, 343.

149. 'Portrait' 27 August 1950. E.H., p. 44.
      'Invented Seasons' ** 1 September 1950.

150. 'The Ballad of Me' 18 October 1950. 'The Dublin Magazine', XXVII, 2, June 1952 E.H., p. 21.

151. 'Another Form of Farewell' ** 19 October 1950.
(In the nightmare of the heart) ** 19 October 1950.

152. 'Lullaby' ** 26 October 1950.
'Words from Any Poet' ** 5 December 1950.
'Love' 5 December 1950. E.H., p. 49.

153. (Time wears and watches, dread is this) **5 December 1950.
'Words to Any Exile' ** 12 December 1950.

154. 'Apocalyptic' ** 12 December 1950. The Apocalypse is the end of the
world. The poem reflects post-war depression and the poet's failure to
secure an university post.
'A Question' 11 January 1951. Nimrod 3, 1, Summer 1965. E.H., p. 33.

155. 'The Anonymous Ghost' ** 12 January 1951.
'Love Lost and Found' ** 15 January 1951.

156. 'Epilogue' ** 16 January 1951.
(Witch woman of small breasts and sulky eyes) ** 24 February 1951.
Addressed to his wife, Madeleine (see also pp. 34, 45, 64, 77, 143, 147,
148, 159, 169, 218, 224, 234, 236, 240, 242, 266, 269, 283, 285, 291, 312,
343). Petrarchan sonnet (see also pp. 1, 12, 36, 41, 61, 80, 86, 91, 108, 119,
124, 138, 140, 234, 254, 255, 260, 266, 276, 282, 302, 305, 311, 339).
'Poem' (In the towns and centuries of youth) 24 February 1951.
Botteghe Oscure, XVII, 1956. E.H., p. 38. *Untitled* in the 'Black Book' (see
also pp. 143, 145, 159, 167, 195, 203, 204, 210, 211, 214, 217, 220, 239,
255, 261, 303, 353).

157. 'Poem on St David's Day, 1951' Written after 24 February, but obviously
not *on* 1 March. '1951' was added before publication. 'Western Mail',
7 March 1951. This daily newspaper (published in Cardiff) has displayed
a fluctuating interest in literature. The poem appeared in the serendipitous
'Wales Day by Day' column.
'Poem for Patricia' ** 2 March 1951. Patricia ('Pat') Power, Jones's
youngest sister (of four) (see also pp. 21, 288, 349), born 29 October 1934,
has been his greatest champion and is keeper of the family archive at Builth
Wells, Powys (see also pp. 21, 33, 64, 143, 294, 297, 326, 343, 346).

158. (In the annunciation and surprise) ** 1 April 1951. A good example of
Jones's postmodernism – the echoes of Yeats (see also pp. 1, 15, 49, 50, 51,
65, 66, 75, 77, 87, 89, 90, 92, 99, 120, 147, 182, 198, 234, 245, 250, 260,
264, 302, 307, 318, 337); Shakespeare (see also pp. 17, 33, 55, 56, 58, 79,
81, 89, 129, 138, 229, 235, 261, 264, 270, 276, 288, 297, 311, 344, 345);
Dylan Thomas (see also pp. 4, 20, 30, 33, 40, 52, 53, 54, 57, 58, 64, 87,
96, 104, 106, 112, 116, 117, 119, 170, 186, 201, 225, 232, 234, 245, 272,
278, 279, 284, 292, 313, 345); and Graves (see also pp. 197, 251, 258,
312) come close to literal quotation.
'The Vocabulary of Promise' 1 April 1951. 'The Dublin Magazine',
XXVIII, 1, March 1953. E.H., p. 29.

159. 'Poem for Madeleine' ('To Madeleine' in the 'Black Book' (see also pp. 143, 145, 167, 195, 203, 204, 210, 211, 214, 217, 220, 239, 255, 261, 303, 353)) 1 April 1951. E.H., p. 11. The poet regrets the absence of his wife in South America and feels that he has driven her away. See also pp. 34, 45, 64, 77, 143, 147, 148, 156, 169, 218, 224, 234, 236, 240, 242, 266, 269, 283, 285, 291, 312, 343.

160. 'A Saviour' ** 1–2 April 1951.
    (I dreamed when I was young) ** 2 April 1951.

161. (Elle a les jambes maigres' [She has thin legs]) ** 20 April 1951.
    'Song' (The sensual wind had blown away) ** 20 April 1951.

162. 'The Poet' ** 20 April 1951.

163. (When the world was a wonder) ** 21 April 1951.
    'Song' (There was a lady) ** 21 April 1951. The 'lady' was Pasiphaë. Seduced by Zeus in the form of a white bull, she gave birth to the Minotaur. 'Sheba' – see 1 Kings 10. 'leching' (slang, from 'lechery') – lustful.

164. 'Epigrams' ** 21 April 1951. VI is entitled 'Macarthur's Return': on 11 April 1951, General Douglas Macarthur (1880–1964) was relieved by President Truman of his command of UN forces in Korea. He received a hero's welcome on his return to the USA, but faded from the limelight almost immediately thereafter.

June 1951–April 1959: Portsmouth

165. 'Poem in Several Moods' ** 26–27 June 1951.
    'Death of a Poet' ** 7 July 1951.

166. 'Deathbed' 8 July 1951. S.M.P., p. 12.
    'Reflections on Tragedy'. 18 July, 1951. S.M.P., p. 13.

167. 'The Definitions of Circumstance' 31 July 1951. E.H., p. 40. Dedicated 'To Margot' in the 'Black Book' (see also pp. 143, 145, 159, 195, 203, 204, 210, 211, 214, 217, 220, 239, 255, 261, 303, 353)). The Garden of Eden was 'innocent' until Satan, in the form of the serpent, persuaded Eve to 'eat of the tree of knowledge of good and evil' and she persuaded Adam to eat also (see also pp. 63, 86, 93, 99, 101, 116, 180, 210, 225, 251, 255, 257, 265, 266, 284, 318, 361, 367, 368). They were expelled from Paradise, and mankind then became subject to death. See Genesis 3. This is a favourite myth of Jones's, who had a strict Nonconformist upbringing which contrasted sharply with his susceptibility to female beauty.

168. 'Song' (There is a country of disorder) 26 August 1951. Botteghe Oscure XVII, 1956. E.H., p. 66.
    'Sonnet to Pam' ** 26 August 1951. Pam Richards and her husband, Ted, an ex-naval officer, were lifelong friends of the poet. (See also pp. 126, 185, 214, 222, 298, 317, 323, 324.)

169. 'Poet' 27 August 1951. E.H., p. 46.

In September 1951, Madeleine and Sian returned from Rio de Janeiro.

169. 'A Song for You and Me' 6 October 1951. S.M.P., p. 14. A fine lyric, strongly influenced by similar poems of W. H. Auden. (See also pp. 8, 12, 13, 17, 20, 23, 26, 33, 48, 58, 64, 76, 78, 79, 80, 108, 147, 175, 177, 181, 183, 186, 195, 204, 233, 271, 316.)

170. 'Four' 13–14 October 1951. S.M.P., p. 15.
'Prayer Against Old Age, *A poem for my thirtieth birthday*' ** 13–14 October 1951. Jones would not be thirty until 21 December, but Dylan Thomas, whom he admired and here virtually imitates, was born on 27 October and his 'Poem in October' ('It was my thirtieth year to heaven') is written in a form similar to that of this poem. (See also pp. 4, 20, 30, 33, 40, 52, 53, 54, 57, 58, 64, 87, 96, 104, 106, 112, 116, 117, 119, 158, 186, 201, 225, 232, 234, 245, 272, 278, 279, 284, 292, 313, 345.)

173. 'A Plea against Armistice' 26 October 1951. E.H., p. 48.
'The Bridegroom' 9 November 1951. E.H., p. 51.

174. 'Thanks' ** 25 November 1951.
'The Formulas' 25 November 1951. S.M.P., p. 16.
'Address to My Face' 6 January 1952. S.M.P., p. 17.

175. 'Ballad' 3 February 1952. Dublin Magazine, XXX, 4, 1955. S.M.P., p. 18. Another example of Auden's influence. (See also pp. 8, 12, 13, 17, 20, 23, 26, 33, 48, 58, 64, 76, 78, 79, 80, 108, 147, 169, 177, 181, 183, 186, 195, 204, 233, 271, 316.)

176. 'Not Much Comfort' ** 19 April 1952.
'Dedicatory Poem' 19 April 1952. Nimrod 3, 1, Summer 1965. E.H., p. 77.

177. 'Willy and Reality' ** 19 April 1952. Cf. W. H. Auden's ballads such as 'Miss Gee'. (See also pp. 8, 12, 13, 17, 20, 23, 26, 33, 48, 58, 64, 76, 78, 79, 80, 108, 147, 169, 175, 181, 183, 186, 195, 204, 233, 271, 316.)

179. 'Short Story' ** 22 June 1952.
'Plaintive' ** 22 June 1952.
'Gorse Idyll' 22 June 1952. E.H., p. 23.
'Love Poem' 22 June 1952. S.M.P., p. 20.

180. 'Data for Dr Kinsey' ** 4 July 1952. Dr Alfred Kinsey (1894–1956) had published his study, 'Sexual Behaviour in the Human Male' in 1948. It was a cause célèbre at that time and of obvious interest to a lyric poet of sexual love.
'Adam' 4 July 1952. S.M.P., p. 22. (See also pp. 63, 86, 93, 99, 101, 116, 167, 210, 225, 251, 255, 257, 265, 266, 284, 318, 361, 367, 368.)
'A Curse' ** 4 July 1952.
'A Lesson in Grammar' 13 August 1952. S.M.P., p. 21.

181. 'The Way of the World' ** 27 August 1952.
     'Song' (Interlocked upon the bed) 27 August 1952. E.H., p. 67.
Influence of Auden. (See also pp. 8, 12, 13, 17, 20, 23, 26, 33, 48, 58, 64,
76, 78, 79, 80, 108, 147, 169, 175, 177, 183, 186, 195, 204, 233, 271,
316.)

182. 'A Late Quarrel' 6 September 1952. S.M.P., p. 23. Influence of Yeats. (See
     also pp. 1, 15, 49, 50, 51, 65, 66, 75, 77, 87, 89, 90, 92, 99, 120, 147,
158, 198, 234, 245, 250, 260, 264, 302, 307, 318, 337.)
     'Hard Luck' ** 20 September 1952.
     'Epigrams' ** 20–21 September 1952. Four of the seven epigrams have
titles: II. 'Gardeners Are Friendly People'; III. 'A Contemporary'; V.
'Mother and Daughter'; VI. 'My Mirror Loves Me, Anyway'.

183. 'The Pride of the Morning' 30 September 1952. Poetry, Chicago, 85, 5,
     February 1955. E.H., p. 69. Cf. Auden's 'As I walked out one evening . . .
     ' (see also pp. 8, 12, 13, 17, 20, 23, 26, 33, 48, 58, 64, 76, 78, 79, 80, 108,
147, 169, 175, 177, 181, 186, 195, 204, 233, 271, 316).

184. 'Voyages' 30 September 1952. S.M.P., p. 24.
     'Two' 18–19 October 1952. E.H., p. 54.

185. 'Stare-in-the-Face' 19 October 1952. E.H., p. 52.
     'The Last Regret' (for Ted) 8 December 1952. S.M.P., p. 25. Ted Richards
(see also pp. 126, 168, 214, 222, 298, 317, 323, 324) kept a café, The Welsh
Kitchen, at Borth, near Aberystwyth, and owned a boat, the Spanish Lady,
aboard which, well supplied with beer, he and Jones would go sailing when
the latter moved to Borth in 1948. Both men had served in the Navy during
the Second World War. Jones had been fascinated, from an early age, by
ships and the sea ('A small boy in a small Welsh school/Dreamed over books
that he would go to sea', 'Lucky Jonah', p. 198) but it was the trauma of
service in the Mediterranean theatre, when friends were drowned and he
escaped, that haunted his nightmares and his poetry ever afterwards.

186. 'Song of the Dandy Bones' (for Ted) 8 December 1952. Dublin Magazine,
     XXX, 4, 1955. E.H., p. 68. 'dandy' – 'smart/fine'; 'lubber' – 'land-loving'.
See also pp. 92, 108 above, 141, 225, 231.
     'Villanelle' 8 December 1952. S.M.P., p. 26. This form, favoured also by
Auden, (see also pp. 8, 12, 13, 17, 20, 23, 26, 33, 48, 58, 64, 76, 78, 79,
80, 108, 147, 169, 175, 177, 181, 183, 195, 204, 233, 271, 316) Empson
and Dylan Thomas (see also pp. 4, 20, 30, 33, 40, 52, 53, 54, 57, 58, 64,
87, 96, 104, 106, 112, 116, 117, 119, 158, 170, 201, 225, 232, 234, 245,
272, 278, 279, 284, 292, 313, 345), comprises five three-lined verses and
a quatrain and employs only two rhymes throughout. The first and third
lines of the first stanza are repeated alternately in the succeeding stanzas as
a refrain and form the concluding couplet of the quatrain. Originally the
villanelle was used for light verse, but, characteristically, modern and
postmodern poets employed it for serious themes.

187. 'Stanzas in a Mirror' 4 January 1953. E.H., p. 42.

188. 'Workers of the World, Unite' (*for Stanley*) 4 January 1953. S.M.P., p. 27. The young Jones was a Stalinist, became Secretary of the Labour Club at Aberystwyth and sold the 'Daily Worker' on the streets. In 1948 he said of the communist coup in Czechoslovakia, 'Some people call this rape! I call it sweet seduction'. The title of the poem is the common form of 'Proletarier alle Länder, vereinigt euch!', the concluding words of 'The Communist Manifesto'. Stanley Kowalski ('Stanley the Pole'), one of the 'displaced persons' so common immediately after the Second World War, was a drinking companion of Jones's at Portsmouth.

189. 'Nursery Rhyme' 4 January 1953. S.M.P., p. 29.
     'Critical Encounter' 16–18 April 1953. E.H., p. 47.

190. 'Invocation' 16–18 April 1953. S.M.P., p. 30. 'stilted bird' – heron.
     'A New Song of Old Despair' 16–18 April 1953. Botteghe Oscure XVII, 1956. E.H., p. 70.

191. 'Long-ago Love' 16–18 April 1953. S.M.P., p. 31.

192. 'Homage to Wallace Stevens' 16–18 April 1953. E.H., p. 57. Wallace Stevens (1879–1955) was born in Pennsylvania, educated at Harvard and became a lawyer. His poems are described in *The Oxford Companion to English Literature* (ed) Margaret Drabble (Oxford University Press, Revised edn 1995) as 'enigmatic, elegant, intellectual, and occasionally startling meditations on order and the imagination, on reality, appearance and art', themes that deeply interested Jones. His *Selected Poems* were published in England in 1953, and made a powerful impression on Jones, whose interest in American literature became increasingly important when he joined the University of New South Wales. This poem, although its verse-form is different, is a response to 'The Man with the Blue Guitar', a poem of more than 300 free-verse couplets concerned with the relationship between things as they are and things imagined – a conjunction which, as we have seen above, also interested Jones (see also p. 266).

193. 'For the Marriage of Hugh and Barbara' ** 19 April 1953. The first of what would be a considerable number of occasional tributes to friends on such occasions as marriage and the birth of children. (See also p. 284.) Hugh Meyler was a Welsh doctor; his wife, Barbara, also a doctor, came from Adelaide.

194. 'I Love Your Beautiful Mind, but I Love Especially Your Body' ** 4 June 1953.
     'Lady in a Garden' 4 June 1953. S.M.P., p. 32.

195. 'Problems of Language: Old Man, Young Girl' 4 June 1953. New Statesman XLIX 1245, 15 January 1955. E.H., p. 55. In the 'Black Book' (see also pp. 143, 145, 159, 167, 203, 204, 210, 211, 214, 217, 220, 239, 255, 261, 303, 353), Jones identifies the 'sage' as Ludwig Wittgenstein (1889–1951), who argued initially that the only meaningful use of language is as a picture of

empirical, scientific fact, and later that language has a great range of uses analogous to the tools in a carpenter's bag. The 'poet' Jones identifies as W. H. Auden (1907–73) (see also pp. 8, 12, 13, 17, 20, 23, 26, 33, 48, 58, 64, 76, 78, 79, 80, 108, 147, 169, 175, 177, 181, 183, 186, 204, 233, 271, 316). These identifications are not given in E.H.

'Debate' 4 June 1953. E.H., p. 50.

196. 'Intimations of Mortality' 14 September 1953. E.H., p. 53. The title is a pun on Wordsworth's famous 'Ode on the Intimations of Immortality' (1807). (See also pp. 87, 199, 234, 260, 346, 370.)

'Love Dies as a Tree Grows' 14 September 1953. S.M.P., p. 33. Prose-poem (see also pp. 96, 114).

197. 'Tribute' 14 September 1953. S.M.P., p. 34. Jones was influenced by Robert Graves's thesis, in 'The White Goddess' (1948), that true poets derive their gifts from the Muse, the primitive, matriarchal Moon Goddess ('she, the needed and divine') of whom each loved woman is a version. (See also pp. 158, 251, 258, 312.)

'A Song of the Days' 21 September 1953. E.H., p. 71. The 'five truants' are the five senses.

198. 'Complaint' 17–30 January 1954. S.M.P., p. 35.

'A Young Man Reproves His Elders' 17–30 January 1954. S.M.P., p. 36. Based on Yeats's 'The Scholars', whose first line, 'Bald heads forgetful of their sins', the first line of this poem echoes (see also pp. 1, 15, 49, 50, 51, 65, 66, 75, 77, 87, 89, 90, 92, 99, 120, 147, 158, 182, 234, 245, 250, 260, 264, 302, 307, 318, 337).

199. 'It Is Not Fear' 17–30 January 1954. S.M.P., p. 37. Another Villanelle.

'Old Man's Song' 19 February 1954. 'The Dublin Magazine', XXXI, 3, December 1956 S.M.P., p. 38. 'The child is father to the man' is a slight misquotation ('to' for 'of') from Wordsworth's 'My Heart Leaps up When I Behold' (see also pp. 87, 196, 234, 260, 346, 370).

200. 'Love's Tautology' April 1954. S.M.P., p. 39. 'Tautology' has both an everyday meaning (unnecessarily saying the same thing more than once – e.g. 'I myself, personally') and a logical one (a statement which is always necessarily true). Presumably it is the second sense that is employed here.

'Situation' April 1954. E.H., p. 56. The vowel music of this lyric is extraordinarily beautiful, and is enhanced by the use of alliteration.

201. 'Sailor' 19 April 1954. S.M.P., p. 40. Another example of the after-effects of war-service.

'Remembrance' September 1954. S.M.P., p. 41.

'Poem Dedicated to the Memory of Dylan Thomas' September 1954. E.H. p. 24. Jones was much influenced by the work of Thomas and in 1963 published the perceptive Oliver and Boyd monograph on him. (See also pp. 4, 20, 30, 33, 40, 52, 53, 54, 57, 58, 64, 87, 96, 104, 106, 112, 116, 117, 119, 158, 170, 186, 225, 232, 234, 245, 272, 278, 279, 284, 292, 313,

345.) Thomas had died on 9 November 1953. The style is deliberately a pastiche: e.g. 'Grained in the deep earth' echoes 'Deep with the first dead . . . The grains beyond age' of Thomas's 'A Refusal to Mourn . . . '.

202. 'Merlin's Lament' 13 July 1955. 'The Dublin Magazine', XXX, 4, December 1955 E.H., p. 60. This is the Merlin (see also p. 3) of the King Arthur (see also pp. 44, 228, 337, 343) tradition, based, however, on the (Welsh) legendary poet/prophet, Myrddin.

203. 'A Lesson in Criticism' 13 July 1955. S.M.P., p. 42. Jones was teaching at the Naval School, Portsmouth, when he wrote this poem.
    'Innocent Song for Two Voices'. 22–24 August, 1955. S.M.P., p. 43. A dedication, 'To Paddy', has been cancelled in the 'Black Book' (see also pp. 143, 145, 159, 167, 195, 204, 210, 211, 214, 217, 220, 239, 255, 261, 303, 353).

204. 'One Song of a Mad Prince' September 1955. This poem was first collected (E.H., p. 72) under this ('Black Book' – see also pp. 143, 145, 159, 167, 195, 203, 210, 211, 214, 217, 220, 239, 255, 261, 303, 353) title. It re-appears in S.M.P., p. 57, as the first of the 'Three Songs of a Mad Prince' which give that volume its title. All three songs are Audenesque ballads. (See also pp. 8, 12, 13, 17, 20, 23, 26, 33, 48, 58, 64, 76, 78, 79, 80, 108, 147, 169, 175, 177, 181, 183, 186, 195, 233, 271, 316.)

205. 'A Promise to My Old Age' 9 October 1955. S.M.P., p. 44.
    'A Sonnet Instead of Theology' 9 October 1955. S.M.P., p. 45. 'Charles Sanders Pierce' (*sic*) (1839–1914), was recognized by William James as the inventor of the word 'Pragmatism', which he, Peirce, defined as 'a method of determining the meanings of intellectual concepts . . . upon which reasoning may hinge'. If this is a sonnet at all (in the formal sense), it is a 'stretched' one. It comprises sixteen lines, rhyming ABB CDEEDF GFGHH AA. The note is Jones's.

206. 'The Time of Love' 31 October 1955. S.M.P., p. 46.
    'Sunday on the Beach' (*for Rhiannon*) 17 February 1956. E.H., p. 79. This appears to be the most recently completed poem to be included in this first volume. The poet's second daughter, Rhiannon, had been born in February 1953. (See also pp. 77, 124, 130, 138, 143, 144, 147, 169, 218, 228, 238, 261, 269, 274, 301, 335.)

207. 'Sea Shanty' ** 7 April 1956. Alludes to perhaps the best-known of shanties, 'Blow the Man Down'. A seaman 'on a lee shore' (the shore towards which the wind is blowing) has every chance of becoming 'the ghost of a sailor'.

208. 'The Child at Night' 2 July 1956. S.M.P., p. 47.

209. 'The Lady and the Fir-Tree' (*for Mairit*) 30 July 1956. S.M.P., p. 48. A (literary) ballad of the 'Question and Answer' type. Mairit was a Swedish friend.
    'Poetic Retrospect' 3 October 1956. S.M.P., p. 49.

210. 'The Ring of Language' (*for Hildie*) 28 May 1957. S.M.P., p. 50. In the 'Black Book' (see also pp. 143, 145, 159, 167, 195, 203, 204, 211, 214, 217, 220, 239, 255, 261, 303, 353) this poem and the one which follows it are dated '28 May 56', clearly a mistake (the 'Black Book' contains other examples, noticed and corrected, however, by the poet, of careless dating). The original title, 'The Naming of the Animals', was altered by Jones when he decided to dedicate the poem to 'Hildie', a Finnish friend. W. H. Entwhistle's *Aspects of Language* was published by Faber and Faber in 1953. The second quotation is from Genesis 2: 19–20. In Genesis 2: 17 Adam (see also pp. 63, 86, 93, 99, 101, 116, 167, 180, 225, 251, 255, 257, 265, 266, 284, 318, 361, 367, 368), who has been placed in the Garden of Eden, is warned not to eat of the tree of the knowledge of good and evil. In Genesis 2: 18, God, not Adam, raises the issue of loneliness ('It is not good that the man should be alone') and in Genesis 2: 22 creates Eve. Jones, ever aware of Man's sinful nature, not infrequently identifies with Adam; the reader wonders about Hildie!

211. 'Christening Poem for Alison Morgan' ** 28 May 1957 (but see above). The Anglo-Welsh poet, Robert Morgan (1921–94), at this time teaching boys with special needs at a Portsmouth school, was a friend of the Joneses.
    'A Second Song of a Mad Prince' 19 June 1957. S.M.P., p. 59, where its title is 'Three Songs of a Mad Prince, II'. Dedication '*to Paddy*' cancelled in the 'Black Book' (see also pp. 143, 145, 159, 167, 195, 203, 204, 210, 214, 217, 220, 239, 255, 261, 303, 353).

212. 'Portsmouth at Night: "Hostilities Only" Rating' ** July 1957. A 'hostilities only' rating is an ordinary seaman who has volunteered (as Jones did in 1941) to serve for the duration of a war. 'Snotty' is naval slang for 'midshipman' (based, presumably, on the fact that these trainee officers tended to 'put on airs'). In 1942 Jones had set out from the Royal Naval Barracks, Portsmouth, for service in the Mediterranean.

213. 'The Monster' July 1957. S.M.P., p. 52.
    'Grandparents' (*for Knut Johansen*) 31 August 1957. S.M.P., p. 53. 'Knut Johansen' – see below at p. 214.

214. 'For Louise Bogan' Gasthaus Strassenwirt, Salzburg Seminar, 12 August 1958. Jones entered seven poems only into the 'Black Book' (see also pp. 143, 145, 159, 167, 195, 203, 204, 210, 211, 217, 220, 239, 255, 261, 303, 353) between 3 October 1956 and August 1958 (a period of almost a year), when he attended the Annual Salzburg Seminar. 'I am gloriously drunk with sunshine, wine, talk, the company of other Poets, beautiful women, no responsibilities.' he wrote to Pam and Ted Richards (see also pp. 126, 168, 185, 222, 298, 317, 323, 324). Not only was the Seminar a stimulus to creativity, it led indirectly to the realization of an ambition with his appointment to a lectureship at the Newcastle College of the University of New South Wales in 1959 (see also pp. 86, 143, 218, 224, 225, 226, 237, 239, 244, 252, 284, 291, 299, 300, 301, 302, 303, 309, 312, 326, 327, 328, 333, 343, 353, 358, 365, 370). Louise Bogan (1897–1970) was a US poet and poetry critic of the *New Yorker* from 1931–69. She published Jones's work

in the USA. Knut Johansen (see above p. 213) was a Norwegian member of the Seminar.

'For Roberto Sanesi, il miglior fabbro' Gasthaus Strassenwirt, Salzburg, 14 August 1958. Jones had met the Italian poet, Roberto Sanesi (1931–2001), a close friend of Vernon Watkins (see also p. 292) and Ceri Richards, at Watkins' home earlier in 1958. (See also pp. 217, 218, 219, 220, 225, 292.) In September Jones wrote to his publisher, Hart-Davis (see also pp. 229, 324), that he was working on translations of Sanesi's poetry and would like to include some of them in his next volume. Although Jones included seven in S.M.P., and the two poets became close friends, Mel Gooding's obituary in the *Guardian* in February 2001 contrived to avoid any mention of either fact. 'Il miglior fabbro' is the dedication which T. S. Eliot (see also pp. 1, 3, 9, 17, 18, 33, 107, 121, 137, 234, 336, 345) made to Ezra Pound in publishing *The Waste Land* (1922).

'Third Song of a Mad Prince' 31 August 1958. S.M.P., p. 61. 'Three Songs of a Mad Prince, III' in S.M.P.

216. 'Failure of Narcissus' October 1958. S.M.P., p. 54. The beautiful youth, Narcissus, did not drown: according to Ovid (see also p. 272), his punishment for the death of Echo was to pine away until metamorphosed into the flower that bears his name. See also 'Narcissus', p. 128 above.

'A Woman Who Loved to Look on Running Water' (*for Elizabeth*) October 1958. S.M.P., p. 55.

217. 'The Crab' October 1958. S.M.P., p. 67. In the 'Black Book' (see also pp. 143, 145, 159, 167, 195, 203, 204, 210, 211, 214, 220, 239, 255, 261, 303, 353) each of the translations has, below the title, the words '*from the Italian of Roberto Sanesi*' (see also pp. 214, 218, 219, 220, 225, 292); in S.M.P., seven of the translations form a section preceded by these words. Orpheus (see also p. 94) enchanted the wild beasts with the lyre presented to him by Apollo (see also pp. 26, 28, 312); 'Vertex' (*sic*) is the pointed tip of a cone. Although unable to speak Welsh, Jones was something of a linguist: he wrote a few poems in French and Sanesi regarded his translations as the finest English versions of his poems.

'Not Lack of Children Only' October 1958. S.M.P., p. 56.

April 1959–January 1965: Newcastle, New South Wales

Early in April 1959, T. H. Jones, his wife, Madeleine, and their three children, Sian, Rhiannon and Ruth Myfanwy, sailed for Australia aboard the M.V. *Oceania*.

218. 'The Savage Balance' 19 June 1959. S.M.P., p. 66. Translation from Sanesi. (See also pp. 214, 217, 219, 220, 225, 292.) 'Elytron' (plural 'elytra') – the hard case of a beetle; 'tourbillion' – French for 'whirlwind'; 'petrolic' – a neologism, appears to signify a shimmering of stars analogous to the sheen on the surface of petrol.

'False Dedication' (*to Anita*) 19 June 1959. S.M.P., p. 65. Translation from Sanesi. (See also pp. 214, 217, 219, 220, 225, 292.) 'Demiurge' means 'The' (or 'a') creator.

219. 'Draw An Arch of Light at the Window' 19 June 1959. Translation from Sanesi. (See also pp. 214, 217, 218, 220, 225, 292.) S.M.P., p. 68. Minerva (Greek Athena) was the Roman goddess of wisdom.
     'Statue of Salt and Wall of Hyacinth' 19 June 1959. Translation from Sanesi. S.M.P., p. 69.

220. 'And Resolve Themselves' (*to Gio' Pomodoro* in S.M.P., not in the 'Black Book' (see also pp. 143, 145, 159, 167, 195, 203, 204, 210, 211, 214, 217, 239, 255, 261, 303, 353)) 19 June 1959. Translation from Sanesi. (See also pp. 214, 217, 218, 219, 225, 292.) S.M.P., p. 70.
     'Bewilderment' 19 June 1959. Australian Letters, 2, 4, March 1960. B.D., p.39 (earliest of the poems to be selected for this third volume).

221. 'In the Light of Ordinary Evenings' ** 12 September 1959.
     'The Ditch of Desire' ** 12 September 1959.
     'Not When I Came' 12 September 1959. C.P., p. 228.

222. 'Lucky Jonah' (*for Ted*) 12 September 1959. The dedication is, appropriately, to Ted Richards (see also pp. 126, 168, 185, 214, 298, 317, 323, 324). Meanjin 19, 2, June 1960. B.D., p. 9, the opening poem of this third volume, where it is given a section to itself. Jones's finest and, apart from 'Cotton Mather' (p. 353), most substantial poem, an elegy ('lullaby and catalogue of the drowned') for the dead sailors of the Second World War. Perversely ignored by anthologists and critics until Meic Stephens' Corgi selection *Lucky Jonah and Other Poems* (2004). In March 1942 a troopship had taken him, via the Cape, to Alexandria, where he joined the HMS *Seaham*, a minesweeper, as signals telegraphist, in June 1942. From October 1943 he served ashore at Algiers, Bougie and perhaps also Naples, returning to Britain in 1944. The horrific experiences of this time left him with a neurosis that showed itself in nightmares for the rest of his life and emerges in the poetry particularly in images of drowning. The poem was drafted aboard ship on the way to his new life in Australia – 'Down the blooming Meddy again – just off Messina, in fact' (Messina, the scene of the most horrific of his wartime experiences), he wrote to Pam and Ted Richards on 5 April 1959. The poem marks an important stage in the poet's development, comparable, in its handling of the wartime experience, to 'The Welshman in Exile Speaks' (see p. 244), and see also pp. 53, 185. 'Lucky Jonah' is a double pun, first because, for sailors, a Jonah brings ill-luck. His original, the Old Testament prophet, took a ship to Tarshish to 'flee from the presence of the Lord' (Jonah 1) and caused a shipwreck. Second because of its echo of the poet's surname. 'Crimped' means 'decoyed' or 'impressed' into service. The 'schoolfellow' was Elwyn Davies, who survived two shipwrecks only to be killed in a car accident. 'Charabanced': the short story, 'A Day at the Seaside' ('Dock Leaves', 15, Winter 1954) gives an account of a Chapel treat to Aberystwyth, the nearest seaside to Llanafanfawr (see also pp. 6, 23, 94, 104, 138, 142, 226, 228, 244, 261, 264, 275, 283, 296, 297, 302, 310, 311, 319, 324, 332, 336, 342, 343, 346, 359, 364, 366); 'to the great waters' (Psalms 107: 23 – 'They that go down to the sea in ships: and occupy their business in great

waters'); 'Captain's Requestmen and Defaulters' – sailors who had made formal requests, e.g. for compassionate leave, or who had committed an offence, were brought before the ship's captain for judgement. This defaulter is a nervous lookout; 'Billy Budd' – in the novella by Herman Melville (1819–91) *Billy Budd, Foretopman* (written 1891, published 1924), the hero is unjustly hanged as a mutineer; 'pongos' – naval slang for 'soldiers'; 'One day we caught a submarine . . . ' – during the invasion of Sicily (10 July 1943) Jones's minesweeper captured the Italian submarine, 'Bronzo'. Charts discovered aboard her proved helpful to the invading troops; 'gharri-driver' – a gharri is a wheeled vehicle plying for hire.

224. 'Excuse' (*for Marlene*) 14 October 1959. C.C., p. 53. The earliest poem to be included (posthumously chosen by Madeleine Jones (see also pp. 34, 45, 64, 77, 143, 147, 148, 156, 159, 169, 218, 234, 236, 240, 242, 266, 269, 283, 285, 291, 312, 343) and Gillian Stowell (see also pp. 266, 310, 309, 323, 340)) in that volume. Marlene Norst (see also pp. 239, 327) lectured in the German Department at the Newcastle College (see also pp. 86, 143, 214, 218, 225, 226, 237, 239, 244, 252, 284, 291, 299, 300, 301, 302, 303, 309, 312, 326, 327, 328, 333, 343, 353, 358, 365, 370) of the University of New South Wales and remained a family friend after her move to Sydney in 1964.

225. 'Taut Rigidity of the Senses' 2 December 1959. Translation from Sanesi. (See also pp. 214, 217, 218, 219, 220, 292.) S.M.P., p. 71.
'The Colour of Cockcrowing' (*for Robyn*) 2 December 1959. C.C., p. 83. 'Cockcrowing' is a sound, not a colour, but both sounds and colours have tone: we are in the world of synaesthesia or the interpretation of one sense (sound, here) in terms of another (sight). It is not uncommon for poets to visualize vowels in terms of colour: for Rimbaud, 'A' was black; for Raymond Garlick, apple-green. Dylan Thomas's poem, 'Once It Was The Colour of Saying' is well-known and may have been the stimulus for the title of this one. (See also pp. 4, 20, 30, 33, 40, 52, 53, 54, 57, 58, 64, 87, 96, 104, 106, 112, 116, 117, 119, 158, 170, 186, 201, 232, 234, 245, 272, 278, 279, 284, 292, 313, 345.) The cock crows at dawn, to announce a new day; for Jones Australia was not merely a new country, very different from Wales, it was a new life and the fulfilment of a lifelong ambition. The poem, a great shout of joy, was rightly given a section to itself in the posthumous volume which, equally rightly, bears its name. But there is no such thing as pure joy in Jones's poetry – cockcrow has another, and quite opposite, significance: Matthew 26:34, 'before the cock crow, thou shalt deny me thrice', and the world so exuberantly evoked in the poem is the world *after* the Fall. The animals in the poem's first section include the 'vulture already aware of death' and the death we must all suffer was decreed by God when Adam and Eve (see also pp. 63, 86, 93, 99, 101, 116, 167, 180, 210, 251, 255, 257, 265, 266, 284, 318, 361, 367, 368) ate of the tree of knowledge. Robyn Iverach (see also pp. 307, 370), a female colleague in the English Department at the Newcastle College (see also pp. 86, 143, 214, 218, 224, 226, 237, 239, 244, 252, 284, 291, 299, 300, 301, 302, 303, 309, 312, 326, 327, 328, 333, 343, 353, 358, 365, 370) of

the University of New South Wales, later married Rod Wallace; 'Leviathan' – any huge sea-animal; 'murderous robin' – male robins fight to the death for their territory, and their breasts are red, but they are also an emblem of a joyous season; 'sainted herring' – St Peter was a fisherman, and is associated with various fish, though not usually this one; 'holy salmon'- as the fish is a symbol of Christ ('ichthus'), all fish are in that sense 'holy'.

226. 'A Christmas Poem' ** 24 December 1959. 'Audrey and' Doug Muecke (see also p. 302) was Head of English at the Newcastle College (see also pp. 86, 143, 214, 218, 224, 225, 237, 239, 244, 252, 284, 291, 299, 300, 301, 302, 303, 309, 312, 326, 327, 328, 333, 343, 353, 358, 365, 370) of the University of New South Wales – see also p. 269; 'Christ's blood streams . . . ' in Marlowe's play, 'Dr Faustus', the hero, about to be damned, cries (see lines 1419–20), 'See see where Christ's blood streams in the firmament./One drop would save my soul . . . '; 'every kiss erects another cross': Judas betrayed Christ to the Romans by kissing him; 'Mary of Magdalen' – Christ 'cast seven devils' out of Mary of Magdala, otherwise known as Mary Magdalene; 'breast upon a bloody thorn' – thorn trees are a feature of the Llanafan (see also pp. 6, 23, 94, 104, 138, 142, 222, 228, 244, 261, 264, 275, 283, 296, 297, 302, 310, 311, 319, 324, 332, 336, 342, 343, 346, 359, 364, 366) landscape so familiar to Jones and the thorn is an important emblem in his work. The obvious association is with Christ's crown of thorns, but of almost equal importance is the fable of the nightingale which sang sweetly to death, its body pierced by the thorn against which it was pressed.

227. 'Italian Baroque Music' ** December 1959/January 1960. Louise Bogan, see also p. 214; 'stases' – stoppages; 'epiphany' – a showing forth or manifestation (cf. the showing of the infant Jesus to the Wise Men); 'Rialto' – a district and island of Venice with a famous bridge over the Grand Canal; 'Harri and Doctor Luck' – the poet includes himself in the poem (a joke); 'Oberon' – King of the Fairies; 'in excelsis' – on high (as in 'Gloria in excelsis Deo'); 'kyrie' – 'Lord', as in 'Kyrie eleison' ('Lord, have mercy'); in music the Kyrie is the first part of the Mass.

228. 'Rhiannon' 19 February 1960. Southerly, 21, 1, 1961. B.D., p. 15. To the poet's second daughter, born in 1953. (See also pp. 77, 124, 130, 138, 143, 144, 147, 169, 206, 218, 238, 261, 269, 274, 301, 335.) *The Mabinogion* (see also pp. 37, 337, 343) is the title used by Charlotte Guest for her translation of twelve medieval Welsh tales (Llandovey, 1849 in Welsh and English; 1879 in English only). Rhiannon loved Pwyll, lord of Dyfed, but was betrothed to Gwawl, son of Clud. Eventually she married Pwyll. Ayer"s Rock (Uluru) is the famous monolith in the Northern Territory of Australia. Jones compares it to the 'small hill, Alltyclych' a landmark near his home at Llanafan (see also pp. 6, 23, 94, 104, 138, 142, 222, 226, 244, 261, 264, 275, 283, 296, 297, 302, 310, 311, 319, 324, 332, 336, 342, 343, 346, 359, 364, 366) which, as a child, he used to cross each day on his way to (primary) school.

'On a Painting, "Sunk Lyonesse", by Rae Richards' August 1960. B.D., p. 61. 'Lyonesse' – King Arthur's (see also pp. 44, 202, 337, 343) country, the rich tract of land fabled to stretch between Land's End and the Scillies; 'Rae Richards' – see also pp. 36, 230, 254, 270, 274, 282, 311, 319, 337, 339, 353; 'Blackmur' – Richard Palmer Blackmur (1904–65), American poet and critic.

229. 'The Same Story' (*for Rupert Hart-Davis*) 23 August 1960. (See also 289.) B.D., p. 62. Shakespearean (see also pp. 17, 33, 55, 56, 58, 79, 81, 89, 129, 138, 158, 235, 261, 264, 270, 276, 288, 297, 311, 344, 345) sonnet; (Sir) Rupert Charles Hart-Davis (see also pp. 214, 324), quintessential man of letters, was at the centre of the English literary scene from the 1930s until his death in 1999. After working for Heinemann (1929–33) he became a director of Jonathan Cape. In 1946 he founded his own company, published the work of Blunden, Causely and R.S. Thomas (see also pp. 310, 342) and at one time had seventeen living authors on his list. A very supportive publisher and friend, he published all four volumes of Jones's poetry. The poem is a good example of the guilt that haunted the poet all his life, and in particular when he survived the Second World War in which friends and comrades were killed. His strict Chapel upbringing caused further guilt-feelings about his sexual promiscuity and alcoholism. Sin and guilt are characteristic of his work.

'Thinking to Write an Ode' 24 August 1960. Australian Letters, 4, 1, October 1961; *The Vital Decade*, ed. Dutton and Harris (1968). C.P., p. 229. 'Ode' – a poem dignified in form, content and style.

230. 'On Having My Portrait Painted' (*to Rae*) 4 September 1960. B.D., p. 63. The portrait survives, and was used as the cover illustration for *T. H. Jones, Poet of Exile* by P. Bernard Jones and Don Dale-Jones' (University of Wales Press, 2001). For Rae Richards (see also pp. 86, 228, 250, 254, 270, 274, 282, 311, 319, 337, 339, 353).

231. 'A Rule of Three Sum Wrong' (*for Ivor*) October 1960. (See also 225, 225, 293.) B.D., p. 16. G. M. Hopkins – Gerard Manley Hopkins (1844–89) (see also pp. 138, 141) was one of the poets Jones had long admired and learned from. Ivor Vivian (see also pp. 252, 253, 328) was a Welsh friend, a teacher of mathematics married to Stephanie. He moved to Sydney in 1961.

232. 'Sea-faiths' 3 November 1960. B.D., p. 65. Jones admired and was, in his early work, influenced by Dylan Thomas (1914–53), and in 1963 published a monograph in the Oliver & Boyd *Writers and Critics* series. The quotation is from 'Where Once the Waters of Your Face'; 'spindrift' (a favourite word of Thomas's) – the spray blown from the crests of waves. (see also pp. 4, 20, 30, 33, 40, 52, 53, 54, 57, 58, 64, 87, 96, 104, 106, 112, 116, 117, 119, 158, 170, 186, 201, 225, 234, 245, 272, 278, 279, 284, 292, 313, 345.)

'Money' ** 5 November 1960. Arthur Hugh Clough (1819–61) used the words quoted in 'Dipsychus'; 'pecunia' – the Latin word for 'money'.

233. 'Lost Love, Unwritten Poems' 5 November 1960. C.P., p. 230. A dedication has been scratched out beneath the title – the neat twist at the poem's end presumably explains this (a typically honest irony).

'Fall of an Empire' 17 November 1960. B.D., p. 66. An Audenesque poem. (See also pp. 8, 12, 13, 17, 20, 23, 26, 33, 48, 58, 64, 76, 78, 79, 80, 108, 147, 169, 175, 177, 181, 183, 186, 195, 204, 271, 316.)

234. 'P is for Poetry' 1 December 1960. C.P., p. 231. 'sea-born' – Aphrodite/ Venus was said to have been born from the foam of the sea (see also pp. 37, 38, 42, 46, 56, 86, 109, 111, 307, 363), but the compliment is surely to Madeleine. See also pp. 34, 45, 64, 77, 143, 147, 148, 156, 159, 169, 218, 224, 236, 240, 242, 266, 269, 283, 285, 291, 312, 343.

'Sonnets at Forty' ** 16 February 1961. Jones would not reach the age of forty until 21 December, but was, in Dylan Thomas's (see also pp. 4, 20, 30, 33, 40, 52, 53, 54, 57, 58, 64, 87, 96, 104, 106, 112, 116, 117, 119, 158, 170, 186, 201, 225, 232, 245, 272, 278, 279, 284, 292, 313, 345) phrase, in his fortieth 'year to heaven'. Both sonnets are Petrarchan (see also pp. 1, 12, 36, 41, 61, 80, 86, 91, 108, 119, 124, 138, 140, 156, 254, 255, 260, 266, 276, 282, 302, 305, 311, 339). 'pitch and toss' – a gambling game in which coins are pitched at a mark and the player who gets nearest has the right to toss all the other players' coins in the air and pocket those that come down heads up; 'unsatisfactory way of putting it' – from 'East Coker' by T. S. Eliot (one of the 'Four Quartets'); 'I am not Prince Hamlet' – T. S. Eliot, from 'The Love Song of J. Alfred Prufrock' (see also pp. 1, 3, 9, 17, 18, 33, 107, 121, 137, 214, 336, 345); Dante (Alighieri) (1265–1321) (see also pp. 14, 46) – his 'Divina Commedia' was an influence on British poets from Chaucer on; 'marvellous boy' – William Wordsworth's (1770–1850) (see also pp. 87, 196, 199, 260, 346, 370) phrase, in 'Resolution and Independence', for Thomas Chatterton (1752–70); 'wither into truth' – W. B. Yeats (1865–1939), from 'The Coming of Wisdom with Time' in the *Green Helmet* collection, (1910) (see also pp. 1, 15, 49, 50, 51, 65, 66, 75, 77, 87, 89, 90, 92, 99, 120, 147, 158, 182, 198, 245, 250, 260, 264, 302, 307, 318, 337); (caught) 'in flagrante (delicto)' – '(caught) in the act', an expression often humorously applied to sexual misdemeanour.

235. 'Never Again' 16 February 1961. Nimrod, 3, 1, Summer 1965. B.D., p. 40.
'Country Sentiment' (*for Marie*) ** 16 February, 1961. (See also pp. 271, 276, 297, 309, 322, 340, 363.) Exploits the pun, at least as old as Shakespeare's (see also pp. 17, 33, 55, 56, 58, 79, 81, 89, 129, 138, 158, 229, 261, 264, 270, 276, 288, 297, 311, 344, 345) *Hamlet*, which Jones will use again in 'Country Matters': he lusts for her. Marie Tietze, a New Zealander who helped Jones with references, was the mother of Miranda (see also pp. 297, 309, 322, 363).

236. 'A Different Idiom' ** 16 February 1961. 'country matters' – see above; 'service . . . court' – Jones sometimes amuses himself (and perhaps the object of his affection) by using the language of courtly love.
'They Lie' (*for Madeleine*) 24 February 1961. C.P., p. 232. Whatever his other loves, Jones's love for his wife was the true and abiding one. See also pp. 34, 45, 64, 77, 143, 147, 148, 156, 159, 169, 218, 224, 234, 240, 242, 266, 269, 283, 285, 291, 312, 343.

237. 'Not Young Any Longer' 16 March 1961. B.D., p. 41. In a letter to Professor Dai Phillips at the Sydney College of the University of New South Wales, the poet enclosed a copy of this poem and commented, 'This ought to be dedicated to my girl students, but I dare not.'

'To Michelene' 16 March 1961. B.D., p. 42. 'Jefferson' – Thomas Jefferson (1743–1826), drafted the American Declaration of Independence and was the first Secretary of State and third President of the USA. He spent the years 1782–7 in Paris, which he greatly enjoyed, but did not recommend to his fellow Americans; Mary Tudor (1516–58) declared, after the loss of Calais, then an English possession in France, 'When I am dead and opened, you shall find "Calais" lying in my heart.' Michelene Price was an Assistant Lecturer in the French Department at the Newcastle College (see also pp. 86, 143, 214, 218, 224, 225, 226, 239, 244, 252, 284, 291, 299, 300, 301, 302, 303, 309, 312, 326, 327, 328, 333, 343, 353, 358, 365, 370) of the University of New South Wales. See also p. 284.

'The Poet Writes of the Imminent Death of His Mistress' ** 20 March 1961. 'necrophily' – a morbid love of dead bodies.

238. 'Poem for My Daughters' ** 20 March 1961. (See also pp. 77, 124, 130, 138, 143, 144, 147, 169, 206, 218, 228, 261, 269, 274, 301, 335.)

'A Queen's Lover' 21 March 1961. Australian Letters, 5, 3, April 1963. B.D., p. 43. A dedication has been deleted; 'oblation' – offering.

239. 'She Is Asleep' 21 March 1961. B.D., p. 44.

'Macaronics for Marlene' ** 2 April 1961 – this is the first of twelve poems to be entered into the 'Black Book' (see also pp. 143, 145, 159, 167, 195, 203, 204, 210, 211, 214, 217, 220, 255, 261, 303, 353) on this date: twelve poems in twelve days. Macaronic verse is any form of verse in which two or more languages are mingled. Jones employs German, French, Italian, Welsh and Latin, with a quotation from Heinrich Heine (1797–1856), 'du bist'ne Blume' ('Du bist wie eine Blume' in Heine's poem: 'You are like a flower') and one from Catullus (c.87–c.54 BC), which he misremembers ('Da mi basia mille': 'Kiss me a thousand times over'). 'Mädchen' – 'girl'; 'fach' – literally 'small', but here means 'dear'; 'je t'adore' – 'I love you'; 'Sliante' – Jones's mis-spelling of 'sláinte' (good health – Gaelic); 'cariad' – 'sweetheart'; 'mon amour' – 'my love'; 'Duw' – 'God'; 'd'ocche blau' – 'with eyes (Italian) of blue (German). The final line is English. For Marlene (Norst) see also below and pp. 224, 327.

'The Panther' (in the Jardin des Plantes, Paris) (after Rilke and for Marlene) ** 2 April 1961. The 'Jardin des Plantes' is the French National Museum of Natural History. This is a free translation of Rilke's (Rainer Maria Rilke, 1875–1926, German lyric poet) poem, 'The Panther, Jardin des Plantes, Paris'. The number of alterations to the poem's wording in the 'Black Book' (seven) (see also pp. 143, 145, 159, 167, 195, 203, 204, 210, 211, 214, 217, 220, 255, 261, 303, 353) suggests that sometimes Jones composed directly into it. The inscription 'from Brin – Harri' suggests that the idea for the poem was given to him by Brin Newton John (see also pp. 244, 291, 326, 328, 333, 334), Head of Arts at the Newcastle College of the University of New South Wales (and father of Olivia), who had translated Under Milk Wood into German.

240. 'Lovers' Colloquy' ** 2 April 1961. 'colloquy' – 'conversation'.
      'Are There Any Modern Poets' (*for Madeleine*) 2 April 1961. C.P., p. 233.
      See also pp. 34, 45, 64, 77, 143, 147, 148, 156, 159, 169, 218, 224, 234,
      236, 242, 266, 269, 283, 285, 291, 312, 343.

241. 'You' ** 2 April 1961.
      'Lovers' Quarrel' ** 2 April 1961.
      'The Poet Is A Bastard Just Like Other People' ** 2 April 1961.
      'A Question of Responsibility' ** 2 April 1961.

242. 'The Lover Shows How Conventional He Is' ** 2 April 1961.
      'Waiting For You' (*to Madeleine*) ** 2 April 1961. See also pp. 34, 45,
      64, 77, 143, 147, 148, 156, 159, 169, 218, 224, 234, 236, 240, 266, 269,
      283, 285, 291, 312, 343.
      'A Love Poem, Perhaps' ** 2 April 1961. 'condescension' – 'graciousness'
      here.

243. 'Simply the Chance' ** 2 April 1961.
      'Anniversary' ** 13 April 1961. As Harri and Madeleine had married
      on 14 December 1946, that is not the anniversary celebrated here.

244. 'Sick with Requited Love' 13 April 1961. B.D., p. 45. 'satisfying
      nightmare' is a thought-provoking oxymoron.
      'The Welshman in Exile Speaks' (*for Brin*) (Newton-John). See also pp.
      259, 290, 292, 297, 297. 13 April 1961. Meanjin, 20, 3, September 1961;
      Nimrod, 3, 1, Summer 1965. B.D., p. 17. One of T. H. Jones's finest poems,
      the first in which he finds, suddenly and with complete confidence, his
      central theme and the language that most effectively conveys it. Comparable
      to his ability, aboard ship in the Mediterranean on the way to Australia, to
      come to terms with wartime traumas in 'Lucky Jonah'. Dedicated,
      appropriately, to Brin Newton John (see also pp. 239, 291, 326, 328, 333,
      334), Head of Arts at the Newcastle College (see also pp. 86, 143, 214, 218,
      224, 225, 226, 237, 239, 252, 284, 291, 299, 300, 301, 302, 303, 309, 312,
      326, 327, 328, 333, 343, 353, 358, 365, 370) of the University of New
      South Wales, himself a Welsh exile. 'green bacon' – home-cured bacon,
      more fat than lean; 'old man's voice' – that of his grandfather, Thomas Jones
      Cwm Crogau (1853–1950) (see also pp. 95, 283, 332, 337, 359, 366),
      shepherd, rate-collector and Deacon of his Baptist chapel. Thomas is the
      subject of a number of poems, in one of which ('My Grandfather Going
      Blind', p. 359) the poet describes himself as 'proud ... to call myself
      only/Young Crogau, old Crogau's grandson', and of short stories;
      'Belshazzars' – the prophet Daniel made Belshazzar, king of Babylon,
      tremble shortly before he lost his kingdom to Darius; Daniel, as a Deacon,
      no doubt warned tractor drivers and other locals about their sinful ways;
      'capel' – Welsh for 'chapel'; 'lead me beside the still waters' – Psalms 23: 1,
      the meek and humble members of the congregation; 'sin-eaters' – a sin-eater
      is one who, by eating bread and salt at a funeral, takes upon himself the
      dead man's sins; 'Pisgah' – Llanafan's Baptist chapel (see also pp. 6, 23, 94,
      104, 138, 142, 222, 226, 228, 261, 264, 275, 283, 296, 297, 302, 310, 311,

319, 324, 332, 336, 342, 343, 346, 359, 364, 366), 'the ugliest building I have ever seen', named, as is typical of Nonconformist chapels, after a site in the Holy Land, in this case a mountain.

245. 'Lines for Marion, On the Occasion of her Graduation and her Twentyfirst Birthday' ** 16 April 1961. The poem is to one of his 'girl students', Marion Halligan, novelist, author of the novel 'Self Possession', whose central character, Tom Lloyd, is modelled on T. H. Jones. It refers to a number of texts he has taught and would like her to remember. 'Coole' – 'The Wild Swans at Coole' is both a major poem (a tribute to Lady Augusta Gregory, his patron) and the title of a collection of poems by W. B. Yeats; (see also pp. 1, 15, 49, 50, 51, 65, 66, 75, 77, 87, 89, 90, 92, 99, 120, 147, 158, 182, 198, 234, 250, 260, 264, 302, 307, 318, 337). 'Over Sir John's Hill' is a major poem by Dylan Thomas (1914–53) (see also pp. 4, 20, 30, 33, 40, 52, 53, 54, 57, 58, 64, 87, 96, 104, 106, 112, 116, 117, 119, 158, 170, 186, 201, 225, 232, 234, 272, 278, 279, 284, 292, 313, 345); the 'white whale' is Moby Dick, the eponymous hero of Melville's novel; it is possible that 'lost traveller sleeps' is an echo of Thomas Moore's (1779–1852) sentimental 'She is far from the land where her young hero sleeps'.
'The Moods of the Sea' 17 April 1961. B.D., p. 67. Another major theme, resulting from wartime experience, is the sea, often associated with drowning; 'fountain of birth' – life on earth originated in the seas; 'glaucous' – sea-green.

246. 'Illicit Colloquy' ** 1 May 1961.
'Lines by a Not Too Dejected Lover' ** 1 May 1961. 'Hassan' – posthumously published eastern play by James Elroy Flecker (1884–1915) (see also p. 21).

247. 'She Bit Me, But Not In Anger' ** 1 May 1961. 'guerdon' – reward (such as a knight would receive from his lady).
'Keeping Chooks' ** 1 May 1961. 'chooks' – 'Strine' for 'chickens'.

248. 'Self-Criticism' ** 1 May 1961.
'Love, Poetry, and Middle Age' 1 May 1961. C.P., p. 233 (where stanzas three and four are omitted). Light verse, but very easy and accomplished.

249. 'Recovering From You' ** 1 May 1961.
'Two Coffee Cups' 1 May 1961. B.D., p. 46.

250. 'Tribute to Rae Richards' Painting of Leda and the Swan' ** 1 May 1961. (See also pp. 86, 228, 230, 254, 270, 274, 282, 311, 319, 337, 339, 353.) Zeus, in the form of a swan, raped Leda (see also pp. 49, 127, 254, 264, 309, 320), wife of Tyndareus, king of Sparta. She gave birth to two eggs, from one of which emerged Helen of Sparta/Troy (see also pp. 49, 127, 254, 264, 277, 279, 284, 298, 320) and from the other Castor and Pollux. Jones is influenced here by his admiration of Yeats: 'holding her helpless' echoes 'He holds her helpless breast upon his breast' in Yeats's 'Leda and the Swan'; (see also pp. 1, 15, 49, 50, 51, 65, 66, 75, 77, 87, 89, 90, 92, 99, 120, 147, 158, 182, 198, 234, 245, 260, 264, 302, 307, 318, 337).
'Disorganized' ** 6 May 1961.

251. 'Love Is Different From What You Think It Is' ** 6 May 1961.
     'Homage to Robert Graves' ** 6 May 1961. (See also pp. 158, 197, 258,
     312.) Jones was influenced both by Graves's love lyrics and by his study of
     Celtic myth in 'The White Goddess' (see also pp. 197, 258, 280, 312).
     'Symptoms of Love', the poem referred to here, shows how much Jones had
     learned from Graves, beginning with the dismal thought that Love is a
     'universal migraine', but concluding with the characteristic reversal, 'Take
     courage, Lover!/Could you endure such grief/At any hand but hers?'.
     'Epigram' ** 7 May 1961. 'the oldest one' – Eve betrayed Adam (see
     also pp. 63, 86, 93, 99, 101, 116, 167, 180, 210, 225, 255, 257, 265, 266,
     284, 318, 361, 367, 368) when she persuaded him to disobey God by
     eating of the Tree of Knowledge of Good and Evil.
     'Acceptance of Fate' ** 7 May 1961.

252. 'Can It Be So Long' ** 7 May 1961.
     'Restless' 7 May 1961. C.P., 234.
     'Love in the Antipodes' (for Stephanie) ** 18 May 1961. Stephanie was
     the wife of Ivor Vivian (see also pp. 231, 253, 328), a Welsh friend who
     taught Mathematics at the Newcastle College of the University of New
     South Wales (see also pp. 86, 143, 214, 218, 224, 225, 226, 237, 239, 244,
     284, 291, 299, 300, 301, 302, 303, 309, 312, 326, 327, 328, 333, 343,
     353, 358, 365, 370).

253. 'In Love' (for Stephanie and Ivor). (See also pp. 231, 252, 328.) ** 18 May
     1961.
     'No Name But Love' ** 18 May 1961.

254. 'From the French of Pemette de Guillet' ** 18 May 1961. See also below.
     'The Ship Sonnet' 18 May 1961. Pemette de Guillet (1520–45) French
     lyric poet; Petrarch (Francesco Petrarca, 1304–74), was the most popular
     Italian poet of the English Renaissance. His love poems in praise of Laura
     were particularly influential upon Surrey and Wyatt. The Petrarchan Sonnet
     (ABBA ABBA CDECDE) (see also pp. 1, 12, 36, 41, 61, 80, 86, 91, 108,
     119, 124, 138, 140, 156, 234, 255, 260, 266, 276, 282, 302, 305, 311,
     339), takes its name from him – Jones wrote a number of such sonnets.
     'Tribute to Rae Richards' Painting of Leda and the Swan, II' ** 18 May
     1961. (See also pp. 86, 228, 230, 250, 270, 274, 282, 311, 319, 337, 339,
     353.) Zeus, in the shape of a swan, raped Leda (see also pp. 49, 127, 250,
     264, 309, 320). She gave birth to two eggs, from one of which emerged
     Helen (of Troy) (see also pp. 49, 127, 150, 264, 277, 279, 284, 298, 320)
     and from the other Castor and Pollux.

255. 'In Despite of John Milton, or, What Adam Probably Said to Eve' ** 6 June
     1961. 'Paradise Lost' (1667), by John Milton (1608–1674) (see also pp. 5,
     17, 49, 281, 323, 333, 367) concerns 'Man's first disobedience, and the
     fruit/Of that forbidden tree, whose mortal taste/Brought death into the world
     and all our woe . . . ' and is a deeply serious poem. Not a few of its readers
     might enjoy this good-natured parody. (See also pp. 63, 86, 93, 99, 101, 116,
     167, 180, 210, 225, 251, 257, 265, 266, 284, 318, 361, 367, 368.)

'Wales – New South Wales. May 1961' 6 June 1961. Quadrant, 5, 4, Spring 1961. B.D., p. 18. A Petrarchan sonnet (see also pp. 1, 12, 36, 41, 61, 80, 86, 91, 108, 119, 124, 138, 140, 156, 234, 254, 260, 266, 276, 282, 302, 305, 311, 339). The dating of this poem, set against the title, confirms Jones's procedure of entering into the Exercise books and the 'Black Book' (see also pp. 143, 145, 159, 167, 195, 203, 204, 210, 211, 214, 217, 220, 239, 261, 303, 353) in batches those of the poems (composed over a period of time varying from one to as many as fourteen days) that he thought worth preserving. The poem reflects the sense of guilt at the root of Jones's poems about his Welsh heritage. 'faring' (as in 'seafaring') – 'journey'.

256. 'If This Is Love' ** 6 June 1961. The poignancy of this poem cannot but be deeply felt by anyone in love for the first time whether with the first loved one or (especially outside marriage) any subsequent one.
    'Gratuitous Advice to Aging (sic) Poets' ** 6 June 1961.

257. 'A Sort of Love Poem' 6 June 1961. C.P., p. 235. 'I only want to lie' – 'lie' is almost always an ambiguous word in Jones's poetry (cf. 'Where all my poems lie' – see 'Builth Wells' p. 346).
    'Adam, Thoughtfully, To Eve' 6 June 1961. C.P., p. 236. (See also pp. 63, 86, 93, 99, 101, 116, 167, 180, 210, 225, 251, 255, 265, 266, 284, 318, 361, 367, 368.) 'died' – ambiguous, cf. 'If thou and I/Love so alike, that none doe slacken, none can die.' in Donne's 'The Good-morrow'. (See also pp. 33, 36, 60, 260, 266, 334, 366.)
    'Chambermaid's Song' ** 6 June 1961.

258. 'Fireworks Night' 6 June 1961. The Bulletin, 85, 4329, 2 February 1963. C.P., p. 236.
    'Any Husband To Any Wife' ** 6 June 1961. All husbands (and some wives) will appreciate the serio-comedy of this poem and the accuracy of its observation.
    'Nightmare' ** 6 June 1961. Jones's war service left him with recurrent nightmares. 'hackles' – the hair of a dog's neck, which stands up when the animal is angry or frightened; 'unjust goddess' – the White Goddess (see also pp. 197, 251, 280, 312) (see Robert Graves, who believed that poetry is written in a trance-like state by a truly mad, truth-possessed, male, torn by conflicting feelings of sexual exaltation, disgust and horror, and that each loved woman is a version of the Goddess as Mother, Lover and Layer-out) (see also pp. 158, 197, 251); 'The hag was riding me' – in past times a nightmare was often called 'the night-hag' or 'the riding of the witch'; 'mare' – old Norse 'mara', means 'incubus', an evil demon.

259. 'Jealousy' ** 6 June 1961. 'tremendous anvils' – achievement of (sexual) climax.
    'Perplexed' ** 6 June 1961.
    'Urgency' 6 June 1961. C.P., p. 237. 'pallid pastures' – Hades, in classical mythology the abode of the departed spirits, a place of gloom but not necessarily punishment; 'incorporeality' – bodilessness.

260. 'Between Nightmare and Nightmare' 6 June 1961. B.D., p. 47. A Petrarchan sonnet (see also pp. 1, 12, 36, 41, 61, 80, 86, 91, 108, 119, 124, 138, 140, 156, 234, 254, 255, 266, 276, 282, 302, 305, 311, 339); 'guilt' – because he had survived a war in which comrades had perished and because of his sexual promiscuity; 'melted down like wax' – cf. Psalms 68: 1, 'like as wax melteth at the fire, so let the ungodly perish'.

'There Are Some Connexions Between Life and Literature' ** 6 June 1961. A virtuoso (and hilarious) literary performance. 'Donne' – John Donne (?1571–1631), poet of sexual, but also Divine love: there are two echoes in this first couplet, the first to the poet's famous comment on his secret marriage to Ann More, for which he was briefly imprisoned, 'John Donne, Ann Donne, undone', the second to his poem, 'Hymn to God in My Sickness': 'When thou has done (Donne), thou hast not done,/For I have more (sins)'; (see also pp. 33, 36, 60, 257, 266, 334, 366); Abelard (1079–1142), an eminent scholar, became tutor to the beautiful Heloise, they fell in love and a son was born. When her father discovered this he had Abelard castrated and Heloise became a nun; Robert Devereux (1567–1601), a favourite of the ageing Elizabeth I, was executed for treason; Martha Blount (pronounced 'blunt') (1690–1762), was a close friend of the poet, Alexander Pope (1688–1744) (see also p. 269); Lord Byron (1788–1824) had a child by his half-sister, Augusta; William Wordsworth (1770–1850) (see also pp. 87, 196, 199, 234, 346, 370) as a young man had a daughter by Annette Vallon, daughter of a French surgeon. In later life he had a very close relationship with his own sister, Dorothy; John Keats (1795–1821) (see also pp. 127, 320, 345) was passionately in love with Fanny Brawne (1800–65). He died of tuberculosis; W. B. Yeats (1865–1939) (see also pp. 1, 15, 49, 50, 51, 65, 66, 75, 77, 87, 89, 90, 92, 99, 120, 147, 158, 182, 198, 234, 245, 250, 264, 302, 307, 318, 337) loved the nationalist revolutionary, Maud Gonne, but she did not return his affection and he married Georgie Hyde-Lees; Oscar Wilde (1854–1900) (see also p. 324) was imprisoned in 1895 for homosexual offences, but in ancient Athens homosexuality was normal for such 'sages' as Socrates and Plato; Robert Burns (1759–96) was famously promiscuous.

261. 'Now That I Love You Truly' ** 6 June 1961. 'Remembered horrors of remembered seas;/Or by contrast a legendary landscape/Contoured by language and by love': these lines define the war and Llanafan (see also pp. 6, 23, 94, 104, 138, 142, 222, 226, 228, 244, 264, 275, 283, 296, 297, 302, 310, 311, 319, 324, 332, 336, 342, 343, 346, 359, 364, 366) experiences that inspire so much of Jones's work; 'Circe' – the enchantress who turned the followers of Odysseus/Ulysses (see also pp. 45, 46, 262) into swine. Jones transforms himself by indulging in his memories.

'Ruth Myfanwy' 6 June 1961, the sixteenth poem to be entered into the 'Black Book' (see also pp. 143, 145, 159, 167, 195, 203, 204, 210, 211, 214, 217, 220, 239, 255, 303, 353) since 18 May. B.D. 19. Ruth was born in Portsmouth in October 1954. (See also pp. 77, 124, 130, 138, 143, 144, 147, 169, 206, 218, 228, 238, 269, 274, 301, 335.) 'Ben Jonson's phrase': 'For a good poet's made, as well as born.' ('To the memory of My Beloved, the Author, Mr William Shakespeare' – see also pp. 17, 33, 55, 56, 58, 79,

81, 89, 129, 138, 158, 229, 235, 264, 270, 276, 288, 297, 311, 344, 345);
'Bible' – 'Ruth' is the eighth book of the Old Testament.

262. 'Ulysses in Ithaca' ** 27 June 1961. Penelope, wife of Ulysses (Latin 'Odysseus') (see also pp. 45, 46, 261), at their home in Ithaca, remained faithful to him during his 'ten good years' at the siege of Troy and the further ten years it took him to get back to Ithaca.
    'In This Degenerate Age' 27 June 1961. C.P., p. 237. 'disturbances' – Solomon (see also pp. 44, 62) was said to have had 700 wives and 300 concubines; it is not clear whether the Queen of Sheba, whose famous visit was made for political reasons, had a relationship with him, though legend says that she had.
    'Who'd Be An Erotic Poet, Anyway?' ** 27 June 1961. 'member' – penis.

263. 'Mr Jones As The Transported Poet' (*to Gwen*) 27 June 1961. The Bulletin, 83, 4275, 20 January 1962. B.D., p. 20. 'transported' – the obvious reference is to the transportation of convicts, but as so often in Jones's poetry, there is a pun here: he is a poet given to intense emotion. Gwen Murphet (Hughes) – Australian artist, writer, singer and poet, born in Wales. 'She persuaded us to move to Australia', said Madeleine Mitchell (Jones).
    'Outrageous' ** 22 July 1961.
    'Drunk on Duty' ** 22 July 1961. Excessive alcohol may make a man temporarily (or even permanently) impotent.

264. 'A Confusion of Bright Women' 22 July 1961. Meanjin, 22, 2, June 1963 (as 'Confusion of Bright Women'). B.D., p. 48. The title may owe something to Shakespeare's *A Midsummer Night's Dream*, I. i. 148, 'So quick bright things come to confusion'; (see also pp. 17, 33, 55, 56, 58, 79, 81, 89, 129, 138, 158, 229, 235, 261, 270, 276, 288, 297, 311, 344, 345); 'daughters of the swan' – from 'Among School Children' by W. B. Yeats: 'For even daughters of the swan can share/Something of every paddler's heritage'. (See also pp. 1, 15, 49, 50, 51, 65, 66, 75, 77, 87, 89, 90, 92, 99, 120, 147, 158, 182, 198, 234, 245, 250, 260, 302, 307, 318, 337.) Zeus, in the form of a swan, raped Leda (see also pp. 49, 127, 250, 254, 309, 320), as a result of which she gave birth to two eggs. Helen of Troy was born from one (see also pp. 49, 127, 250, 254, 277, 279, 284, 298, 320), Castor and Pollux from the other; 'a mole like Imogen'; in Shakespeare's tragedy, 'Cymbeline', the villainous Iachimo convinces Posthumus, Imogen's husband, that he has seduced her by revealing that 'under her breast . . . lies a mole . . . I kiss'd it'.
    'Llanafan Unrevisited' 27 July 1961. Meanjin, 22, 2, June 1963; Poetry Magazine, 2, 1965. B.D., p. 21. The poem evokes the landscape and religion in which Jones grew up (see also pp. 6, 23, 94, 104, 138, 142, 222, 226, 228, 244, 261, 275, 283, 296, 297, 302, 310, 311, 319, 324, 332, 336, 342, 343, 346, 359, 364, 366).

265. 'Adam's Song After Paradise' (*to A.D. Hope*) 28 July 1961. B.D., p. 49. A.D. Hope: Alec Derwent Hope, 1907–2000, best known for elegies and satires. Jones met him in 1959. (See also pp. 266, 335.) Sex became sinful when Eve persuaded Adam (see also pp. 63, 86, 93, 99, 101, 116, 167,

180, 210, 225, 251, 255, 257, 266, 284, 318, 361, 367, 368) to eat of the tree of knowledge of good and evil Genesis 3:7: 'And the eyes of them both were opened, and they knew that they were naked . . . '.

266. 'The Mirror of Herself'(*for Jill*). Jill Stowell and John, her husband, were friends of the Joneses (see also pp. 224, 301, 309, 323, 340). Jill helped Madeleine (Jones) Mitchell (see also pp. 34, 45, 64, 77, 143, 147, 148, 156, 159, 169, 218, 224, 234, 236, 240, 242, 269, 283, 285, 291, 312, 343) edit the posthumous volume, *The Colour of Cockcrowing*. 28 July 1961. The Bulletin, 83, 4273, 6 January 1962. B.D., p. 50. Wallace Stevens (1879–1955) – see '111', p. 192 (above). The misquotation ('a' for 'the') is from Wallace Stevens *Notes toward a Supreme Fiction 1942*, section IV: 'The first idea was not our own. Adam/In Eden was the father of Descartes/And Eve made air *the* mirror of herself,/Of her sons and daughters.' (See also pp. 63, 86, 93, 99, 101, 116, 167, 180, 210, 225, 251, 255, 257, 265, 284, 318, 361, 367, 368.) 'bright bone . . . hair' echoes the 'bracelet of bright hair about the bone' of Donne's 'The Relic'; (see also pp. 33, 36, 60, 257, 260, 334, 366). 'circumambient' – surrounding.
   'Exile' ** August 1961. Petrarchan sonnet (see also pp. 1, 12, 36, 41, 61, 80, 86, 91, 108, 119, 124, 138, 140, 156, 234, 254, 255, 260, 276, 282, 302, 305, 311, 339). For A. D. Hope (see also pp. 265, 335). 'Man Friday' – the young savage found by Robinson Crusoe on a Friday, his faithful servant and companion on the desert island; 'breasts to be maternal' cf. 'Hills like Mam's breasts, homely and tremendous', 'The Welshman in Exile Speaks', p. 244 above.

267. 'I Gave You Roses Once' ** August 1961.
   'Verbalist' August 1961. C.P., p. 238. 'verbalist' – someone skilled in the use of words; 'bedwreck, bedreckoned, bedfound' – these coinages emphasize that this relationship is centred on sex; 'funambulist' – tight-rope walker.

268. 'A Woodland Walk' ** August 1961. 'forest' – pubic hair; 'tree' – penis.
   'A Thought' ** August 1961.
   'The Gold Clarity Of This Moment' August 1961. C.P., p. 239. 'five . . . receptors' – the five senses; 'epistemology' – the theory of knowledge.

269. 'A Birthday Poem for Madeleine' August 1961. B.D., p. 51. See also pp. 34, 45, 64, 77, 143, 147, 148, 156, 159, 169, 218, 224, 234, 236, 240, 242, 266, 283, 285, 291, 312, 343. 'tall daughters' – Sian was now thirteen, Rhiannon, eight and Ruth, nearly seven. (See also pp. 77, 124, 130, 138, 143, 144, 147, 169, 206, 218, 228, 238, 261, 274, 301, 335.)
   'Mr Pope' 23 September 1961. Quadrant, 6, 4, Spring 1962. B.D., p. 68. Alexander Pope (1688–1744) satirical and moralistic Augustan poet. 'morals' – a reference to his 'Moral Essays'; 'writing . . . dunces' – Pope (see also p. 260) was savagely critical, most notably in the 'Dunciad' (1743), of bad writing; 'commination' – denunciation; 'literacy . . . personality' – although written over forty years ago, this poem is up-to-date in its identification of two contemporary diseases: semi-literacy in speech and writing, and the cult of the

(however disreputable) personality; 'Twickenham' – in 1718 Pope moved there with his mother and spent much time in the development of his garden.

270. 'A Birthday Wish for a Painter' ** 23 September 1961. Shakespearean (see also pp. 17, 33, 55, 56, 58, 79, 81, 89, 129, 138, 158, 229, 235, 261, 264, 276, 288, 297, 311, 344, 345) sonnet. The painter is Rae Richards (see also pp. 86, 228, 230, 250, 254, 274, 282, 311, 319, 337, 339, 353).

271. 'Obviously for Somebody' ** 12 October 1961. Another exploration of sexual intercourse, with obvious puns. 'easily on your back' recalls Auden's 'easily you move, easily your head . . . ' ('A Bride in the Thirties'). (See also pp. 8, 12, 13, 17, 20, 23, 26, 33, 48, 58, 64, 76, 78, 79, 80, 108, 147, 169, 175, 177, 181, 183, 186, 195, 204, 233, 316.)
   'Tutor' (for Marie) (See also pp. 235, 276, 297, 309, 322, 340, 363.) 12 October 1961. Australian Highway, November 1963. 'ten years' – Jones had been teaching since 1951, when he joined the staff of the Dockyard School, Portsmouth; 'hwyl' – cadence (Welsh).

272. 'Lines for the Early Stages of a Love Affair' ** 12 October 1961. 'Hercules' – famous for strength and bravery, but he lived for three years among women when he was in bondage to Omphale, queen of Lydia; 'tithe' – one tenth; 'Don Juan' – in Mozart's opera, 'Don Giovanni', this legendary rake, roué and libertine was said to have 1,003 mistresses in Spain alone; Ovid, BC43–AD18, famous for his licentious poem, 'Ars Amatoria' ('The Art of Love') (see also p. 216).
   'Doublecross' ** 12 October 1961. The quotation is from Dylan Thomas's 'Before I Knocked', a poem in which he identifies with Christ, 'Who took my flesh and bone for armour/And doublecrossed my mother's womb'. (See also pp. 4, 20, 30, 33, 40, 52, 53, 54, 57, 58, 64, 87, 96, 104, 106, 112, 116, 117, 119, 158, 170, 186, 201, 225, 232, 234, 245, 278, 279, 284, 292, 313, 345.) 'Doublecross' can signify 'doubly sanctify' as well as 'betray'. Any lover is potentially a Judas, to betray with a kiss.

273. 'On the Banks of Some River or Other' 12 October 1961. B.D., p. 52.
   'An Affair' ** October 1961.
   'Surprising and Inevitable' ** October 1961. 'come' is used in its sexual sense, of 'reach a climax', as well as its everyday one.
   'A Poem for Flowers, Perhaps' ** October 1961. A 'perfumed garden' of a poem exploiting analogies such as 'garden' for vagina and 'rose' for nipple.

274. 'Scansion' ** October 1961. 'come' and 'death' carry their sexual significance; 'scansion' – means both 'looking at' and 'analyzing the rhythm of'.
   'For a Painting of Clea' ** October 1961. Apparently for Rae Richards (see also pp. 86, 228, 230, 250, 254, 270, 282, 311, 319, 337, 339, 353) and her daughter.
   'Entire' ** 24 October 1961. 'entire' is used of a male animal that has not been castrated; 'resurrection' (rising again) has the obvious sexual significance.

'Even Fathers Can Be Honest' ** 24 October 1961. It is not unusual for
fathers to be jealous of their daughters' boyfriends. Jones's daughters, Sian,
Rhiannon and Ruth were thirteen, eight and seven at this time. (See also
pp. 77, 124, 130, 138, 143, 144, 147, 169, 206, 218, 228, 238, 261, 269,
301, 3358.)

275. 'Portrait Gallery' 24 October 1961. B.D., p. 22. The thinly disguised
portraits here caused the kind of reaction in Llanafan (see also pp. 6, 23,
94, 104, 138, 142, 222, 226, 228, 244, 261, 264, 283, 296, 297, 302, 310,
311, 319, 324, 332, 336, 342, 343, 346, 359, 364, 366) that some of D.H.
Lawrence's creations caused at Eastwood.
  'From Whence Cometh My Help' 26 October 1961. C.P., p. 240. The
title is taken from Psalm 121:1 – 'I will lift up mine eyes unto the hills: from
whence cometh my help.' It was only when he was far from Llanafan (see
also pp. 6, 23, 94, 104, 138, 142, 222, 226, 228, 244, 261, 264, 283, 296,
297, 302, 310, 311, 319, 324, 332, 336, 342, 343, 346, 359, 364, 366)
that Jones's experiences there became accessible for creative purposes. Such
'hiraeth' (nostalgia) is (perhaps) particularly common among Welsh
writers. 'in deserts' – when he was serving in the Far East during the
Second World War; 'lumper' – the bumpkin that he was when young; 'out
and down' – out to the Far East, down to Australia; 'appetency' – longing;
'ineluctably' – inescapably.

276. 'Advertisement' (for Marie) (See also pp. 235, 271, 297, 309, 322, 340,
363.) ** 11 November 1961. Petrarchan sonnet (see also pp. 1, 12, 36, 41,
61, 80, 86, 91, 108, 119, 124, 138, 140, 156, 234, 254, 255, 260, 266,
282, 302, 305, 311, 339). 'world enough and time' – from Andrew
Marvell's (1621–78) 'To His Coy Mistress', 'had we but world enough and
time/This coyness, lady, were no crime'; 'approaching time' – death.
  'Glory Be' ** 11 November 1961. A Shakespearean (see also pp. 17, 33,
55, 56, 58, 79, 81, 89, 129, 138, 158, 229, 235, 261, 264, 270, 288, 297,
311, 344, 345) sonnet.

277. 'In Memoriam Ernest Hemingway' 11 November 1961. Hemingway
(1899–1961) shot himself in July, 1961. Jones admired him as a man who
lived, loved and drank hard. 'Pappa' – Hemingway's nickname for himself
in his later years; 'Paris was liberated' – Hemingway was certainly among
the first Allied personnel to enter Paris near the end of the Second World
War; 'stiff' – strong, as in 'a stiff drink'.
  'Country Matters' ** 11 November 1961. See also 'Country Sentiment',
p. 235 above. The quotation is from Hamlet, III. ii, where Hamlet, talking
to Ophelia, has used the ambiguous phrase 'shall I lie in your lap' and
purports to believe that she thought he meant have sexual intercourse with
her.
  'Land of My Fathers' 11 November 1961. B.D., p. 23. 'Land of My
Fathers' ('Hen Wlad fy Nhadau' – 'The Ancient Land of My Fathers') is the
Welsh National Anthem. 'blue/Salt acres' – the Mediterranean, where
Jones served during the Second World War; 'Menelaus', 'Paris', 'Helen' –
Paris, visiting the court of Menelaus, fell in love with his wife, Helen (see

also pp. 49, 127, 250, 254, 264, 279, 284, 298, 320), and carried her off to Troy, as a result of which occurred the ten-year war which ended with Troy's destruction by the Greeks; 'ancient, sunburnt country' – Australia; 'can never be content' – all Welsh people in exile feel the 'hiraeth', a longing for their native land; 'sings and kills' – Jones's guilt feelings caused by the gap between his strict religious upbringing and his 'sinful' life in Australia.

278. 'Owl and Echo' 11 November 1961. 11 November 1961. B.D., p. 69. 'I am the owl and the echo' – from Dylan Thomas's (1914–53) surrealistic short story, 'A Prospect of the Sea', title-story of the 1955 volume. (See also pp. 4, 20, 30, 33, 40, 52, 53, 54, 57, 58, 64, 87, 96, 104, 106, 112, 116, 117, 119, 158, 170, 186, 201, 225, 232, 234, 245, 272, 279, 284, 292, 313, 345.) As Ted Hughes ('The Thought-fox') images a thought as a fox, here Jones images the poet in the act of composition as a wise owl identifying its prey, the poem, and then capturing it under the inspiration ('stroke') of the Muse. 'wising' – applying the owl's traditional wisdom to the task in hand; 'soundstruck' – hearing the sound of the prey.

   'Wordless' ** 21/22 November 1961. A 'triad' is a group of three lines (in this case pairs of lines, each pair alliterating on a different consonant – 'w', 'l', 'd') in different metres.

279. 'Storms Etc.' 21/22 November 1961. C.P., p. 241. 'stands' – has the usual sexual overtone; 'spindrift' – the spray blown from the crests of waves.

   'The Different Skies' ** 21/22 November 1961. 'preaching heron' echoes Dylan Thomas's 'heron priested' (see also pp. 4, 20, 30, 33, 40, 52, 53, 54, 57, 58, 64, 87, 96, 104, 106, 112, 116, 117, 119, 158, 170, 186, 201, 225, 232, 234, 245, 272, 278, 284, 292, 313, 345); 'Helen' – of Troy (see also pp. 49, 127, 250, 254, 264, 277, 284, 298, 320); 'lies' – a not uncommon pun.

280. 'Unknown to Lexicologists' ** 21/22 November 1961. 'lexicologist' – one who studies language; 'White Goddess' – the Muse (see also pp. 197, 251, 258, 312), matriarchal Moon Goddess of whom each loved woman is a version. The reference is playful here, but elsewhere serious.

   'Never An Armistice' 21/22 November 1961. Nimrod, 1, 2, Winter 1963. C.P., p. 242. Winter is metaphorical here – November is not winter in Australia. The poem is about the never-ending 'warfare' between married couples/lovers. 'die' – sexually, not literally.

281. 'They Also Serve' ** 21/22 November 1961. The title is a reference to the last line of John Milton's 'Sonnet on his Blindness', 'They also serve who only stand and wait', but Milton's deeply serious line is travestied, 'stand' here meaning 'have an erection'. (See also pp. 5, 17, 49, 255, 323, 333, 367.)

   'Veteran' 21–22 November 1961. B.D., p. 53. Love presented in terms of knight errantry. 'sulk among the tents' – in the 'Iliad' the Greek champion, Achilles sulked in his tent, refusing to fight, when his concubine, Briseis, was taken from him by his commanding officer, Agamemnon.

282. 'On Seeing An Australian Play' ** 25 November 1961. 'Gallipoli' – many Australian soldiers died there in the Dardanelles Campaign (February 1915–January 1916); 'Dammo' – Damn! (Welsh); 'play for Wales' – at rugby, of course; 'Saesneg' – English.

    'Rain Forest' (to Rae) ** 10 December 1961. Petrarchan sonnet (see also pp. 1, 12, 36, 41, 61, 80, 86, 91, 108, 119, 124, 138, 140, 156, 234, 254, 255, 260, 266, 276, 302, 305, 311, 339) with alexandrine (twelve syllable) final line. Rae Richards: see also pp. 86, 228, 230, 250, 254, 270, 274, 311, 319, 337, 339, 353. 'bushed' – tired/lost in the bush.

283. 'There Is Something In What The Psychologists Say' (to Madeleine) ** 10 December 1961. See also pp. 34, 45, 64, 77, 143, 147, 148, 156, 159, 169, 218, 224, 234, 236, 240, 242, 266, 269, 285, 291, 312, 343. 'lubber' – as in 'landlubber'; 'lies' – both 'untruths' and 'love-makings'.

    'My Grandmother Died in the Early Hours of the Morning' 10 December 1961. B.D., p. 24. The achieved 'simplicity' of style and the Llanafan theme (see also pp. 6, 23, 94, 104, 138, 142, 222, 226, 228, 244, 261, 264, 275, 296, 297, 302, 310, 311, 319, 324, 332, 336, 342, 343, 346, 359, 364, 366) are characteristic of Jones's mature work. Mari Jones had died on 2 October 1938, when the poet was seventeen; his grandfather, Thomas, died on 27 June 1950 (see also pp. 95, 332, 337, 359, 366).

284. 'Memories of a Country Childhood' 1961. C.P., p. 242. 'Pasiphae' – Zeus, in the form of a bull, had intercourse with the wife of Minos, King of Crete. As a result, the monstrous Minotaur was born; 'burning Troy' – Agamemnon burning Troy for the sake of his wife, Helen (see also pp. 49, 127, 250, 254, 264, 277, 279, 298, 320), whom Paris, Prince of Troy, had abducted; 'we were expelled' – the expulsion of Adam and Eve (see also pp. 63, 86, 93, 99, 101, 116, 167, 180, 210, 225, 251, 255, 257, 265, 266, 318, 361, 367, 368) involved that also of all their descendants; 'dies' – pun on physical death and the 'little death' after intercourse.

    'A Christmas Poem for Michelene' ** 1961. Michelene Price (see also p. 237) was an assistant lecturer in the French Department at the Newcastle College (see also pp. 86, 143, 214, 218, 224, 225, 226, 237, 239, 244, 252, 291, 299, 300, 301, 302, 303, 309, 312, 326, 327, 328, 333, 343, 353, 358, 365, 370) of the University of New South Wales.

    'Poet at Night' (for Barbara) 30 December 1961. (see also p. 193) 'witness fingers' – the trick of employing a noun as adjective is characteristic of Dylan Thomas. (See also pp. 4, 20, 30, 33, 40, 52, 53, 54, 57, 58, 64, 87, 96, 104, 106, 112, 116, 117, 119, 158, 170, 186, 201, 225, 232, 234, 245, 272, 278, 279, 292, 313, 345.) Barbara Michael was a neighbour of the Joneses in Merewether.

285. 'This Wedded Gentleman' ** 30 December 1961. 'long time bound' – fifteen years: Jones married in 1946.

    'Once' (for Madeleine) ** 1961. See also pp. 34, 45, 64, 77, 143, 147, 148, 156, 159, 169, 218, 224, 234, 236, 240, 242, 266, 269, 283, 291, 312, 343. 'womankind/Who wanted to separate us' – see the short story, 'My Grandfather Would Have Me Be a Poet'.

286. 'A Poem Which Is Better Without A Title' ** 1961. 'implumis' – without feathers.
     'Taliesin Broods Upon the Father of Harvard' ** 1961. Taliesin was a late sixth century Welsh poet. The founder of Harvard was John Harvard (born in London, 1607 – died in Boston, Massachusetts, 1638). New England was settled by Puritans driven out of England who developed schools and the universities of Harvard (1636) and Yale (1638).

287. 'The Hunger of This Love' 4 January 1962. Poetry Magazine, 1, 1965. C.P., p. 243. 'wedding salt' – an emblem of purity; 'asperge' – sprinkle.

288. 'Not Blessed' ** 10 January 1962.
     'Late Spring in Wales' (for Pat). 12 January 1962. B.D., p. 25. Shakespearean (see also pp. 17, 33, 55, 56, 58, 79, 81, 89, 129, 138, 158, 229, 235, 261, 264, 270, 276, 297, 311, 344, 345); sonnet. 'Pat' – Patricia Power née Jones, the poet's youngest sister. See also pp. 21, 157, 349. 'dogma' – doctrine.

289. 'In the Tremble of the Year' ** 1 February 1962. 'fair field . . . parable' – perhaps a hint at the 'fair field full of folk' in William Langland's (?1330–?1400) 'Piers the Plowman'.
     'Ever' 1 February 1962. B.D., p. 54.
     'Ancestor, Old Lady' 1 February 1962. B.D., p. 26. 'To beast' – into a beast.

290. 'A Little Elegy' ** 1 February 1962. 'sharded' – shattered.

291. 'And In The Woods To Walk' ** 1 February 1962.
     'Only' (to Madeleine) ** 3 February 1962. See also pp. 34, 45, 64, 77, 143, 147, 148, 156, 159, 169, 218, 224, 234, 236, 240, 242, 266, 269, 283, 285, 312, 343.
     'The Beast at the Door' (to Brin). 13 February 1962. Quadrant, 7, 2, Autumn 1963; Poetry Magazine, 2, 1965; Nimrod 3, 1, Summer 1965. B.D., p. 79. Title poem of Jones's third volume of poems (1963). 'Brin' – Newton-John (see also pp. 239, 244, 326, 328, 333, 334), former Squadron Leader, Head of the Arts Department at the Newcastle College (see also pp. 86, 143, 214, 218, 224, 225, 226, 237, 239, 244, 252, 284, 299, 300, 301, 302, 303, 309, 312, 326, 327, 328, 333, 343, 353, 358, 365, 370) of the University of New South Wales, with whom the ex-sailor, Jones, had a somewhat uneasy relationship; 'big-pilled' – with large testicles.

292. 'Reluctant' February–March 1962. B.D., p. 27. Vernon Watkins (1906–67) (see also p. 214), Anglo-Welsh poet, close friend of Dylan Thomas (see also pp. 4, 20, 30, 33, 40, 52, 53, 54, 57, 58, 64, 87, 96, 104, 106, 112, 116, 117, 119, 158, 170, 186, 201, 225, 232, 234, 245, 272, 278, 279, 284, 313, 345.). It was at Watkins' home that Jones first met Roberto Sanesi (see also pp. 214, 217, 218, 219, 220, 225), a number of whose poems he translated. The quotation is from 'The Tolling' in The Death Bell (Faber and Faber, 1954).

293. 'Soil' ** February–March 1962.
    'The Pendulum' February–March 1962 C.P., p. 244. 'troll' – in Scandinavian mythology, a giant; plays a similar role here to the beast in 'The Beast at the Door' (p. 291); 'my quick' – my life.

294. 'Bronwen' ** February–March 1962. 'Bronwen' – literally 'white-breasted'; 'lumper' – bumpkin'; 'Rhondda' – T. H. Jones's mother (see also pp. 16, 319), Ruth, came from the Rhondda and there was a natural link between the valley and the Llanwrtyd/Builth area (see also pp. 21, 33, 64, 143, 157, 297, 326, 343, 346); 'chapel doctrine' – the fundamentalist idea that sex is sinful; 'tup' – a ram; 'seared' – shamed; 'ach y fi' – Welsh expression of disgust; 'moithering' – wandering/going astray. The poem is reminiscent of Jones's short stories, particularly 'Saturday Night'.

296. 'Head in the Clouds' 14 March 1962. B.D., p. 28. Pencarreg and Penrhiw: Llanafan hill-farms (see also pp. 6, 23, 94, 104, 138, 142, 222, 226, 228, 244, 261, 264, 275, 283, 297, 302, 310, 311, 319, 324, 332, 336, 342, 343, 346, 359, 364, 366).

297. 'For Miranda' (*born 9 March 1962*) ** 15 March 1962. T. H. Jones's Uncle Daniel had been the last 'Bardd Gwlad' (local poet) of Llanafan (see also pp. 6, 23, 94, 104, 138, 142, 222, 226, 228, 244, 261, 264, 275, 283, 296, 302, 310, 311, 319, 324, 332, 336, 342, 343, 346, 359, 364, 366) and Jones, wherever he was, celebrated 'local' events such as births and marriages. Miranda (see also pp. 235, 309, 322, 363) was the daughter of Marie Tietze, a New Zealander who helped Jones check references. (See also pp. 235, 271, 276, 309, 322, 340, 363). Prospero, the magician, was Miranda's father and Ferdinand eventually her husband in Shakespeare's (see also pp. 17, 33, 55, 56, 58, 79, 81, 89, 129, 138, 158, 229, 235, 261, 264, 270, 276, 288, 311, 344, 345) play, *The Tempest*.
    'Cwchwefri' 15 March 1962. B.D., p. 29. The river Chwefri (Chwefru) joins the Wye at Builth Wells (see also pp. 21, 33, 64, 143, 157, 294, 326, 343, 346). Its upper course is on the opposite (western) side of the hill, Alltyclych, to Cwm Crogau, where T. H. Jones was born; 'six o'clock news' – then on the Home Service of BBC radio, the most respected source of information during the Second World War and for years thereafter.

298. 'To Helen (*in a very proper spirit*) ** 5–6 April 1962. 'spirit' – a pun; Helen, thy beauty is to me' is the first line of Edgar Allen Poe's (1809–49) poem with the same title (see also pp. 49, 127, 250, 254, 264, 277, 279, 284, 320). It continues, 'Like those Nicean barks of yore'; 'iambically' – the rhythm of the poem is iambic, i.e. consists of a series of poetic feet of which the first stress is weak and the second strong; the ingenious reader may be able to supply the words covered by 'Etc' e.g. 'virginity' at the end of the first stanza; 'Bushmills' is a well-known (and potent) Irish whisky.
    'Worthy Is The Lamb' ** 5–6 April 1962. 'The Lamb' is Christ: see John 1:29 – 'Behold the Lamb of God, which taketh away the sins of the world' and Revelation 5:12 – 'Worthy is the Lamb that was slain . . . ', but there is also a pun on the fact that Glyn is a shepherd; 'Worthy is the Lamb' is

the title of Ted Richards' (See also pp. 126, 168, 185, 214, 222, 317, 323, 324) most anthologized short story; 'Cwmuchaf' – 'the upper valley'; 'Messiah' – Handel's (1685–1759) famous oratorio, a favourite of Welsh (and other) choirs.

299. 'Thou Shalt Not' ** 5–6 April 1962. 'Thou shalt not . . . ' the words that introduce most of the Ten Commandments; 'base of the scrum' – a position in rugby frequently filled by players better endowed physically than mentally or spiritually; 'the one sheep' – the one sinner who is saved: St Luke 15: 6–7, 'Joy shall be in heaven over one sinner that repenteth, more than over ninety and nine just persons, which need no repentance'. This poem and the previous one are characteristic of Jones's serio-comic (cf. Caradoc Evans, 1878–1945) treatment of chapel hypocrisy.

'That Impossible She' (*to Ialene*) ** 5–6 April 1962. A hilarious evocation of the various snags, physical and mental, attendant on a relationship between the sexes. The omission of the final stop is deliberate. Ialene's husband, Warren Hogan, taught Economics at the Newcastle College (see also pp. 86, 143, 214, 218, 224, 225, 226, 237, 239, 244, 252, 284, 291, 300, 301, 302, 303, 309, 312, 326, 327, 328, 333, 343, 353, 358, 365, 370) of the University of New South Wales; they were New Zealanders.

300. 'A New Ballad of Old Ireland' ** 5–6 April 1962. 'Ringsend' – port area of Dublin; 'Joyce' – James Joyce (1882–1941) (see also p. 139) portrays Dublin in detail in his novel, 'Ulysses' (1922); 'Beckett' – Samuel Beckett (1906–89), another Dubliner: his first published work was an essay on Joyce; 'Brian Boru' (926–1014) – famous King of Ireland, AD 1002; 'Hart' – presumably Jones's English Department colleague, Clive Hart.

'Stormy Night in Newcastle, N.S.W.' 5–6 April 1962. Nimrod, 1, 1, Summer 1962. B.D., p. 30. 'Newcastle' – Jones's home in Australia (see also pp. 86, 143, 214, 218, 224, 225, 226, 237, 239, 244, 252, 284, 291, 299, 301, 302, 303, 309, 312, 326, 327, 328, 333, 343, 353, 358, 365, 370).

301. 'For Vanessa Stowell, Born 6 April 1962' ** 23 April 1962. John and Jill Stowell were close friends of the Jones family at Newcastle (see also pp. 86, 143, 214, 218, 224, 225, 226, 237, 239, 244, 252, 284, 291, 299, 300, 302, 303, 309, 312, 326, 327, 328, 333, 343, 353, 358, 365, 370). See also pp. 224, 266, 309, 323, 340).

'For An Unborn Daughter' ** 23 April 1962. (See also pp. 77, 124, 130, 138, 143, 144, 147, 169, 206, 218, 228, 238, 261, 269, 274, 335.)

302. 'Improbable Land' 23 April 1962. C.C., p. 17. Petrarchan sonnet (see also pp. 1, 12, 36, 41, 61, 80, 86, 91, 108, 119, 124, 138, 140, 156, 234, 254, 255, 260, 266, 276, 282, 305, 311, 339). A perspective of rainy Llanafan (see also pp. 6, 23, 94, 104, 138, 142, 222, 226, 228, 244, 261, 264, 275, 283, 296, 297, 310, 311, 319, 324, 332, 336, 342, 343, 346, 359, 364, 366) from sunny Australia.

'The Poet Meditates Upon Byzantium' (*for Doug Muecke*) ** 28 April 1962. Doug Muecke – Head of English at the Newcastle College (see also pp. 86, 143, 214, 218, 224, 225, 226, 237, 239, 244, 252, 284, 291, 299,

300, 301, 303, 309, 312, 326, 327, 328, 333, 343, 353, 358, 365, 370) of the University of New South Wales; 'Byzantium' – Jones is thinking less of the former Constantinople than of Yeats's idealized, symbolic city in his 'Byzantium' and 'Sailing to Byzantium'; 'gong' is a reference to Yeats's 'gong-tormented sea' in 'Byzantium' and 'Old men' to the opening line of 'Sailing to Byzantium', 'That is no country for old men . . . ' (see also pp. 1, 15, 49, 50, 51, 65, 66, 75, 77, 87, 89, 90, 92, 99, 120, 147, 158, 182, 198, 234, 245, 250, 260, 264, 307, 318, 337).

303. 'Three Verses for a Twentyfirst Birthday' ** Not in 'Black Book' (see also pp. 143, 145, 159, 167, 195, 203, 204, 210, 211, 214, 217, 220, 239, 255, 261, 353) – included here as an example of verse which the poet considered too 'occasional' for preservation. 'To Julian with best wishes Harri 31 May 1962'. Julian Croft (1941–) was a graduate and postgraduate student taught by Jones at the Newcastle College (see also pp. 86, 143, 214, 218, 224, 225, 226, 237, 239, 244, 252, 284, 291, 299, 300, 301, 302, 309, 312, 326, 327, 328, 333, 343, 353, 358, 365, 370) of the University of New South Wales, and later an academic. He wrote the Writers of Wales monograph on T.H. Jones (1976) and co-edited the *Collected Poems of T. Harri Jones* (1977); 'Rough Johnson' – Dr Samuel Johnson (1709–84), notoriously rough in conversation; wrote a poem entitled 'One-and Twenty'.

304. 'Impeccable Strategy Let Down By Fallible Tactics (But Not Irreparably)' ** 13 June 1962.

305. 'The Green Tree' 13 June 1962. C.P., p. 245. 'reticulate' – netted; 'lissome' – flexible.
    'Old Compulsions'. 13 June 1962. Nimrod, 1, 1, Summer 1962. B.D., p. 31. Petrarchan sonnet (see also pp. 1, 12, 36, 41, 61, 80, 86, 91, 108, 119, 124, 138, 140, 156, 234, 254, 255, 260, 266, 276, 282, 302, 311, 339). 'We' means the Welsh.
    'The Minstrel Boy' 13 June 1962. B.D., p. 70. Title from Thomas Moore's (1779–1852) popular song. A minstrel was a wandering entertainer/poet; 'antic' – grotesque; 'leman' – whore.

306. 'Love's Overtones' 13 June 1962. C.P., p. 246. 'overtones' – subtleties; 'depredations' – damage; 'civility' – appropriateness; 'sea-change' – a reference to the song 'Full Fathom Five' in 'The Tempest', where the drowned father's bones 'are coral made'.
    'Useless Advice to a Young Man Hopelessly in Love' 14 June 1962. Meanjin, 22, 2, June 1963. C.P., p. 247.

307. 'Prothalamion' (*for Robyn*) May 1962 (*sic*: apparently entered out of sequence). ** Robyn Iverach (see also pp. 225, 370) was the colleague in the English Department to whom 'The Colour of Cockcrowing' is dedicated'; this poem celebrates her marriage to Rod Wallace. 'prothalamion' – a word apparently coined by Edmund Spenser (1552?–1599) (see also pp. 17, 46) from the Latin 'pro' (before) and Greek 'thalamus' (a bride-chamber), for his poem of that name in honour of the double wedding in 1596 between Lady

Elizabeth and Lady Katharine Somerset, daughters of the Earl of Worcester, and Henry Gilford and William Peter, Esquires.

'A Celebratory Poem for Robyn and Rod' ** June 1962. In honour of the same occasion. 'dolphin and swan' – in medieval art the dolphin symbolizes social love; swans were in classical legend (and in Spenser's 'Prothalamion') said to draw the chariot of Venus, goddess of love (see also pp. 37, 38, 42, 46, 56, 86, 109, 111, 234, 363). It is interesting to note that W. B. Yeats (see also pp. 1, 15, 49, 50, 51, 65, 66, 75, 77, 87, 89, 90, 92, 99, 120, 147, 158, 182, 198, 234, 245, 250, 260, 264, 302, 318, 337), much admired by Jones, used both dolphins and swans symbolically in his work.

308. 'Simply to Write' 16 June 1962. B.D., p. 71. The use, or absence of the comma between 'write' and 'simply' enables Jones to interplay two meanings of the refrain: 'just to write/to concentrate on writing' and 'to avoid complexity in writing'. A comparison between early poems and later ones such as this reveals how, in his mature work, he had learned 'to write simply'.

309. 'A Dog Speaks To His Mistress' ** 9 August 1962.

'Lines for a Double Christening: Miranda Tietze and Vanessa Stowell 30 June, 1962' 9 August 1962. B.D., p. 72. Jill Stowell remembers of this time at the Newcastle College (see also pp. 86, 143, 214, 218, 224, 225, 226, 237, 239, 244, 252, 284, 291, 299, 300, 301, 302, 303, 312, 326, 327, 328, 333, 343, 353, 358, 365, 370) of the University of New South Wales that 'Most of us were young, nesting and producing babies far from our relatives . . . Harri loved babies . . . He was . . . one of my first visitors when Vanessa was born'. For Tietze (Marie) see also pp. 235, 271, 276, 297, 322, 340, 363. For Stowell see also pp. 224, 266, 301, 323, 340).

'Love's Mythology' 9 August 1962. B.D., p. 55. 'swan, dolphin, lion' – Zeus, in the form of a swan, made love with Leda (see also pp. 49, 127, 250, 254, 264, 320); dolphins enjoy riding the waves; the fond lovers, Hippomenes and Atalanta, were changed into lions by Cybele, goddess of fertility.

310. 'In Memoriam' 9 August 1962. B.D., p. 32. Francis Higginson (1586–1630), a Puritan divine, emigrated to Salem in 1629 and perished, with many others, as a result of the hardships endured during their first winter in the USA. 'New England's Plantation' (1630) is the journal of his first few months in Salem. Daniel Jones, the poet's uncle, as hill-farmer, Baptist Deacon and 'Bardd Gwlad' (local poet) had much in common with Higginson. 'kestrelled' – soared like a hawk; 'Allt-y-clych' (Hill of the Bell) – a landmark near the poet's home in Llanafanfawr; 'Isaiah' – Old Testament prophet; 'Abergwesyn' – hamlet in a depopulated area near Llanafanfawr (see also pp. 6, 23, 94, 104, 138, 142, 222, 226, 228, 244, 261, 264, 275, 283, 296, 297, 302, 311, 319, 324, 332, 336, 342, 343, 346, 359, 364, 366); 'jasper city' – the New or Heavenly Jerusalem, with walls of jasper (diamond) symbolic of true or ideal religion; 'thank God' – the truly religious man is supposed to be grateful for his suffering because it develops his soul and brings him closer to God. This poem may be

compared with the early work of R. S. Thomas (see also pp. 229, 342), who, however, viewed from the outside the harsh life of the depopulated rural Wales in which Jones grew up and where Jones developed a guilt which, it may be argued, eventually killed him.

311. 'Traditional' ** September 1962.
      'Pastoral' September 1962. C.P., p. 248 (where 'feg' is misprinted 'fog'). A modified Shakespearean (see also (see also pp. 17, 33, 55, 56, 58, 79, 81, 89, 129, 138, 158, 229, 235, 261, 264, 270, 276, 288, 297, 344, 345)) Sonnet. 'feg' is a Llanafan (see also pp. 6, 23, 94, 104, 138, 142, 222, 226, 228, 244, 261, 264, 275, 283, 296, 297, 302, 310, 319, 324, 332, 336, 342, 343, 346, 359, 364, 366) dialect word for rough grass of no use to man or sheep; 'this one swift thing' – castration: male sheep, apart from the best specimens, kept for breeding, are generally neutered.
      'A Birthday Sonnet' (for Rae) ** September 1962. For Rae Richards, see also pp. 86, 228, 230, 250, 254, 270, 274, 282, 319, 337, 339, 353. Petrarchan sonnet (see also pp. 1, 12, 36, 41, 61, 80, 86, 91, 108, 119, 124, 138, 140, 156, 234, 254, 255, 260, 266, 276, 282, 302, 305, 339).

312. 'Lines for the Death of an Alcoholic' 22 September 1962. B.D., p. 73. 'Newcastle University College was notorious for its drinking habits', Jones's widow has said, and Jones drank both to solace his neuroses and to release his poetry (see also pp. 86, 143, 214, 218, 224, 225, 226, 237, 239, 244, 252, 284, 291, 299, 300, 301, 302, 303, 309, 326, 327, 328, 333, 343, 353, 358, 365, 370). He knew very well what he was doing and, as this poem shows, did not in any sense spare himself – a characteristic of 'confessional' poets.
      'Cwmchwefri Rocks' (for Madeleine) 22 September 1962. B.D., p. 33. See also pp. 34, 45, 64, 77, 143, 147, 148, 156, 159, 169, 218, 224, 234, 236, 240, 242, 266, 269, 283, 285, 291, 343. Cwmchwefri Rocks stand above the river Chwefru in whose valley Jones was born; 'God' here is the relentless Calvinistic deity of the Chapel; 'goddess' – the White Goddess (see also pp. 197, 251, 258, 280), Mother, Lover and Layer-out, present in every woman a man loves (see Robert Graves's book of the same name) (see also pp. 158, 197, 251, 258); 'Apollo' – Greek god of song and music (see also pp. 26, 28, 217), a quite opposite deity; 'Jahveh' – the relentless, unforgiving God of the Old Testament; 'thorn' – the claw of the bird of prey; 'Ceridwen' – one of the manifestations of the White Goddess; 'dies' – in the sexual as well as the mortal sense.

313. 'Swansea' 28 July 1962. B.D., p. 35. 'Landor in Italy' – Walter Savage Landor, who lived in Italy from 1815–35; claimed that Swansea Bay was more beautiful than the Bay of Naples; 'all too affable/Ghost' – Dylan Thomas (1914–53), like Jones a sociable and drinking man: Jones admired, learned from and grew out of Thomas's poetry, and wrote the fine Oliver and Boyd critical monograph (see also pp. 4, 20, 30, 33, 40, 52, 53, 54, 57, 58, 64, 87, 96, 104, 106, 112, 116, 117, 119, 158, 170, 186, 201, 225, 232, 234, 245, 272, 278, 279, 284, 292, 345); (Stéphane) 'Mallarmé' (1842–98), one of the founders of modern European poetry, wrote, in his poem 'The

Tomb of Edgar Poe', that the effect of Poe's verse on his readers was to make them imagine that 'they had drunk of some foul mixture brewed/In Circe's madding cup, with sorcery imbued'; 'St Helen's, Sketty and Cwmdonkin Park' – areas of Swansea: Dylan Thomas grew up in a house in Cwmdonkin Drive, played as a child in the nearby Park and wrote 'The Hunchback in the Park', a poem based on that childhood experience; 'Iesu' – Welsh for 'Jesus'; 'bloody air-raids' – Swansea was 'blitzed' by German bombers during the Second World War, the first raid in June 1940, and the worst the 'Three Nights Blitz' of 19–21 February 1941, when 230 people were killed.

314. 'The Nightmare of King Theseus' 11 October 1962. B.D., p. 74. As a young man, Theseus (see also p. 120), later King of Athens, entered the Labyrinth in Crete containing the monstrous Minotaur. Ariadne, daughter of Minos, King of Crete, supplied him with a sword and a ball of thread which he paid out as he advanced so as to be able to find his way back after killing the monster.
     'Heart, Mind and Body' 11 October 1962. C.P., p. 249. 'internecine' – disputatious.

315. 'With the Sea's Volubility' 11 October 1962. 'volubility' – fluency; 'salt' – wit and good sense.
     'Dark Rival' 12 November 1962. B.D., p. 62. The 'mirror' image is common in the early poems and has to do with the neurosis caused by experience of warfare. The 'rival' is Jones's 'other' or 'darker' self.

316. 'But if it be a Boy You Shall Put Him to the Sea – Traditional' 12 November 1962. C.C., p., 18. Reminiscent of Auden's (see also pp. 8, 12, 13, 17, 20, 23, 26, 33, 48, 58, 64, 76, 78, 79, 80, 108, 147, 169, 175, 177, 181, 183, 186, 195, 204, 233, 271) early, formal verse in traditional forms. Jones was born among mountains, went to sea during the Second World War and never achieved the 'civility' represented by gardens. 'lecherous' – presumably in its desire for the bodies of the drowned; 'last and salt oblivion' – drowning, a common and, in view of the poet's death by drowning, deeply ironical image.
     'Poem for the Winter Solstice' ** 12 November 1962. The winter solstice is the shortest day of the year; 'insurrected' – uprisen. The poem brings together the sexual 'death' following orgasm, winter (the death of the year), and the deathlike experience of sleep.

317. 'The Kingdom of Terror' 15 November 1962. Nimrod, 1, 2, Winter 1963.
     'To Ted Richards' 15 November 1962. (See also pp. 126, 168, 185, 214, 222, 298, 323, 324.) C.C., p. 54. Richards was the ex-naval-officer friend of the Joneses.

318. 'Belated Welcome for Mary' ** December 1962. 'hiraeth' – nostalgia for one's native Wales. Mary Davies emigrated to Australia from Aberystwyth in 1961.
     'Letter Writing is a Lost Art' ** December 1962. Katharine Tynan (1861–1931) – poet and novelist, friend of W. B. Yeats (1865–1939) (see also pp. 1, 15, 49, 50, 51, 65, 66, 75, 77, 87, 89, 90, 92, 99, 120, 147,

158, 182, 198, 234, 245, 250, 260, 264, 302, 307, 337); 'felicitous postlaparian' – delightfully sexy: after the fall of Adam and Eve, sex, and therefore any aspect of male or female attractiveness, became sinful (see also pp. 63, 86, 93, 99, 101, 116, 167, 180, 210, 225, 251, 255, 257, 265, 266, 284, 361, 367, 368); 'amanuensis' – secretary.

319. 'To My Mother' December 1962. Poetry Magazine, 2, 1965. B.D., p. 76. Ruth Jones (see also pp. 16, 294) lived until 1971. 'God was a loud voice' – he was brought up in a strictly religious atmosphere; 'thorn' – a favourite image of the Llanafan landscape (see also pp. 6, 23, 94, 104, 138, 142, 222, 226, 228, 244, 261, 264, 275, 283, 296, 297, 302, 310, 311, 324, 332, 336, 342, 343, 346, 359, 364, 366) and religion. The vowel and consonant music of this poem is very powerful, and most memorably enunciated in a recording made by the poet.

'Australian Christmas' (*for Rae*) December 1962. ** Dedicated to Rae Richards, painter (see also pp. 86, 228, 230, 250, 254, 270, 274, 282, 311, 337, 339, 353); 'fair' – a pun: Rae was a beautiful blonde.

320. 'On Re-reading Old Myths' 23 December 1963. C.C., p. 55. The poem's juggling of some of the world's most resonant myths is a bravura, tragic-comic performance. John Keats (1795–1821) (see also pp. 127, 260, 345) wrote his famous sonnet, 'On First Looking into Chapman's Homer', in 1814, aged nineteen. He was so impressed by Chapman's translation that he felt like 'stout Cortez' and his men, 'Silent upon a peak in Darien' (Panama) when they discovered the Pacific Ocean. (In fact the explorer who discovered the Pacific was Balboa, in 1513). 'rabid ingurgitation of barbiturates' – desperate swallowing of sleeping-tablets (polysyllabic humour cf. 'felicitous postlapsarian curls' in 'Letter Writing . . . ' above); 'wooden . . . cow' – Pasiphäe, daughter of Minos, King of Crete, hid inside a wooden cow made for her by Daedalus in order to have intercourse with a white bull; 'swan's glory' – Zeus, in the form of a swan, had intercourse with Leda (see also pp. 49, 127, 250, 254, 264, 309) on the banks of the river Eurotas; 'tear his eyeballs out' – when Oedipus discovered that he had killed his father and married his mother he was so horrified that he blinded himself; 'your wife' – Helen (see also pp. 49, 127, 250, 254, 264, 277, 279, 284, 298), daughter of Leda and wife of Menelaus, was abducted by Paris of Troy, thus causing the war between Greeks and Trojans on 'the windy plains'; 'recusant' – disobedient (presumably, here, of doctor's orders).

'On Re-reading the Twenty third Psalm' 15 February 1963. C.C., p. 19. The travesty of the well-known psalm is a postmodernist technique deriving from the use by modernist poets of unacknowledged quotation or half-quotation. The lines travestied here are: 'He maketh me to lie down in green pastures; he leadeth me beside the still waters', 'though I walk through the valley of the shadow of death', 'thy rod and thy staff they comfort me' and 'surely goodness and mercy shall follow me all the days of my life'. Jones abandoned, but could never escape the faith he grew up in. 'Gutsily taking more than a proper tithe' – it was not uncommon for a chapel preacher to visit families of his congregation at meal-times and take full advantage of the hospitality which they dared not refuse.

321. 'Marriage a la Mode' ** 9 March 1963. The title is the same as that of John Dryden's (1631–1700) tragic-comedy produced in 1672.

322. 'To Miranda On Her First Birthday' ** 9 March 1963. The subject of the poem is Miranda Tietze (see also pp. 235, 297, 309, 363), daughter of Marie Tietze. (See also pp. 235, 271, 276, 297, 309, 340, 363.) 'Over the hills and far away' is an appropriate quotation from the nursery rhyme, 'Tom He Was a Piper's Son' (1795).
     'Letter to a Dead Friend' ** 22 March 1963.

323. 'Prayer to the Steep Atlantick Stream' (*for the natives of Borth*) 22 March 1963. B.D., p. 36. The title is an allusion to a line from Milton's 'Comus' (see also pp. 5, 17, 49, 255, 281, 333, 367). Borth is the seaside village north of Aberystwyth where in the late 1940's Jones spent happy times with his friends, Ted and Pam Richards. (See also pp. 126, 168, 185, 214, 222, 298, 317, 324.) The hiraeth ('nostalgia') is typical of the later poetry.
     'Not That I Don't Like Kingsley Amis' (*to Jill and John* [Stowell]) See also pp. 224, 266, 301, 309, 340. 22 March 1963. Australian Highway, November 1963. Kingsley Amis (1922–95), novelist and poet, presented a satiric and patronizing view of Wales and the Welsh. This may have had something to do with his experiences as a young lecturer at Swansea. This poem amusingly catches the Amis tone. 'WEA' – Workers' Educational Association, a provider of further and higher education for (especially) working adults. Jones worked for the Association during his time at Portsmouth. (Franz) 'Kafka' (1883–1924) – German-speaking Jewish novelist, the reading of whose work has been viewed as a badge of the (aspiring) intellectual. (Thomas) 'Mann' (1875–1955) – German novelist and essayist. 'John Wain' (1925–94), poet, critic and novelist associated with Amis as a 'Movement' poet. 'Glamorgan were county champions' – Glamorgan Cricket Club won the County Championship for the first time in 1948.

324. 'To The Keeper Of The Welsh Kitchen' ** 22 March 1963. 'The Welsh Kitchen' was Ted Richards' café at Borth, near Aberystwyth. (See also pp. 126, 163, 185, 214, 222, 298, 317, 323.)
     'To Rupert Hart-Davis' (*on the receipt of The Letters of Oscar Wilde*) ** 22 March 1963. (See also p. 260.) Hart-Davis was Jones's generous publisher and friend. In 1962 he both edited and published the *Letters of Oscar Wilde*. (See also pp. 214, 229.)
     'One Memory' 22 March 1963. B.D., p. 58. The memory is of winter at Llanafanfawr (see also pp. 6, 23, 94, 104, 138, 142, 222, 226, 228, 244, 261, 264, 275, 283, 296, 297, 302, 310, 311, 319, 332, 336, 342, 343, 346, 359, 364, 366).

325. 'Have You Ever Been Frightened?' ** 22 March 1963. 'Stukas' – Second World War German dive-bombers, which were fitted with sirens to increase the apprehension they caused – 'Stuka' is an abbreviation of 'Sturzkampfflugzeug', the German word for 'dive-bomber'; 'dot-dash dash-dot' – Jones's position aboard ship was signals telegraphist; 'E-boats' – abbreviation of 'Enemy War Motorboats', the German equivalent of the

British M.T.B. (Motor Torpedo Boat); 'Texan' – when the USA entered the Second World War there was, from time to time, friction between their servicemen and those of Britain; 'weasel' – an animal ferocious, and noisy, in defence of its young.

326. 'Hwyl Fawr, Brin' ** 22 March 1963. Brin (Newton-John) – Head of Arts (see also pp. 239, 244, 291, 328, 333, 334) at Newcastle University College (see also pp. 86, 143, 214, 218, 224, 225, 226, 237, 239, 244, 252, 284, 291, 299, 300, 301, 302, 303, 309, 312, 327, 328, 333, 343, 353, 358, 365, 370); 'hwyl fawr, bachgen' – all the best, boy/boyo/old chap (etc.); 'ring factitiously' – sound artificial/false.

'Ambivalent Poem in the Old Manner' (*To Whom Else*) ** 22 March 1963. 'O western winde . . . ' – slightly inaccurate reference to an anonymous love-poem from the *Oxford Book of English Verse* (1st edn, 1921): 'Western wind, when wilt thou blow,/The small rain down can rain?/Christ, if my love were in my arms/And I in my bed again!'.

'A Man Without Eyelids' 29/30 March 1963. B.D., p. 75. A memory of war service in Egypt, where afflictions of the eyes were common. 'Mr' – presumably the Headmaster of Builth County School (see also pp. 21, 33, 64, 143, 157, 294, 297, 343, 346), the redoubtable Mr P. G. Davies, B.Sc., M.A. (Oxon.).

327. 'Salute to Marlene from Down in the Valleys' (*Welsh accent obligatory*) ** 30 March 1963. 'mun' – man; 'Duw' – (my) God! For Marlene (Norst) – see also pp. 224, 239.

'Thanks to Jean and Norman for Coming Here' ** 30 March 1963. Norman Talbot, rival 'working class' poet, a member of the Faculty of Arts at the Newcastle College (see also pp. 86, 143, 214, 218, 224, 225, 226, 237, 239, 244, 252, 284, 291, 299, 300, 301, 302, 303, 309, 312, 326, 328, 333, 343, 353, 358, 365, 370) of the University of New South Wales and writer of a memorable obituary to Jones, 'The Seafolding of Harri Jones'. (See also p3589.)

'The Second Critical Encounter' (*to Marlene*) (See also pp. 200, 213, 213, 291.) 28 June 1963. C.C., p. 56. A shrewd critic as well as a fine poet, Jones here accurately assesses his own development as poet. For the first 'critical encounter', see p. 169; see also 'Simply to Write', p. 274.

328. 'One Reason for Disliking Englishmen' ** 28 June 1963. 'hirsute' – hairy; 'Wing-Co' – Royal Air Force Wing Commander; the 'Englishman' is Brin Newton-John (see also pp. 239, 244, 291, 326, 333, 334), Head of the Arts Department at the Newcastle College (see also pp. 86, 143, 214, 218, 224, 225, 226, 237, 239, 244, 252, 284, 291, 299, 300, 301, 302, 303, 309, 312, 326, 327, 333, 343, 353, 358, 365, 370) of the University of New South Wales.

'To, And For, Caroline' ** 28 June 1963. 'hwyl fawr' – best wishes; 'Ivor' – Caroline was Ivor Vivian's wife (see also pp. 231, 252, 253).

329. 'Sawmill Incident' (*to Alan Mullard, Timberman*) 28 June 1963. C.C., p. 57. 'finger' – the amputated digit, sometimes known as the 'feeling

finger', is the one used in sexual foreplay. Mullard, also a potter, was a friend of the Joneses.

'Infidelity' 28 June 1963. The Bulletin, 86, 4426, 19 December 1964.

'Welsh Pastoral Elegy' 28 June 1963. Australian Highway, 1964. C.C., p. 20. 'rods' – the rod, pole or perch is an obsolete unit of measurement, $5\frac{1}{2}$ yards.

330. 'Adrift' 28 June 1963. C.C., p. 21. The Bulletin, 86, 4426, 19 December 1964.

331. 'Lower Deck Attitude Illustrated' (*Persons with O.L.Q. requested not to read*) ** 28 June 1963. O.L.Q. – Organisational Leadership Quality; 'Lower deck' – where the Ordinary Seamen are quartered; 'Flag Lieutenant' – officer who acts as aide to the Admiral; 'wardroom' – officers' quarters; 'Asdic' – sailors responsible for operating the submarine-detection apparatus named after the body which sponsored it, the Allied (or Anti-) Submarine Detection Investigation Committee; 'bo's'n' (boatswain) – warrant officer; 'Cox'n' (Coxswain) – petty officer; 'E.R.A.' – Engine Room Artificer; 'Leatherneck' – sailor's name for a soldier or marine.

'In The Shadow Of Your Hair' 28 June 1963. C.C., p. 58.

332. 'Spoiled Preacher' (*to many contemporaries, and some in especial*) 28 June 1963. C.C., p. 22. 'Chwefru' – stream that runs through the middle of Llanafanfawr (see also pp. 6, 23, 94, 104, 138, 142, 222, 226, 228, 244, 261, 264, 275, 283, 296, 297, 302, 310, 311, 319, 324, 336, 342, 343, 346, 359, 364, 366): it was used for (Nonconformist) baptisms and sheep-dipping; 'Christmas Evans' – 1776–1838, Baptist preacher and hymn-writer; 'Evan Jones' – 1777–1819, Baptist preacher famous for his Calvinistic pamphlets. His family came from Eglwyswrw in Pembrokeshire. Excommunicated in 1810 for public drunkenness; 'grandfather' – Thomas Jones (see also pp. 95, 244, 283, 337, 359, 366), 'Crogau', scholar, shepherd, rate-collector and Deacon of his Baptist chapel; 'notches' – system of identifying the owners of sheep; 'McTurk's man' – T. H. Jones's uncle, Jack Jones, worked as a shepherd for McTurk, a land-owner at Abercraf, Powys.

333. 'Rape' (*A Footnote by Satan to Paradise Lost*) ** 28 June 1963. 'Paradise Lost' – Milton's (1608–74) (see also pp. 5, 17, 49, 255, 281, 323, 367) epic poem in which Satan, in the form of a snake, brings about the Fall of Mankind; 'Confucius' – Kung Fu-tse (550–480 BC), Chinese philosopher to whom are jokingly attributed many vulgar witticisms in the form, 'Confucius, he say, "When rape inevitable, relax"'.

'For A Good Marriage' (*to Valerie and Brin*) (See also pp. 239, 244, 291, 326, 328, 334.) ** 28 June 1963. Brin Newton-John was Head of Arts at Newcastle University College (see also pp. 86, 143, 214, 218, 224, 225, 226, 237, 239, 244, 252, 284, 291, 299, 300, 301, 302, 303, 309, 312, 326, 327, 328, 343, 353, 358, 365, 370); Valerie is a clinical psychologist.

334. 'With Love, For Love' (*to Valerie and Brin*) ** 28 June 1963. 'a little room'
– an allusion to John Donne's (1571?–1631) poem (see also pp. 33, 36, 60,
257, 260, 266, 366), 'The Good-Morrow', which contains the lines 'For
love . . . makes one little roome an every where'. For Brin Newton John
and Valerie, see also pp. 239, 244, 291, 326, 328, 333.
     'Eyes, Hair, Sea, Fall' 15 July 1963. C.C., p. 59. Southerly, 25, 3, 1965.
'ambuscade' – trap; 'spindrift' – spray blown by the wind from the crests
of waves; 'Argosies' – treasure-ships; 'sere' – dry; 'lies' – as almost always
in Jones's love poems, this word carries the obvious double meaning.

335. 'On A Daughter' (*for James McAuley*) 15 July 1963. C.C., p. 60. The
Bulletin, 86, 4391, 18 April 1964; Quadrant, 1964. (See also pp. 77, 124,
130, 138, 143, 144, 147, 169, 206, 218, 228, 238, 261, 269, 274, 301.)
McAuley was a poet and editor of the magazine, 'Quadrant'. Jones was
introduced to him by the older Australian poet, A. D. Hope (see also pp.
265, 266); 'guilt' – Calvinistic sense of original sin.
     'With Hunger, With Anger' 3 September 1963. C.C., p. 74.

336. 'A Small Vision of Hell' 3 September 1963. Nimrod, 1964. C.C., p. 61.
'breastless' – cf. T. S. Eliot, 'Whispers of Immortality': 'breastless creatures
underground/Leaned backward with a lipless grin.' (see also pp. 1, 3, 9, 17,
18, 33, 107, 121, 137, 214, 234, 345). 'hairless snake' – penis.
     'Welsh Childhood' The Australian, November 1964. C.C., p. 24. The
Llanafanfawr scene (see also pp. 6, 23, 94, 104, 138, 142, 222, 226, 228,
244, 261, 264, 275, 283, 296, 297, 302, 310, 311, 319, 324, 332, 342,
343, 346, 359, 364, 366) with usual sense of sin/guilt.

337. 'Instructions To A Painter: For Her Birthday' ** 16–19 September 1963.
'remembering . . . ' see above p. 337, 'On a Painting, "Sunk Lyonesse" by
Rae Richards'; for Rae Richards, see also pp. 86, 228, 230, 250, 254, 270,
274, 282, 311, 319, 339, 353); 'Tintagel' – ruined castle in Cornwall,
traditional birthplace of King Arthur (see also pp. 44, 202, 228, 343);
'Kynge Arthur Ys Nat Dede' – the ancient prophecy that Arthur would one
day return; 'Gawain' (in the 'Mabinogion', Gwalchmai (see also pp. 37,
228, 343)) – King Arthur's nephew; 'Gwenhwyfar' – Welsh name of Queen
Guinevere; 'perjured sails' – it was not the sails that were perjured, but
Tristram's wife: wounded by a poisoned weapon, Tristram sent for Iseult
(Isolde) from Ireland to heal him; it was arranged that if she was aboard
the returning ship, a white sail would be hoisted, if not, a black; in fact, the
sail was white, but the jealous wife reported it to be black, and Tristram
died; 'gongs and dolphins' – an allusion to the final line of W. B. Yeats's
poem, 'Byzantium': 'That dolphin-torn, that gong-tormented sea'. (See also
pp. 1, 15, 49, 50, 51, 65, 66, 75, 77, 87, 89, 90, 92, 99, 120, 147, 158,
182, 198, 234, 245, 250, 260, 264, 302, 307, 318.)
     'With A Distant Bow To Mrs Hemans' (I.M. Tomos Jones Crogau)
16–19 September 1963. C.C., p. 25. Southerly 24, 2, 1964. 'Mrs Hemans'
– Mrs Felicia Dorothea Hemans (1793–1835), sentimental Victorian poet
whose first volume was titled 'Domestic Affections'. Her poems were
popular recitation pieces for Eisteddfodau; 'I.M.' – In Memoriam; as a

child, Jones had a closer relationship with his grandfather (see also pp. 95, 244, 283, 332, 359, 366) than with his father: see e.g. the short story 'My Grandfather Would have Me Be a Poet'.

338. 'With Thanks' ** (late) 1963.
'Taffy Was Transported' (late) 1963. C.C., p. 26. 'transported' means both deeply affected and shipped (as convicts were in the nineteenth century) to Australia: 'Sion' – Mount Hermon, a lofty peak in the Middle East: both 'Sion' and 'Hermon' are common names for Welsh chapels; 'Jahveh' – Jehovah, the harsh god of the Old Testament; 'crooked star' – the Southern Cross.

339. 'Recriminations Over' (late) 1963. C.C., p. 62. The Bulletin, 86, 4405, 25 July 1964.
'Christmas Once More' ** (December) 1963. Petrarchan sonnet (see also pp. 1, 12, 36, 41, 61, 80, 86, 91, 108, 119, 124, 138, 140, 156, 234, 254, 255, 260, 266, 276, 282, 302, 305, 311); 'a painter' – Rae Richards (see also pp. 86, 228, 230, 250, 254, 270, 274, 282, 311, 319, 337, 353).

340. 'Instead of a Christmas Card' for Jill & Marie ** (December) 1963. 'Jill' is Jill Stowell (see also pp. 224, 266, 301, 309, 323); 'Marie' – Marie Tietze. (See also pp. 235, 271, 276, 297, 309, 322, 363.)
'A Sailor Who Reads Books Sends A Christmas Card To His Dead Sweetheart' (for Anna) Christmas Eve 1963. C.C., p. 63. 'Platonic' – philosophical. Anna Rutherford, one of Jones's brightest students, subsequently taught English Studies in Denmark See also p. 353.

341. 'No Regrets' ** 1 January 1964.
'My Country, My Grief' 1 January 1964. C.C., p. 26. 'guilt' – because of the severe religion in which he was brought up.

342. 'Back?' 14 January 1964. C.C. p. 28. Meanjin 24, 1, March 1965. R. S. Thomas (1913–2000) (see also pp. 229, 310), the finest Welsh poet of the twentieth century, and one of the finest writing anywhere in English, began his ministry in a rural area comparable to Llanafanfawr (see also pp. 6, 23, 94, 104, 138, 142, 222, 226, 228, 244, 261, 264, 275, 283, 296, 297, 302, 310, 311, 319, 324, 332, 336, 343, 346, 359, 364, 366) and his early poetry depicts scenes and characters similar to those of Jones's. Jones's admiration of Thomas was not returned; 'birded' – musical; 'Glyn Dwr' – Owain Glyndŵr (c.1354–c.1416), outstanding Welsh military leader whose rising against Henry IV in 1401 was not finally suppressed until 1413; 'Saunders Lewis's aerodrome' – Saunders Lewis (1893–1985), dramatist, poet, literary historian and critic was, in 1925, one of the founders of the Welsh Nationalist Party, Plaid Cymru. In 1936, with D. J. Williams and Lewis Valentine, he committed a token act of arson at the R.A.F. bombing school at Penyberth, Caernarfonshire; 'match at Swansea' – Jones played rugby at school and, like all true Welshmen, remained interested in it thereafter: Swansea was then a first class club.

343. 'Welsh Bastard' (*to David Jones*) 26 January 1964. C.C., p. 30. The 'I' of this poem is Jones, but he is also the archetypal Welshman, oppressed, defeated and defiant down the ages. 'David Jones' (1895–1974), artist and modernist Anglo-Welsh writer who, in his 'war-book', *In Parenthesis*, makes use of Aneirin's long poem, *Y Gododdin*, which commemorates the heroic deeds of the war-band that assaulted Catraeth (Catterick); 'Camlann' – battle which took place c.539, probably at Camboglanna on the Roman Wall, and in which Arthur (see also pp. 44, 202, 228, 343 below) and Mordred died; 'Sarn Elen' – Roman road in Cardiganshire and other counties, and hamlet near Llanafan associated with the fourth century Elen Luyddog (Elen of the Hosts), heroine of *The Dream of Macsen Wledig*, one of the two historical tales in the *Mabinogion* (see also pp. 37, 228, 337); 'Blodeuedd' (Blodeuwedd) – beautiful, faithless wife of Lleu Llawgyffes in the same work; 'Nest' (fl. 1100–1120) – daughter of Rhys ap Tewdwr, renowned for her beauty; 'last Llewelyn' – Llywelyn ap Gruffudd (c.1225–82), 'The Last Prince' ('Y Llyw Olaf'), killed by English troops at Cilmeri, west of Builth Wells (see also pp. 21, 33, 64, 143, 157, 294, 297, 326, 346); 'bloody minded Tudor' – Henry VII; 'Agincourt' – Welsh archers distinguished themselves at this battle; 'Cynddylan' – early seventh century king of Powys; 'Pengwern' –'Eryr Pengwern' (The Eagle of Pengwern) – poem in which are described the screaming birds of prey which feast on fallen warriors, in particular Heledd's brother, Cynddylan.

'Anoeth bid Bedd I Arthur' 26 January 1964. Australian Highway, December 1964. C.C., p. 31. 'The Stanzas of the Graves' (*Englynion y Beddau*) – a collection of poems (in the *Black Book of Carmarthen*) which name the graves of heroes; 'March' (ap Meirchion) – early legendary hero, perhaps based on a son of the King of Glamorgan; 'Gwythur' and 'Gwgan' – Celtic warriors of the time of Arthur (see also pp. 44, 202, 228, 343 above); 'Epoch and Artist' (1959) – a collection of essays on various subjects, including Wales; 'my grave' – Jones's body was cremated in Newcastle, New South Wales (see also pp. 86, 143, 214, 218, 224, 225, 226, 237, 239, 244, 252, 284, 291, 299, 300, 301, 302, 303, 309, 312, 326, 327, 328, 333, 353, 358, 365, 370) and his ashes interred in the churchyard of Llanfihangel Brynpabuan, Llanafan (see also pp. 6, 23, 94, 104, 138, 142, 222, 226, 228, 244, 261, 264, 275, 283, 296, 297, 302, 310, 311, 319, 324, 332, 336, 342, 346, 359, 364, 366), where a small stone commemorates him; 'quondam and futurus' – once and future (king), a phrase applied to Arthur. Jones wrote many poems to his wife, Madeleine (see also pp. 34, 45, 64, 77, 143, 147, 148, 156, 159, 169, 218, 224, 234, 236, 240, 242, 266, 269, 283, 285, 291, 312), but this is the finest, most resonant and saddest of them all, using postmodern technique to associate some of the greatest and most tragic events of Welsh history with his own life, love and death.

344. 'The Hedgeschoolmaster Talks To Himself' 11 February 1964. C.C., p. 32. Quadrant, 9, 1, Jan–Feb 1965. 'Hedge-schoolmaster' – a hedge-school was an open-air school, common in Ireland during the seventeenth and eighteenth centuries because of the ban on Catholic education and the Irish language: like Shakespeare's (see also pp. 17, 33, 55, 56, 58, 79, 81, 89, 129,

138, 158, 229, 235, 261, 264, 270, 276, 288, 297, 311, 345) melancholy Jacques, the poet finds 'sermons in stones' and 'books in the running brooks'.

'Petrarch Did Not Write Like This' 28 May 1964. C.C., p. 65. The love-poems of Petrarch (1304–74) (see also pp. 1, 12, 36, 41, 61, 80, 86, 91, 108, 119, 124, 138, 140, 156, 234, 254, 255, 260, 266, 276, 282, 302, 305, 311, 339) neither are, nor could be anything like as risqué as this rondeau- or rondel-like poem.

345. 'On Being Asked to Contribute To A "Theatre and Drama" Issue Of Meanjin' ** 28 May 1964. 'Meanjin' – Australian literary magazine; 'Nahum Tate' – (1652–1715), playwright, mainly of adaptations, one of them of 'King Lear'; 'Keats did King Lear' – John Keats (1795–1821) (see also pp. 127, 260, 320) wrote sonnets entitled 'On Sitting Down to Read *King Lear* Again' and 'On First Looking into Chapman's Homer'; 'Kate' – the heroine of Shakespeare's (see also pp. 17, 33, 55, 56, 58, 79, 81, 89, 129, 138, 158, 229, 235, 261, 264, 270, 276, 288, 297, 311, 344) *The Taming of the Shrew*; 'Burtoned' – a reference to the Welsh actor, Richard Burton (1925–84), who starred with his then wife, Elizabeth Taylor, in a film version of the play, and to English beer brewed at Burton-on-Trent; 'Browning' – Robert Browning (1812–89), English poet; 'Pound' – Ezra Pound (1885–1972) – American poet, friend of T. S. Eliot (see also pp. 1, 3, 9, 17, 18, 33, 107, 121, 137, 214, 234, 336); 'Dylan' – Dylan Thomas (1914–53), Anglo-Welsh poet – 'too late, Cock' is a quotation from his 'Under Milk Wood' (see also pp. 4, 20, 30, 33, 40, 52, 53, 54, 57, 58, 64, 87, 96, 104, 106, 112, 116, 117, 119, 158, 170, 186, 201, 225, 232, 234, 245, 272, 278, 279, 284, 292, 313); 'Gautier' – Théophile Gautier (1811–72), French poet, novelist, critic and journalist.

346. 'The Solitary Wanderer' 28 May 1964. Nimrod, 3, 1, Summer 1965. C.C., p. 33. 'evil eye of the toad' – toads were once thought to be poisonous.

'Builth Wells' 28 May 1964. C.C., p. 34. Builth Wells is a small town situated on the River Wye in the county of Powys (formerly Breconshire). In 1933 Jones began to attend the County School, living in lodgings during the week and returning to Llanafanfawr (see also pp. 6, 23, 94, 104, 138, 142, 222, 226, 228, 244, 261, 264, 275, 283, 296, 297, 302, 310, 311, 319, 324, 332, 336, 342, 343, 359, 364, 366) at weekends. See also pp. 21, 33, 64, 143, 157, 294, 297, 326, 343, 'Builth'; 'French letters' – contraceptive sheaths; 'sylvan Wye' – 'How oft, in spirit, have I turned to thee, O sylvan Wye!': Wordsworth, *Lines composed a few miles above Tintern Abbey* (see also pp. 87, 196, 199, 234, 260, 370); 'Buallt' – the Welsh name of Builth is Llanfair-ym-muallt, 'muallt' being a mutation of the initial consonant following the preposition; 'Groe' – the municipal park and courting area; 'great footballer' – there were several of these, both rugby and soccer players; 'choir' – a choir conducted by 'Llew Buallt' (E. Evans) won at the National Eisteddfod in the 1880s.

347. 'But That Was In Another Country' 28 May 1964. Australian Letters, 1965. C.P., p. 250. 'bounden' – obligatory (cf. 'bounden duty'), with a sense of man's enslavement to woman.

348. 'Not on this Continent' June 1964. C.P., p. 251.
     'Treatment' ** June 1964. The 'treatment' of the title was for alcoholism. The note on Semyon Yaklovevich is the poet's.

349. 'For David Jonathan Power' ** June 1964. Jones youngest sister, Patricia (see also pp. 21, 157, 288), married Glyn Power in 1961; their elder son, David Jonathan, was born in June 1964.

350. 'Another Love' June 1964. C.C., p. 66. The 'love' of the poem is, presumably, poetry.
     'Unsuccesful Attempt At Suicide' ** September 1964.

351. '"Here is the peace of the fathers". – Hart Crane' September 1964. C.C., p. 67. (Harold) Hart Crane, 1899–1932, alcoholic US poet who committed suicide by leaping into the sea.
     'After the Quarrel' ** 16 September 1964. Poignant revelation of the strains caused by alcoholism.

352. 'Disorderly Spring' September 1964. Poetry Magazine, 1, 1965. C.C., p. 68. Australian spring is British autumn.
     'A Failed Marriage' ** September 1964. 'bound sticks' – the pain of the relationship resembles bearing a bundle of sticks upon one's back; 'ignominy' – love has degenerated beyond even unsatisfactory sex.

353. 'An Apology of a Sort' (to Rae) ** September 1964. The dedicatee is Rae Richards, the artist. (See also pp. 86, 228, 230, 250, 254, 270, 274, 282, 311, 319, 337, 339.)
     'Cotton Mather Remembers the Trial of Elizabeth How: Salem, Massachusetts, 30 June 1692' 25/26 September 1964. C.C., p. 45 (section II of that volume). Also published by Nimrod Publications, Newcastle, N.S.W., as 'Nimrod Pamphlets No.1 1964'. The last poem to be entered into the 'Black Book' (see also pp. 143, 145, 159, 167, 195, 203, 204, 210, 211, 214, 217, 220, 239, 255, 261, 303), and followed by the inscription, 'Newcastle N.S.W. September 1964', (see also pp. 86, 143, 214, 218, 224, 225, 226, 237, 239, 244, 252, 284, 291, 299, 300, 301, 302, 303, 309, 312, 326, 327, 328, 333, 343, 358, 365, 370) this is, in a sense, the poet's epitaph. In 'Spoiled Preacher' we see him speculating on the religious career he might have followed; here he identifies with Cotton Mather. Anna Rutherford (one of his brightest students – see also p. 340 above) described Jones as 'Not a religious man in the conventional sense, yet one of the most religious people I ever met . . . ' and refers to 'his desperate search for a faith, and the fear and defeat he felt in his inability to find it'. Cotton Mather (1663–1728) was the most famous of the New England Puritans and a central figure in the Salem Witch Trials (1692) after which twenty people, most of them women, were hanged. Elizabeth How was examined on 31 May and executed on 19 July. Although Mather believed in 'possession by the devil', he recognized that the Trials were used by some to repay secular grievances and would have preferred the problem to have been resolved by prayer and fasting. The poem is a dramatic monologue by Mather in a pastiche of his own style, and something of the

state of Jones's mind in the last months of his life may be gained by contrasting the nightmarish content and bleak blank verse of this work with the exuberance, five years earlier, of 'The Colour of Cockcrowing'. 'The Devil in Massachusetts' by Marion L. Starkey was published by Knopf (New York) in 1949. 'Indian wilderness' – the land settled by the Puritans had originally belonged to the 'Red' Indians; 'folio-writers' – anti-Puritan religious pamphleteers; 'obloquy' – slander; 'Tacitus despite Tertullian' – born *c*.AD 150, Tertullian, one of the greatest of early Christian writers in Latin, was opposed to the introduction of classical writers such as Tacitus into Christian schools; 'Goody' – Goodwife: the wife of a 'Goodman' (Yeoman); 'Ipswich' – settlement north of Salem; 'Newbery' – settlement north of Ipswich; 'Acts' – 'The Acts of the Apostles', the fifth book of the New Testament; 'a book' – *The Wonders of the Invisible World* (1693); 'Essex County' – both the settlements and the administrative areas of this part of Massachusetts were named after towns and counties of England from which the persecuted Puritans had fled: north of Boston can be found e.g. Gloucester, Portsmouth, Exeter etc.; 'mazes' – perplexities/ bewilderment.

358. 'Towards a Homage to Norman Talbot' 30 September–1 October 1964. C.C., p. 69. MS. Norman Talbot: Australian, rival 'working class' poet, a member of the Faculty of Arts at the Newcastle College (see also pp. 86, 143, 214, 218, 224, 225, 226, 237, 239, 244, 252, 284, 291, 299, 300, 301, 302, 303, 309, 312, 326, 327, 328, 333, 343, 353, 365, 370) of the University of New South Wales and writer of a memorable obituary to Jones, 'The Seafolding of Harri Jones' (see also p. 327); 'decrescent volutes' – descending spirals; 'alation' – flying; 'discrete' – separate.

359. 'Bird on a Jaunt' 4 October 1964. C.C., p. 73. The bird (symbolic of the poet), is, of course, a cock.
    'My Grandfather Going Blind' 4 October 1964. C.C., p. 38. Meanjin 24, 1, March 1965; Penguin Book of Australian Verse, 1972 (as 'My Grandfather Goes Blind'). One of Jones's finest poems, rooted, as so often, in the 'land of his heart', Llanafanfawr (see also pp. 6, 23, 94, 104, 138, 142, 222, 226, 228, 244, 261, 264, 275, 283, 296, 297, 302, 310, 311, 319, 324, 332, 336, 342, 343, 346, 364, 366), its deceptively plain language so different from the complexity of the apprentice work. As a child (see short stories such as 'My Grandfather Would Have Me Be a Poet'), he had a closer relationship with Thomas Jones, Crogau (1853–1950) (see also pp. 95, 244, 283, 332, 337, 366), than with either of his parents. ('Mari') Mary Jones, his grandmother (1855–1938); 'thorny' – tough: the image is derived from the stunted, wind-blown hawthorn trees characteristic of the hilly Llanafan landscape; cf. 'Thorn', p. 371 below.

360. 'Word Is All' 4 October 1964. Poetry Magazine, 1, 1965. C.C., p. 37. 'that bare poem,/True as home' is an accurate description of the best of these final poems; 'cwm' – valley; 'stumbled' – ruinous.

361. 'A Welsh Poet Finds a Proper Story' C.C., p. 80. 4 October 1964. 'story' – the Garden of Eden (Wales and the poet's childhood there), Adam, Eve (see

also pp. 63, 86, 93, 99, 101, 116, 167, 180, 210, 225, 251, 255, 257, 265, 266, 284, 318, 367, 368), temptation, sexual guilt, fall and banishment/exile from the Garden, the central myth of Jones's poetry.

'You Can Have More Than One Breakdown If You Try Hard Enough' ** 4 October 1964. A bitterly honest 'confessional' poem of a sick man. 'prick' – of a hypodermic; 'stew' – possibly an allusion to the story of Atreus, of the House of Pelops, who revenged himself on Thyestes by killing the latter's two sons and serving him their flesh at a banquet.

362. 'Perennial Complaint of a Writer ** 4 October 1964.

363. 'Advice to a Knight' 1964. C.C., p. 73. 'as they might be' – archaic for 'as if they might be'.

'To Miranda Crossing the Seas' ** 1964 Perhaps the most beautiful of the occasional poems. Miranda (see also pp. 235, 297, 309, 322) was the daughter of Marie Tietze (see also pp. 235, 271, 276, 297, 309, 322, 340). 'mother of beauty' – Aphrodite (Venus), goddess of love and beauty, was, in one myth, supposed to have been born from the foam of the sea. (See also pp. 37, 38, 42, 46, 56, 86, 109, 111, 234, 307.)

364. 'Small Protest from a Native' University of Wales Review, 1964. A briefly revived version of the *Welsh Anvil*, annual journal of the Guild of Graduates of the University of Wales, a federal institution of seven colleges, each of which awarded its own degree under the university's auspices. When, in 1964, a committee report recommended defederalisation into four separate universities, the *University of Wales Review* was established to defend the decision of the University Court against this. This poem is Jones's response as a graduate of University College, Aberystwyth. 'Llangammarch (Wells)' and Abergwesyn': small communities not far from Llanafanfawr (see also pp. 6, 23, 94, 104, 138, 142, 222, 226, 228, 244, 261, 264, 275, 283, 296, 297, 302, 310, 311, 319, 324, 332, 336, 342, 343, 346, 359, 366); 'Aber' – the affectionate abbreviation by which that university is known to its students and ex-students.

365. 'On Taking Part in a Recital of Baroque Music and Poetry at Newcastle Cathedral, Sunday, 4 October 1964' ** 6 October 1964. (See also pp. 86, 143, 214, 218, 224, 225, 226, 237, 239, 244, 252, 284, 291, 299, 300, 301, 302, 303, 309, 312, 326, 327, 328, 333, 343, 353, 358, 370.) More, perhaps, than any other, this almost incoherent poem shows the anguish caused to Jones by the stern religion in which he had grown up and could never reject, though he could equally never accept it. 'Book' – the Bible; 'paradox' – a self-contradictory statement, e.g. 'Dying to life'; 'oxymoron' – a figure of speech, such as 'hurry slowly', in which contradictory terms are combined; 'judas . . . garden . . . kissed' – Judas Iscariot, the disciple who betrayed Christ, did so by kissing Him in the Garden of Gethsemane to identify him for waiting Roman soldiers; 'manquake' – the lectern is shaking with the intensity of the poet's performance (and perhaps nervousness); 'His Dove' – the Holy Spirit, or Holy Ghost, third member, along with the Father and the Son, of the Holy Trinity or God in three persons'; 'angels wrestle' – in Genesis 32: 24–30, the Angel of

the Covenant appeared as a man and Jacob wrestled with him all night. As a result, Jacob's name was changed to Israel.

366. 'For My Grandfather' 11 October 1964. C.C., 39. (See also pp. 95, 244, 283, 332, 337, 359.) 'pulpitwalkers, pathtakers' – the poet's ancestors included shepherds who were also deacons of their Chapel; 'Allt-y-clych' – the 'Hill of bells' across which Jones, as a child, walked to school; 'Alpha and Omega' – the first and last letters of the Greek alphabet; 'fire . . . thornbush' – God spoke to Moses out of a burning bush, telling him to lead the Israelites out of their captivity in Egypt; 'pleached' – folded/bound (a term in traditional hedging, cf. 'pleached arbour' or 'pleached walk'); 'went down to the sea, the great waters' – Jones served in the Navy during the Second World War: Psalm 104:23 – 'They that go down to the sea in ships: and occupy their business in great waters; These men see the works of the Lord: and his wonders in the deep'; 'rhymed in the antipodes' – the poem was written in Australia; 'Cwmcrogau' – the valley and smallholding at Llanafanfawr (see also pp. 6, 23, 94, 104, 138, 142, 222, 226, 228, 244, 261, 264, 275, 283, 296, 297, 302, 310, 311, 319, 324, 332, 336, 342, 343, 346, 359, 364) where Jones grew up.

'Girl Reading John Donne' 1 October 1964. The Australian, November 1964; Nimrod, 3, 1, Summer 1965. C.C., p. 75. Although this poem alludes to three love-poems of John Donne (1572–1631) (see also pp. 33, 36, 60, 257, 260, 266, 334), the poem which the 'almost anonymous' lecturer has prescribed is 'The Extasie', which begins with praise of spiritual love, but concludes with the necessity of sexual intercourse: 'So must pure lovers soules descend . . . Else a great Prince in prison lies'. Line six alludes to 'The Good-morrow' ('And now good morrow to our waking soules'); 'his favourite Elegie' is the wonderfully sensual 'To his Mistris going to Bed', the most relevant lines of which are 'Licence my roaving hands, and let them go,/Before, behind, between, above, below./O my America! My new-found-land'; 'canicule and sear' – great heat and burning ('canicule' refers to the 'dog-days', the hottest period of summer in the northern hemisphere); 'elsewhere' – the poet shares the frustration of the lover in 'The Extasie'.

367. 'Adam and Eve Hear the Thunder' October 1964. C.C., p. 77. (See also pp. 63, 86, 93, 99, 101, 116, 167, 180, 210, 225, 251, 255, 257, 265, 266, 284, 318, 361, 368.) Eve has offered Adam the fruit of the Tree of Knowledge of Good and Evil, and he has eaten it, bringing, as Milton ('Paradise Lost', Bk 1, line 3) puts it, 'death into the world and all our woe' (see also pp. 5, 17, 49, 255, 281, 323, 333); 'prerogative . . . cancelled' – they have lost, through their sinful disobedience, the privilege of sexual love free of guilt; descant' – song; 'ineluctable' – inescapable.

368. 'Mountain Death' October 1964. Poetry Magazine, 1, 1965. C.C., p. 36. 'reticence' - mountains *say* nothing, do not communicate, and man is lonely among them; 'maculate' – spotted or soiled (the season appears to be winter); 'thorn' – suffering and, ultimately, death; 'unrequiting' – indifferent/unresponsive.

'Adam Wonders About Eve' October 1964. C.C., p. 78. (See also pp. 63, 86, 93, 99, 101, 116, 167, 180, 210, 225, 251, 255, 257, 265, 266, 284, 318, 361, 367.) Eve is tempting Adam to eat the Forbidden Fruit. 'palpable' – able to be touched/attractive.

369. 'Against Wantonness' October 1964. C.C., p. 79. 'divining-rod' – instrument for discovering e.g. water, but here means penis; 'blushes' – *before* the Fall, sex was entirely sinless and void of embarrassment, but afterwards a source of shame; 'kiss the rod' – accept, even welcome the punishment.
    'After Divorce' October 1964. C.C., p. 71. 'shade' – ghost.

370. 'For Robyn Going Abroad' ** December 1964. Robyn (Iverach) Wallace was the colleague in the English Department at the Newcastle College (see also pp. 86, 143, 214, 218, 224, 225, 226, 237, 239, 244, 252, 284, 291, 299, 300, 301, 302, 303, 309, 312, 326, 327, 328, 333, 343, 353, 358, 365) of the University of New South Wales to whom the poem, 'The Colour of Cockcrowing' is dedicated. (See also pp. 225, 307.)
    'A Storm in Childhood' ? December 1964. C.C., p. 40. The poem has the kind of powerful simplicity one associates with the best of Wordsworth (see also pp. 87, 196, 199, 234, 260, 346). 'sins' – conveys a sense of the stern, Calvinistic religion in which Jones was brought up and which, it may be argued, in its clash with his sexuality, destroyed him.

371. 'Thorn' C.C., p. 35. ? December 1964. Perhaps the last poem Jones composed, and appropriately the final poem in this volume. He had reached the point where endurance was all that remained to him, and took for his symbol the tough, bristling, gnarled tree which struggles for survival on the hills of Powys – but in spring makes the land glorious with its blossom.

* * *

On the morning of 29 January 1965, the body of T. H. Jones was found floating in the Bogey Hole, a bathing pool carved out of solid rock by convicts on the shore of the Pacific Ocean near Newcastle, New South Wales. In 1966 the posthumous volume, *The Colour of Cockcrowing*, edited by his widow, Madeleine, and a friend, Jill Stowell, was published by Hart-Davis.

Index

INDEX OF TITLES

A

Aberystwyth, March 1946	31
Acceptance of Fate	251
Acrobat	2
Across the Unresponsive Oceans	47
Adam	180
Adam and Eve Hear the Thunder	367
Adam, Thoughtfully, to Eve	257
Adam Wonders About Eve	368
Adam's Song After Paradise	265
Address to My Face	174
Adrift	330
Advertisement	276
Advice from a Friend	142
Advice to a Knight	363
Affair, An	273
Afraid of being converted like St. Paul	134
After Divorce	369
After The Funeral With None to Praise	52
After The Quarrel	351
Against Wantonness	369
Agony Is Not to Be Encountered In Islands	48
Allegory	123
All Passion Spent	119
All the torn and blistered fields	133
Alone	57
Ambivalent Poem in the Old Manner	326
Amends	128
Ancestor, Old Lady	289
Ancestral	94
And In The Woods to Walk	291
And I Would Send You Argosies Of Words	37
And Resolve Themselves	220
Anglo-Welsh, The	126
Anniversary	243

Annunciation   126
Anoeth Bid Bedd I Arthur   343
Anonymous Ghost, The   155
Another Form of Farewell   151
Another Love   350
Any Husband to any Wife   258
Apocalyptic   154
Apologia pro carmina sua   54
Apology of a Sort, An   353
Are There any Modern Poets?   240
Art Poetique   92
At midnight in deserted towns   97
Attainment   130
At the close of a winter day   62
Aubade   103
Australian Christmas   319

                                    B

Back?   342
Ballad   175
Ballad of Me, The   150
Beast at the Door, The   291
Beauty lies with the fool, The   88
Because Of That Great Company   49
Before The Bright Bird Write His Epitaph   8
Belated Welcome for Mary   318
Beneath the surface of decay   122
Benghazi, Christmas 1942   44
Between Nightmare and Nightmare   260
Bewilderment   220
Beyond this murder   120
Biography   80
Bird On A Jaunt   359
Birthday Poem for Madeleine, A   269
Birthday Sonnet, A   311
Birthday Wish for a Painter, A   270
Birth of Venus   111
Bodies are Poems   40
Bridegroom, The   173
Bronwen   294
Brothel In Algiers: Wartime   90
Builth   33
Builth Wells   346
Burning against the lyric dark   111
'But if it be a Boy You Shall Put Him to the Sea'   316
But That Was In Another Country   347
But that was yesterday   15

C

Calling Within Us the Spring   2
Can It Be So Long?   252
Celebratory Poem for Robyn And Rod, A   307
Chambermaid's Song   257
Child at Night, The   208
Children in the Park   123
Christening Poem for Alison Morgan   211
Christmas Once More   339
Christmas Poem, A   226
Christmas Poem for Michelene, A   284
Colour of Cockcrowing, The   225
Complaint   198
Confusion Of Bright Women, A   264
Conquest of the West, the   79
Contemplation   6
Contemporary, A (Epigram III, Second Set)   192
Contradiction of your images, The   118
Cool Pity Covers Us   3
Cotton Mather Remembers The Trial Of Elizabeth How: Salem,
    Massachusetts, 30 June 1692   353
Country Drunkard, The   94
Country Matters   277
Country of Hurt, The   102
Country Sentiment   235
Crab, The   217
Critical Encounter   189
Curse, A   180
Cwmchwefri   297
Cwmchwefri Rocks   312

D

Dark Rival   315
Darlings   21
Data for Dr Kinsey   180
Dear Lady   17
Deathbed   166
Death Is Within Us Like A Child   74
Death of a Poet   165
Debate   195
Dedicatory Poem   176
Definitions of Circumstance, The   167
Desertion   16
Difference   135
Different Idiom, A   236
Different Skies, The   279
Dilemma   140

Disorderly Spring   352
Disorganized   250
Ditch of Desire, The   221
Djinn-Master Solomon   44
Dog Speaks to His Mistress, A   309
Do Not Look for Me In That Foreign Place   50
Doublecross   272
Draw An Arch of Light at the Window   219
Drunk on Duty   263

E

Easter Poem   115
Eclogue   95
Elegy   86
Elle à les jambes maigres   161
Enemies, The   42
Enemy In The Heart, The   29
Ennui, Mediterranean   85
Entire   274
Epigram   251
Epigrams   164
Epigrams (Second Set)   182
Epilogue   156
Epitaphs   4
Epithalamion   40
Erotic Season, The   100
Even Fathers Can Be Honest   274
Ever   289
Excuse   224
Exercise In Blank Verse: The Dancing Girl   14
Exile   266
Eyes, Hair, Sea, Fall   334

F

Failed Marriage, A   352
Failure of Narcissus   216
Fall of an Empire   233
False Dedication   218
Fear Not The Pettiness Of Time   7
Ferdinand to Miranda   58
Fireworks Night   258
First Kiss   37
For A Dead Sailor   58
For A Good Marriage   333
For an Unborn Daughter   301
For a Painting of Clea   274
For a Play (Chorus for the Undefeated)   97

For A Proud Beauty   27
For David Jonathan Power   349
For Louise Bogan   214
For Miranda   297
For My Grandfather   366
For My Unborn Child   77
For Rachel   145
For Roberto Sanesi, Il Miglior Fabbro   214
For Robyn Going Abroad   370
For Sian   144
For the Marriage of Hugh and Barbara   193
For Vanessa Stowell, Born 6 April 1962   301
Formulas, The   174
Found Love   30
Four   170
From a Play?   90
From Brooding On The Possible Event   56
From My Singing Sullenness   36
From the French of Pemette de Guillet   254
From What High Heaven   44
From Whence Cometh My Help   275

G

Gardeners are Friendly People (Epigram II, Second Set)   182
Garden of Eden   93
Genesis   116
Girl Reading John Donne   366
Glory Be   276
Gold Clarity Of This Moment, The   268
Gorse Idyll   179
Grandparents   213
Gratuitous Advice to Aging Poets   256
Greenness Of The Heart, The   61
Green Tree, The   305
Grief's Unscarred Wounds   39

H

Hard Luck   182
Have You Ever Been Frightened?   325
Head in the Clouds   296
Heart, Mind, And Body   314
Heart of the Winter, The   78
Hedgeschoolmaster Talks to Himself, The   344
He Had A Certain Seagreen Speech   32
'Here is the Peace of the Fathers' – Hart Crane   351
Here on the Atlas   142
Hiraeth   119

History	81
Homage	28
Homage to Robert Graves	251
Homage to Wallace Stevens	192
Hot Summer In The Blood	52
Hunger of This Love, The	287
Hwyl Fawr, Brin	326

I

I am the spindrift ghost	96
I dreamed when I was young	160
I Gave You Roses Once	267
I Have Been One That Loved	18
I have watched his pale hands	133
I Love Your Beautiful Mind, but I Love Especially Your Body	194
I Remember The House	9
I See the Sad Cities	47
I Would Have You Remain	56
I Would Not Have You Otherwise	48
I Would Send You Words	42
If I Should Lyrically Lament	54
If This Is Love	256
Idyll	36
Illicit Colloquy	246
Image	137
Images Of Adventure And Desire	45
Impeccable Strategy Let Down By Fallible Tactics (But Not Irreparably)	304
Improbable Land	302
Inaccessibility	19
In Despite of John Milton, or, What Adam Probably Said to Eve	255
In Love	253
In love's outrageous slums	98
In Memoriam	310
In Memoriam Ernest Hemingway	277
In my beginning	116
In my returning	33
In the annunciation	158
In the demented wood	120
In the duality of man	2
In the Light of Ordinary Evenings	221
In the Nightmare of the Heart	151
In The Shadow Of Your Hair	331
In the Tremble of the Year	289
In This Blind Time	105
In This Degenerate Age	262
In This White Courtyard	11
Infidelity	329
Infirm, Infirm	139

Innocent Song for Two Voices   203
Instead of a Christmas Card   340
Instructions to A Painter: for Her Birthday   337
Intimations of Mortality   196
Invented Seasons   149
Invocation, Lady, the stilted bird   190
Invocation, Unlatch Those Lids   17
Italian Baroque Music   227
It Is Not Death I Fear   52
It Is Not Fear   199
It Was A Lovely Lady   14
It Was Always Easy   42
It Was A Voice Serene   19
It Was A Winter Night And Cold to The Heart   60

J

Jack Christ Was Kind to Me   11
Jealousy   259
Journey From a War   12
Judgement Day   92

K

Keeping Chooks   247
Kingdom of Terror, The   317

L

Lady and the Fir-Tree, The   209
Lady in a Garden   194
Lake Woman's Song   110
Lament   20
Land of My Fathers   277
Landward   4
Last Regret, The   185
Late Love   46
Late Quarrel, A   182
Late Spring in Wales   288
Legends   81
Legends Ago   38
Lesson in Criticism, A   203
Lesson in Grammar, A   180
Let Me Make You a Poem That Is Everywhere   60
Letter to a Dead Friend   322
Letter Writing is a Lost Art   318
Limbs Of Summer In Their Glory, the   54
Lines by a Not Too Dejected Lover   246
Lines for A Double Christening   309
Lines for A Play   137

Lines for Marion   245
Lines for the Death of an Alcoholic   312
Lines for the Early Stages of a Love Affair   272
L'Invitation au Voyage   129
Little Elegy, A   290
Llanafan Unrevisited   264
Loitering Hounds, The   142
Lone Mister In The Park, the   57
Long-Ago Love   191
Lost Love   96
Lost Love, Unwritten Poems   233
Lost on the floor   118
Love   152
Love Dies as a Tree Grows   196
Love Gone   20
Love In The Antipodes   252
Love Is Different From What You Think It Is   251
Love is Like the Lion's Tooth   75
Love Lost and Found   155
Love Poem   179
Love Poem, Perhaps, A   242
Love, Poetry, and Middle Age   248
Love Song (Be Human Only Now)   10
Love Song (The nightingales of former lovers)   136
Love's Mythology   309
Love's Overtones   306
Love's Tautology   200
Love's Weather Changed to Thunder In My Ears   54
Lover Shows How Conventional He Is, The   242
Lovers' Colloquy   240
Lovers' Quarrel   241
Lower Deck Attitude Illustrated   331
Lucky Jonah   222
Lullaby   152

M

Macaronics for Marlene   239
Macarthur's Return (Epigrams, VI)   164
Man may feel, A   127
Man Without Eyelids, A   326
Marriage a la Mode   321
Martyrdom   143
Mediterranean: Wartime   107
Memories of a Country Childhood   284
Merlin's Lament   202
Metamorphosis   30
Midnight Words, The   117
Miles of Water, The   124
Mind Alone Has Not Its Own Defence, The   61

Minstrel Boy, The   305
Mirror and mask abound   109
Mirror of Herself, The   266
Money   232
Monster, The   213
Moods of the Sea, The   245
Moondappled Memories   12
Morning over the Valleys   82
Mother and Daughter (Epigram V, Second Set)   183
Mountain Death   368
Mountain Scene   15
Mr Jones As The Transported Poet   263
Mr Pope   269
My Angel   133
My Country, My Grief   341
My Daughter Asleep   138
My Grandfather Going Blind   359
My Grandmother Died in the Early Hours of the Morning   283
My Heart Is Now An Unlocked Lucky Room   33
My Mirror Loves Me, Anyway (Epigram VI, Second Set)   183

N

Narcissus   128
Nature of Love, The   119
Need for Pardon, The   91
Never Again   235
Never an Armistice   280
Never that love shall languish   133
New Ballad of Old Ireland, A   300
New Song of Old Despair, A   190
Nightmare of King Theseus, The   314
Nightmare, Terror: nightmare: and my crawling skin   258
Nightmare, The dragons crawl about the mountains   89
No More for You and I, My Love   3
No Name But Love   253
No Pity Nor Prophylactic   35
No Regrets   341
No Songs Or Sonnets   5
Nonconformist Hills, The   142
Nostalgia, The gaudy summers of my youth   108
Nostalgia, Waves Whelm Me Westward from this Antique Sea   16
Not Blessed   288
Not in that drunken morning   117
Not Lack of Children Only   217
Not Much Comfort   176
Not on this Continent   348
Not That I Don't Like Kingsley Amis   323
Not When I Came   221

Not, where he lay   114
Not Young Any Longer   237
Now After Many Journeys   34
Now Is the Time to Remember the Other Landscapes   48
Now let me circumambulate dead charms   109
Now That I Love You Truly   261
Now The Expected Ambush   134
Nursery Rhyme   189

O

O Broken By Bright Eyes My Crusoe Mind   46
O Light, O Menace   146
O Mariner, Return   114
Obviously for Somebody   271
Ode   113
Of Course That Was No Country for Young Men   50
Oh! Who Would Follow Singing Seas to His Death   53
Oh! You Who Have Been There   8
Old Compulsions   305
Old Man Murmured, An   136
Old Man's Song   199
Old Story, An   130
On A Daughter   335
On A Painting, 'Sunk Lyonesse', By Rae Richards   228
On Being Asked to Contribute to A 'Theatre And Drama' Issue
    Of Meanjin   345
On Having My Portrait Painted   230
On Re-Reading Old Myths   320
On Re-Reading The Twenty Third Psalm   320
On Seeing an Australian Play   282
On Taking Part In A Recital Of Baroque Music And Poetry At
    Newcastle Cathedral, Sunday, 4 October 1964   363
On the Banks of Some River or Other   273
On the Death of Yeats   147
Once   285
Once in a time   127
Once I Wanted to Make   37
One Memory   324
One Reason for Disliking Englishmen   328
One Song of a Mad Prince   204
Only   291
Oracle, The   129
Orestes   110
Orpheus   94
Out of Wales   143
Outrageous   263
Owl and Echo   278

P

P Is for Poetry	234
Pacifist, The	1
Pale Hands You Loved	140
Panther, The	239
Pastoral	311
Pathetic Fallacy	131
Pay No More Adulation	32
Peace	80
Pendulum, The	293
Perennial Complaint of a Writer	362
Perplexed	259
Persuasion of Light, The	144
Petrarch Did Not Write Like This	344
Place of Failure, The	132
Plaintive	179
Plea against Armistice, A	173
Poem, Awkward or innocent	103
Poem, Back to the loved sky and the humped hills,	104
Poem Dedicated to the Memory of Dylan Thomas	201
Poem for A Birthday	125
Poem for Flowers, Perhaps, A	273
Poem for Madeleine	159
Poem for My Daughters	238
Poem for Patricia	157
Poem for The Winter Solstice	316
Poem for Wales	23
Poem, From these five witnesses	98
Poem, Heart-madness and the labouring craft	112
Poem, I am the poet walking in the wind	35
Poem, I have gone walking in dishevelled fields	140
Poem In Absence	106
Poem in Several Moods	165
Poem, in that rich dark, that midnight wood	84
Poem, in the mean parishes of my desire	76
Poem, in the towns and centuries of youth	156
Poem, mortal, miraculous	72
Poem, O girl merry as apples	132
Poem On St David's Day, 1951	157
Poem, The animal sleep in winter	112
Poem, The hand that dreams of poems	64
Poem, The innocent frenzy of the wind	79
Poem, The lying calendar of youth	111
Poem, The Sensual Landscape In His Mind	82
Poem Which Is Better Without A Title, A	286
Poem, Wild in the ambush and agony of love	102
Poems In Separation	63
Poet at Night	284
Poet is a Bastard Just Like Other People, The	241

Poet Meditates Upon Byzantium, The   302
Poet, The   162
Poet Writes on the Imminent Death of His Mistress, The   237
Poet (Gartered with love and gadded with ambition)   169
Poet (To Die Is But to Be A Breaking Wave)   74
Poetic Retrospect   209
Portrait (By Foreign Calculation Led to Infer)   149
Portrait (Inhibited, He Walks His Narrow Stage)   45
Portrait Gallery   275
Portrait Of The Artist As A Young Man   139
Portsmouth at Night: 'Hostilities Only' Rating   212
Prayer against old age   170
Prayer to The Steep Atlantick Stream   323
Prayer (For Those Who Have Been Lost In Innocent Woods)   145
Prayer (Purge Me Those Images Of Idol Days)   39
Pride of the Morning, The   183
Prince Hamlet – But Not With Very Much to Say   56
Princes of This World, The   135
Prisoner, The   96
Problems of Language: Old Man, Young Girl   195
Prologue to 'Love for Love'   76
Promise to My Old Age, A   205
Prothalamion   307

Q

Queen's Lover, A   238
Question, A   154
Question Of Responsibility, A   241

R

Rain Forest   282
Rape   333
Reaching Towards The Light   4
Recovering From You   249
Recriminations Over   339
Reflections on Tragedy   166
Refusing Now to Sing   49
Reluctant   292
Remembrance   201
Renunciation   43
Reply   134
Requiescat   21
Restless   252
Restlessly Seeking   135
Rhiannon   228
Ring of Language, The   210
Rivers and Revolutions   136

Rule of Three Sum Wrong, A	231
Ruth Myfanwy	261

S

Sailor	201
Sailor Speaks, the	75
Sailor Who Reads Books Sends a Christmas Card to His Dead Sweetheart, A	340
Sailor's Return	16
Salute to Marlene From Down in the Valleys	327
Salvationist's Dream	10
Same Story, The	229
Savage Balance, The	218
Saviour, A	160
Sawmill Incident	329
Scansion	274
Sea-faiths	232
Sea Shanty	207
Sea Voices	27
Seascape	121
Second Critical Encounter, The	327
Second Song of a Mad Prince, A	211
Seeking The Last Deformity	51
Seeking to make a music of the myth	108
Self-Criticism	248
Separated Limbs Are Lovelier, The	54
Sestina for Sian Crossing the Seas	147
Shapes of Pity, The	99
She Bit Me, But Not In Anger	247
She is Asleep	239
Ship Sonnet, The	254
Short Story	179
Sickbed Fantasy	132
Sick With Requited Love	244
Similes In Exile	8
Simply the Chance	243
Simply to Write	308
Singing Wonder Of The Stars, The	9
Situation	200
Small indifferent birds, The	112
Small Protest from a Native	364
Small Vision Of Hell, A	336
So I Beget You In A Lyric Mood	55
So I Was Ruined In That Hectic Summer	55
Soil	293
Solitary Wanderer, The	346
Song, By violent, ambiguous ways	77
Song, Commend we that Prodigious Grief	147

Song for a Time Of Trouble   122
Song for Rachel   101
Song for You and Me, A   169
Song, Interlocked upon the bed   181
Song, Once, beneath a morbid sun   131
Song, O who unribbed me where I lay   101
Song of Hope   26
Song of the Dandy Bones   186
Song Of The Days, A   197
Song, Ten weathers at my finger-tips   83
Song, The sensual wind had blown away   161
Song, There is a country of disorder   168
Song, There was a lady loved a bull   163
Song, Were I As Wise As Solomon   62
Sonnet for my Daughter's Childhood   124
Sonnet, No rich complexity of flower or woman   89
Sonnet Instead of Theology, A   205
Sonnet On A Lost Mistress   1
Sonnet to Pam   168
Sonnets at Forty   234
Sort Of Love Poem, A   257
Speech for A Play   141
Spoiled Preacher   332
Spring Sonnet   138
Stages to A Modern Prelude: 'The Uncreated Conscience'   87
Stanzas in a Mirror   187
Stanzas in Dejection   82
Stare-in-the-Face   185
Statue of Salt and Wall of Hyacinth   219
Storm In Childhood, A   370
Storms Etc   279
Stormy Night In Newcastle, N.S.W.   300
Summer Of Birds Made The Wild Morning Wonder, A   57
Sunday on the Beach   206
Surprising and Inevitable   273
Surrender That Which Is Already Given   48
Swansea   313
Sweet Sleeper, Do Not Wake   18

T

Taffy Was Transported   338
Taliesin Broods Upon the Founder of Harvard   286
Taut Rigidity of the Senses   225
Thanks   174
Thanks to Jean And Norman for Coming Here   327
That Impossible She   299
That Other I, The Unhappy Lover And Proud Talker   40
There Are Some Connections Between Life And Literature   260

There is a Country 141
There is No Way 143
There Is Something In What The Psychologists Say 283
They Also Serve 281
They Lie 236
Thinking to Write an Ode 229
Third Song of a Mad Prince 214
This Circling Dancer Is The Whirling World 65
This Hero Now 13
This Wedded Gentleman 285
Thorn 371
Thou Shalt Not 299
Though body on body press 118
Though We Lie Now In This Dead Land 61
Thought, A 268
Three Verses for A Twentyfirst Birthday 303
Time of Love, The 206
Time wears and watches 153
To, and for, Caroline 328
To Helen 298
To Madeleine 148
To Michelene 237
To Miranda Crossing the Seas 363
To Miranda On Her First Birthday 322
To My Mother 319
To Rupert Hart-Davis 324
To Ted Richards 317
To the Keeper of the Welsh Kitchen 324
Tomorrow is an island 122
Tonight I see an image 79
Towards a Homage to Norman Talbot 358
Traced On The Dark Skies Of My Mind 47
Traditional 311
Treatment 348
Tribute 197
Tribute to Rae Richards' Painting of Leda and the Swan 250
Tribute to Rae Richards' Painting of Leda and the Swan, II 254
Tutor 271
Two 184
Two Coffee Cups 249
Two Poems, I 41
Two Poems, II 41

U

Ulysses 46
Ulysses in Ithaca 262
Unfaithful 129
Unknown to Lexicologists 280

Unsuccessful Attempt at Suicide   350
Urgency   259
Useless Advice to a Young Man Hopelessly in Love   306
Utter the pangs of grass   124

                                    V

Venus Anadyomene   86
Verbalist   267
Veteran   281
Villanelle   186
Vocabulary of Promise, The   158
Voyages   184

                                    W

Waiting for You   242
Waiting The Onslaught Of The Light   7
Wales-New South Wales. May   1961
                                                         255
War Generation   120
War Widow   59
Way of the World, The   181
We Are In Love   36
Weasel At The Heart, The   66
Welsh Bastard   343
Welsh Childhood   336
Welshman in Exile Speaks, The   244
Welsh Pastoral Elegy   329
Welsh Poet Finds a Proper Story, A   360
Were I That Cold Commemorative Ghost   38
What Original Or Rare   32
When In The Tousled Bed We Lie   60
When the bone cried   107
When the world was a wonder   163
When we were young we felt the tortured cities   12
Where My Seafellow In A Windless Humour   106
Where No Light Breaks   53
Who Dealt In Dogmas Of Delight   49
Who'd Be an Erotic Poet, Anyway?   262
Why Should I Be Afraid?   3
Willy and Reality   177
Winter   99
Winter Beeches   10
Winter Can Be Deceitful   51
Winter's Shadowed Hour   50
Wish, A   45
Wish for My Eldest Daughter, A   130
Witch Woman   156

With A Distant Bow to Mrs Hemans   337
With Hunger, With Anger   335
With Love, for Love   334
With rags of honour   129
With Thanks   338
With the Sea's Volubility   315
Woman And Some Men, A   74
Woman Who Loved to Look on Running Water, A   216
Woodland Walk, A   268
Word Is All   360
Wordless   278
Words from Any Poet   152
Words to Any Exile   153
Workers of the World, Unite   188
World In The Mirror, The   137
Worthy is the Lamb   298
Wounded Water, The   100

Y

You Can Have More Than One Breakdown If You Try Hard Enough   361
You (Could With Love's Rhetoric)   29
You (Your small voice frightens me)   241
Young Man Reproves His Elders, A   198
Young Men Who Admire Themselves In Mountain Pools, the   47

INDEX OF FIRST LINES

A

A clamour in the night	126
A comedy we offer you tonight	76
A dark woman, passionate in a public place	74
A dream which I translated to a painted stage	87
A female voice out of the East	79
A finch sang in the hazels	319
A flat sea smugs in	350
A gentle man in a long wind	358
A girl against a background, holding	274
A government has fallen with a crash	164
A good whisky, a good girl, a good	277
A man may feel what Homer sung	127
A man without eyelids – I call him a man	326
A picture of a town beside a river	346
A rocket soars, explodes, and dies away	258
A stammering repetition of your name	331
A summer of birds made the wild morning wonder	57
A woman who loved to look on running water	216
Absence is pride, the unforgiving warfare	106
Accused of, praised for, being an erotic poet	248
Across the unresponsive oceans and the listless lands	47
Afraid of being converted like St Paul	134
After barbaric centuries and lands	119
After his grief he woke	33
After my many bitter journeys	75
After the bickering among the trophies	173
After the funeral with none to praise	52
Agony is not to be encountered in islands	48
Ah, it was cold that water and a cheat.	216
Alison is now your name	211
All night in the ready fields	289
All other quarrels being now forgotten	182
All statements that I make may be defined	300
All their bravado in that grove	367
All the torn and blistered fields	133
All we are is epitaphs	4
Aloysius stroked his finely modelled head	182
Always, it seems, I wanted to tell, compulsive	229
Ambiguous omens	97
An anniversary poem you said: what should	243
An ocean or embrace away	159
An old man murmured a country prayer	136
An old ram, slithering along the feg	311
An old reticence of mountains	368
And having come	132
'And how do you react to exile?' Politely	263

And I remember how I named 265
And I would send you argosies of words 37
And if I did mean country matters 277
And many were afraid and hid their faces 92
And my grave, when you make it 343
And so fawn-like she came 14
And this preposterous inversion 252
And you invite me to your bed 253
Anguish is my country 341
Around me, my books leer, lour 362
As if it weren't enough 340
As I walked out in the pride of the morning 183
As I was going by the sweet legend 175
As malefactors once were branded, so 247
As the night rains away 284
Askew a bar, aslant 317
Assailed by various weathers and temptations 123
Assassin, lover, from your exile 153
At midnight, in deserted towns 97
At that miraculous unlooked-for moment 37
At the close of a winter day 62
At wedding-feast or country fair 95
Attended by multitudes of wishes 193
Autumn was always cold, and so was spring 255
Autumnal Hamlet sees the spies of grief 82
Awkward or innocent 103

B

Back is the question 342
Back to the loved sky and the humped hills 104
Bald witnesses observant of my plight 198
Ballad the idiom of my ancestry 366
'Balls, old boy,' he said, and he spread 328
Because of that great company 49
Be dancers first: go gay 238
Be human only now, and warm 10
Before the bright bird write his epitaph of wing 8
Before time began 157
Beggars snuffle in doorways 152
Being a boy from the hills, brought up 244
Being older now I said ('For a Proud Beauty') 27
Being older now I said ('Metamorphosis') 30
Being the youngest of a poet's three daughters 261
Being thus analytical, no wilder ghost 151
Believing in no grief save that alone 41
Beneath the surface of decay 122
Beyond the promise and deceit of seasons 129
Beyond this murder 120

Blind days I ravelled unforgettable 314
Boasting merely of the bodily contact 257
Bodies are poems lovers learn 40
Brutal comedian of my common act 137
Burning against the lyric dark 111
But never until the meeting making hour 40
But no regrets: upon the lithe response 341
But not in mine. See Daniel wear the sky 310
But that was yesterday 15
By foreign calculation led to infer 149
By violent, ambiguous ways 77

C

Calling within us the spring 2
Can it be so long – twenty four hours 252
Caught by the glory of her sensual head 369
Caught in the singing foliage of youth 75
Caught young, I grew to be a pretty boy 305
Children do not read the clock 199
Christmas again – shall I decline? 340
Christmas once more, and once more I accept 339
Cloudburst, sunblast, tiderip, bedwrack 275
Coiled within us waiting for release 26
Cold comfort when the blue yawn of the sea 222
Comedians are born, they say, not made 303
Commend we that prodigious grief 147
Cool pity covers us 3
Could with love's rhetoric 29

D

Darling, you would have floated in your hair 301
Darlings 21
Dazedly watching from a railway window 16
Deadlocked and still indubitably two 184
Dear departer, I do not wish 370
Dear Jean, wife of a poet and occasion of poetry 327
Dear Lady 17
Dear, stay a little while that I 237
Death is within us like a child 74
Debts, sick children, your own morning cough 262
Devoted – the word was yours. I had said 273
Diluted voices in the neighbouring room 132
Discreet old age, I'd often said 180
Disorderly spring once more 352
Disorganized 250
Distinguished and remote, the formulas arranged 174
Djinn-master Solomon 44

Do not despond: some over-obvious tricks   309
Do not look for me in that foreign place   50
Draw, winter, an arch of light at the window   219
Drinking in bars around the sunlit harbours   107
Drowned meadows, submarine   351
Drunk on duty, not for the first time   263

E

Easy now on a beach, he notes the sea   201
Eating the bread of the world   336
Elle à les jambes maigres comme le remords   161
Emblems of blood and the bloodthirsty moon   154
Eve's first laughter shook the leaves   189

F

Fairflesh, used, still wanted. Not for sale   276
Fascinated by murder and by mirrors   128
Fear not the pettiness of time   7
Flowers, forest, in the downing rain   282
Flowers of stone and thorn in a   220
For I would give you   242
For nine moons cradled in grace   309
For those who have been lost in innocent woods   145
Four corners of the room I'm in   170
From brooding on the possible event   56
From gorse and cinder hills I Adamed out   201
From my singing sullenness   36
From shabby towns or lucid pastures   120
From these five witnesses   98
From what high heaven of thought   44
Fuck me, said the Admiral's wife, and the Able   331
Furious nativity   111

G

Gartered with love and gadded with ambition   169
Get fucked, is what I remember you saying.   322
Ghosted with sailors, the sleeping city   212
Girls were betrayed by men in the old stories   251
God, as we know him in a world of fact   205
Grandfather Adam, who first tried   369
Grief's unscarred wounds are treasured up   39

H

Half awake, I heard you murmur to my side   257
Having contrived a history of crisis   140

Having in mind that ambuscade of hair 334
Head in the clouds to you is a worn phrase 296
Heart-madness and the labouring craft 112
He drew the hyperbolic draperies 94
He found the countless pities of the sea 58
He had a certain seagreen speech 32
He had been long away; too long, too long 266
He will not come again 20
Helen, thy beauty is to me 298
Her arms bare, and her eyes naked 366
Her hair was like the sunlit gorse 179
Here is the feature and fashion knows not bruise 138
Here on the atlas of my suffering 142
Here stone and sky are married 15
Hiraeth is a word that costs 318
Hot summer in the blood 52
Hours ago he woke up the sky 359
How should that famous man have come 147
Hwyl fawr, bach – the words must have been said 326

I

I am the poet walking in the wind 35
I am the spindrift ghost 96
I blame it all on those headhurting books 224
I could not bear 329
I crumple under the hurt hump of marriage 352
I dreamed when I was young that I might make 160
I gave you roses once – do you remember 267
I had a cock, and he was tall 247
I had always thought it right and proper 274
I have been one that loved 18
I have been walking above Cwmchwefri 297
I have come far now from the kiss of frost 157
I have forsaken them all 43
I have gone walking in dishevelled fields 140
I have played so many rôles – swan, dolphin, lion 309
I have watched his pale hands shuffling money in the moonlight 133
I heard the water talking like a woman 273
I knew a doctor 348
I knew those rigid kings 202
'I love my husband too.' How many wives 241
I never learned to say it properly 180
I remember the house 9
I said I did not mean to make you jealous 268
I saw my blood run down the stairs 211
I see the sad cities but I cannot reach them 47
I sent a letter to my love 204
I sent a letter to my love – wrote it in the wrong language 318

I set a rage apart	170
I sit, trying to look nonchalant	230
I slur through the dingle, cwm	360
I stayed too late: my waiting was too slow	344
I straddled the world	350
I thought I'd come upon the scene too late	345
I took for emblem the upland moors and the rocky	264
I tried to keep the summer in my head	209
I used to talk in quite a different idiom	236
I walked abroad in my kingdom	214
I walked with a bare mind	344
I was always defeated	343
I was on me way to Ringsend	300
I who was never handsome nor very tall	46
I would have you remain	56
I would make a sullen claim	292
I would not ache tonight	57
I would not have you otherwise	48
I would send you words	42
I would walk always in gardens	45
I've never cried	337
If I make a dark song	64
If I should lyrically lament	54
If I were blessed, my rage would praise	288
If not of this, then of some other despair	306
If this is love, to feel in absence	256
If you should come, a slack-loined ghost	185
Ignore, ignore. Forget, and sidle out	351
Images of adventure and desire	45
Impatient, debonair	173
In a cold season	78
In a perhaps momentary confusion	220
In countries where no sea-faiths were	232
In country sentiment I said I loved you	235
In love's outrageous slums	98
In my beginning was the sweat of sleep	116
In my returning, the proud, flowered walking	33
In no proud walking	31
In that rich dark, that midnight wood	84
In the afternoon, the Indian summer	6
In the annunciation and surprise	158
In the cold splendour of that rocky place	312
In the conspiracy of love	58
In the corruption of the distances	165
In the demented wood	120
In the dissolving churches of her smiles	30
In the ditch of desire your true man I lay	221
In the duality of man	2
In the heart alone is the last enemy	29

In the indeed and always countries 291
In the last chapter he grew sick and died, 81
In the light of ordinary evenings 221
In the mean parishes of my desire 76
In the mornings where my mercies were 184
In the nightmare of the heart 151
In the room of the curse and the web of prayer 166
In the shop-front of your magnificence 41
In the towns and centuries of youth 156
In the tremble of the year, the uncertain moment 289
In this blind time 105
In this poisonous intimacy of trees and wind 219
In this white courtyard where the not-to-be-imprisoned sun 11
In times of public strain and stress 164
In your great kingdom of uncertainties 124
Inadequate but still importunate 281
Infirm, infirm, but all too passionate 139
Inhibited, he walks his narrow stage 45
Insulting people is so easy, insulting 271
Intense, a fawn, hearing mad sounds 214
Interlocked upon the bed 181
Intimations of honour and of fear 139
Invented seasons, known by snakespit, cuckoocall 149
Invested by you in that royal sleep 238
Is there such a word as gnatchen? 280
It is a terrible thing to be young, young 306
It is easy to grow up 364
It is not death I fear 52
It is not fear but knowing what to fear 199
It is the verbalist in me concedes 267
It was a confusion of bright women troubled 264
It was a cuckooed land going gravely 288
It was against the custom of the country 338
It was a lovely lady came riding by 14
It was always easy to imagine idylls 42
It was always the colour of cockcrowing 225
It was at first merely the inconvenience 269
It was at the wave's foot the crab was scrabbling 217
It was a voice serene and placid as 19
It was a winter night and cold to the heart 60
It was bound to come; and I grew 241
It was cold in that room, after the cold hours 283
It was indeed its anonymity 155
It was not in the lubber lands 186
It was spring, we were in the country, we were together 311
It was that great man Thomas Jefferson 237
It was to make the words perform 228
It was your sign to believe in a future 218
It would be a hard, a bitter man 363
It's no good: not on this continent 348

J

Jack Christ was kind to me, a poor thief ... 11
Just as the doors are closing ... 227

L

Lady, the stilted bird who gave me love ... 190
Landor in Italy longed for an old bay ... 313
Landward you linger, and the western air ... 4
Language is always dogma, said the sage ... 195
Legends ago ... 38
Let her remember in outrageous youth ... 130
Let me make you a poem that is everywhere ... 60
Lipless, breastless, they importuned me with ... 336
Locked in the green house of the dark ... 208
Loneliness came quietly like a pain ... 90
Long dedicated to the service of the goddess ... 251
Look, I tell you he let that bloody saw ... 329
Lost in the curls and tendrils of your forest ... 268
Lost on the floor of darkness ... 118
Lousy Byzantiums of the mind ... 302
Love should have been as harsh and challenging ... 251
Love, that old, notorious country ... 347
Love's weather changed to thunder in my veins ... 54
Low and low ... 152

M

M.A. now, and First Class Honours too. ... 327
Mädchen fach, du bist'ne Blume ... 239
Mary Ann Evans went to bed ... 182
May David be a big boy who ... 349
Millicent, having had her share of sin ... 183
Mimic, you called me, and said I had that comic ... 240
Miranda, may ... 297
Mirror and mask abound ... 109
Moondappled memories of beloved midnights ... 12
Mortal, miraculous ... 84
Mr Pope, full of pain and fine feeling ... 269
My angel slept within my side ... 133
My daughter of the Mabinogion name ... 228
My double darling, witty dismay ... 174
My duty to set down, to propagate ... 353
My father's scowl, grandfather's scowl ... 335
My heart is now an unlocked lucky room ... 33
My intricate and massy image ... 82
My long-ago love goes lightly through the summer ... 191
My love and I held long debate ... 195

My manhood, powdered by your lust 180
My masters and colleagues will come riding by 152
My neighbour foolishly left me alone 182
My neighbour, learning that I lacked for meat 182
My ship goes, laden with forgetfulness 254
My world is upsidedown, and Christmas burns 226
My world is weeping, and the driven blood 63

N

Never again I said shall that invader 235
Never that love shall languish 133
New Englands of the mind: and such choice grain 286
Night is transparent, and the mousing sounds 278
No convert even now to gentleness 176
No, I am not jealous, I said 259
No more for you and I, my love, the warm retreat 3
No more stale rinsings of the sun 312
No pity nor prophylactic 35
No rich complexity of flower or woman 89
No songs or sonnets now take time away 5
No, the landscape never sweetened us 231
No uncompanionable divinity 320
Nostalgic sailors in a dream of gardens 158
Not bald or impotent yet – should one give thanks 234
Not even wanting to be Hercules 272
Not in that drunken morning shall my dew 117
Not lack of children only 217
Not only hers: crisscross from the light 272
Not when I came 221
Not, where he lay 114
Now after many journeys 34
Now in a season of heat and oddly holly 319
Now in midwinter and still at war 280
Now is the news good, and our hearts high 307
Now is the time to remember the other landscapes 48
Now let me circumambulate dead charms 109
Now that I love you truly, I can tell 261
Now the ambitious season of the year 138
Now the expected ambush of spring 134
Now the persuasion of light 144
Now the position has been made quite clear 164
Now told by eight and twenty years 125
Now wisdom comes after idolatry 119
Nursing a brittle passion 96

O

O broken by bright eyes my crusoe mind 46
O girl merry as apples 132
O light, O menace, our unlucky hearts, 146
O mariner, return, return 114
O randy and random I roamed through the town 207
O western winde, when shalt thou – Christ 326
O who unribbed me where I lay 101
Observe the gold clarity of this moment 268
Obsessed by the colours of decay 110
Obsessed by the morbidity of time 131
Of course I've been frightened; by such 325
Of course that was no country for young men 50
Oh! who would follow singing seas to his death? 53
Oh! you who have been there, at the end 8
Old compulsions, insistent as rain 305
On Monday it is the waking 197
On the edge of the horrible wood 93
On the horizon a funereal gleam 16
On the mutual bed assume 334
On the worn and public grass 188
Once 285
Once, beneath a morbid sun 131
Once I read Donne to you, and was undone 260
Once I wanted to be a vegetable 291
Once I wanted to make 37
Once I would have fretted, been ill at ease 233
Once I wrote you a simple poem 284
Once in a time of blossoming and air 127
Our Greek imaginations kept the story 250
Our strategy was simple and, I thought 304
Out of invented countries, comic scenes 305
Out of my stubborn passion comes this prayer 77
Outrageous – I didn't even use the word 263
Over there, the hills of Sion 338
Over there there are timid coasts 330

P

Patience, you counselled: when you look for it least 314
Pay no more adulation 32
Penned in the garden of her own disaster 194
Perplexed as always by your absence 259
Persuaded was one way of putting it 274
Pleased with the green extravagance of ocean 130
Pluck me an apple, darling 255
Poems about paintings – after Leda, who? 270
Poets have written much about love's madness 248
Poppy, considering every man a beast 183

Predicaments of landscape, old despairs 234
Prepared for the dark obliteration 316
Pressed in the throng of guilt 137
Prince Hamlet:- but not with very much to say 56
Purge me those images of idol days 39

R

Rain thrashes the house, and I am back 300
Rape is an old-fashioned sort of joke 333
Reaching towards the light 4
Recovering from you, taking 249
Recriminations over, what's to do 339
Refusing now to sing I am cast out 49
Remembering among the unlovely London voices 126
Remembering today the land from which 143
Remote in all his casual brilliancies 160
Removed from the definitions of circumstance 167
Reprove my contraband desires 134
Rest from intolerable living 21
Restless, I rose 252
Restlessly seeking the archaic sea 135
Rhetorician or somnambulist 162
Rhymes, ships, and winter – all a western sea 321
Ride, horseman, confidently astride 283
Rivers and revolutions of my thought 136
Rose uprose, magnificent above 273

S

Safe islanded in ravening seas 19
Scholar, friend, and gentleman – how good to use 324
See Davies, who hates his wife because 275
Seeking the last deformity 51
Seeking to make a music of the myth 108
Shafted body in the sun 203
She believes in manners, I believe in sin 321
She combs and combs her yellow hair 183
She had not strength enough to undergo 129
She said, 'I do not like my belly 240
She that has sweated in my sweat 181
She was, and is 299
She writhes so 368
Similes of sunlight at thought of you occur 8
Simply the chance 243
Sleep recomposes 239
So I beget you in a lyric mood 55
So I was ruined in that hectic summer 55
So I went 246

So tired his eyes are grown from the bars passing 239
So you sit down, lean and slippered, expecting 320
Some frosty farmers fathered me to fare 277
Something there is not cured with a kiss 186
Sometimes in the sweaty and stained night 332
Sometimes, when one has almost given up 273
Sprawlheels again, easily on your back 271
Stare-in-the-face said to me 185
Stare, stare, said the soldier 101
Storms I had been through before, heaved 279
Strange things have happened in her ambient 197
Strut, arrogant frame, your pride of bones 205
Summer for the lovers, a gift of sun 66
Surrender that which is already given 48
Sweat and the hot blood tell his genesis 116
Sweet cheat – if I sound like a bloody bird 286
Sweet sleeper, do not wake 18

T

Taut rigidity of the senses that strangle life 225
Ten weathers at my finger-tips 83
Terror: nightmare: and my crawling skin 258
That morning Adam named the animals 210
That other I, the unhappy lover and proud talker 40
That tribute should be annual does not mean 311
The ambushed and didactic years 144
The animal sleep in winter 112
The assumption of convenient passion 141
The augury of this am 194
The ballad's wormy eye 190
The bauble and glint and glitter of it 232
The beauty lies with the fool 88
The bitter thoughts that flowered in the garden 91
The blind old empires crumble to decay 81
The bridge to that romantic country 85
The bull upon the cow: in those rough days 284
The contradiction of your images 118
The country drunkard desiring 94
The crude constructions of fortuitous dream 192
The delicate and reluctant deer 324
The definition of being young 237
The disappearance of old honesty 276
The dragons crawl about the mountains 89
The early Fathers of the Church were all 164
The enemies are walking, walking 42
The gaudy summers of my youth 108
The golden hammers of my tongue beat out 92
The great proconsul hurries home 64

The greenness of the heart 61
The hairs on my belly are wet with your sweat 179
The hand that dreams of poems at my side 64
The hunger of this love 287
The imperception of your absences 179
The innocent frenzy of the wind 79
The landscape and the myth escape me now 119
The lecherous and griefless sea 316
The lectern firms me; the Book's ever a strong prop 365
The limbs of summer in their glory 54
The lineaments of my improbable land 302
The lion sleeps upon the stair 10
The listless waters 121
The loitering hounds of the sea 142
The lone mister in the park 57
The long legs of my love were walking like swans 36
The lying calendar of youth 111
The meaning of fear is not apparent 166
The miles of water 124
The mind alone has not its own defence. 61
The moment has gone by 145
The moods of the sea I celebrate 245
The nightingales of former lovers 136
The nonconformist hills have kept 142
The old extravagance of love eludes us 96
The one day of the year – but every day 282
The poem reminded this one of a moth 203
The priestess writhes, breathes heavily 129
The princes of this world 135
The puritan, the profiteer, the pimp 164
The ravening of this ghost 155
The secret scripture of the grass 99
The sensual landscape in his mind 82
The sensual wind had blown away 161
The separated limbs are lovelier 54
The shapes of pity reluctantly displayed 99
The sick poet in his tower, 123
The singing wonder of the stars 9
The small, indifferent birds 112
The speaking voices of the sea 27
The storm without, the storm within 209
The story told in the beginning garden 361
The thorn is punished by the October wind 371
The time I expect was summer 201
The time, the time, the time of love 206
The various poems answer for my hero 86
The war being only, when you look at it, a state of mind 12
The weather altered in your long delay 140
The whinnying animals of sleep 103

The wideawake sky went on for ever and ever   150
The wind was clouting the beach   206
The windy oceans that around me sorrow   63
The woman supine on the bed   179
The world in the mirror has a different life   137
The wounded water lies like broken sleep   100
The year returns, turns   337
The young men who admired themselves in mountain pools   47
There are old stories, some declare   307
There is a country of disorder   168
There is a country of no suffering,   141
There is no way that does not lead to water   143
There is, we say, nothing extraordinary   245
There on that hot, unlucky bed   196
There was a chemistry I knew   20
There was a lady loved a bull   163
There was a time, not over-long ago   1
There were no gods among that bitten grass   128
There were omens of course, but mostly unheeded   233
These are your mourners, now your world is cast   290
These disturbances now I dedicate   176
These wan woods now are winter's care   10
They lie, who tell me love is such   236
They were tidy and unrumpled   257
Thief   246
Thinking to write an ode, to avoid elegy   229
This bitter friend would have me understand   142
This black, this person, self-dissolving   218
This circling dancer is the whirling world   65
This critic was too subtle is my guess   189
This hero now, a gauche cynic   13
This is a house inhabited by the young   213
This is a poem I must make for you   23
This is authentic dark. Startling the air   143
This is the country of hurt   102
This wedded gentleman now for a long time bound   285
Thou shalt not: little Howells   299
Though body on body press   118
Though we lie now in this dead land   61
Time wears and watches; dread is this   153
To be in love – this is to suffer   253
To be magical, and yet direct.   308
To content him who thus torments me   254
To die is but to be a breaking wave   74
To have been content with ordinary things   251
To have this at least in common with Solomon   262
To those who, keeping like ourselves   113
To you, unequalled, unimpaired   322
Today the erotic season begins   100

Tomorrow is an island   122
Tomorrow round the corner   187
Tonight I see an image   79
Touching your flesh, or merely dreaming   274
Traced on the dark skies of my mind   47
Trample on that sea-born innocence   86
Turn with the turning world, and hear   117
Twin, dark rival, supplanter   315
Two coffee cups as paradigm   249

U

Ulysses, self-satisfied though travel-weary   46
Under different skies: the loved and rainy   279
Under God's violent unsleeping eye   135
Under his downy arm's   28
Under the burn and toil   293
Under this sky, and this compulsion   242
Under you now the enchanting waters foretell   147
Unlatch those lids   17
Unreal this ruined city in the unredeeming   44
Up there, in Cwmuchaf, Glyn   298
Urgency was what I always felt with you   259
Utter the pangs of grass   124

V

Vagrant through jewelled nights of Asia   130
Vanessa, heiress of an honoured name   301
Virgins and heroes in his eclectic youth   80

W

Waiting for you   242
Waiting for you in coffee-rooms, in bars   258
Waiting the onslaught of the light   7
Waking with the taste still of your nipples   262
Walking alone in the garden of day   180
Walking, alone with sentiment, his twisted stick   346
Walking between nightmare and nightmare   260
Waves whelm me westwards from this antique sea   16
We are descended in more senses than one   266
We are in love. The miracle is this   36
We had taken the long way home, a mile   370
Wear modest armour; and walk quietly   363
Were I as wise as Solomon   62
Were I that cold commemorative ghost   38
What I have found between your thighs   148

What I really meant was this 154
What is it that begins, or ends, in this room at midnight? 196
What original or rare 32
What should we blame 294
What then if there were no power to crave 80
What will come 293
When a rhymer forgets to rhyme 353
When I have paid my debt to time and terror 168
When in the tousled bed we lie 60
When I see old heads bowed in shame 1
When that great girl lies down to cool her thighs 254
When the beast came to the door 291
When the bone cried 107
When the cataracts came down, he remembered 359
When the lion brings to the broken city 122
When the sea-monster came to visit us 213
When the world was a wonder, the weather was gay 163
When this lust lies beyond geography 174
When we were young we felt the tortured cities 12
Where my seafellow in a windless humour 106
Where no light breaks 53
Where the dark sisters paid 90
Where we were born, a windy place 94
Whether upon his own dishevelled bed 244
Who dealt in dogmas of delight 49
Who would want to pardon 169
Whose hands were blessing on my breasts 59
Why does the trouble of your sleep 198
Why should I be afraid? 3
Wild in the ambush and agony of love 102
Willy was a wishful thinker 177
Wilt, wanton, if you will 278
Winter can be deceitful 51
Winter's shadowed hour 50
Wishes are cheap, and life is ruinous 333
Witch woman of small breasts and sulky eyes 156
With hunger, with anger, I shouted for images 335
With rags of honour 129
Witness the paradise upon the mountain 115

Y

Yes, Evans was all right, decent type 323
Yes, I have written my poem 156
You call yourself 'old lady' and the phrase 214
You could, I suppose, make some parable 329
You have to be forty and half impotent 256
You know that old and angry look of hers 289

You said, 'All those bloody poems   241
You said, looking at some poems, 'These are good'   327
You told me, being violent in the extreme   165
You've had, broken, enough. The watchful, kind   361
You walked into our lives, beautifully   328
You'd remember that summer when the barbarians   324
You'd think you'd easily recognize   317
Young man, lover, poet; how easy to foretell   315
Young man, when you pasture   110
Young veteran, and still presumptuous   281
Your eyes are telling the weather back   200
Your heart is an acrobat that will not stand still   2
Your small voice frightens me   241